KS1
5–7
Years

Master Maths at Home

Addition and Subtraction

Scan the QR code to help your child's learning at home.

mastermathsathome.com

How to use this book

Maths — No Problem! created **Master Maths at Home** to help children develop fluency in the subject and a rich understanding of core concepts.

Key features of the Master Maths at Home books include:

- Carefully designed lessons that provide structure but also allow flexibility in how they're used. For example, some children may want to write numbers, while others might want to trace.
- Speech bubbles containing content designed to spark diverse conversations, with many discussion points that don't have obvious 'right' or 'wrong' answers.
- Rich illustrations that will guide children to a discussion of shapes and units of measurement, allowing them to make connections to the wider world around them.
- Exercises that allow a flexible approach and can be adapted to suit any child's cognitive or functional ability.
- Clearly laid out pages that encourage children to practise a range of higher-order skills.
- A community of friendly and relatable characters who introduce each lesson and come along as your child progresses through the series.

You can see more guidance on how to use these books at **mastermathsathome.com**.

We're excited to share all the ways you can learn maths!

Maths — No Problem!
mastermathsathome.com
www.mathsnoproblem.com
hello@mathsnoproblem.com

First published in Great Britain in 2022 by
Dorling Kindersley Limited
One Embassy Gardens, 8 Viaduct Gardens, London SW11 7BW
A Penguin Random House Company

The authorised representative in the EEA is Dorling Kindersley Verlag GmbH. Amulfstr. 124, 80636 Munich, Germany

10 9 8 7 6 5 4 3 2 1
001–327069–Jan/22

A CIP catalogue record for this book is available from the British Library.

ISBN: 978-0-24153-911-8
Printed and bound in China

For the curious
www.dk.com

This book was made with Forest Stewardship Council™ certified paper – one small step in DK's commitment to a sustainable future. For more information go to www.dk.com/our-green-pledge

Acknowledgements
The publisher would like to thank the authors and consultants Andy Psarianos, Judy Hornigold, Adam Gifford and Dr Anne Hermanson.

The Castledown typeface has been used with permission from the Colophon Foundry.

Contents

Ruby
Elliott
Amira
Charles
Lulu
Sam
Oak
Holly
Ravi
Emma
Jacob
Hannah

Reading and writing to 100

Lesson 1

Starter

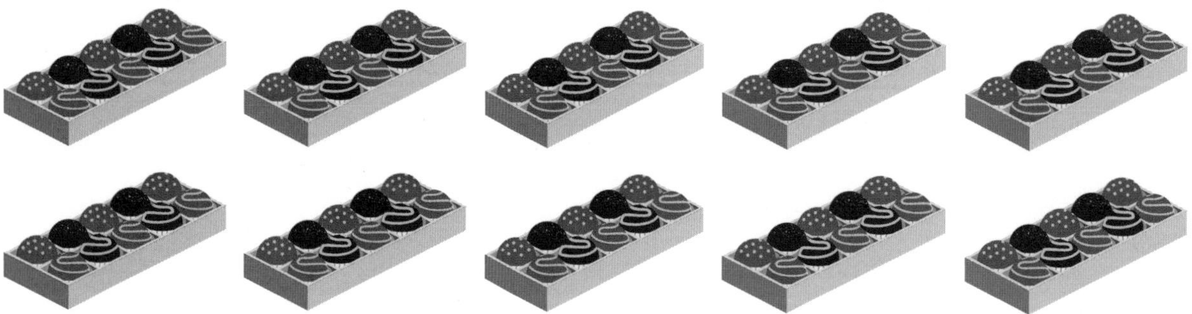

How many chocolates are there in total?

Example

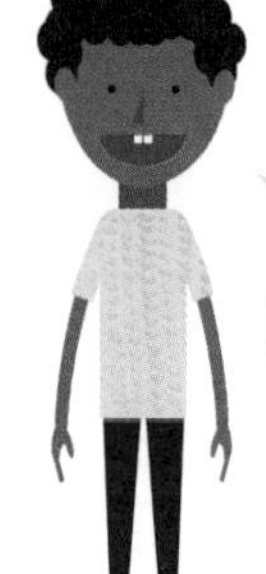

There are 10 boxes of chocolates.

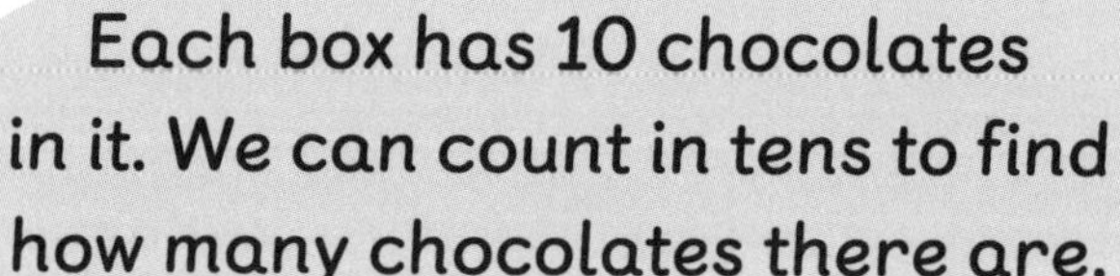

Each box has 10 chocolates in it. We can count in tens to find how many chocolates there are.

Ten, twenty, thirty, forty...

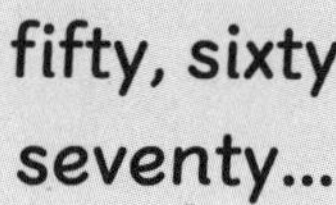

fifty, sixty seventy...

eighty, ninety, one hundred. There are 100 chocolates in total.

Practice

Count and trace the numbers in words and in numerals.

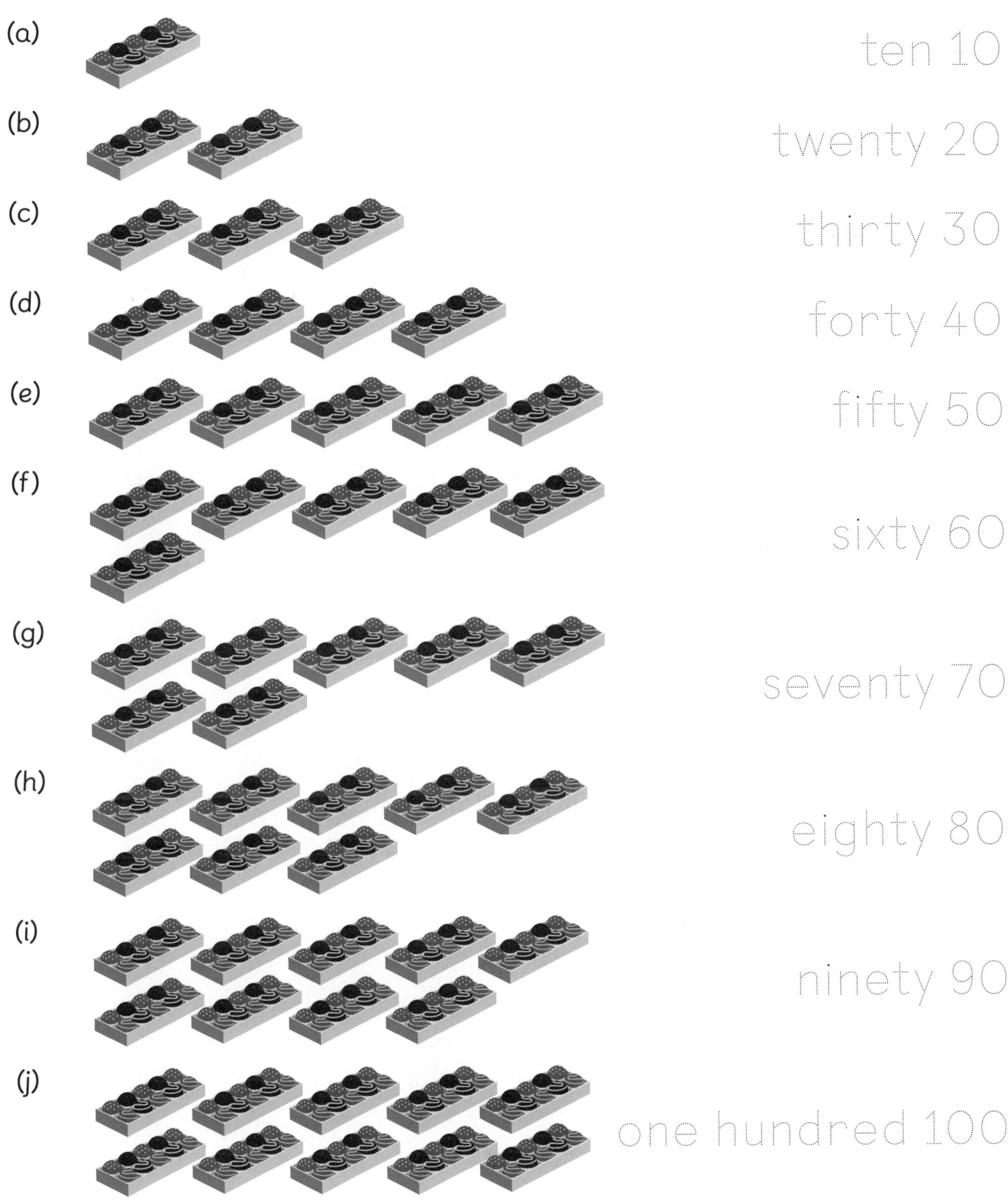

(a) ten 10

(b) twenty 20

(c) thirty 30

(d) forty 40

(e) fifty 50

(f) sixty 60

(g) seventy 70

(h) eighty 80

(i) ninety 90

(j) one hundred 100

Place value

Lesson 2

Starter

How many  are there?

Example

Each one of these is 10 of .

There are 3 tens. 10, 20, 30

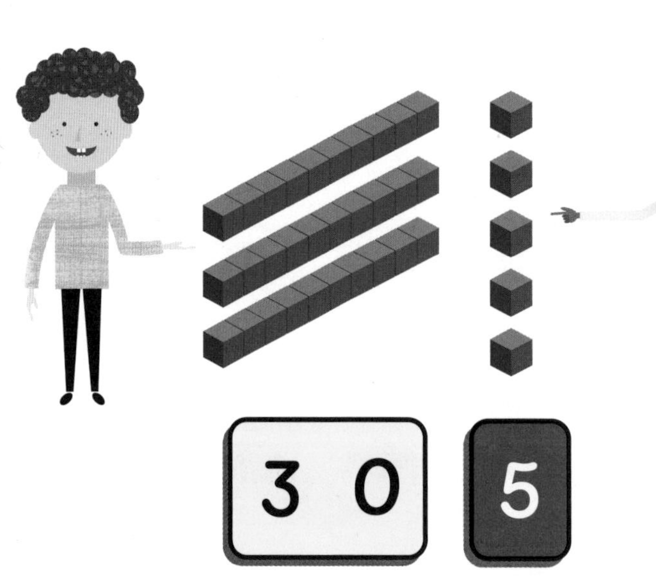

There are 5 .

31, 32, 33, 34, 35

We can also show 35 in a number bond this way.

There are 35 .

35 = 3 tens and 5 ones
The digit 3 stands for 30.
The digit 5 stands for 5.

tens	ones
3	5

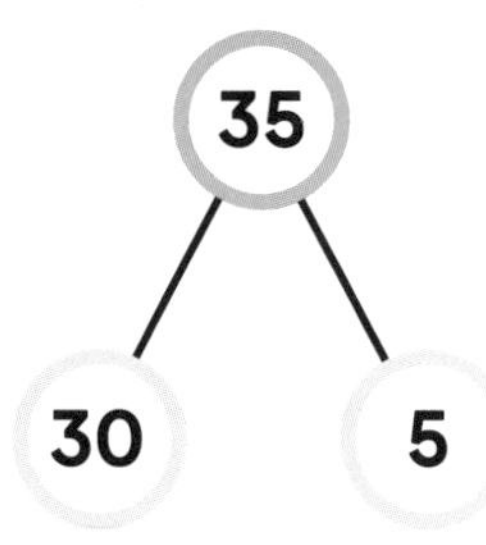

Practice

The children are counting in tens and ones.
Can you help them by filling in the missing numbers?

1

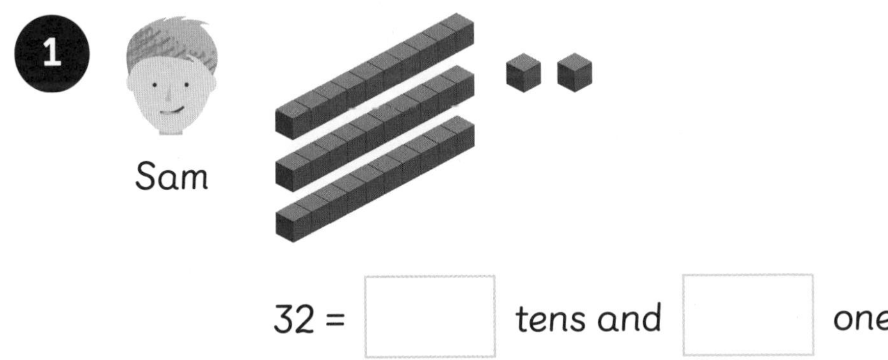

32 = ☐ tens and ☐ ones

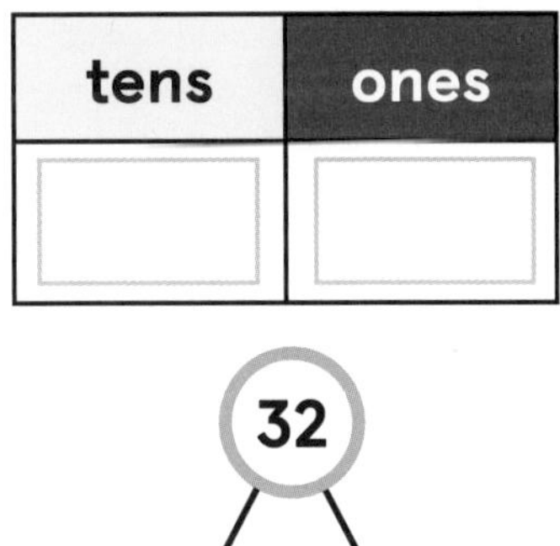

tens	ones

2

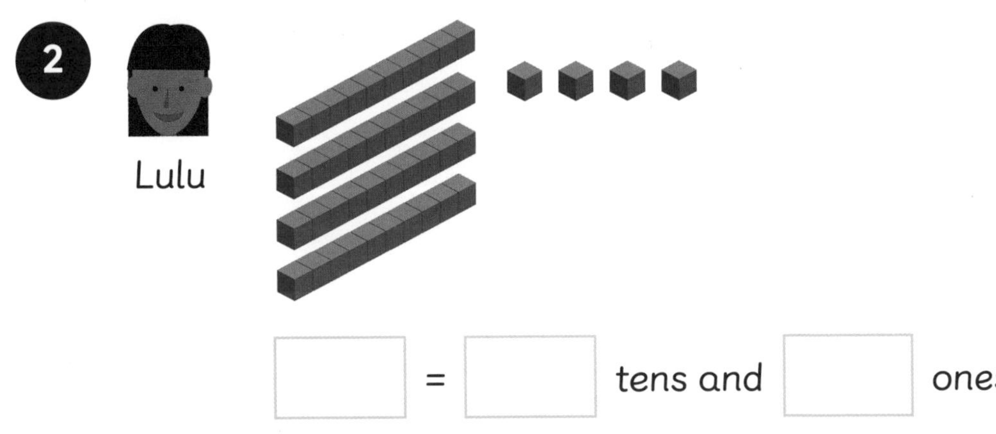

☐ = ☐ tens and ☐ ones

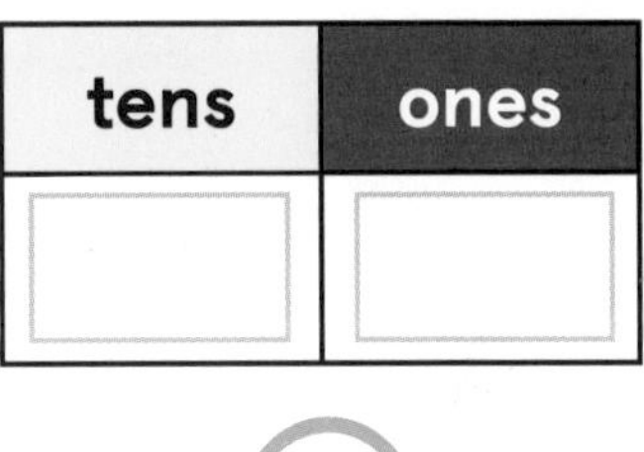

tens	ones

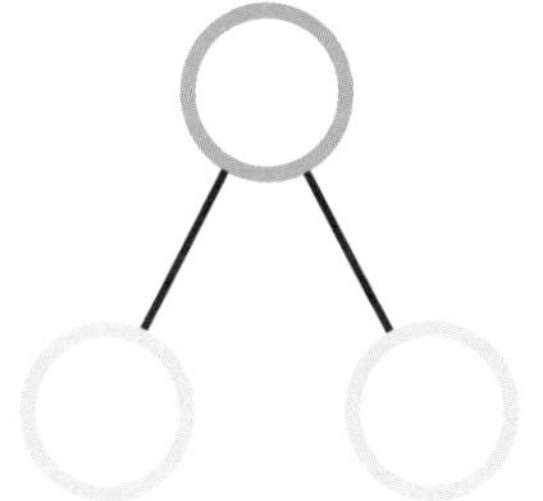

3

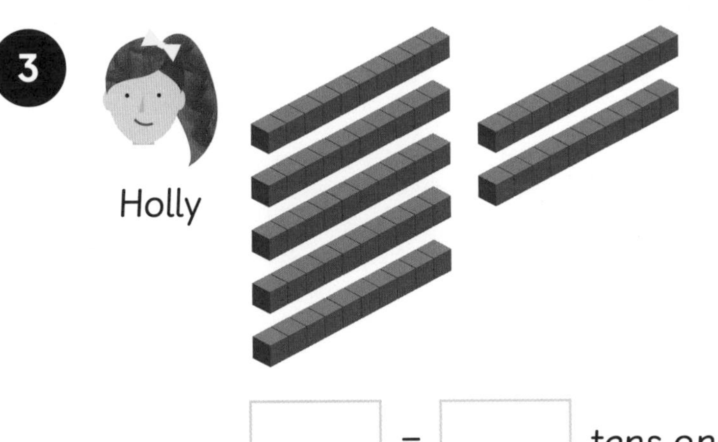

☐ = ☐ tens and ☐ ones

tens	ones

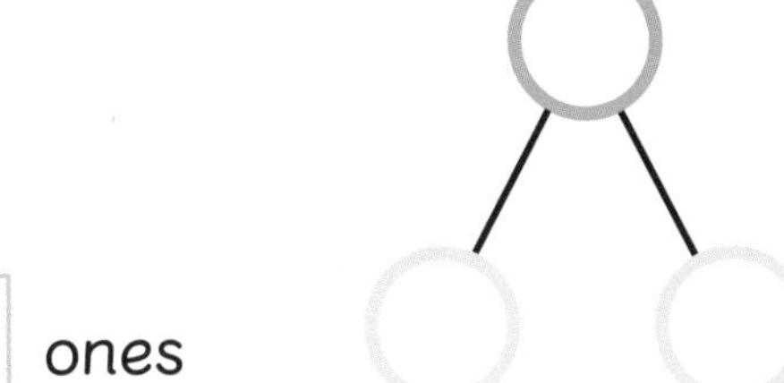

Comparing numbers

Lesson 3

Starter

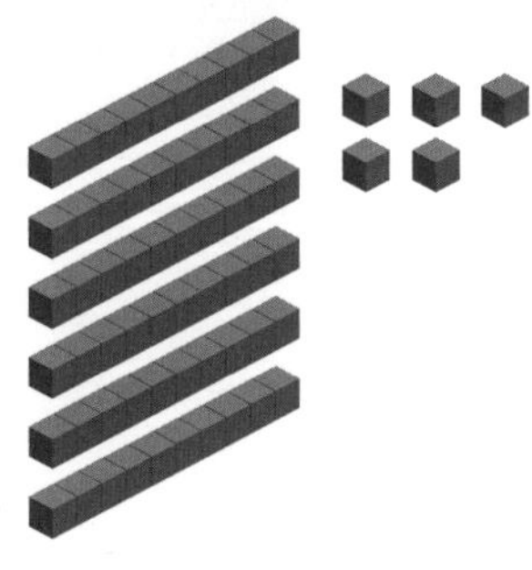

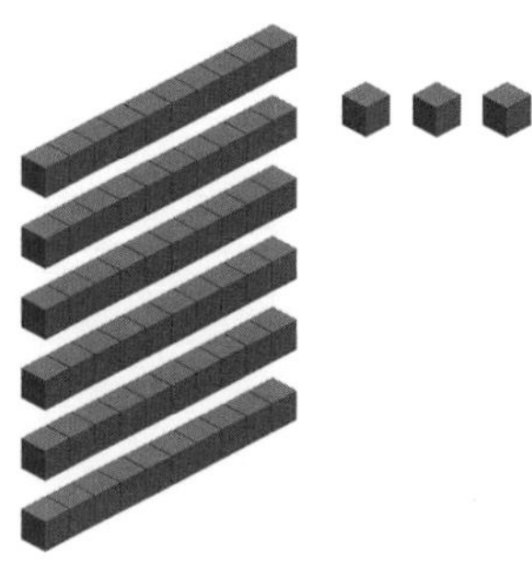

Which number is the greatest?
Which number is the smallest?

Example

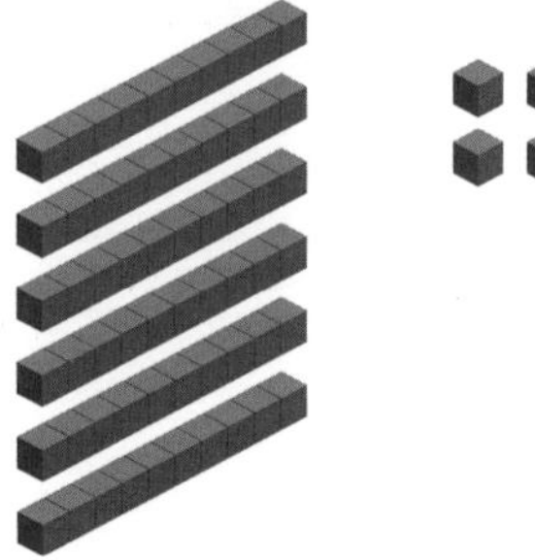

tens	ones
6	5

65

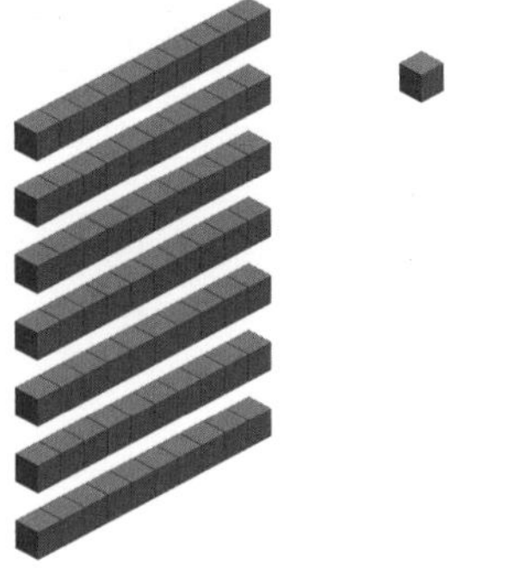

tens	ones
7	1

71

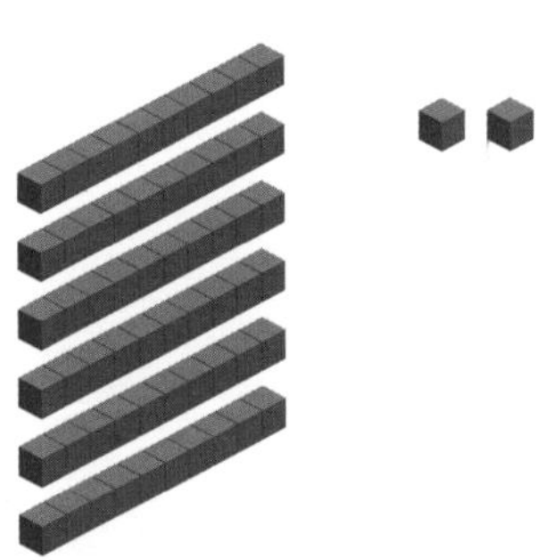

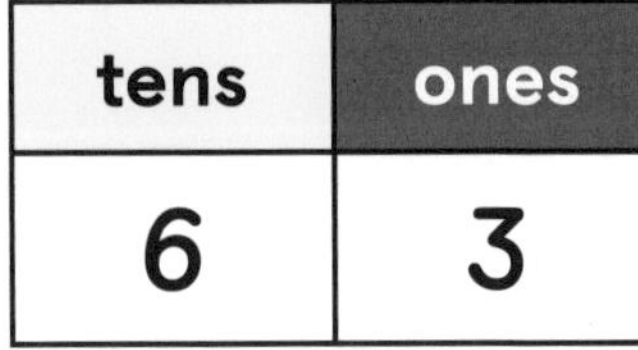

tens	ones
6	3

63

We need to compare the tens first. 65 and 63 both have 6 tens. 71 has 7 tens.

7 tens is more than 6 tens. 71 has the most tens.

71 is greater than 65.
71 > 65

71 is greater than 63.
71 > 63

71 is the greatest number.

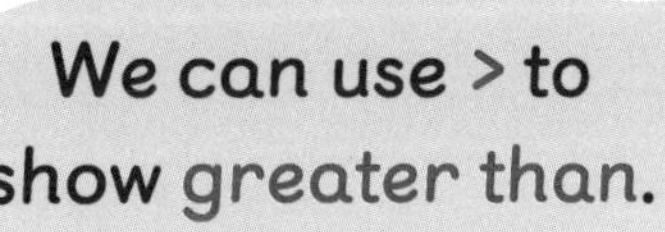

We need to compare the ones next. 65 has 5 ones. 63 has 3 ones. 3 ones is less than 5 ones.

63 is less than 65.

We can use < to show less than.

63 is less than 65.
63 < 65
63 is the smallest number.

We can also use a number line to compare the numbers.

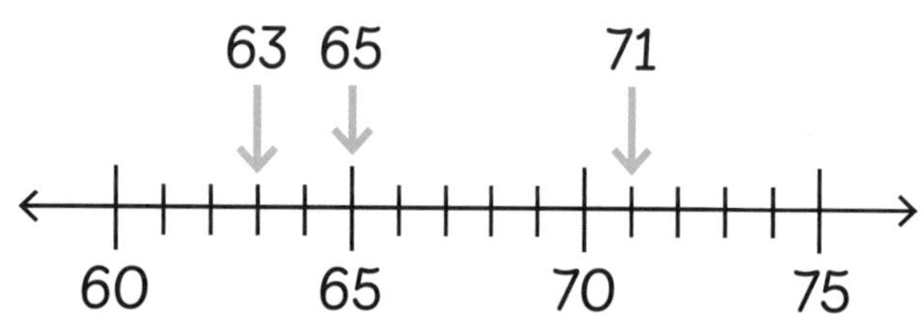

We can order the numbers in two ways.

71, 65, 63 greatest → smallest	63, 65, 71 smallest → greatest

Practice

1 Count in tens and ones.
Compare the numbers and fill in the blanks.

tens	ones

☐ = ☐ tens and ☐ ones

tens	ones

☐ = ☐ tens and ☐ ones

☐ is less than ☐ .

2 Fill in the blanks on the number line using the numbers given. Compare the numbers using > or <.

(a) 31, 39, 34

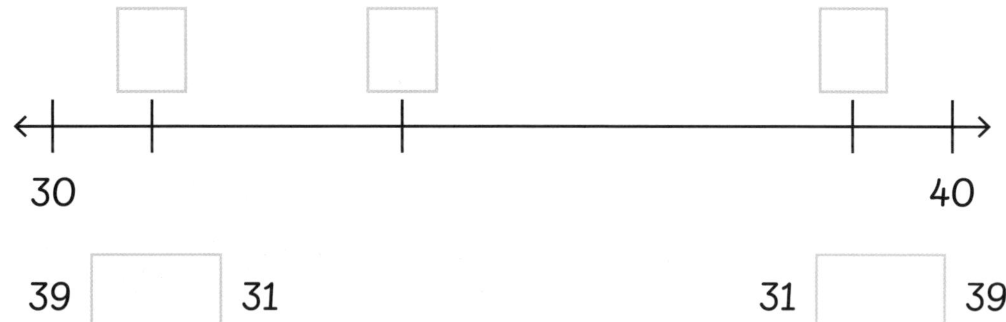

39 ☐ 31 31 ☐ 39

(b) 53, 46, 58, 41

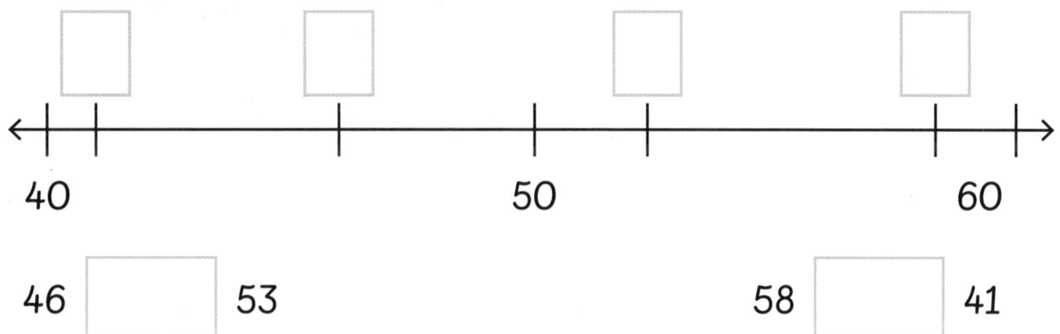

46 ☐ 53 58 ☐ 41

3 Put the numbers in order, starting with the smallest.

98, 79, 85

☐, ☐, ☐

4 Put the numbers in order, starting with the greatest.

23, 11, 24

☐, ☐, ☐

5 Use > or < to fill in the blanks.

(a) 12 ☐ 56 (b) 64 ☐ 46 (c) 78 ☐ 87

Patterns

Lesson 4

Starter

Emma is placing drink packs on the shelf.
She has put 4 packs on the shelf so far.
How many drinks are on the shelf?

Example

There are 4 drink packs on the shelf. Each pack has 5 drinks.

We can count in fives.
I can use a number line to help.
5, 10, 15, 20
There are 20 drinks on the shelf.

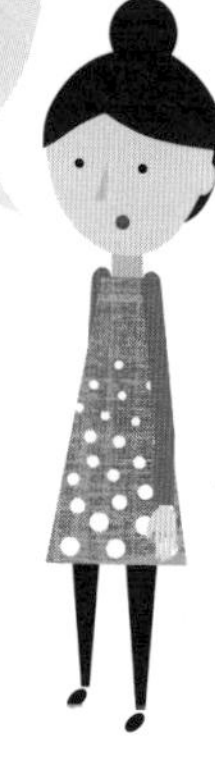

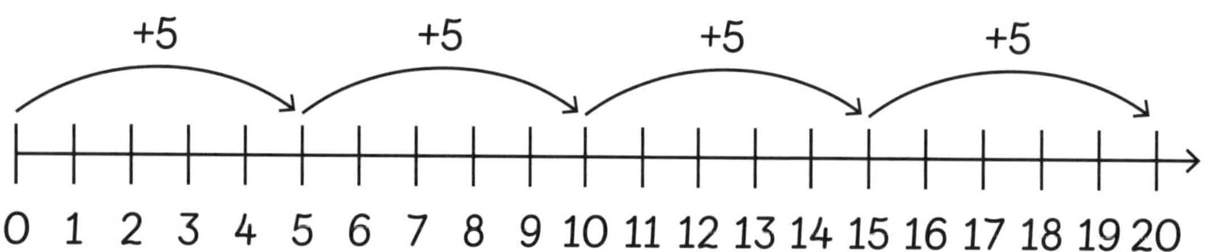

What if Emma puts the other 2 drink packs on the shelf? How many drinks will be on the shelf?

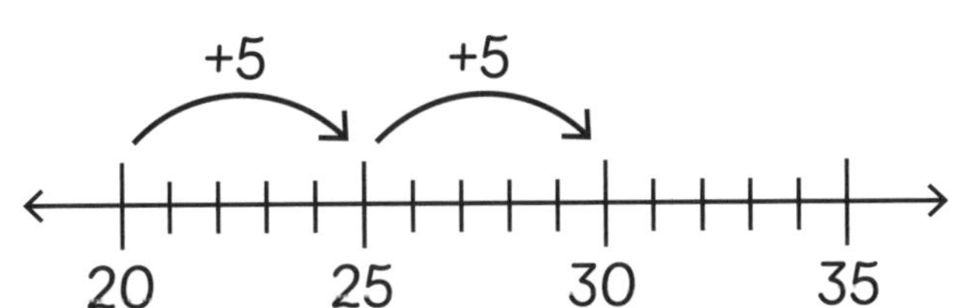

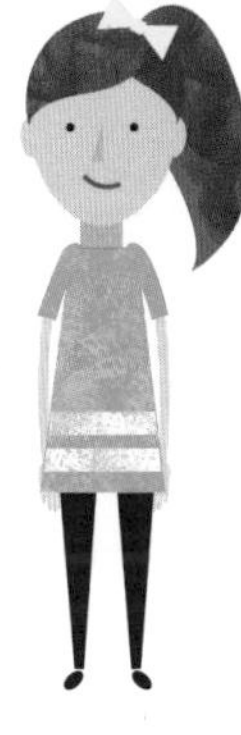

There will be 30 drinks on the shelf.

Practice

Fill in the blanks.

1 How many crisp packs are on the shelf?

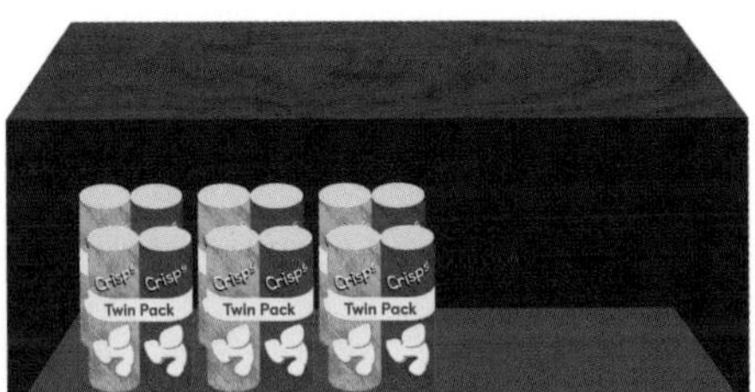

2, 4, 6, 8, 10, ☐

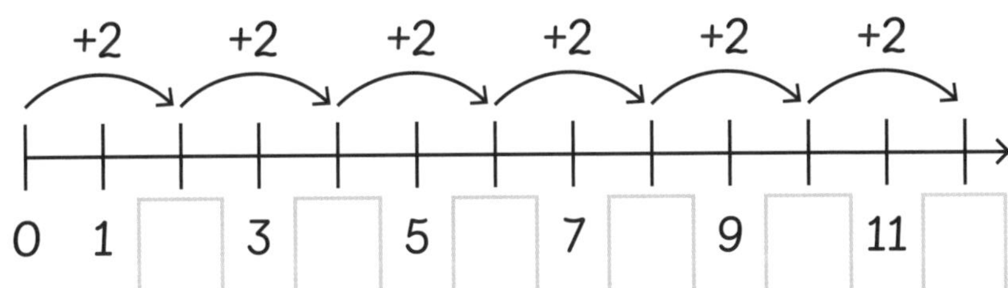

2

(a) ☐ ← 3 less — 27 — 3 more → ☐

(b) ☐ ← 3 less — 30 — 3 more → ☐

(c) ☐ ← 5 less — 35 — 5 more → ☐

(d) ☐ ← 5 less — 86 — 5 more → ☐

(e) ☐ ← 3 less — 62 — 3 more → ☐

Adding ones

Lesson 5

Starter

How many crayons are there in total?

Example

There are 42 crayons on the table. Amira is holding 3 crayons.

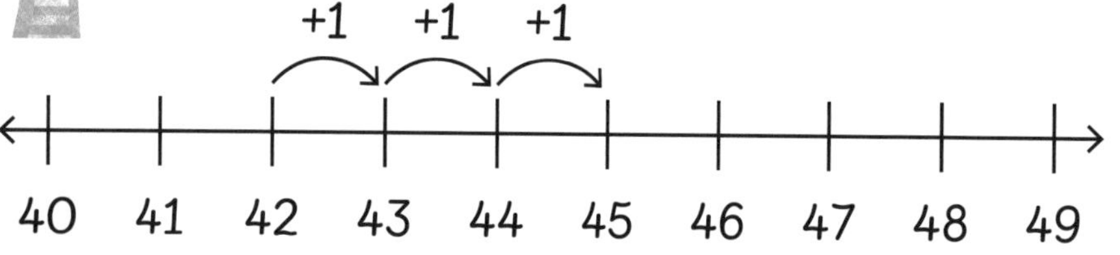

I can count on from 42. 43, 44, 45

There is another way.

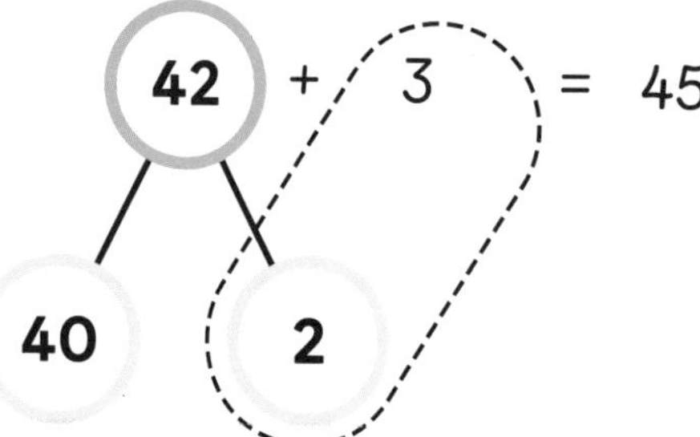

I can split 42 into 40 and 2. I can then add the ones.

Practice

Add and fill in the blanks.

1 Use the number lines to help you count on.

(a) 15 + 2 = ☐

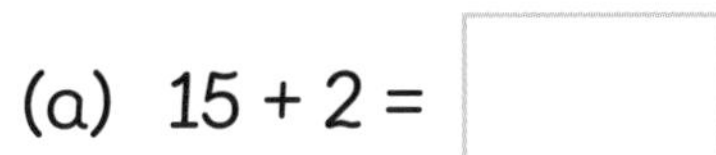

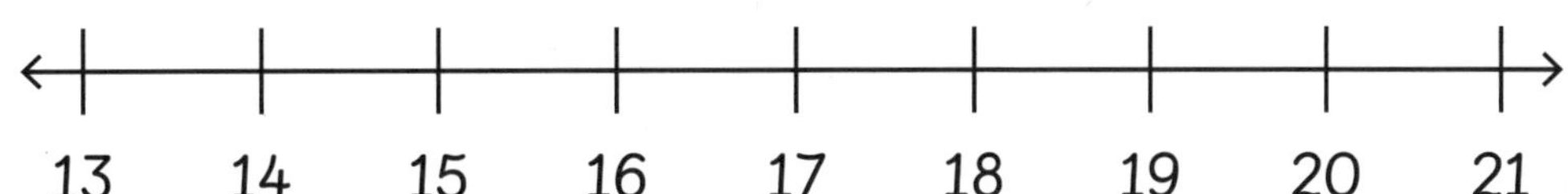

(b) 72 + 7 = ☐

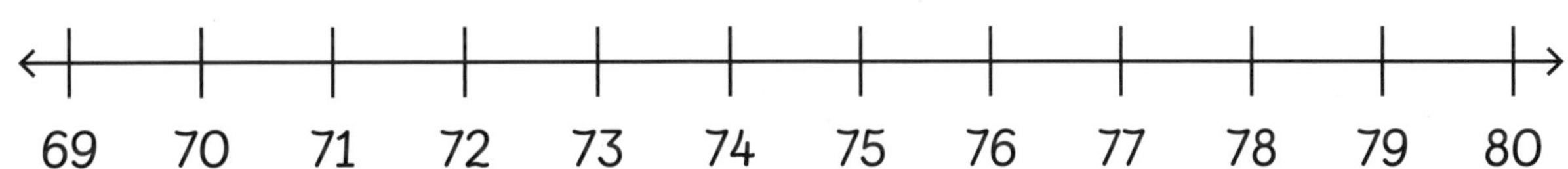

2 (a) **47** + 2 = ☐ 47 and 2 make ☐.

47 → **40**, **7**

(b) **62** + 7 = ☐ 62 and 7 make ☐.

62 → **60**, ☐

(c) 3 + **82** = ☐ 3 and 82 make ☐.

82 → ☐, ☐

Adding tens

Lesson 6

Starter

How many apples does the grocer have for sale?

Example

Each box has 10 apples.

4 tens + 3 tens = 7 tens

There are 4 boxes of red apples. There are 3 boxes of green apples.

40 + 30 = 70
The grocer has 70 apples for sale.

Practice

Add and fill in the blanks.

1 (a) 2 + 5 = ☐

(b) 20 + 50 = ☐

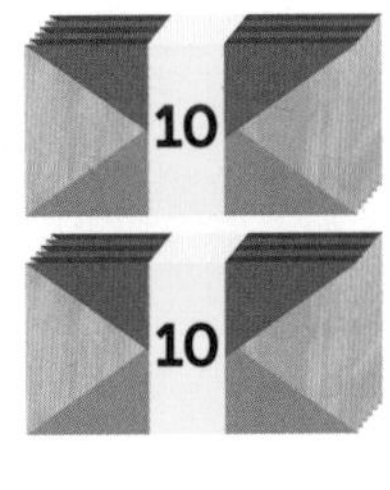

2 (a) 7 + 2 = ☐

(b) 70 + 20 = ☐

(c) 30 + 30 = ☐

(d) 70 + 30 = ☐

3 (a) 2 ones + 4 ones = ☐ ones

(b) 4 tens + 2 tens = ☐ tens

(c) 5 tens + 5 tens = ☐

(d) 6 tens + 5 ones = ☐

Adding in columns

Lesson 7

Starter

I have 53 cards.

I have 40 cards.

How can we add 53 + 40?

Example

I can count on in tens starting from 53. 63, 73, 83, 93

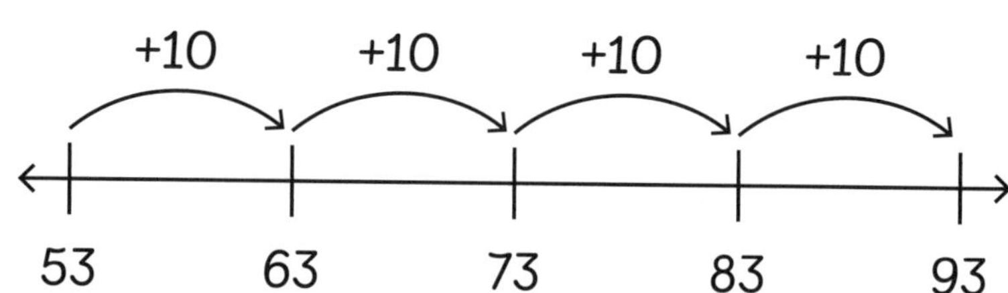

I can add the tens and then add the ones.

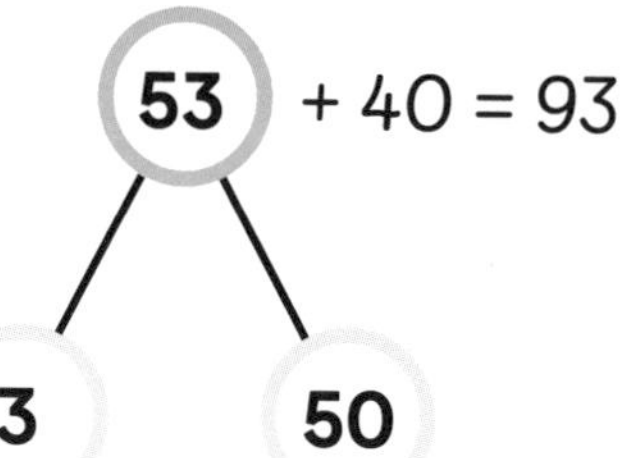

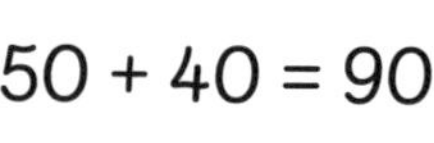

50 + 40 = 90
90 + 3 = 93

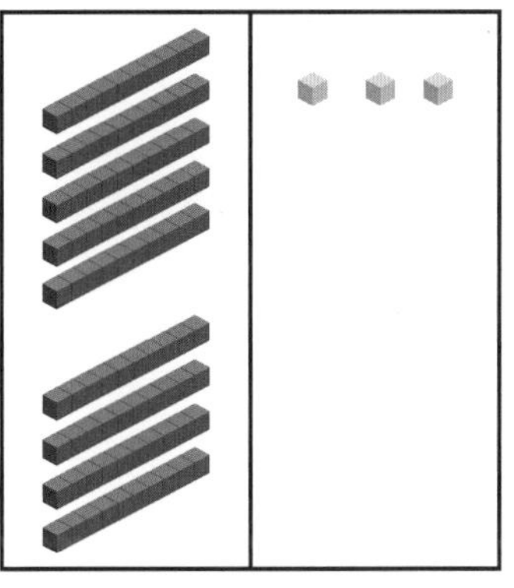

Here's another way to add.
Start with the ones.

3 ones + 0 ones = 3 ones
3 + 0 = 3

	tens	ones
	5	3
+	4	0
		3

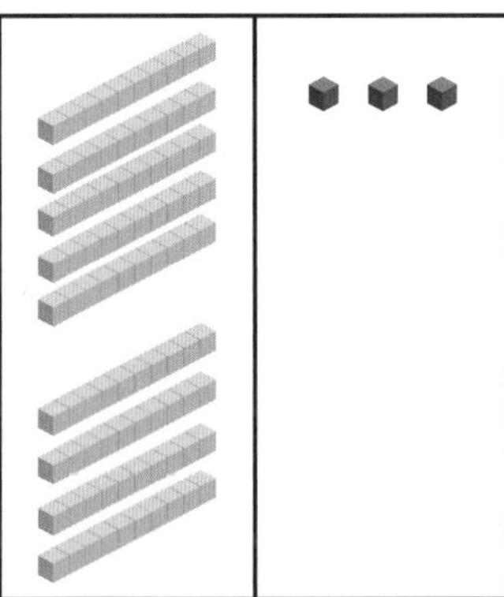

Add the tens.

5 tens + 4 tens = 9 tens
50 + 40 = 90

	tens	ones
	5	3
+	4	0
	9	3

9 tens + 3 ones = 93
The friends have collected 93 cards altogether.

Practice

1 Fill in the blanks.

(a) 17 + 20 = ☐

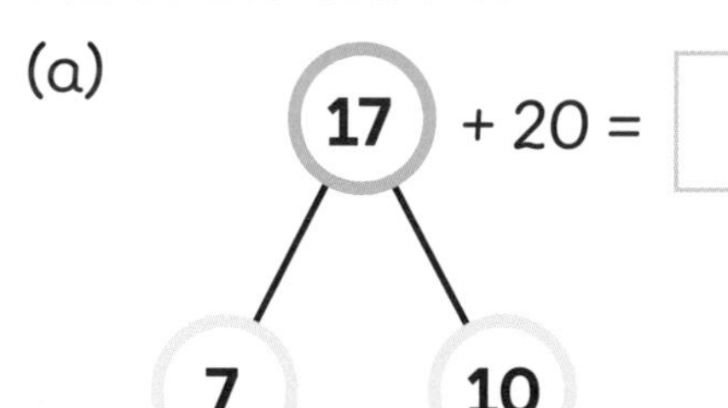
17
7
10

(b) 46 + 30 = ☐

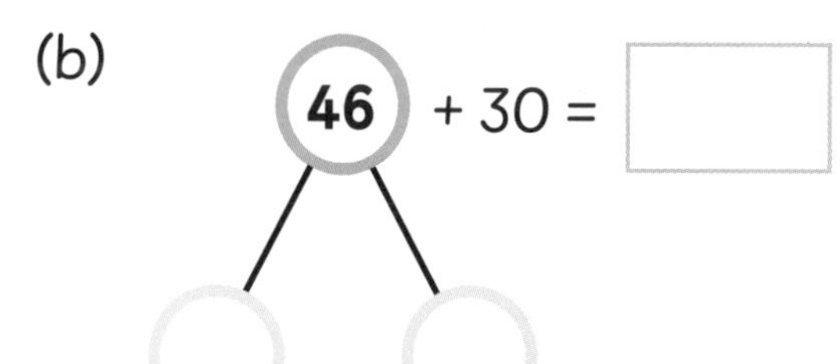
46

2 Add.

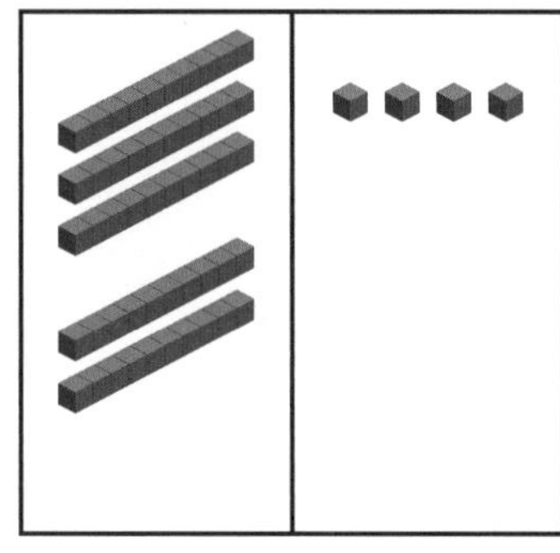

	tens	ones
	3	4
+	2	0
	☐	☐

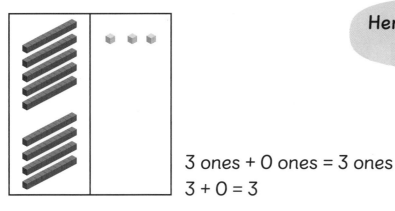

Adding in columns without renaming

Lesson 8

Starter

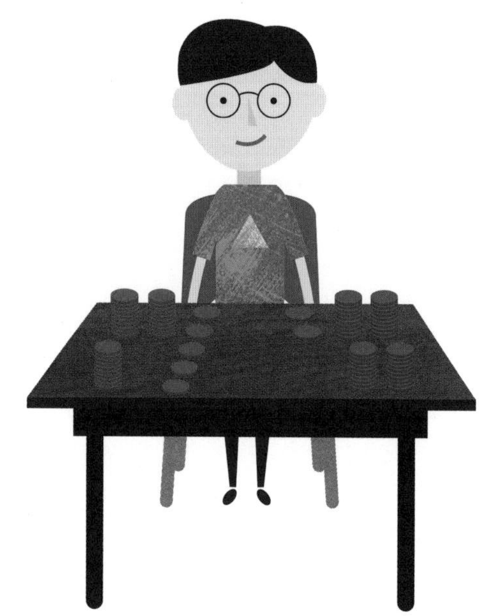

How many counters does Charles have altogether?

Example

Charles has 35 red counters and 42 blue counters.

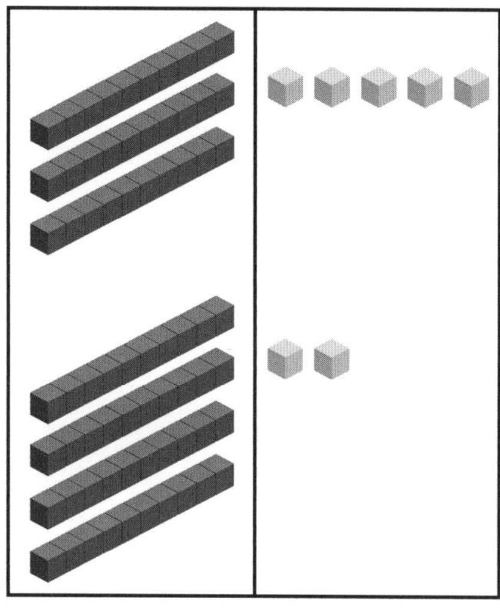

	tens	ones
	3	5
+	4	2
		7

5 ones + 2 ones = 7 ones
5 + 2 = 7

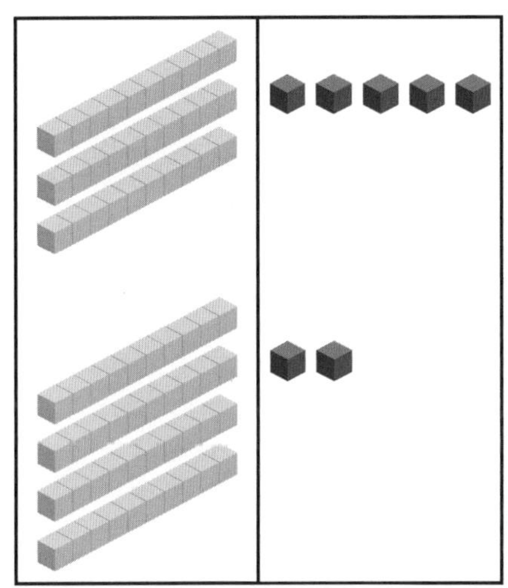

	tens	ones
	3	5
+	4	2
	7	7

3 tens + 4 tens = 7 tens
30 + 40 = 70

35 and 42 make 77.
35 + 42 = 77
Charles has 77 counters altogether.

Practice

Add and fill in the blanks.

1 (a) 51 + 23 = ___

(b) 72 + 26 = ___

2 (a) 37 + 42 = ___

	tens	ones
	3	7
+	4	2

(b) 64 + 35 = ___

	tens	ones
	6	4
+	3	5

Adding in columns with renaming (part 1)

Lesson 9

Starter

Jacob read 36 pages of his book last week.
He has read 7 pages this week.
How many pages has Jacob read altogether?

Example

36 + 7 = ?

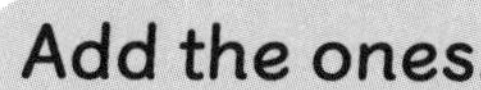

Method 1

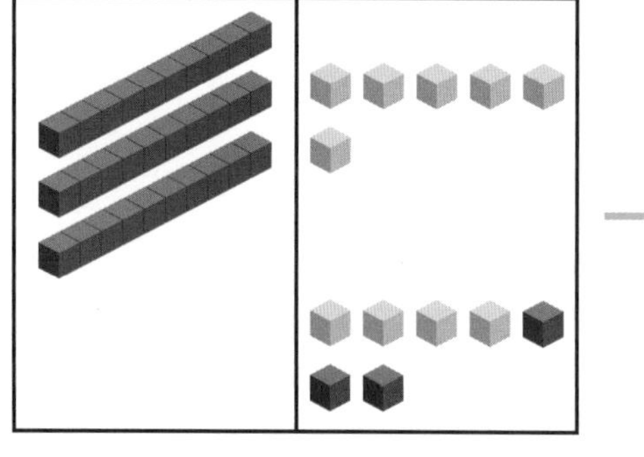

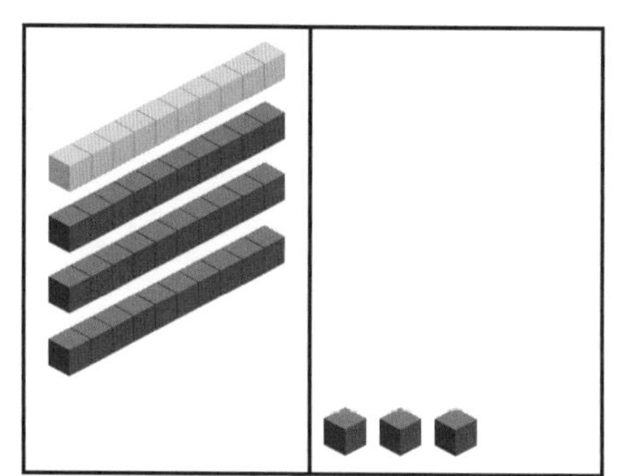

	tens	ones
	3	6
+		7
	1	3

6 ones + 7 ones = 13 ones
Rename the ones.
13 ones = 1 ten and 3 ones

10 ones are equal to 1 ten.

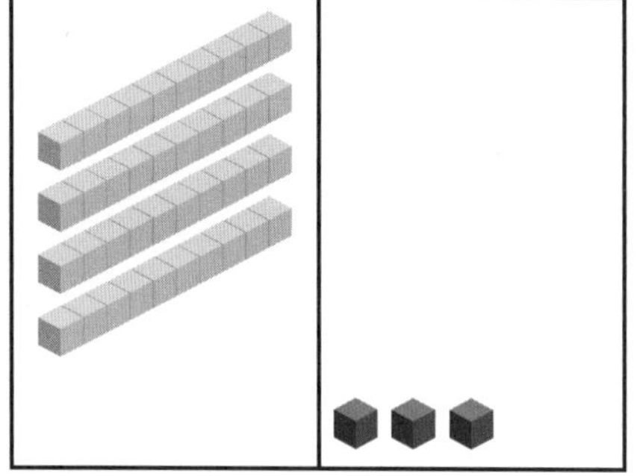

	tens	ones
	3	6
+		7
	1	3
+	3	0
	4	3

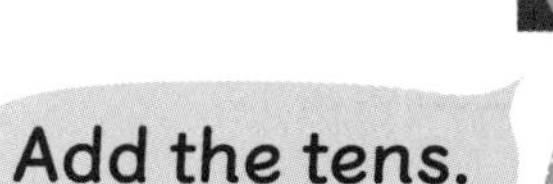

3 tens + 1 ten = 4 tens
30 + 10 = 40
36 + 7 = 43

Method 2

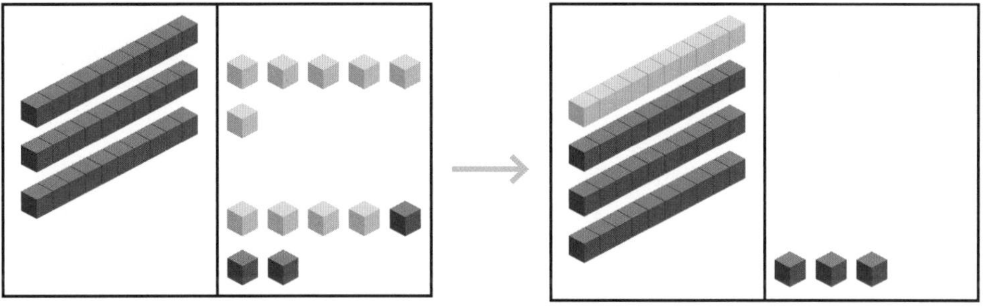

	tens	ones
	[1]3	6
+		7
		3

6 ones + 7 ones = 13 ones

Rename the ones.

13 ones = 1 ten and 3 ones

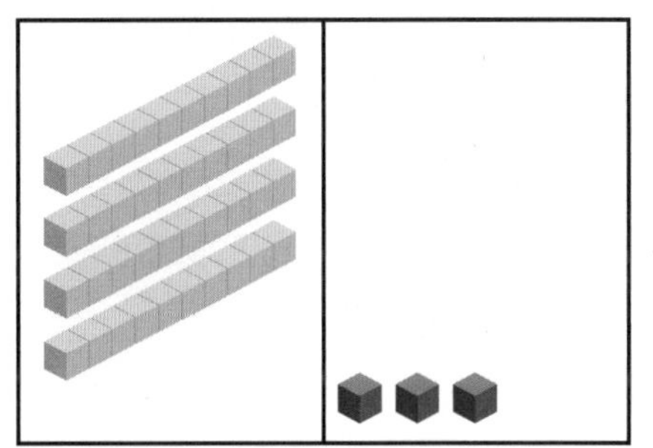

	tens	ones
	[1]3	6
+		7
	4	3

3 tens + 1 ten = 4 tens

30 + 10 = 40

36 + 7 = 43

Jacob has read 43 pages altogether.

Practice

Add and fill in the blanks.

1 57 + 8

	tens	ones
	5	7
+		8
	☐	☐
+	☐	☐
	☐	☐

2 9 + 23

	tens	ones
		9
+	2	3
	☐	☐
+	☐	☐
	☐	☐

Adding in columns with renaming (part 2)

Lesson 10

Starter

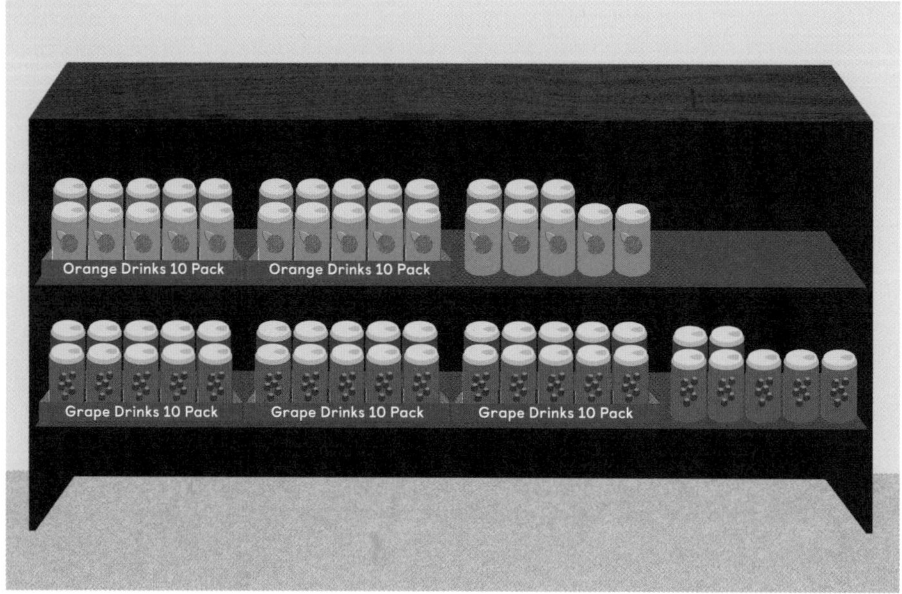

A shop has 28 orange drinks and 37 grape drinks.
How many drinks does the shop have in total?

Example

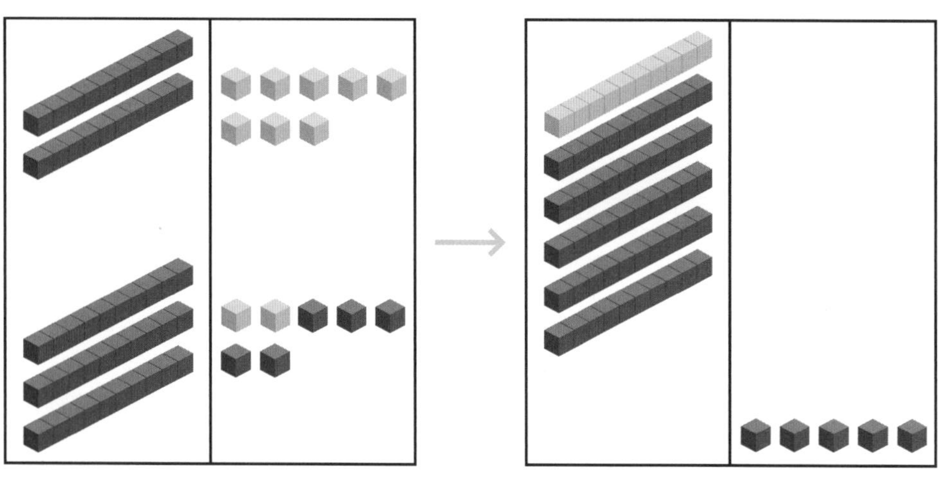

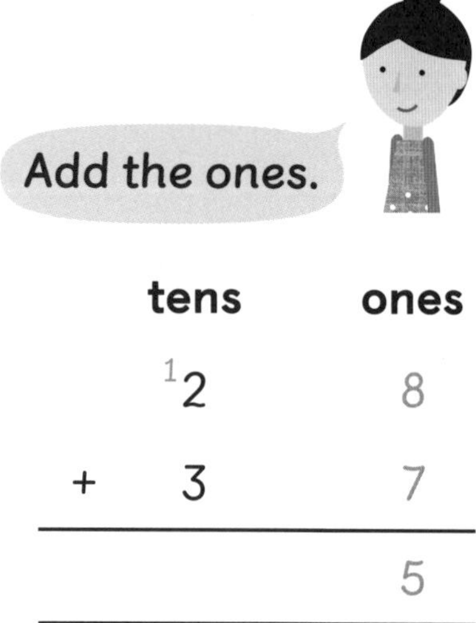

	tens	ones
	[1] 2	8
+	3	7
		5

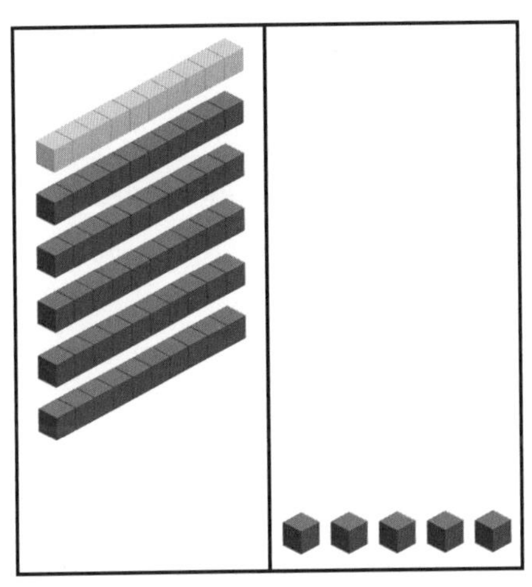

	tens	ones
	$^{1}2$	8
+	3	7
	6	5

Add the tens.

2 tens + 3 tens + 1 ten = 6 tens

20 + 30 + 10 = 60

28 + 37 = 65

The shop has 65 drinks in total.

Practice

Add and fill in the blanks.

1. 27 + 15

	tens	ones
	2	7
+	1	5
	☐	☐

2. 18 + 19

	tens	ones
	1	8
+	1	9
	☐	☐

3. 37 + 47

	tens	ones
	3	7
+	4	7
	☐	☐

4. 66 + 28

	tens	ones
	6	6
+	2	8
	☐	☐

Adding three numbers

Lesson
11

Starter

How many doughnuts are there altogether?

Example

I can use a number line to help me count on.

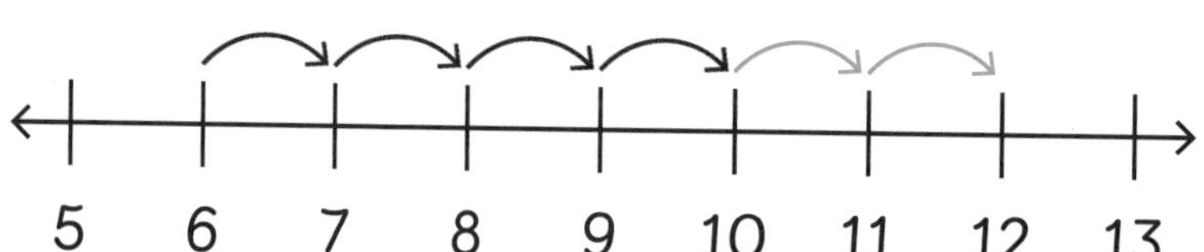

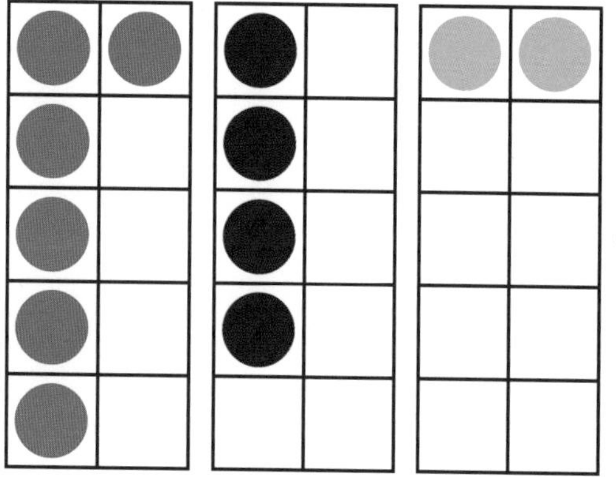
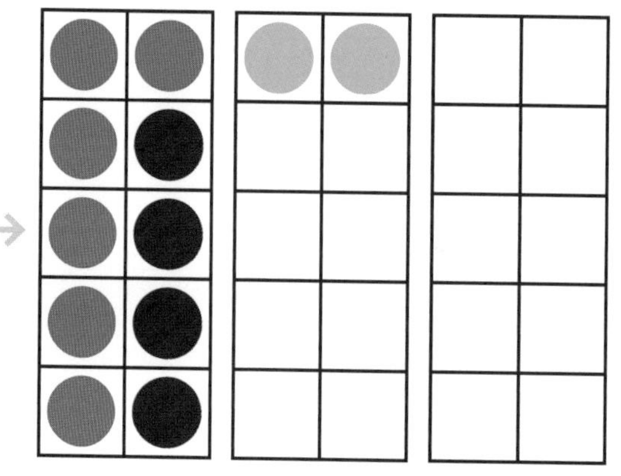

$6 + 4 + 2 = 10 + 2$

$= 12$

I can use ten frames and make 10.

There are 12 doughnuts altogether.

Practice

1 Make 10. Shade the ten frames and fill in the blanks.

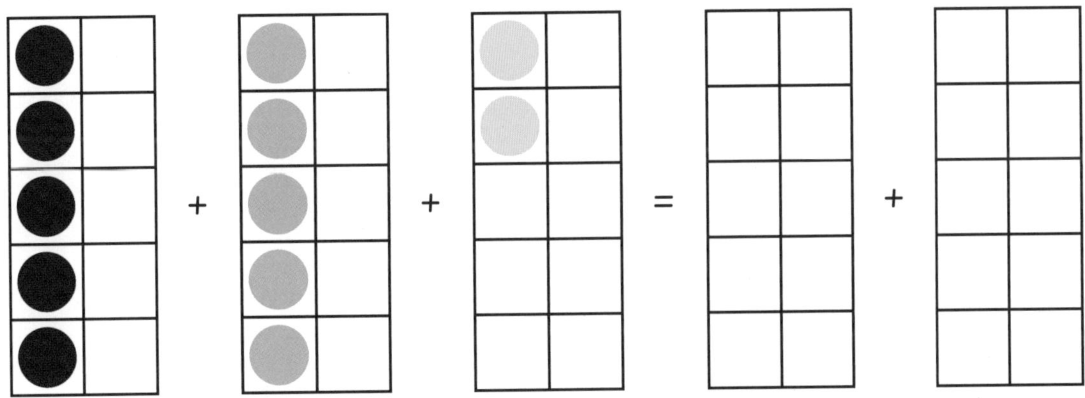

☐ + ☐

= ☐

2 Make 10. Add and fill in the blanks.

(a) 7 + 3 + 2 = ☐ + ☐

= ☐

(b) 4 + 8 + 2 = ☐ + ☐

= ☐

(c) 6 + 3 + 4 = ☐ + ☐

= ☐

(d) 5 + 4 + 5 = ☐ + ☐

= ☐

3 Add and fill in the blanks.

(a) 7 + 7 + 3 = ☐

(b) 5 + 6 + 9 = ☐

(c) 8 + 4 + 8 = ☐

(d) 7 + 6 + 7 = ☐

(e) 9 + 6 + 8 = ☐

(f) 7 + 7 + 9 = ☐

Subtracting ones

Lesson 12

Starter

The shop has 26 chocolates. Charles buys 3 chocolates. How many chocolates are left in the shop?

Example

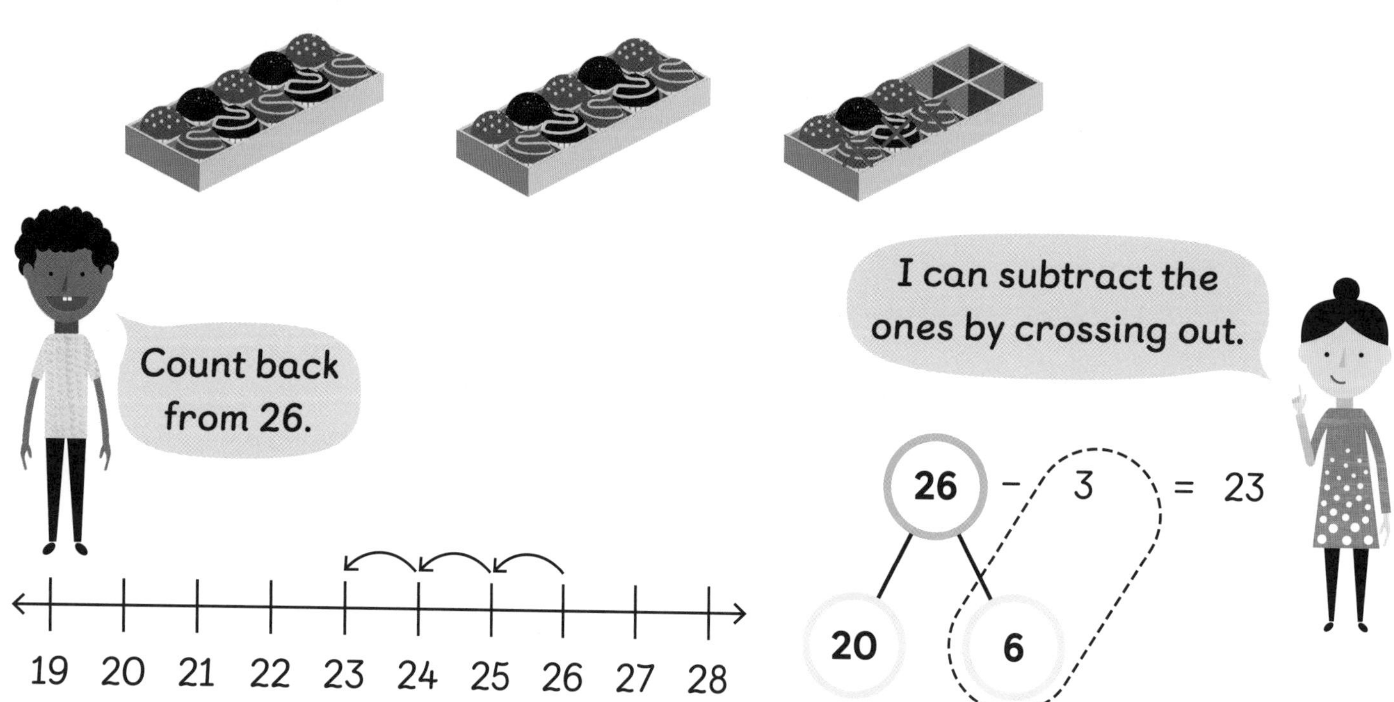

Count back from 26.
19 20 21 22 23 24 25 26 27 28
I can subtract the ones by crossing out.
26 − 3 = 23
20
6

There are 23 chocolates left in the shop.

Practice

Subtract and fill in the blanks.

1 Use the number lines to help you count back.

(a) 37 − 5 = ☐

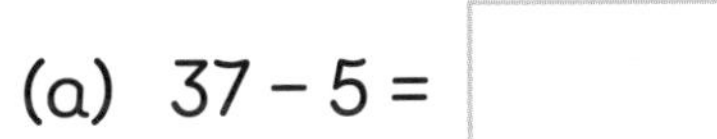

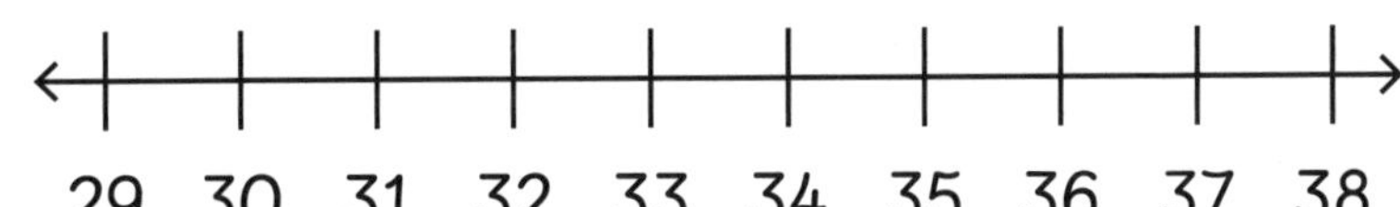

(b) 58 − 4 = ☐

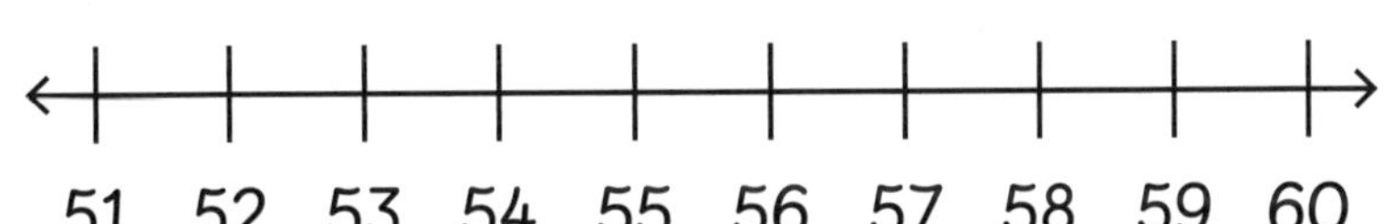

2 (a) 27 − 4 = ☐ 27 subtract 4 is equal to ☐ .

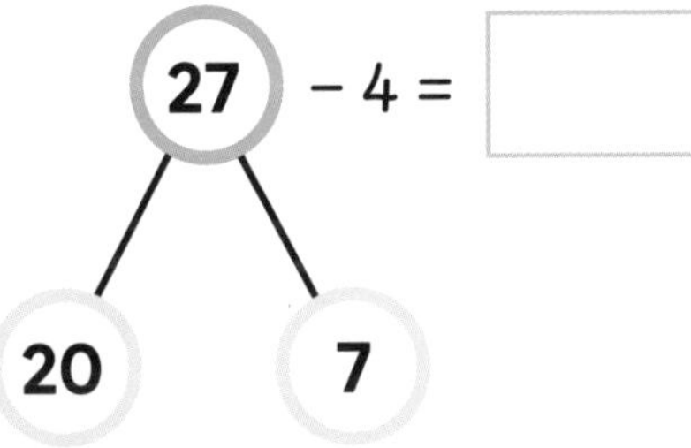

(b) 68 − 5 = ☐ 68 subtract 5 is equal to ☐ .

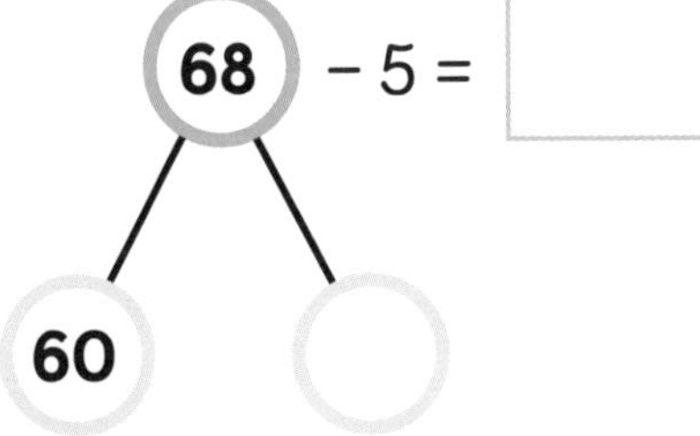

Subtracting tens

Starter

There are 6 boxes of fish fingers for sale at a shop.
Elliott buys 2 of the boxes.
How many fish fingers are left at the shop?

Example

Each box has 10 fish fingers.

The shop has sold 2 boxes. There are now 4 boxes left.

I can use a number line to count back in tens.

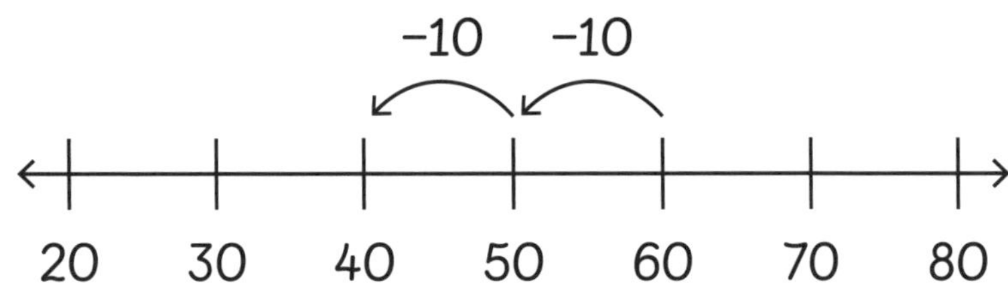

6 tens – 2 tens = 4 tens

60 – 20 = 40

There are 40 fish fingers left at the shop.

Practice

Subtract and fill in the blanks.

1 Use the number lines to help you count back in tens.

(a) 80 – 30 = ☐

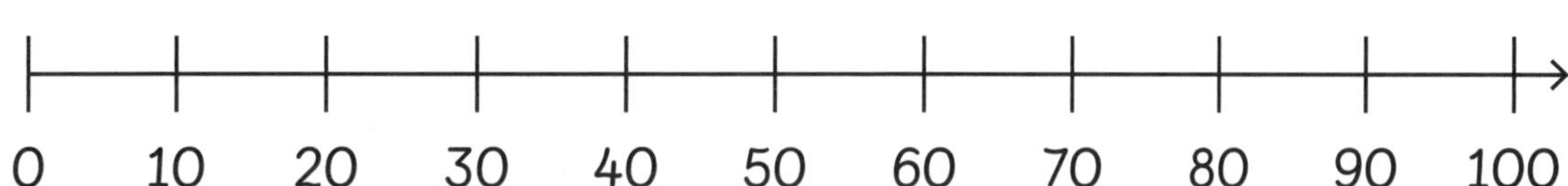

(b) 50 – 40 = ☐

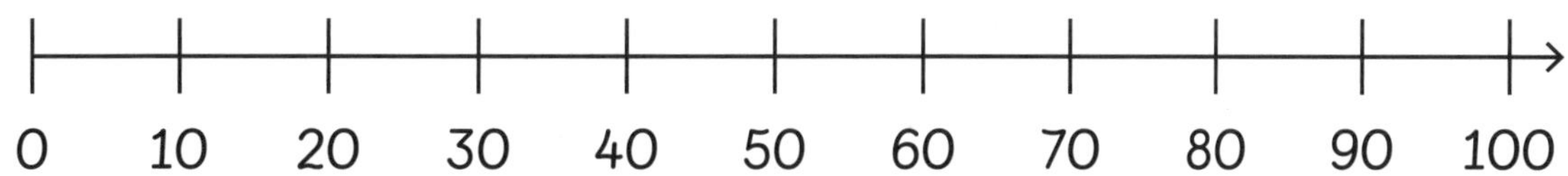

2 (a) 9 – 5 = ☐

9 tens – 5 tens = ☐ tens

90 – 50 = ☐

(b) 8 – 4 = ☐

8 tens – 4 tens = ☐ tens

80 – 40 = ☐

Subtracting in columns

Lesson 14

Starter

Sam has 55 coins in his collection. He gives 30 of his coins to his little brother. How many coins does Sam have left?

Example

55 – 30 = ?

55 – 30 = 25

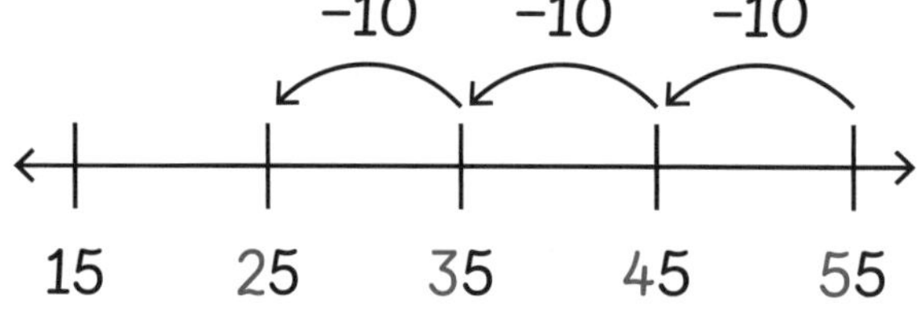

50 – 30 = 20
20 + 5 = 25
55 – 30 = 25

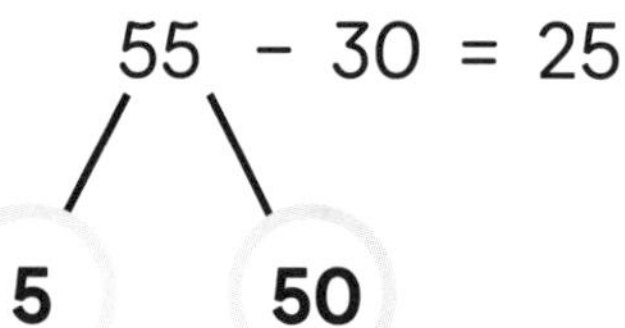

Subtract the tens, then add the ones.

5 ones – 0 ones = 5 ones, 5 – 0 = 5

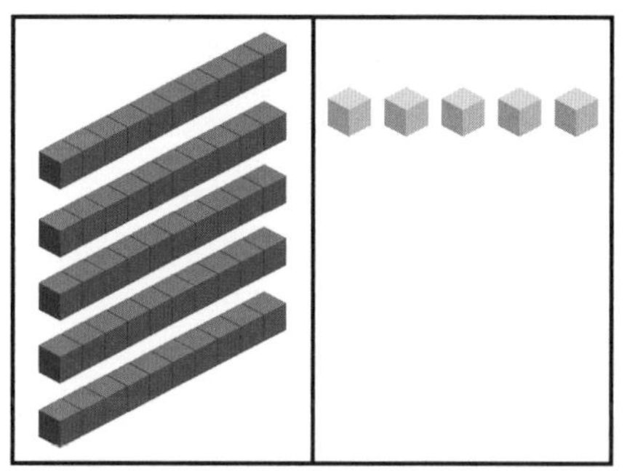

	tens	ones
	5	5
–	3	0
		5

Subtract the ones.

5 tens – 3 tens = 2 tens, 50 – 30 = 20
55 – 30 = 25

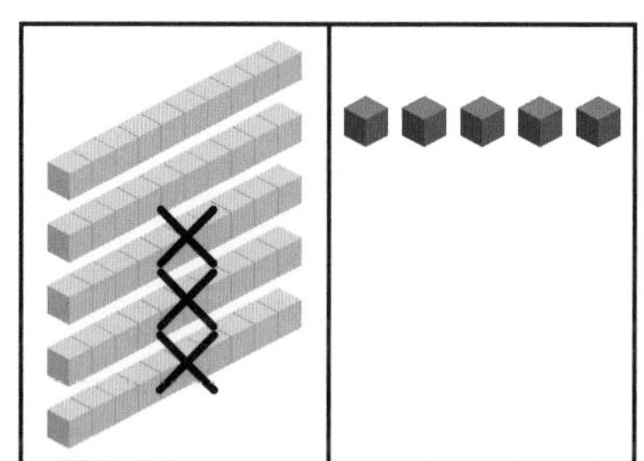

	tens	ones
	5	5
–	3	0
	2	5

Subtract the tens.

Sam has 25 coins left.

Practice

Subtract and fill in the blanks.

1. 58 – 20

	tens	ones
	5	8
–	2	0
	☐	☐

2. 87 – 70

	tens	ones
	8	7
–	7	0
	☐	☐

3. 55 – 20

	tens	ones
	5	5
–	2	0
	☐	☐

4. 72 – 30

	tens	ones
	7	2
–	3	0
	☐	☐

Subtracting in columns without renaming

Lesson 15

Starter

There are 45 elephants in a herd.
23 of the elephants are bulls.
How many of the elephants are not bulls?

A male elephant is called a bull.

Example

45 − 23 = ?

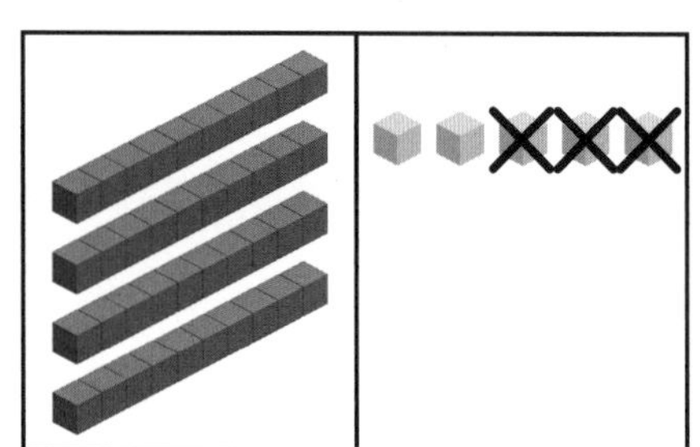

	tens	ones
	4	5
−	2	3
		2

Subtract the ones.

5 ones − 3 ones = 2 ones
5 − 3 = 2

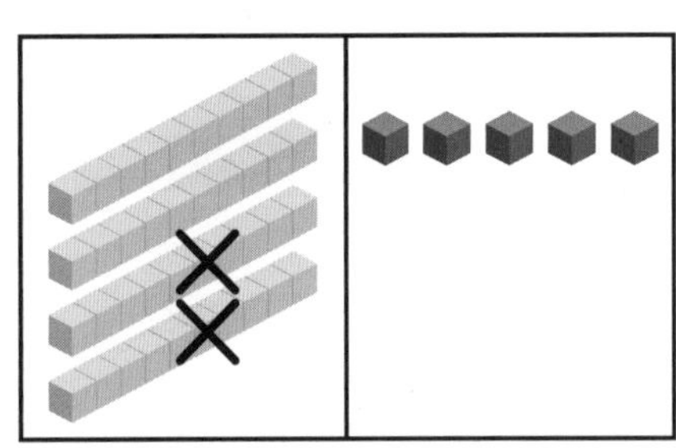

	tens	ones
	4	5
−	2	3
	2	2

4 tens − 2 tens = 2 tens
40 − 20 = 20
45 − 23 = 22

22 elephants are not bulls.

Practice

Subtract and fill in the blanks.

1 48 − 15

	tens	ones
	4	8
−	1	5
	☐	☐

2 53 − 12

	tens	ones
	5	3
−	1	2
	☐	☐

3 66 − 33

	tens	ones
	6	6
−	3	3
	☐	☐

4 64 − 54

	tens	ones
	6	4
−	5	4
	☐	☐

Subtracting in columns with renaming (part 1)

Starter

There are 42 monkeys in a troop.
6 of them are on the ground.
How many monkeys are not on the ground?

Example

42 − 6 = ?

Method 1

Take 6 away from 10.

42 − 6 = 36

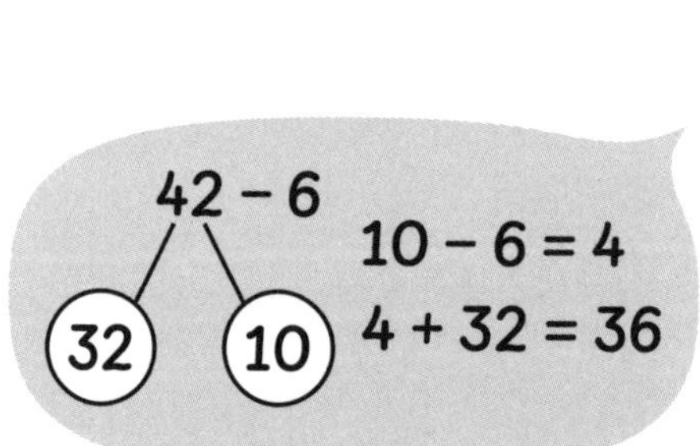

Method 2

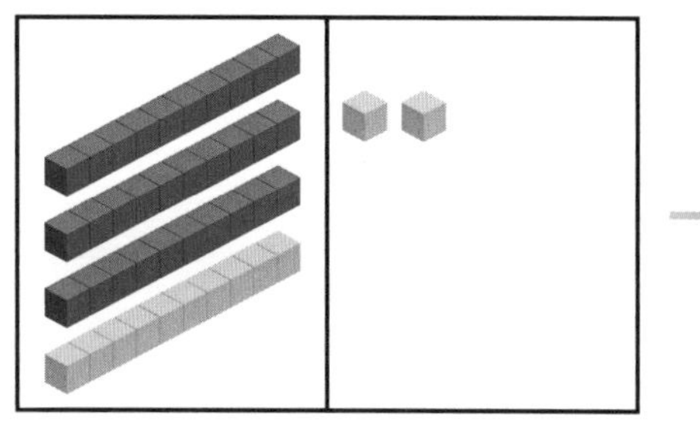

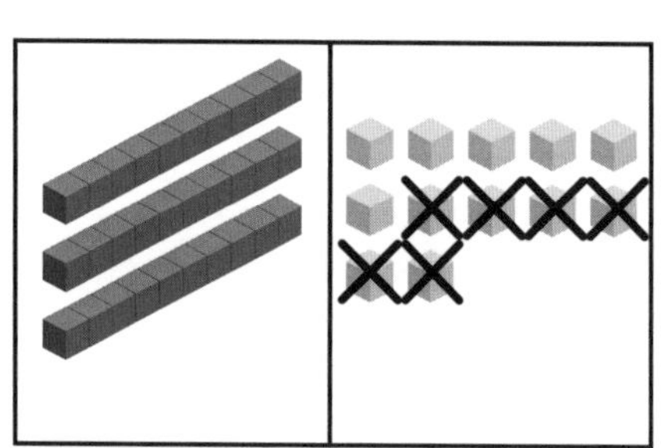

	tens	ones
	~~4~~ 3	~~2~~ 12
−		6
		6

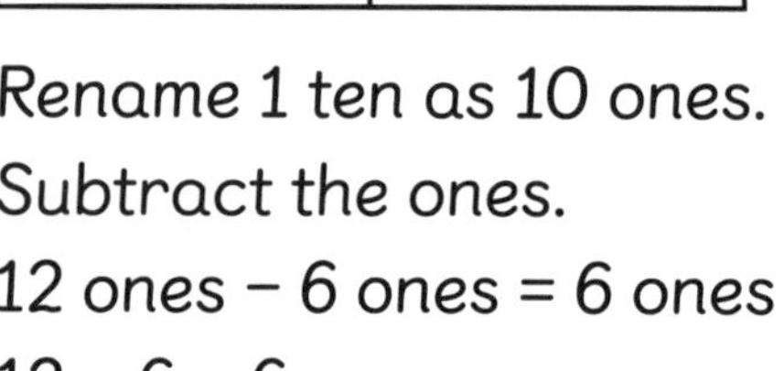

Rename 1 ten as 10 ones.
Subtract the ones.
12 ones − 6 ones = 6 ones
12 − 6 = 6

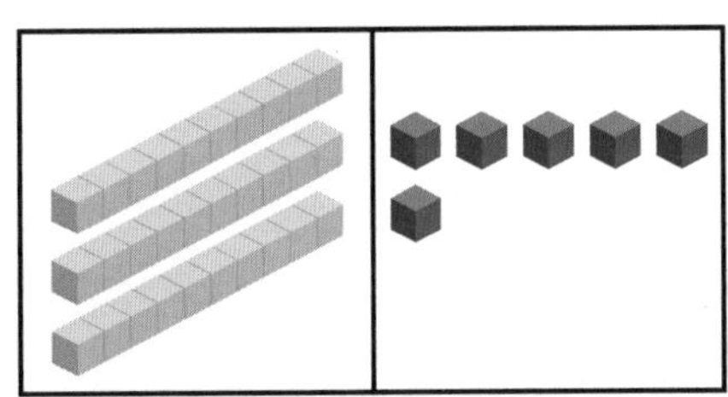

	tens	ones
	~~4~~ 3	~~2~~ 12
−		6
	3	6

Subtract the tens.
3 tens − 0 tens = 3 tens
30 − 0 = 30
42 − 6 = 36

36 monkeys are not on the ground.

Practice

Subtract and fill in the blanks.

1 53 − 5 = ☐

2 44 − 8 = ☐

3 35 − 7 = ☐

4 72 − 8 = ☐

5

	tens	ones
	2	1
−		3
	☐	☐

6

	tens	ones
	8	5
−		6
	☐	☐

Subtracting in columns with renaming (part 2)

Starter

There are 42 doughnuts for sale at a bakery.
Charles and his dad buy 24 doughnuts for a party.
How many doughnuts are left at the bakery?

Example

42 – 24 = ?

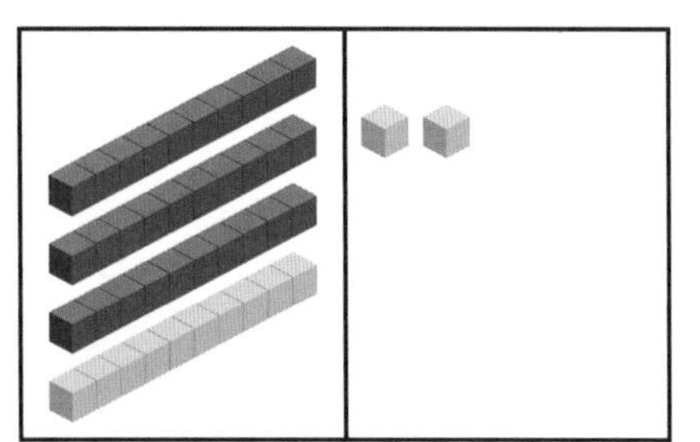

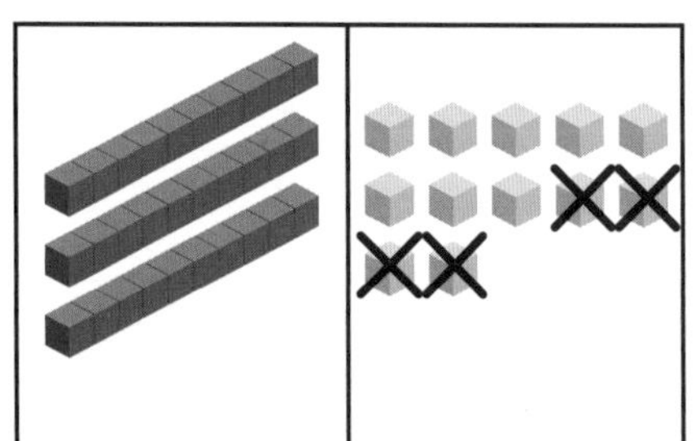

	tens	ones
	$^{3}\cancel{4}$	$^{12}\cancel{2}$
–	2	4
		8

Rename 1 ten as 10 ones.
Subtract the ones.
12 ones – 4 ones = 8 ones
12 – 4 = 8

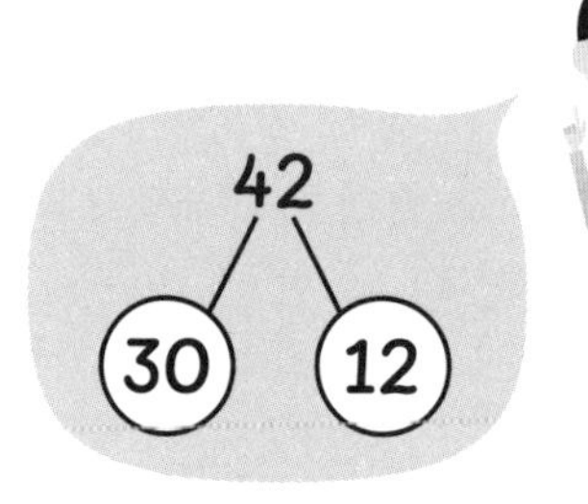

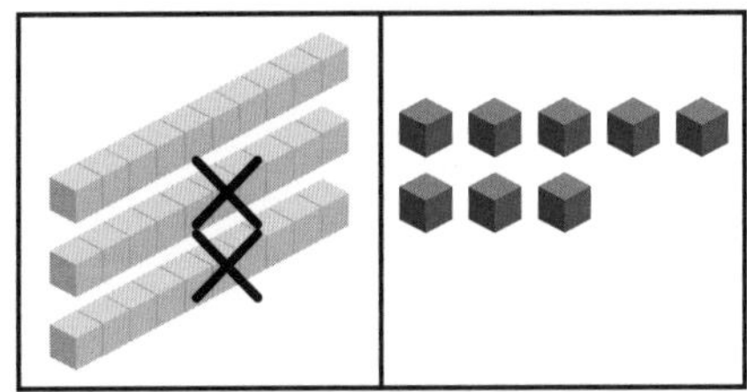

	tens	ones
	~~4~~ 3	~~2~~ 12
−	2	4
	1	8

Subtract the tens.
3 tens − 2 tens = 1 ten
30 − 20 = 10
42 − 24 = 18

18 doughnuts are left at the bakery.

Practice

Subtract and fill in the blanks.

1 74 − 35 = ☐

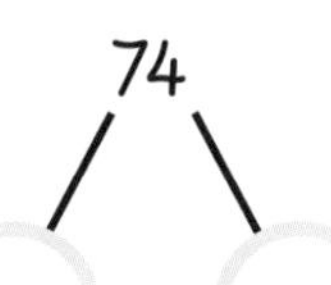

2

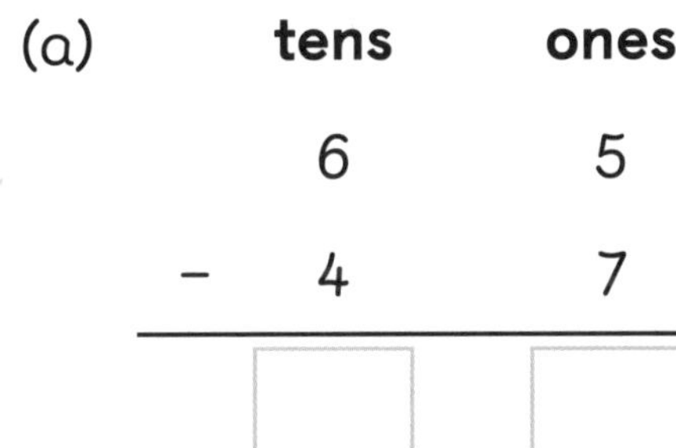

(a)

	tens	ones
	6	5
−	4	7
	☐	☐

(b)

	tens	ones
	9	5
−	1	6
	☐	☐

(c)

	tens	ones
	3	2
−	1	8
	☐	☐

(d)

	tens	ones
	9	1
−	8	9
	☐	☐

Review and challenge

1 Fill in the blanks.

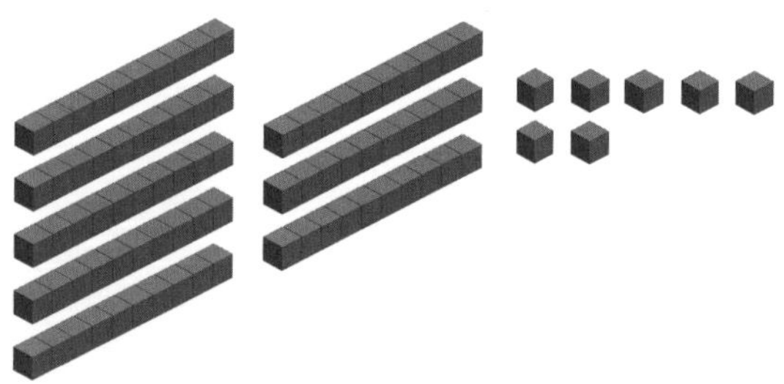

tens	ones

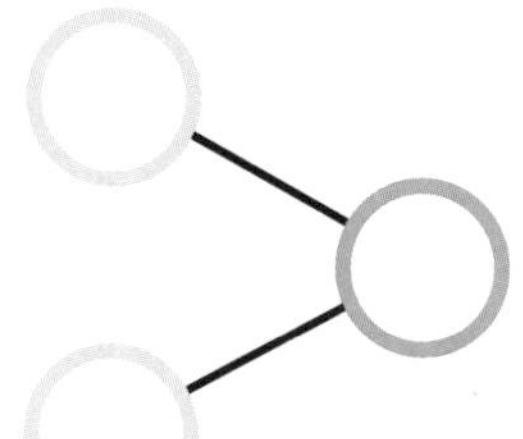

☐ = ☐ tens and ☐ ones

2 Fill in the blanks.

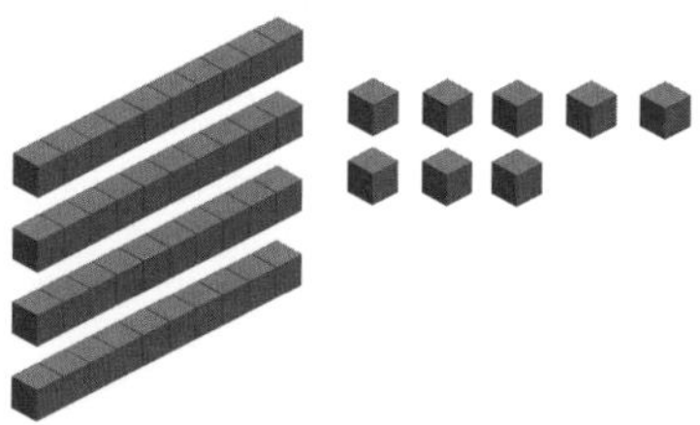

tens	ones

☐ = ☐ tens and ☐ ones

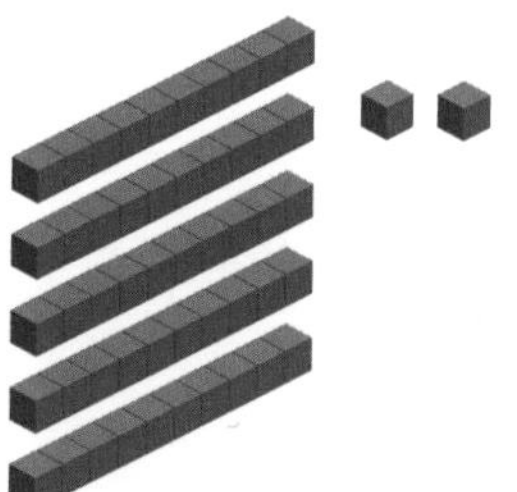

tens	ones

☐ = ☐ tens and ☐ ones

☐ is less than ☐.

3 Put the numbers in order, starting with the smallest.

78, 29, 65

☐, ☐, ☐

4 Put the numbers in order, starting with the greatest.

54, 41, 56

☐, ☐, ☐

5 Use > or < to fill in the blanks.

(a) 25 ☐ 36 (b) 56 ☐ 65 (c) 39  41

6 Fill in the blanks.

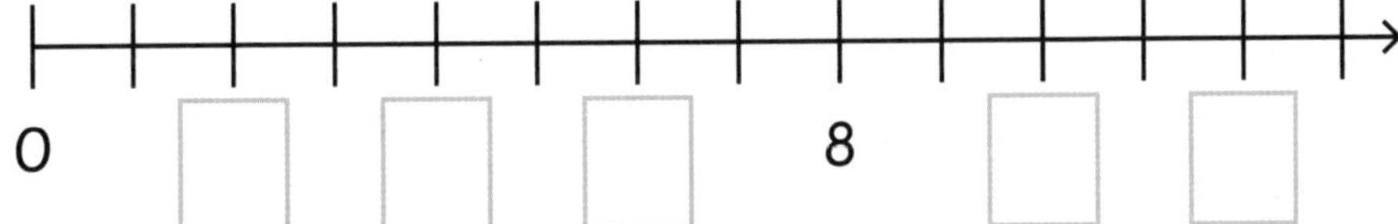

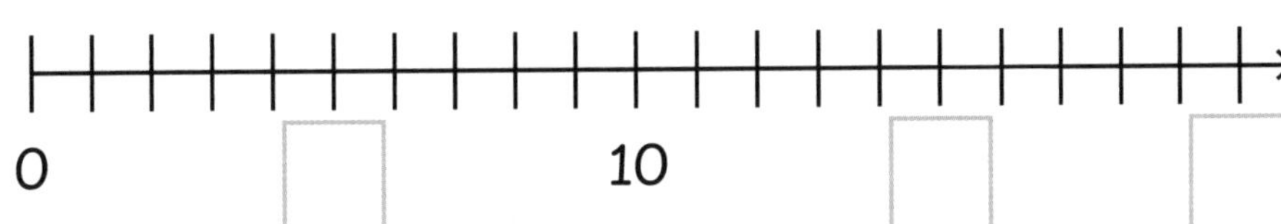

7 Add and fill in the blanks.

(a) 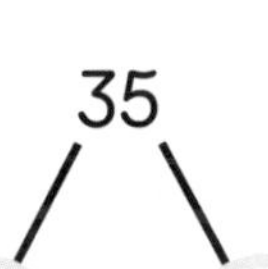

\+ 24 = ☐

(b) 53 + 24 = ☐

Solve.

8 Emma took 45 photographs of the animals at the wildlife park.
Ruby took 38 photographs.
How many photographs did they take in total?

They took ☐ photographs in total.

9 Subtract and fill in the blanks.

(a) 65 − 16 = ☐

(b) 76 − 28 = ☐

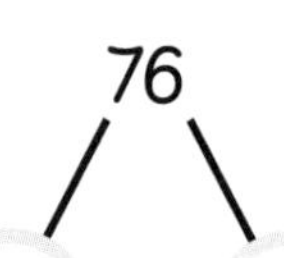

10 Add and fill in the blanks.

(a) 3 + 4 + 6 = ☐

(b) 8 + 4 + 8 = ☐

(c) 9 + 0 + 7 = ☐

(d) 8 + 5 + 7 = ☐

11 Write the missing numbers.

(a) 12 + 7 = 10 + ☐

(b) ☐ + 2 = 6 + 6

(c) 27 − 8 = 9 + ☐

12 Add or subtract.

(a)

	tens	ones
	5	8
−	2	5
	☐	☐

(b)

	tens	ones
	6	3
−	3	6
	☐	☐

(c)

	tens	ones
	6	0
−	4	4
	☐	☐

(d)

	tens	ones
	5	5
+	2	5
	☐	☐

(e)

	tens	ones
	3	9
+	4	8
	☐	☐

(f)

	tens	ones
	7	0
−	5	9
	☐	☐

13 Ravi has 32 stamps in his collection.
Sam has 10 more stamps than Ravi has.

(a) How many stamps does Sam have?

Sam has ☐ stamps.

(b) How many stamps do the children have altogether?

The children have ☐ stamps altogether.

14 60 children go on a school trip. 35 of the children get on the first bus and the rest of the children get on the second bus.

(a) How many children are on the second bus?

There are ☐ children on the second bus.

(b) Which bus has more children?

The ☐ bus has more children.

(c) How many more children are on this bus?

The ☐ bus has ☐ more children than the ☐ bus.

Answers

Page 7 **1** 32 = 3 tens and 2 ones 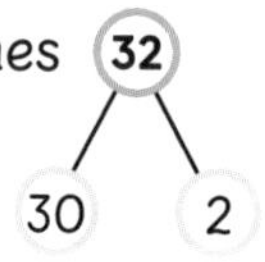

2 44 = 4 tens and 4 ones 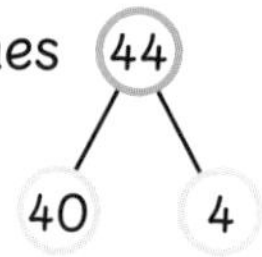

3 70 = 7 tens and 0 ones 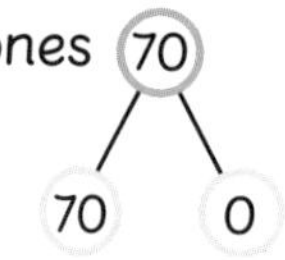

Page 10 **1** 58 = 5 tens and 8 ones, 62 = 6 tens and 2 ones, 58 is less than 62.

Page 11 **2 (a)** 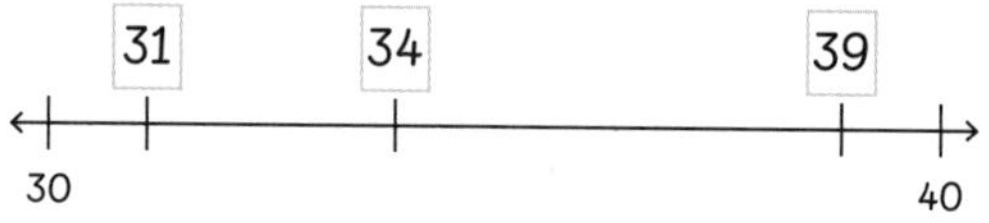

39 > 31 31 < 39

(b) 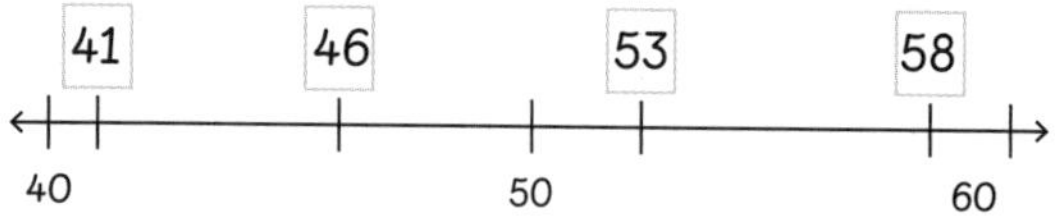

46 < 53 58 > 41

3 79, 85, 98 **4** 24, 23, 11 **5 (a)** 12 < 56 **(b)** 64 > 46 **(c)** 78 < 87

Page 13 **1** 12, 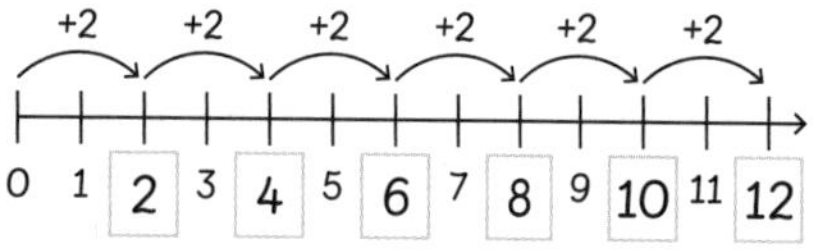

2 (a) 24, 30 **(b)** 27, 33 **(c)** 30, 40 **(d)** 81, 91 **(e)** 59, 65

Page 15 **1 (a)** 17 **(b)** 79 **2 (a)** 49; 47 and 2 make 49 **(b)** 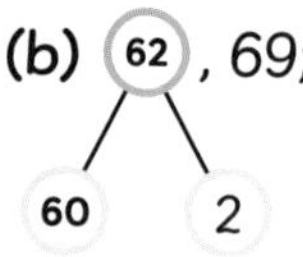

, 69; 62 and 7 make 69.

(c) 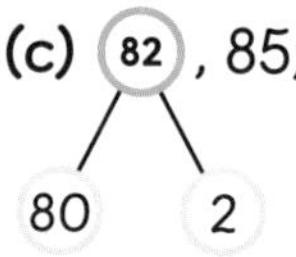

, 85; 3 and 82 make 85.

Page 17 **1 (a)** 7 **(b)** 70 **2 (a)** 9 **(b)** 90 **(c)** 60 **(d)** 100 **3 (a)** 6 ones **(b)** 6 tens **(c)** 100 **(d)** 65

Page 19 **1 (a)** 37 **(b)** 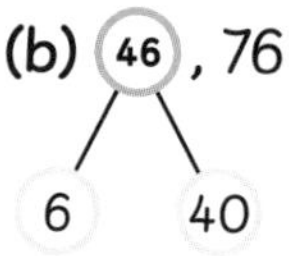

, 76 **2** 54

Page 21 **1 (a)** 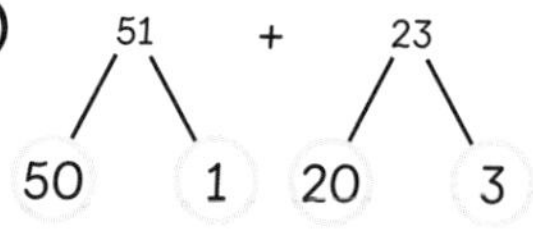

= 74 **(b)** 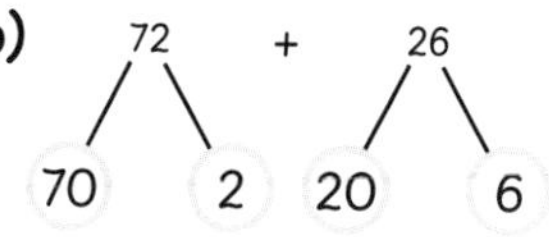

= 98 **2 (a)** 79 **(b)** 99

Page 23 **1**

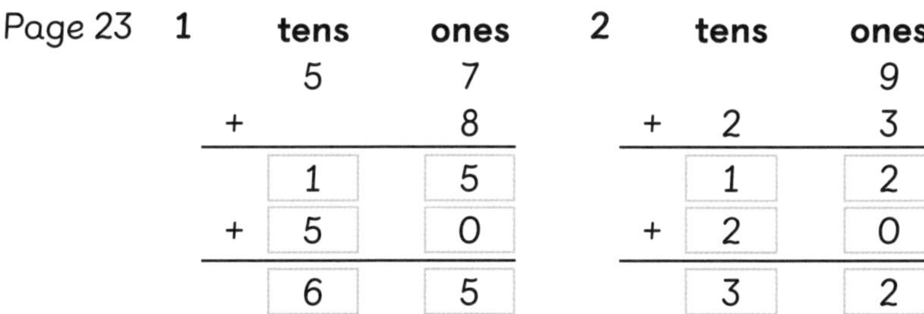

	tens	ones
	5	7
+		8
	1	5
+	5	0
	6	5

2

	tens	ones
		9
+	2	3
	1	2
+	2	0
	3	2

Page 25 **1** 42 **2** 37 **3** 84 **4** 94

Page 27 **1**

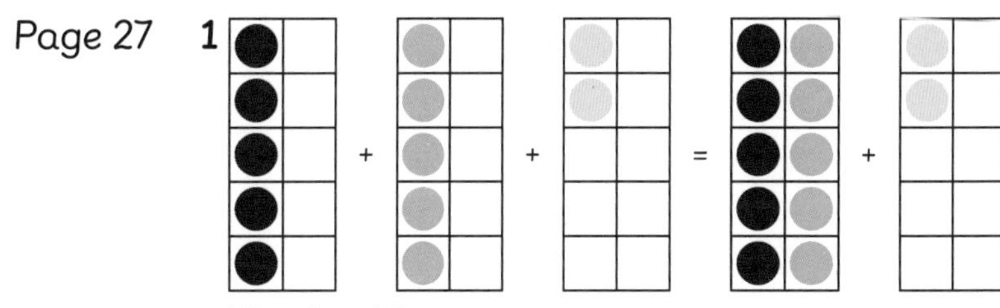

10 + 2 = 12

2 (a) 10 + 2 = 12 **(b)** 10 + 4 = 14 **(c)** 10 + 3 = 13 **(d)** 10 + 4 = 14

3 (a) 17 **(b)** 20 **(c)** 20 **(d)** 20 **(e)** 23 **(f)** 23

Page 29 **1 (a)** 32 **(b)** 54 **2 (a)** 23; 27 subtract 4 is equal to 23.

(b) 68 (60, 8), 63; 68 subtract 5 is equal to 63.

Page 31 **1 (a)** 50 **(b)** 10 **2 (a)** 4, 4 tens, 40 **(b)** 4, 4 tens, 40

Page 33 **1** 38 **2** 17 **3** 35 **4** 42

Page 35 **1** 33 **2** 41 **3** 33 **4** 10

Page 37 **1** 53 (43, 10), 48 **2** 44 (34, 10), 36 **3** 35 (25, 10), 28 **4** 72 (62, 10), 64

5

	tens	ones
	$^{1}\cancel{2}$	$^{11}\cancel{1}$
−		3
	1	8

6

	tens	ones
	$^{7}\cancel{8}$	$^{15}\cancel{5}$
−		6
	7	9

Page 39 **1** 74 (60, 14) − 35 (30, 5) = 39

2 (a)

	tens	ones
	$^{5}\cancel{6}$	$^{15}\cancel{5}$
−	4	7
	1	8

(b)

	tens	ones
	$^{8}\cancel{9}$	$^{15}\cancel{5}$
−	1	6
	7	9

(c)

	tens	ones
	$^{2}\cancel{3}$	$^{12}\cancel{2}$
−	1	8
	1	4

(d)

	tens	ones
	$^{8}\cancel{9}$	$^{11}\cancel{1}$
−	8	9
		2

Answers continued

Page 40 **1** 87 = 8 tens and 7 ones, 80 — 87 — 7

2 48 = 4 tens and 8 ones; 52 = 5 tens and 2 ones; 48 is less than 52. **3** 29, 65, 78

Page 41 **4** 56, 54, 41 **5 (a)** 25 < 36 **(b)** 56 < 65 **(c)** 39 < 41

6 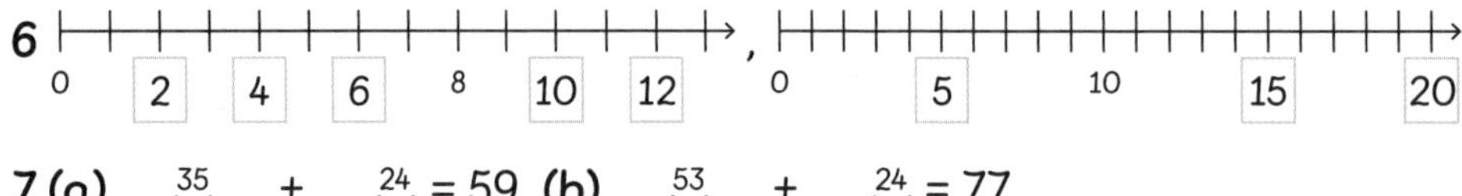

7 (a) 35 (30, 5) + 24 (20, 4) = 59 **(b)** 53 (50, 3) + 24 (20, 4) = 77

Page 42 **8** They took 83 photographs in total.

9 (a) 65 (50, 15) − 16 (10, 6) = 49 **(b)** 76 (60, 16) − 28 (20, 8) = 48

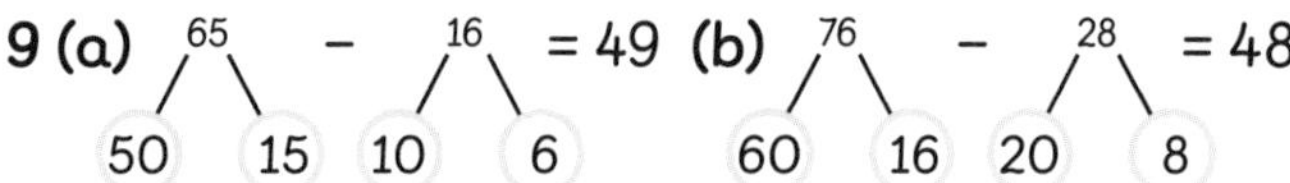

10 (a) 13 **(b)** 20 **(c)** 16 **(d)** 20

Page 43 **11 (a)** 9 **(b)** 10 **(c)** 10 **12 (a)** 33 **(b)** 27 **(c)** 16 **(d)** 80 **(e)** 87 **(f)** 11

Page 44 **13 (a)** 32 + 10 = 42. Sam has 42 stamps. **(b)** 32 + 42 = 74. The children have 74 stamps altogether.

Page 45 **14 (a)** 60 − 35 = 25. There are 25 children on the second bus. **(b)** The first bus has more children. **(c)** 35 − 25 = 10. The first bus has 10 more children than the second bus.

KS1
5–7
Years

Master Maths at Home

Fractions

Scan the QR code to help your child's learning at home.

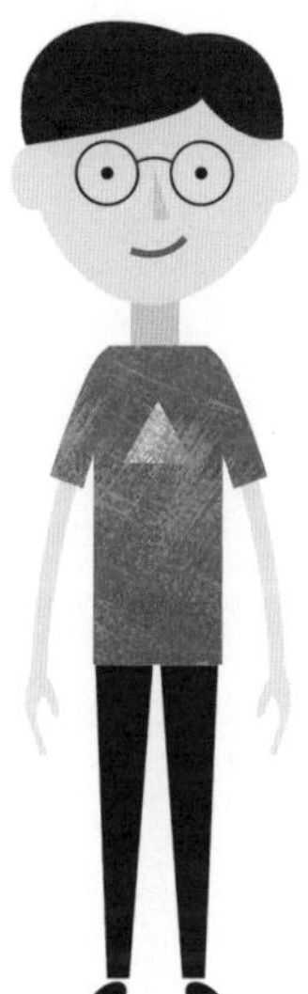

MATHS
NO PROBLEM!

mastermathsathome.com

How to use this book

Maths — No Problem! created **Master Maths at Home** to help children develop fluency in the subject and a rich understanding of core concepts.

Key features of the Master Maths at Home books include:

- Carefully designed lessons that provide structure but also allow flexibility in how they're used. For example, some children may want to write numbers, while others might want to trace.
- Speech bubbles containing content designed to spark diverse conversations, with many discussion points that don't have obvious 'right' or 'wrong' answers.
- Rich illustrations that will guide children to a discussion of shapes and units of measurement, allowing them to make connections to the wider world around them.
- Exercises that allow a flexible approach and can be adapted to suit any child's cognitive or functional ability.
- Clearly laid out pages that encourage children to practise a range of higher-order skills.
- A community of friendly and relatable characters who introduce each lesson and come along as your child progresses through the series.

You can see more guidance on how to use these books at **mastermathsathome.com**.

We're excited to share all the ways you can learn maths!

Maths — No Problem!
mastermathsathome.com
www.mathsnoproblem.com
hello@mathsnoproblem.com

First published in Great Britain in 2022 by
Dorling Kindersley Limited
One Embassy Gardens, 8 Viaduct Gardens, London SW11 7BW
A Penguin Random House Company

The authorised representative in the EEA is Dorling Kindersley Verlag GmbH. Arnulfstr. 124, 80636 Munich, Germany

10 9 8 7 6 5 4 3 2 1
001–327070–Jan/22

This book was made with Forest Stewardship Council™ certified paper - one small step in DK's commitment to a sustainable future. For more information go to www.dk.com/our-green-pledge

A CIP catalogue record for this book is available from the British Library.

ISBN: 978-0-24153-912-5
Printed and bound in China

For the curious
www.dk.com

Acknowledgements
The publisher would like to thank the authors and consultants Andy Psarianos, Judy Hornigold, Adam Gifford and Dr Anne Hermanson.

The Castledown typeface has been used with permission from the Colophon Foundry.

Contents

Ruby
Elliott
Amira
Charles
Lulu
Sam
Oak
Holly
Ravi
Emma
Jacob
Hannah

Equal parts

Lesson 1

Starter

Four friends want to share a pizza so everyone gets the same amount.
Ruby cuts the square pizza this way.

I think all these pieces are the same amount. All 4 pieces are equal.

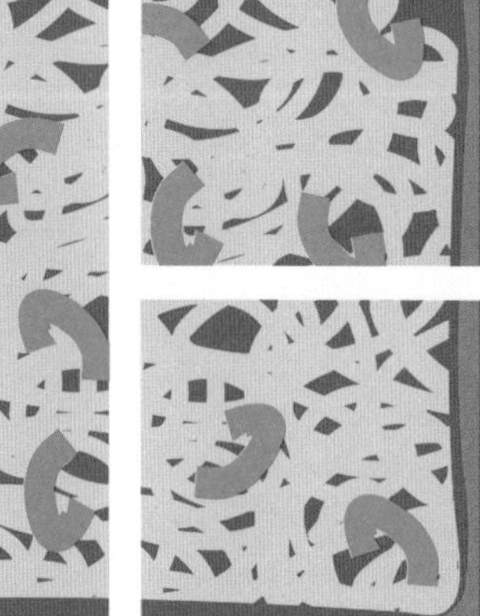

The pieces are different shapes. I don't think they are the same size.

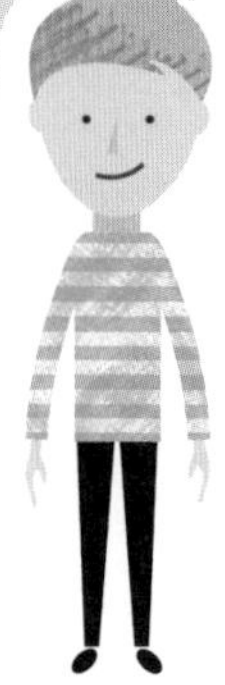

Who is correct?

Example

First I cut the pizza in 2 equal parts like this.

step 1

I then cut one of the pieces into 2 smaller equal pieces.

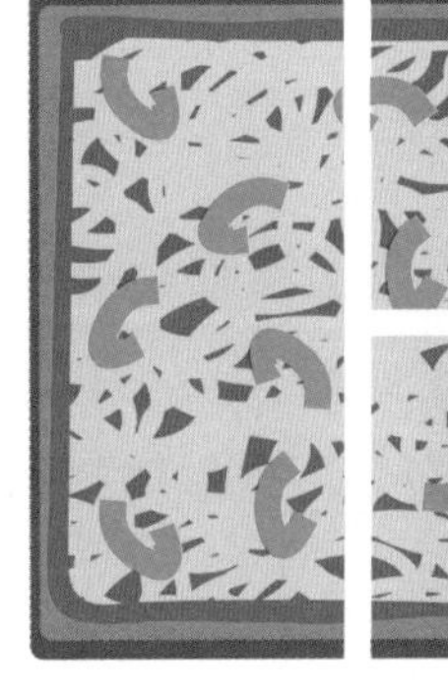

step 2

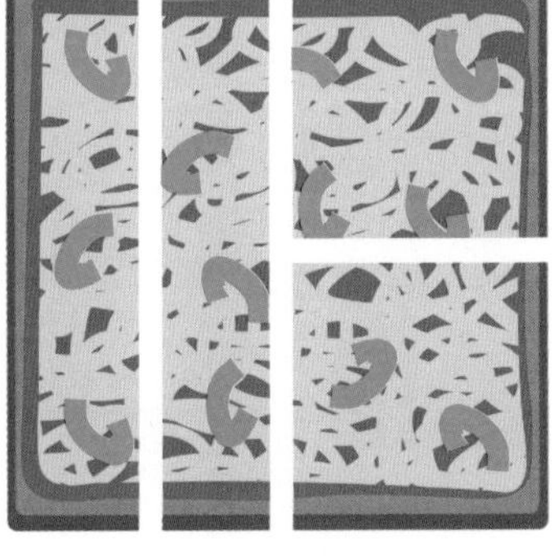

Then I cut the other piece into 2 smaller equal pieces in another way.

step 3

I think [girl] is correct. The pieces don't look the same but they are the same size.

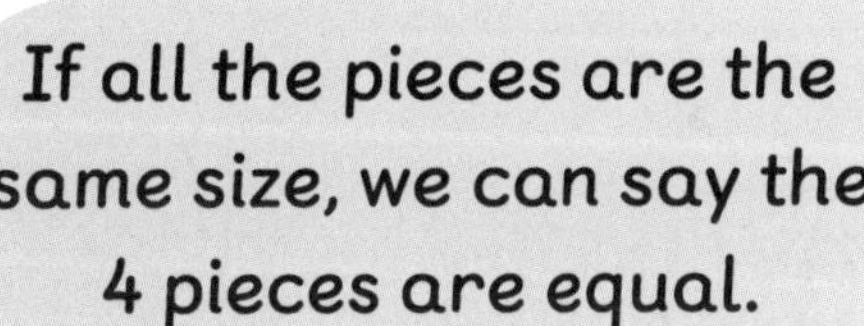

If all the pieces are the same size, we can say the 4 pieces are equal.

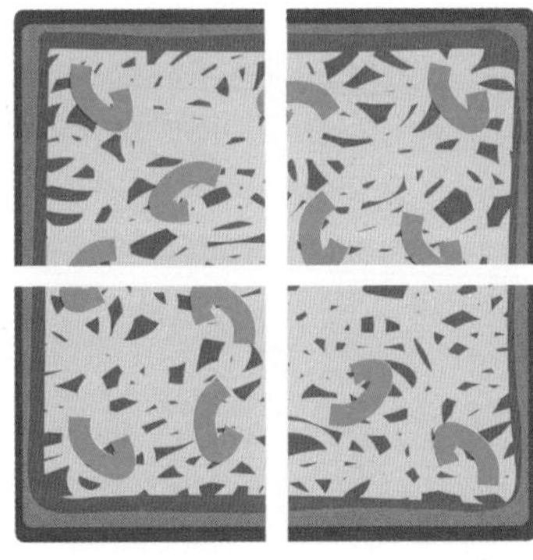

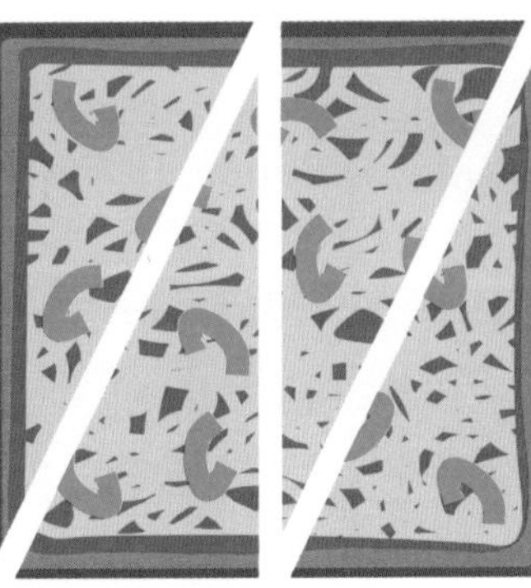

These are some other ways that Ruby could have cut the pizza.

Are all these pieces equal?

Practice

1 Draw lines to cut each shape into 2 equal parts.
Try to find more than 1 way.

(a)

(b)

2 Draw lines to cut each shape into 4 equal parts.
Try to find more than 1 way.

(a)

(b)

3 Circle the shapes that show equal parts.

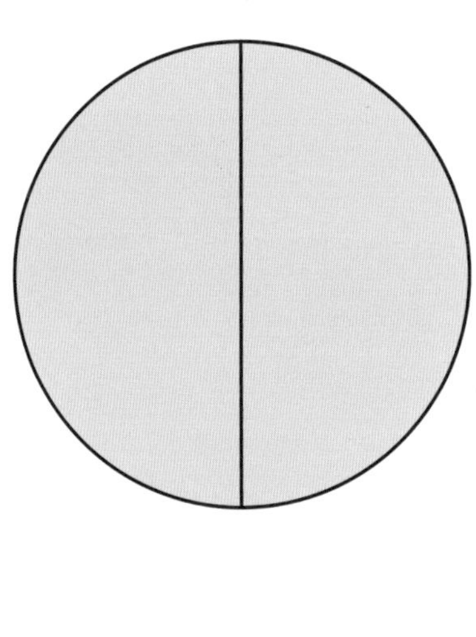

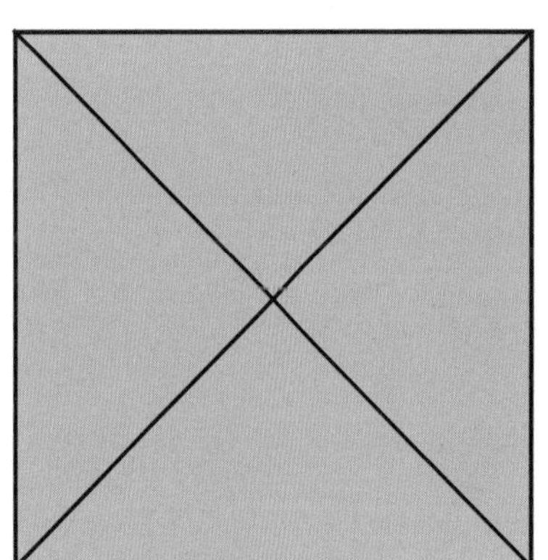

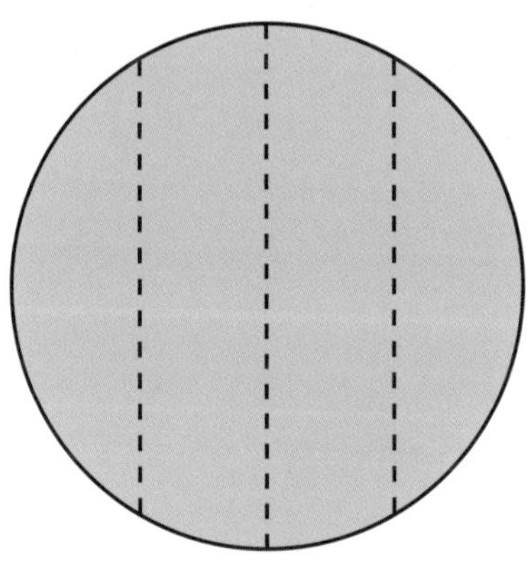

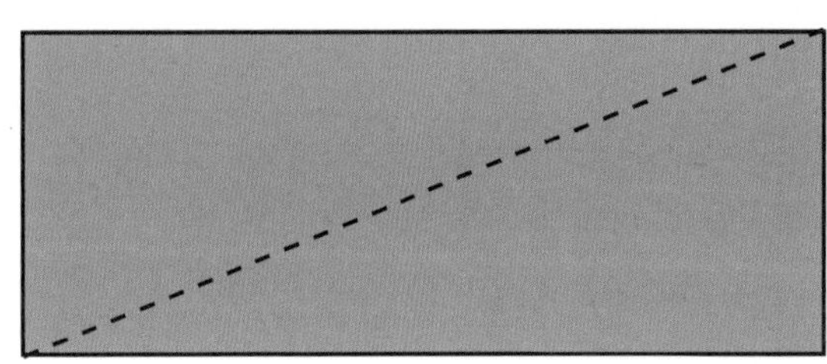

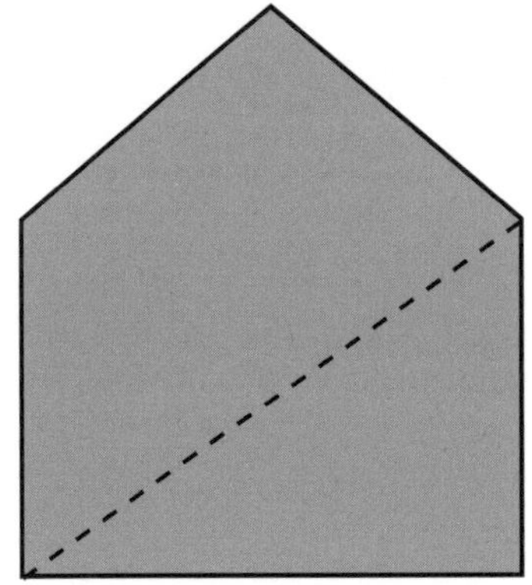

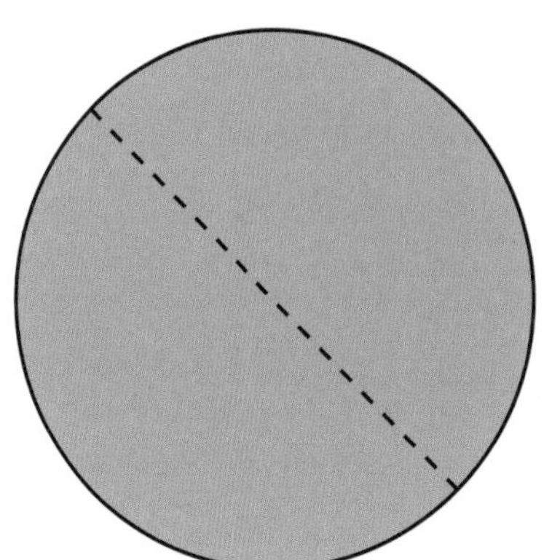

Halves and quarters

Lesson 2

Starter

Can you help Elliott fold a piece of paper into 2 equal parts?

What about folding the piece of paper into 4 equal parts?

Example

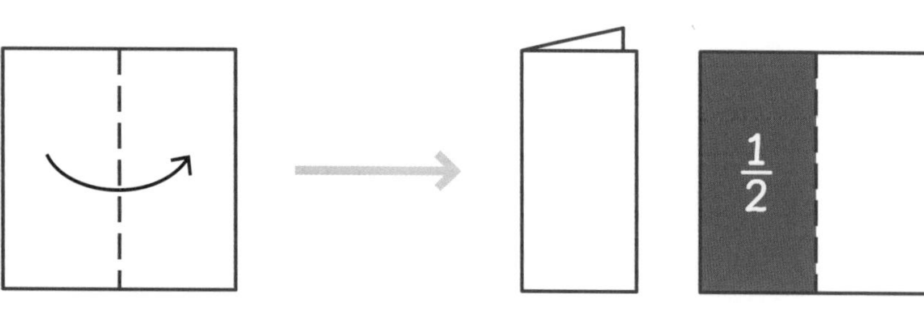

Fold the square piece of paper to show 2 equal parts.

There are 2 equal parts.
Each piece is 1 half of the whole paper.
Each piece is 1 part out of 2 equal parts.

We can write this as $\frac{1}{2}$.

We say **one half**.

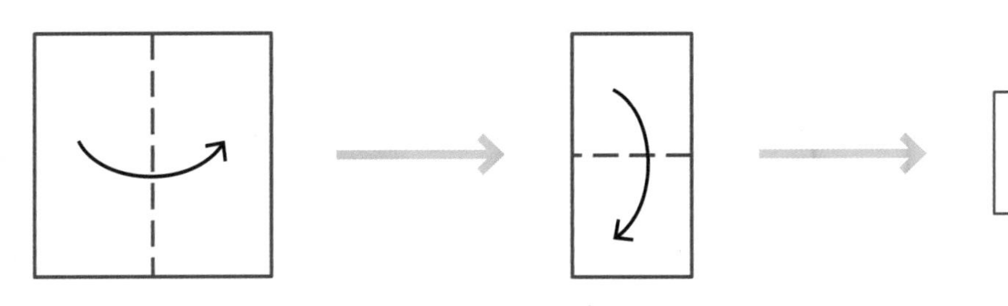

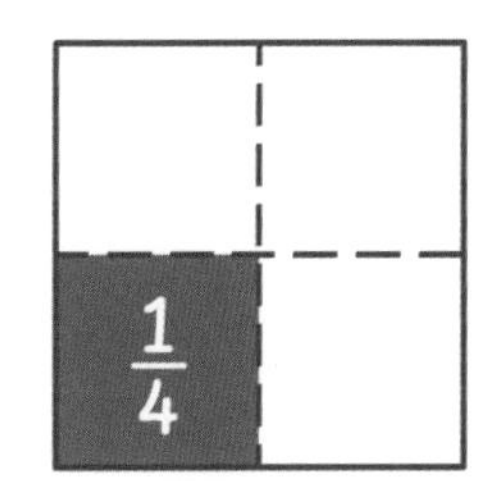

There are 4 equal parts.
Each piece is 1 quarter of the whole paper.
Each piece is 1 part out of 4 equal parts.

We can write this as $\frac{1}{4}$.

We say **one quarter**.

Fold the paper this way to make 4 equal parts.

Practice

Match the pictures that show $\frac{1}{2}$ and $\frac{1}{4}$.

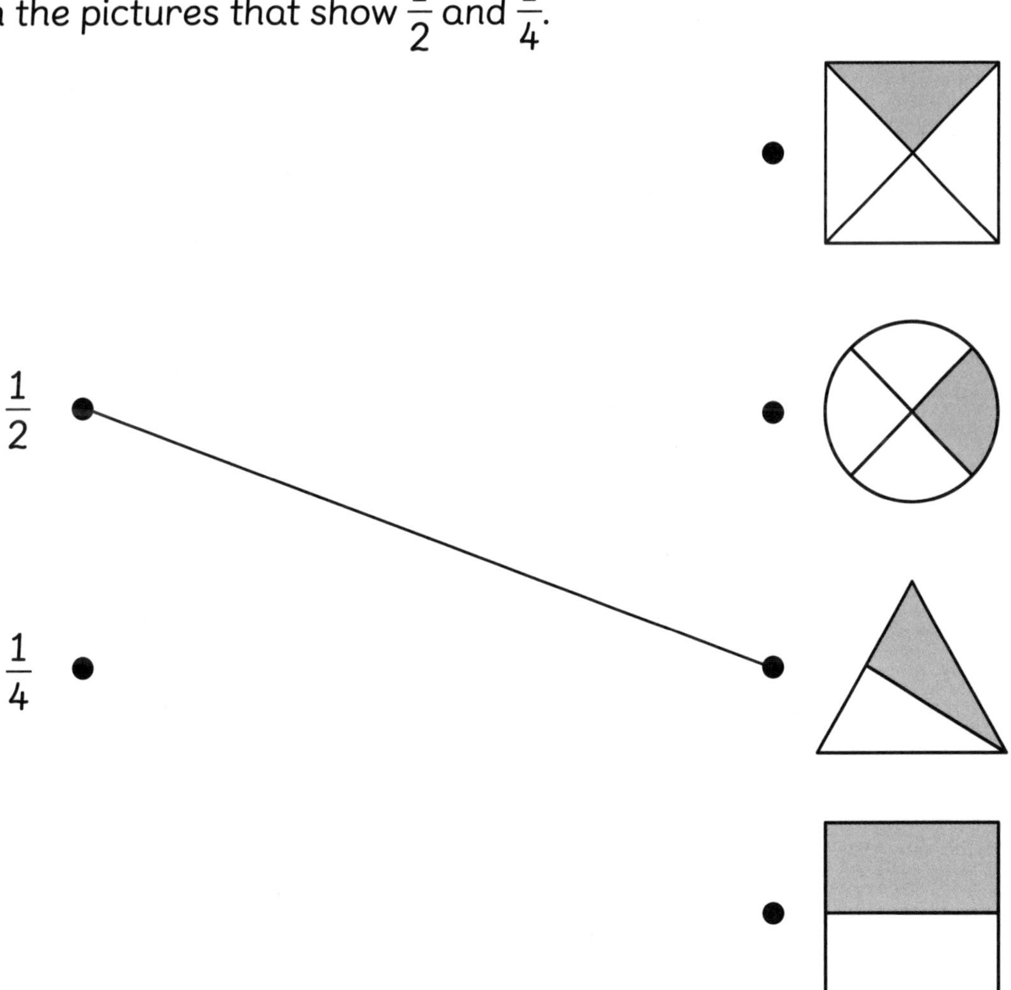

Thirds

Lesson 3

Starter

2 parts of the strip of paper are shaded.

How much of the paper is not shaded?

Example

The strip of paper is divided into 3 equal parts.
Each piece is called a **third**.

$\frac{1}{3}$	$\frac{1}{3}$	$\frac{1}{3}$

1 third = $\frac{1}{3}$

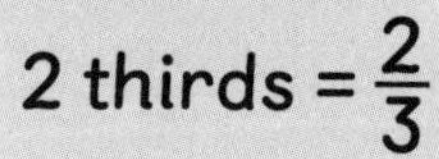

2 thirds of the paper is shaded.
1 third of the paper is not shaded.

$\frac{1}{3}$ of the paper is not shaded.

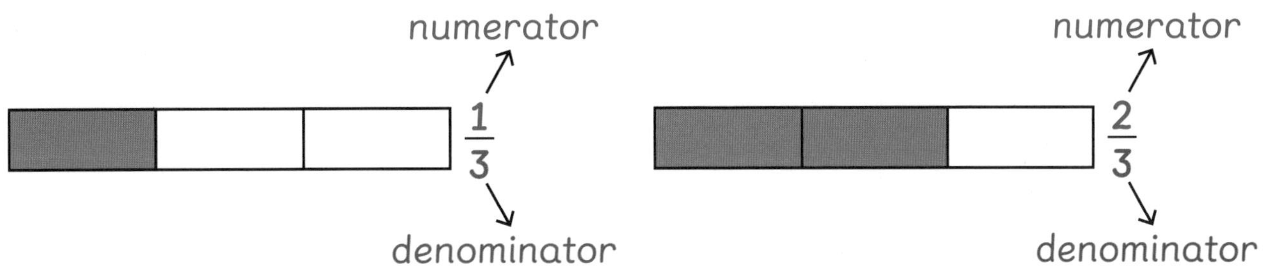

The **numerator** tells us the number of parts.
The **denominator** tells us the number of equal parts the item is divided into.

Practice

What fraction of each shape is shaded?

1

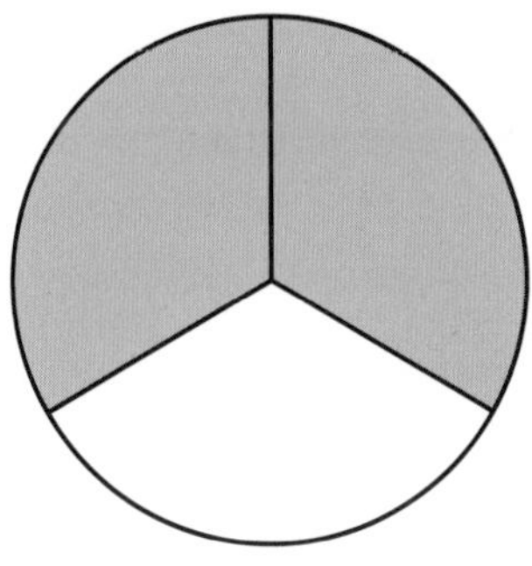

$\frac{\square}{3}$ ☐ thirds

2

$\frac{\square}{3}$ ☐ third

3

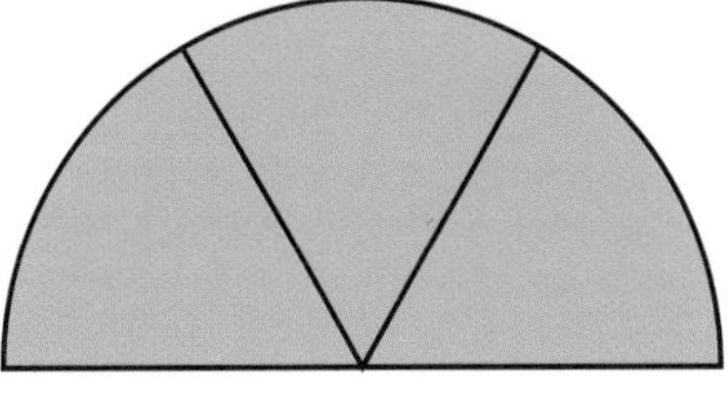

$\frac{\square}{3}$ ☐ thirds

Recognise, name and write fractions

Lesson 4

Starter

How much of each strip is shaded?

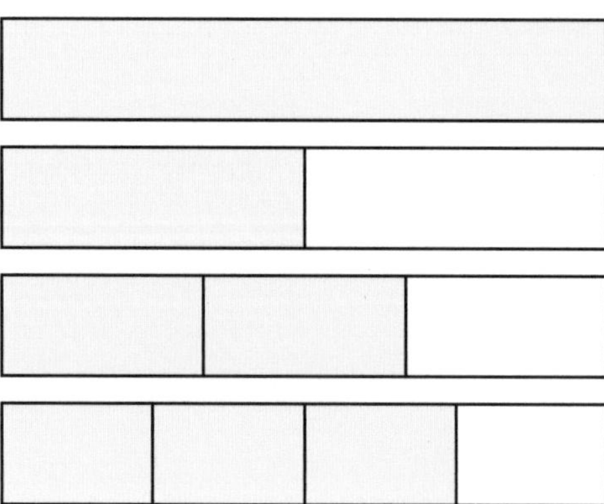

Example

1

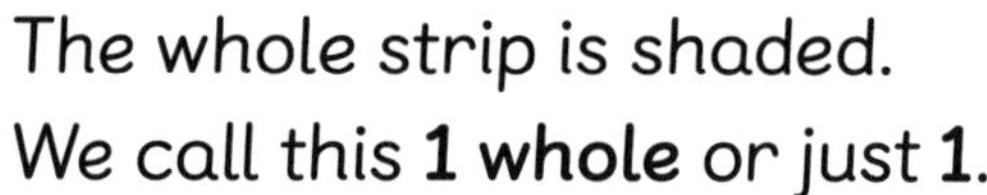

The whole strip is shaded.
We call this **1 whole** or just **1**.

$\frac{1}{2}$	$\frac{1}{2}$

The strip is in two equal parts.
We call these parts **halves**.
1 half is shaded.
We write 1 half like this $\frac{1}{2}$.

When we cut 1 whole into parts, we can name the parts. The parts must be equal before we can name them.

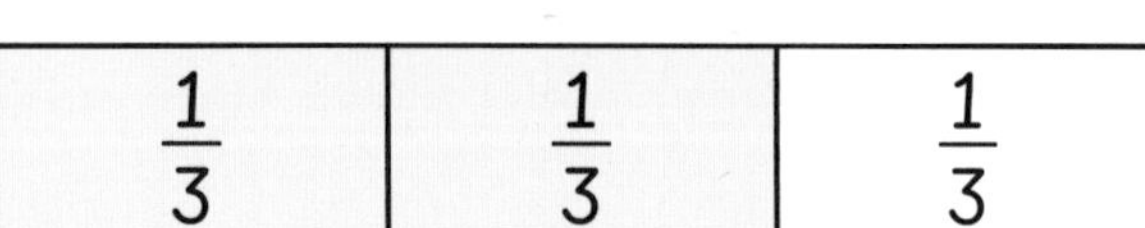

$\frac{1}{3}$	$\frac{1}{3}$	$\frac{1}{3}$

The strip is in three equal parts.
We call these parts **thirds**.
2 thirds are shaded.
We write 2 thirds like this $\frac{2}{3}$.

$\frac{1}{4}$	$\frac{1}{4}$	$\frac{1}{4}$	$\frac{1}{4}$

The strip is in four equal parts.
We call these parts **quarters**.
3 quarters are shaded.
We write 3 quarters like this $\frac{3}{4}$.

$\frac{3}{4}$
The numerator is 3.
The denominator is 4.

Practice

1 What fraction of each shape is shaded?

(a)

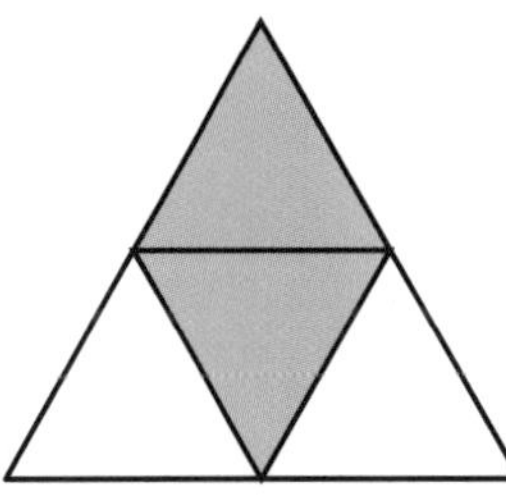

[ ] out of [ ] parts are shaded.

[ ] is the numerator.

[ ] is the denominator.

(b)

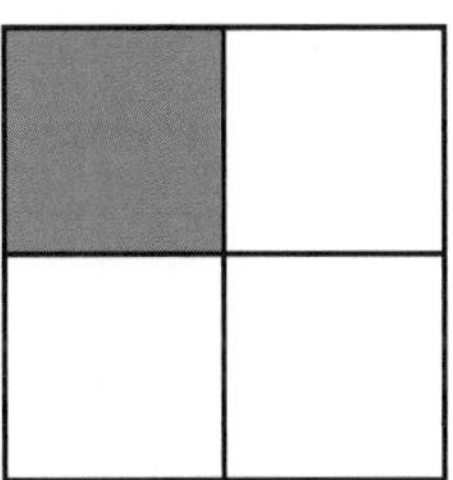

[ ] out of [ ] parts is shaded.

[ ] is the numerator.

[ ] is the denominator.

(c)

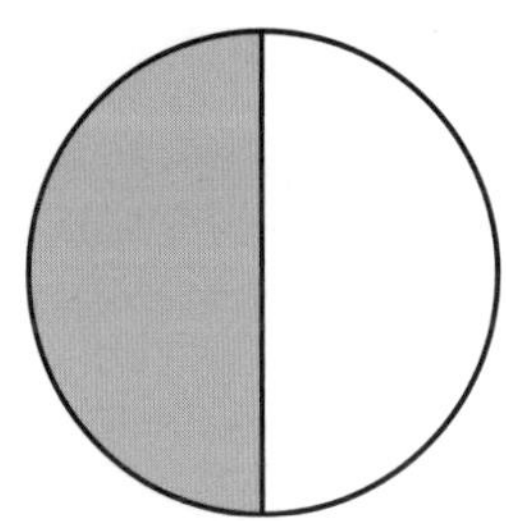

[ ] out of [ ] parts is shaded.

[ ] is the numerator.

[ ] is the denominator.

2 What fraction of the shape is shaded?
What fraction of the shape is not shaded?

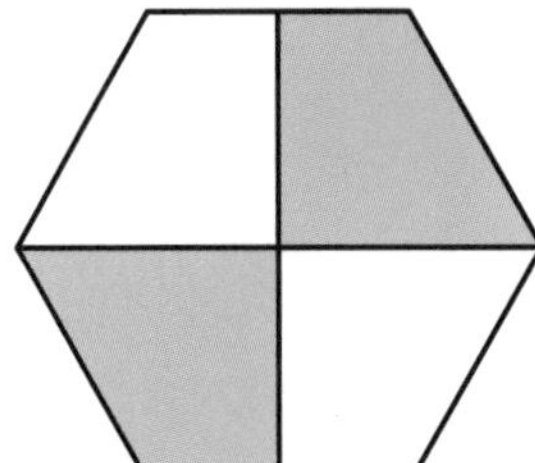

shaded

not shaded

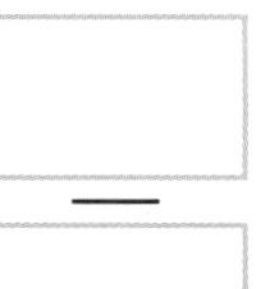

Equal fractions

Lesson 5

Starter

I ate 1 piece of my tart.

I ate 2 pieces of my tart.

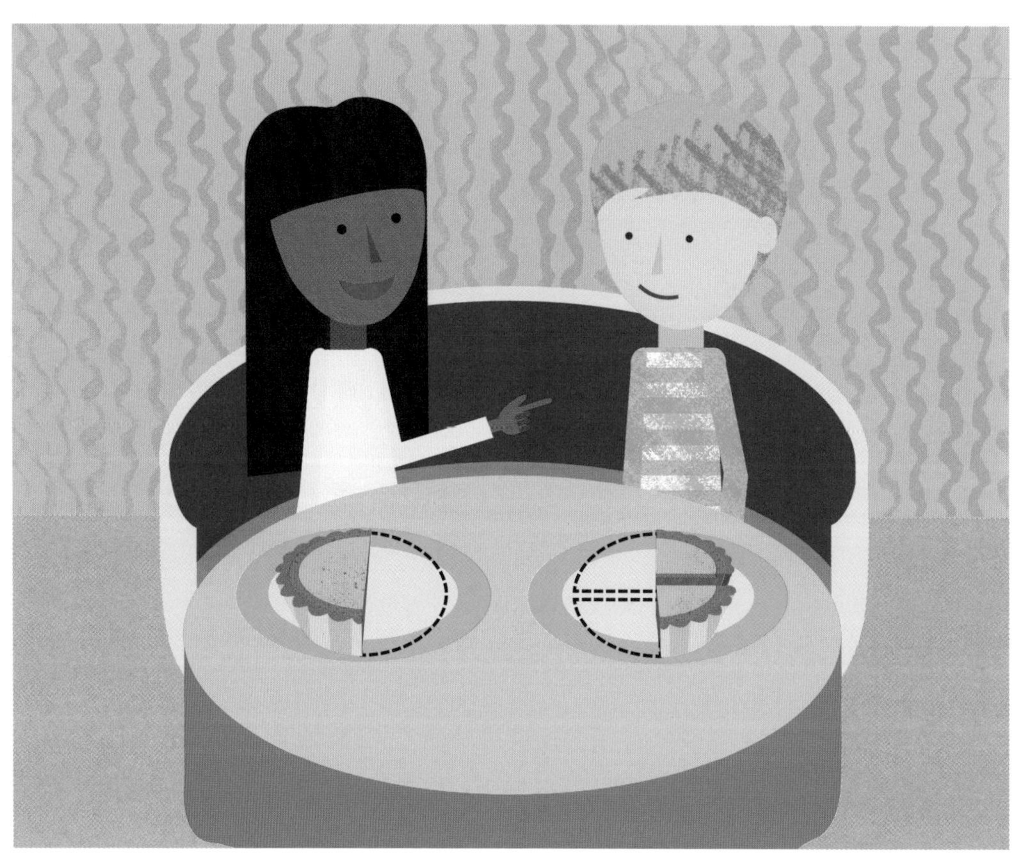

Did they eat the same amount of tart?

Example

I cut my tart into 2 equal pieces. Each piece is $\frac{1}{2}$ of the whole tart. I ate 1 of these pieces.

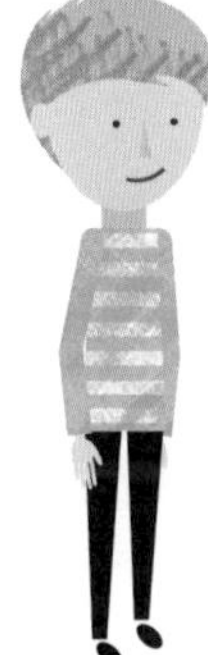

I cut my tart into 4 equal pieces. Each piece is $\frac{1}{4}$ of the whole tart. I ate 2 of these pieces.

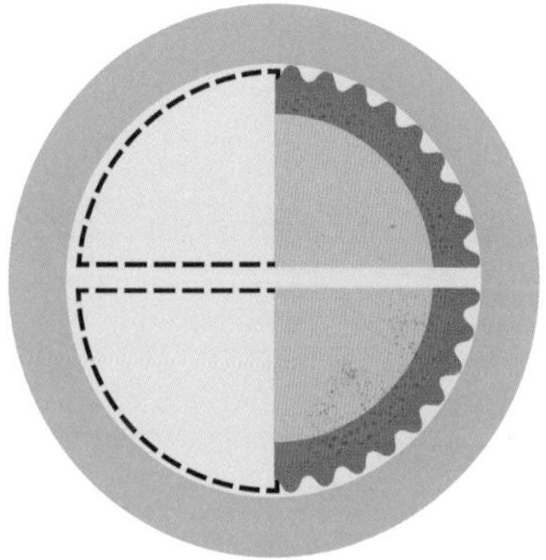

 and  ate the same amount of tart.

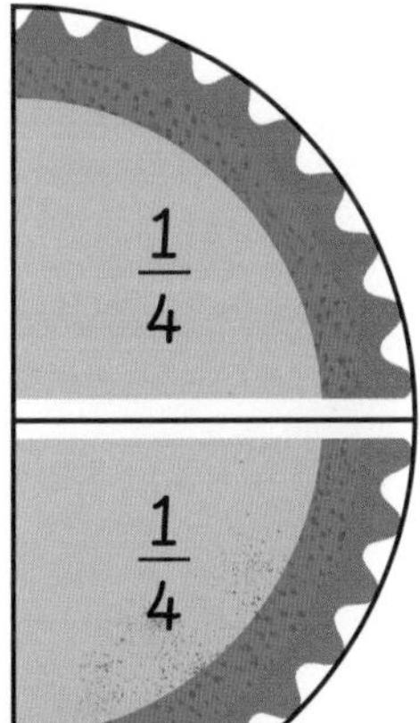

$\frac{2}{4} = \frac{1}{2}$

2 quarters of the tart is the same as 1 half of the tart.

Practice

1 Match the fractions to make 1 whole.

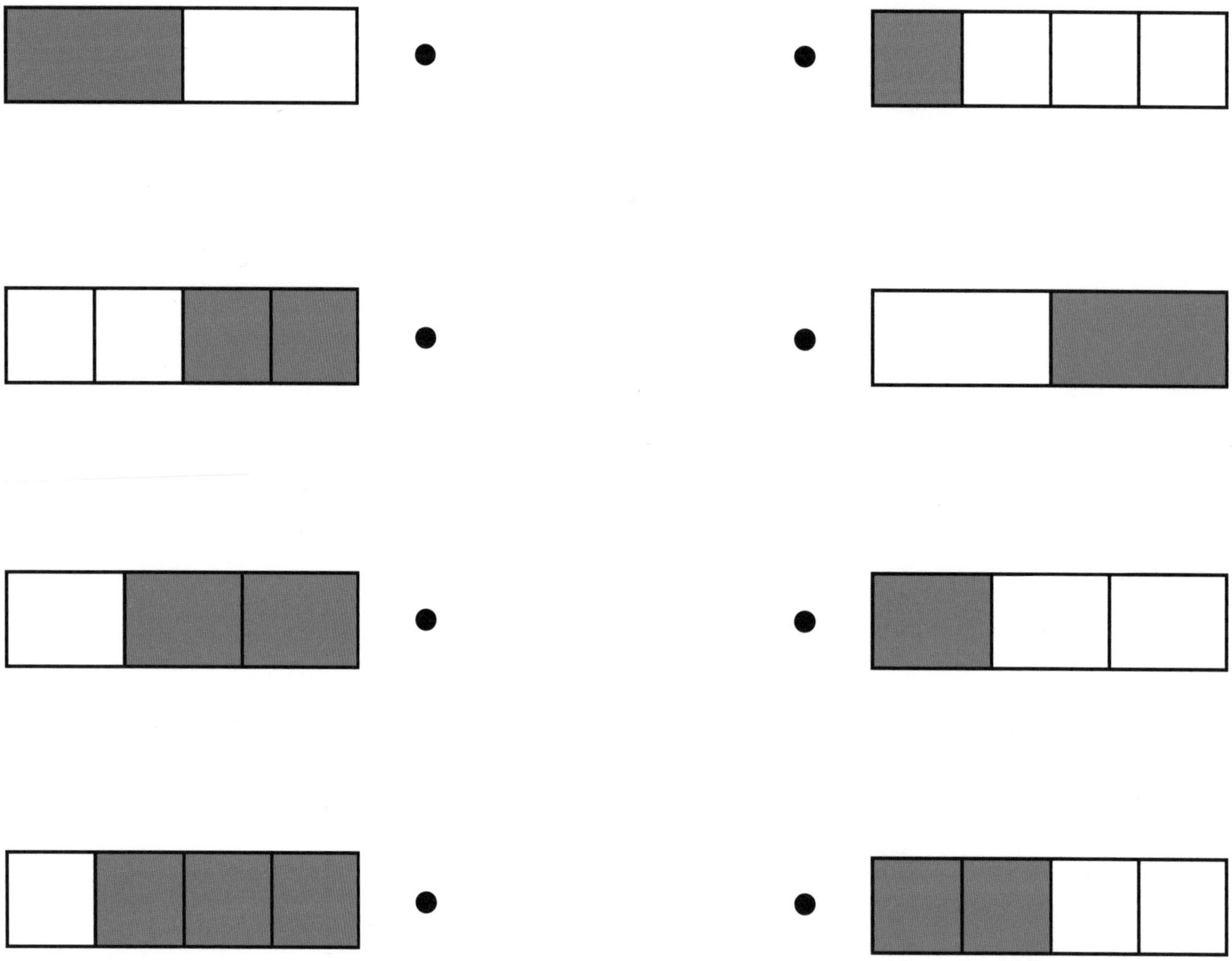

2 Use the chart to help you fill in the blanks.

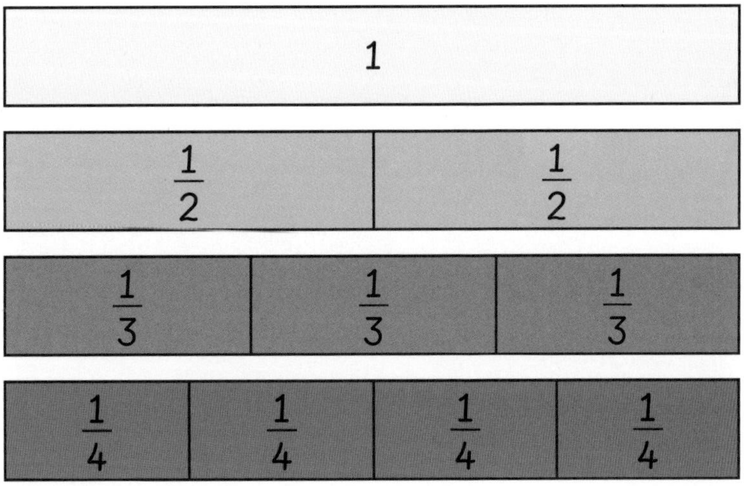

1			
$\frac{1}{2}$		$\frac{1}{2}$	
$\frac{1}{3}$	$\frac{1}{3}$	$\frac{1}{3}$	
$\frac{1}{4}$	$\frac{1}{4}$	$\frac{1}{4}$	$\frac{1}{4}$

(a) $\frac{\square}{2} = 1$

(b) $\frac{\square}{3} = 1$

(c) $\frac{3}{\square} = 1$

(d) $\frac{\square}{4} = 1$

(e) $\frac{1}{\square} = \frac{2}{4}$

(f) $\frac{\square}{4} = \frac{1}{2}$

Comparing like fractions

Lesson 6

Starter

Charles and Ruby both cut their pizzas into 4 equal-sized pieces.

Ruby eats 2 slices and Charles eats 1 slice.

Who eats more pizza?

Example

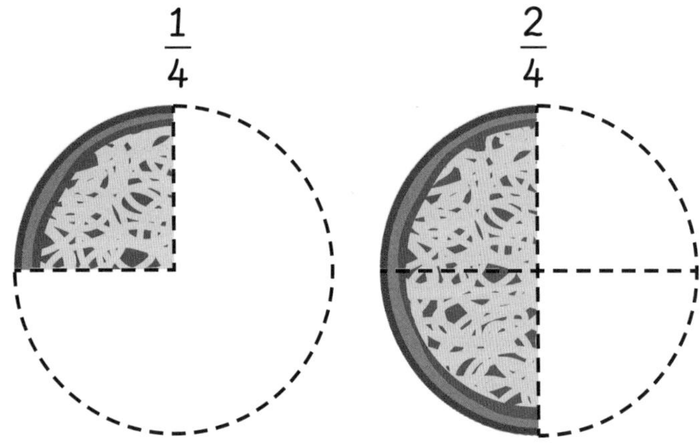

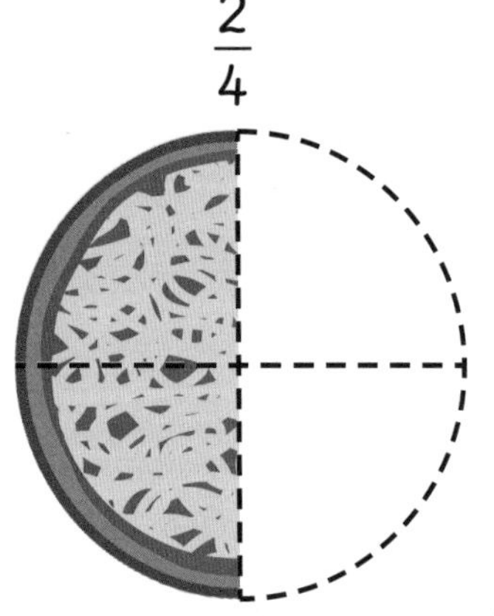

A piece of pizza is called a **slice**.

$\frac{2}{4} > \frac{1}{4}$

Ruby eats more pizza than Charles.

$\frac{2}{4}$ is greater than $\frac{1}{4}$. We use > to mean **greater than** and < to mean **less than**.

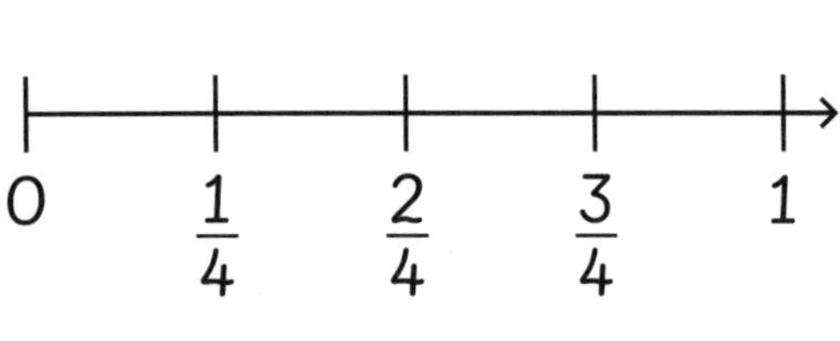

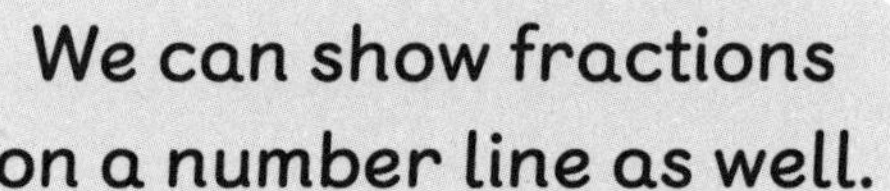

We can show fractions on a number line as well.

Practice

1 Shade and fill in the blanks.

$\frac{1}{4}$

$\frac{3}{4}$

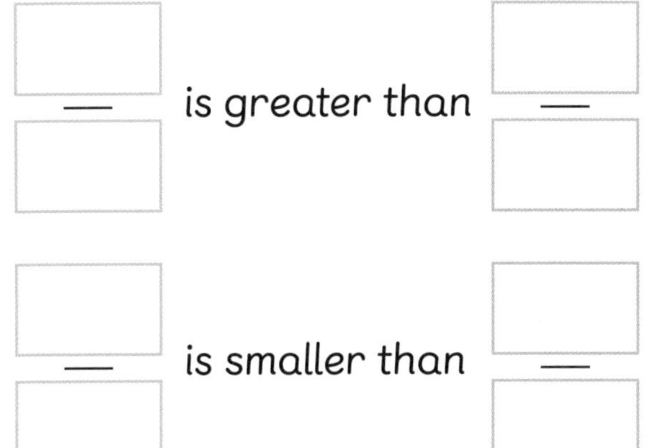

2 Arrange the fractions in order.

(a) Start with the greatest.

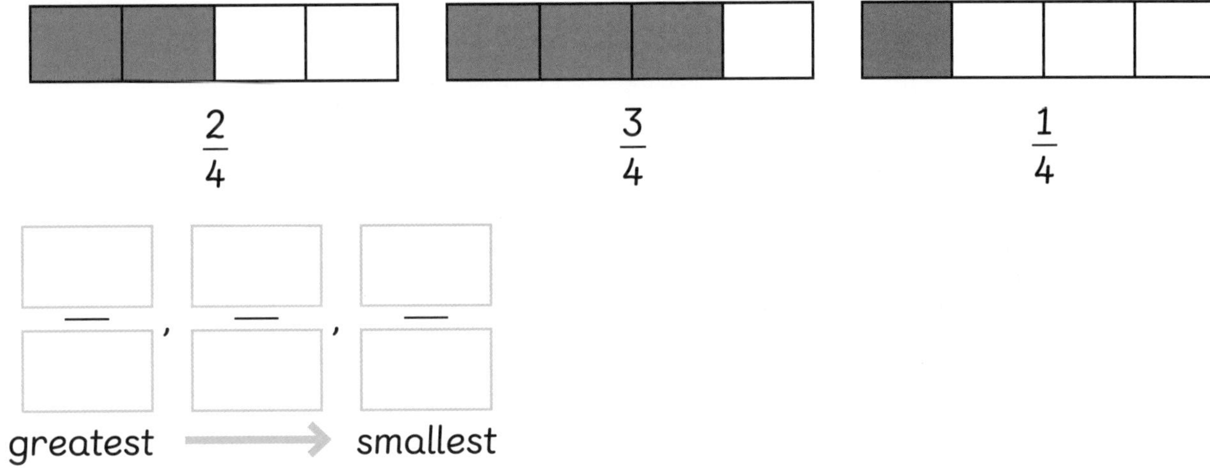

greatest → smallest

(b) Start with the smallest.

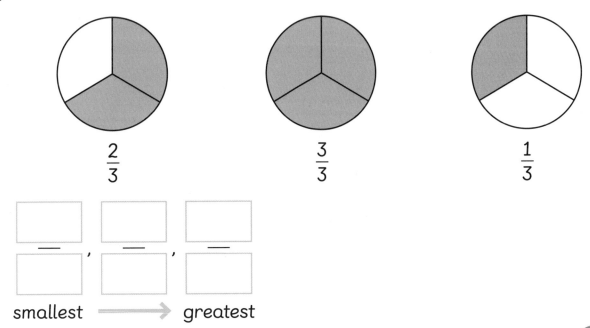

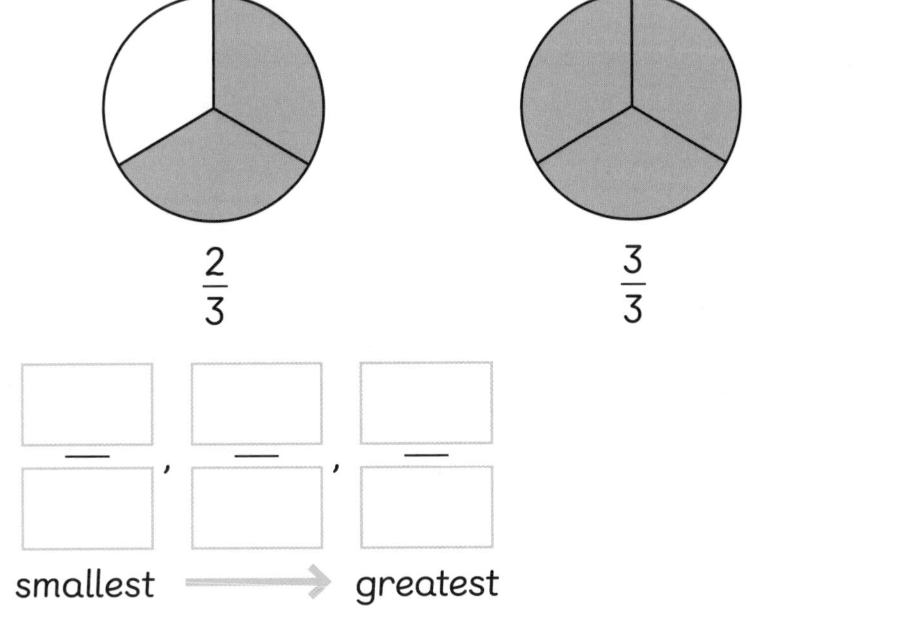

Comparing unlike fractions

Starter

I think $\frac{1}{3}$ is more than $\frac{1}{2}$.

I don't agree. I think $\frac{1}{2}$ is more than $\frac{1}{3}$.

Who is correct?

Example

I can draw number lines to check.

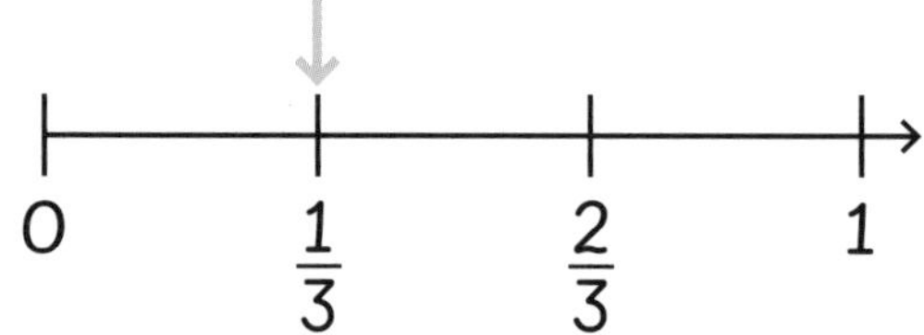

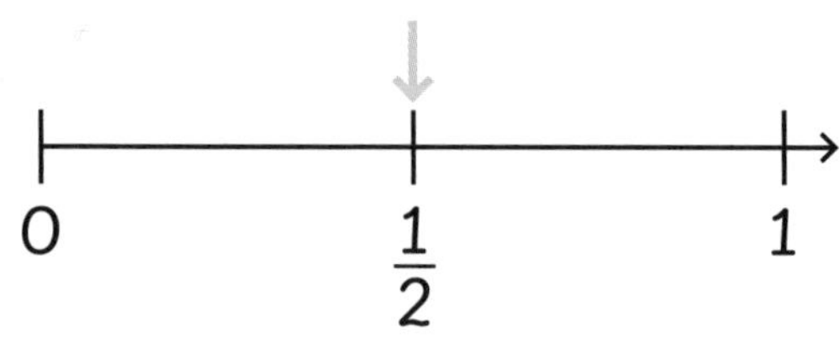

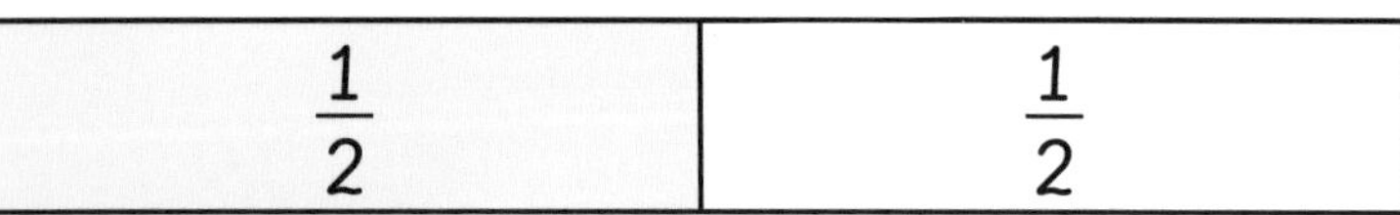

I like to use paper strips.

 is correct.

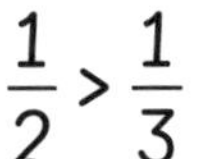

1 half is more than 1 third.

Practice

1 Fill in the blanks. Use > or <.

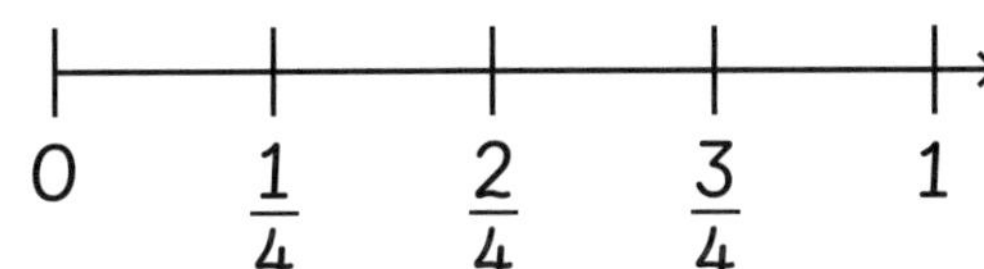

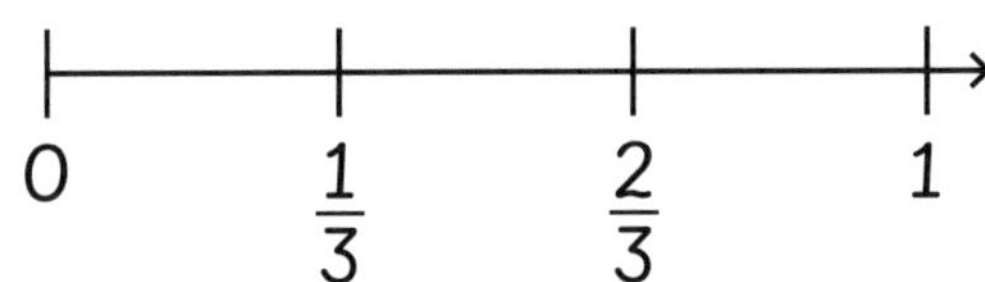

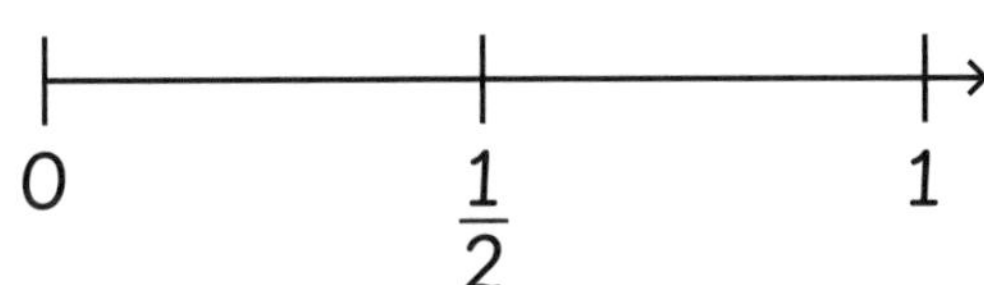

(a) $\frac{1}{4}$ ☐ $\frac{1}{2}$ (b) $\frac{1}{3}$ ☐ $\frac{1}{4}$ (c) $\frac{1}{3}$ ☐ $\frac{1}{2}$

2 Arrange the fractions in order.
Start with the smallest.

$\frac{1}{4}$ $\frac{1}{2}$ $\frac{1}{3}$

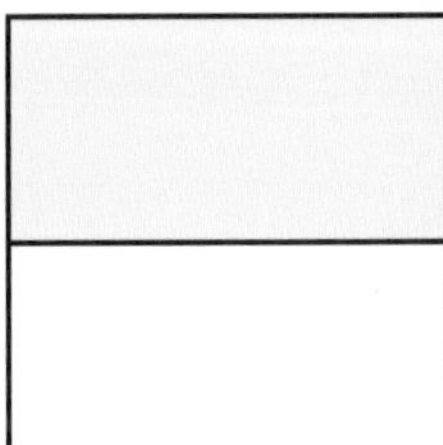

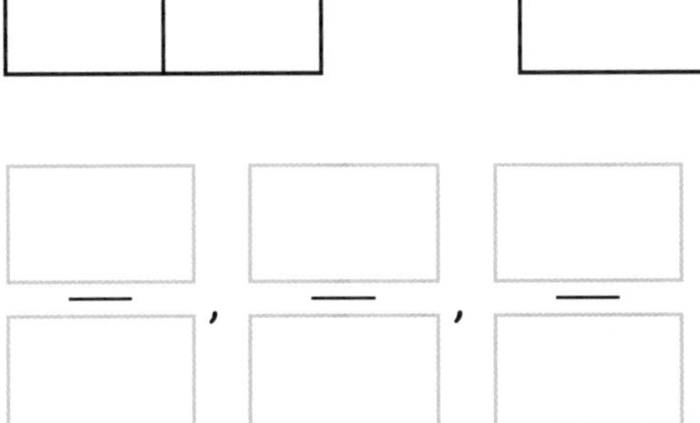

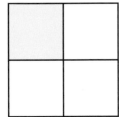

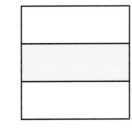

smallest → greatest

Whole numbers and fractions

Lesson 8

Starter

Ravi and Emma want to share 3 muffins equally. How much does each of them get?

Example

Each of them gets a whole muffin.

They also get $\frac{1}{2}$ of a muffin each.

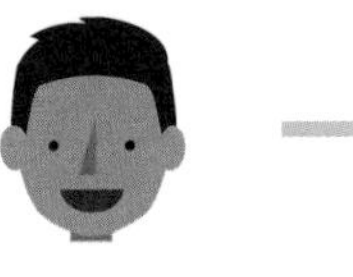

They both get 1 whole muffin and 1 half of a muffin.

They both get $1\frac{1}{2}$ muffins.

Practice

Count the number of pieces and fill in the blanks.

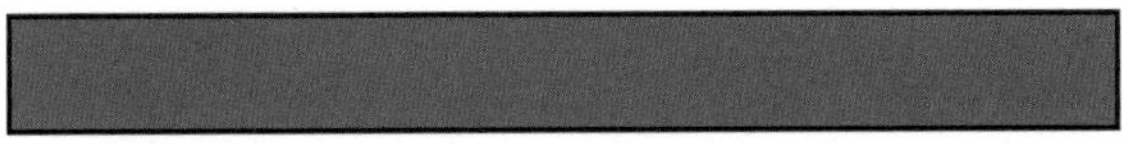

This is one piece.

1

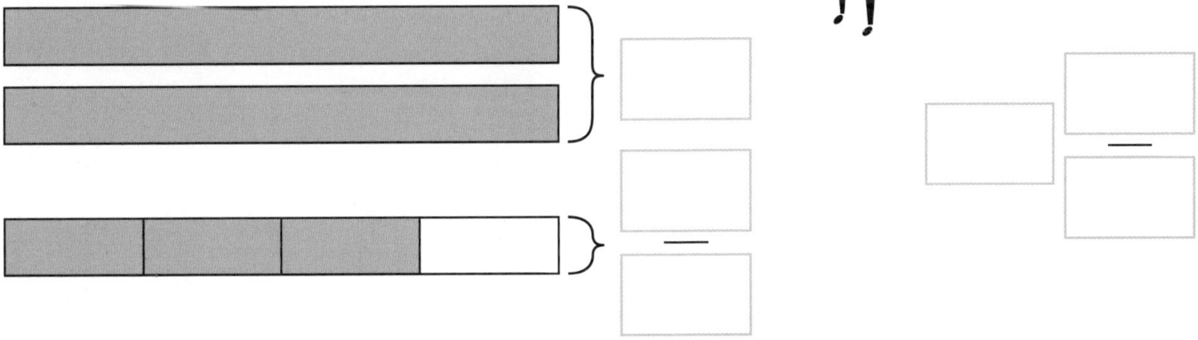

2

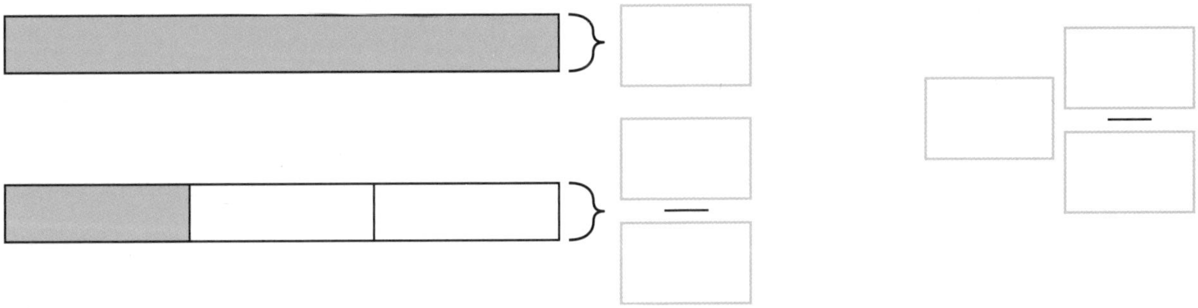

3

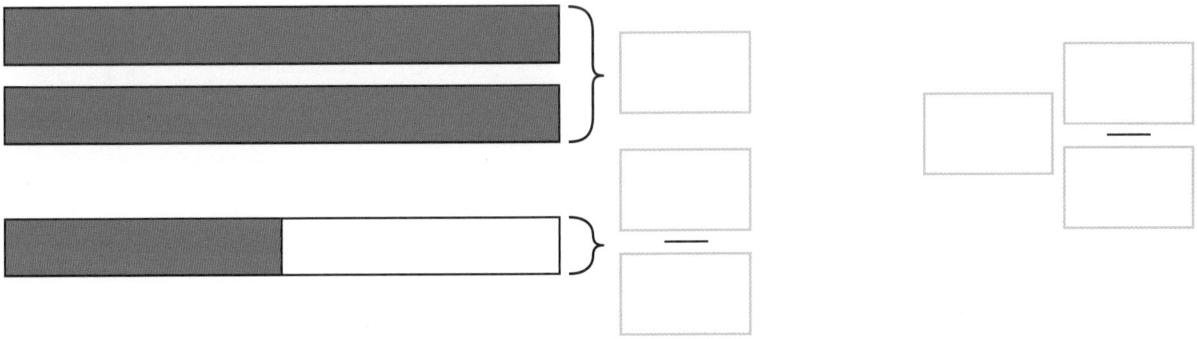

4

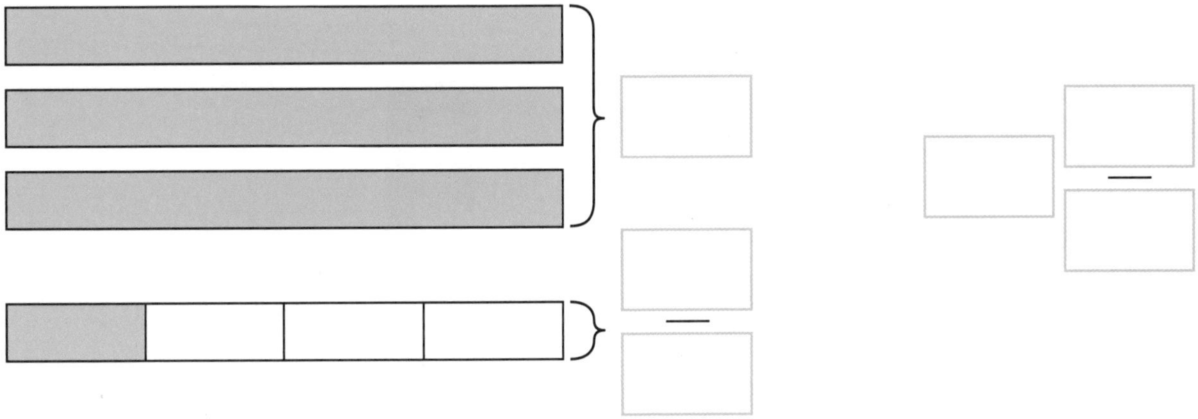

Counting in halves

Lesson 9

Starter

Sam and his mum buy some watermelon for the school picnic. How much watermelon do they buy?

Example

This is a whole watermelon. They buy 2 of these.

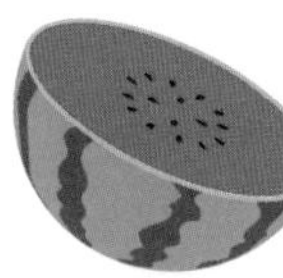

This is 1 half of a watermelon. They buy one of these.

They buy $2\frac{1}{2}$ watermelons. We say two and a half watermelons.

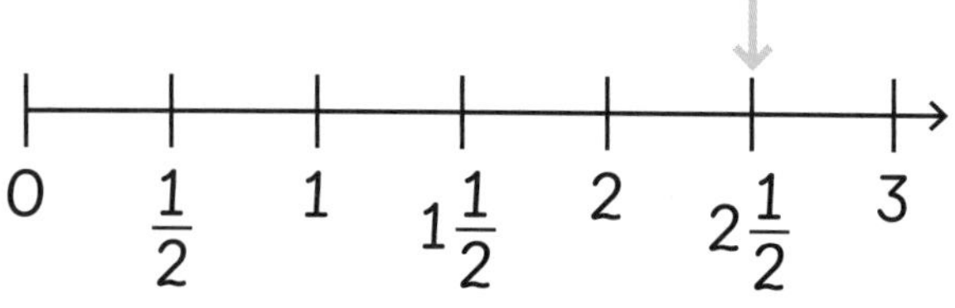

We can show $2\frac{1}{2}$ on a number line like this.

Practice

1 How many pieces are there? Fill in the blanks.

(a)

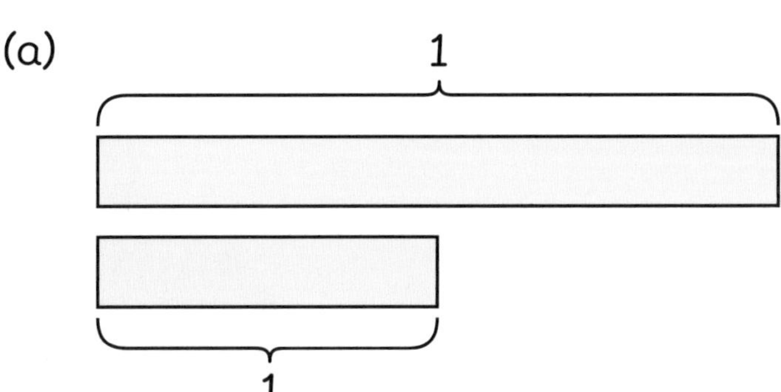

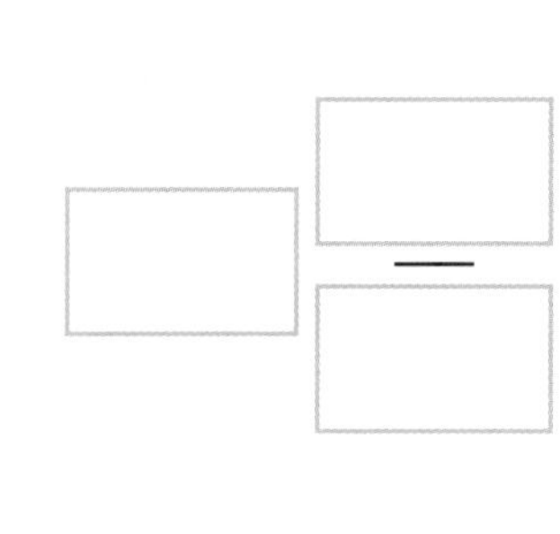

(b)

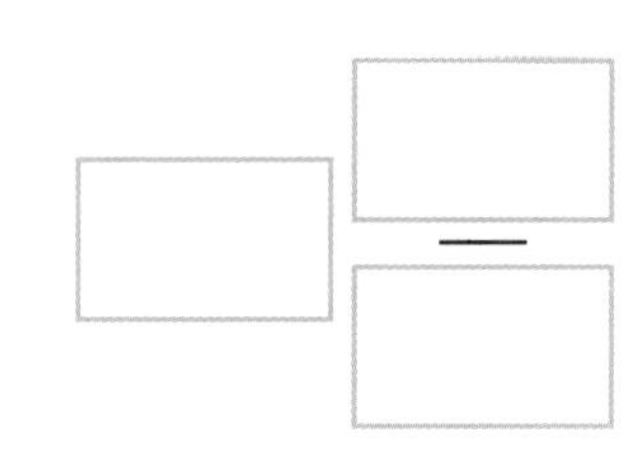

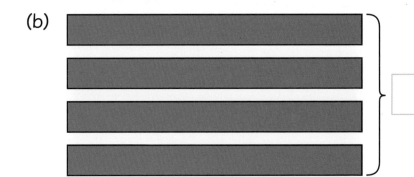

(c)

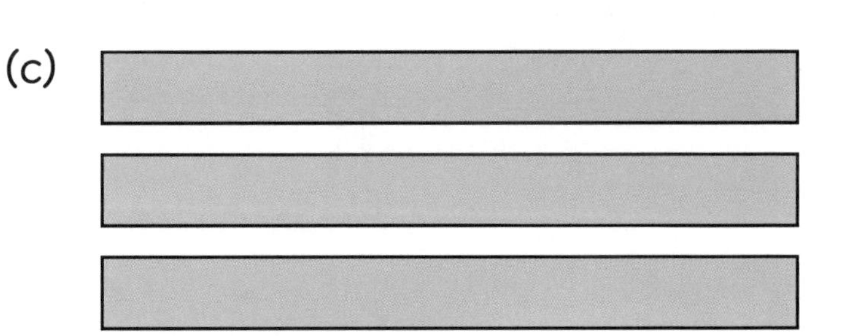

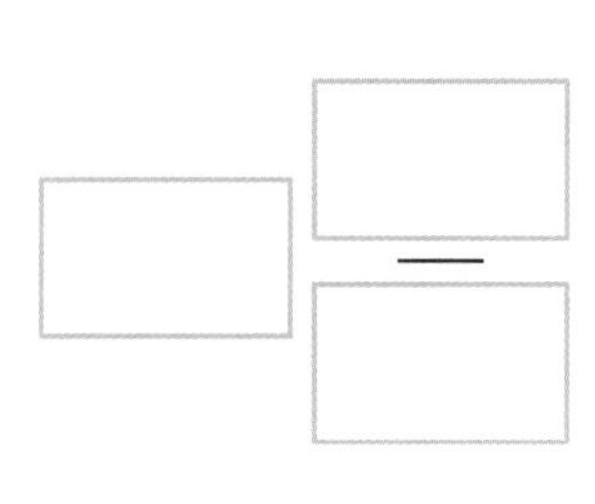

2 Fill in the blanks.

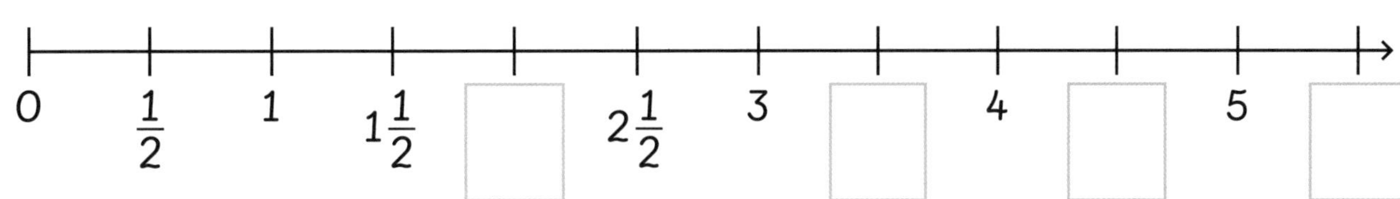

Counting in quarters

Starter

How much watermelon does the shopkeeper have left at the end of the day?

Example

This is 1 whole watermelon.
This is 1 quarter of a watermelon.

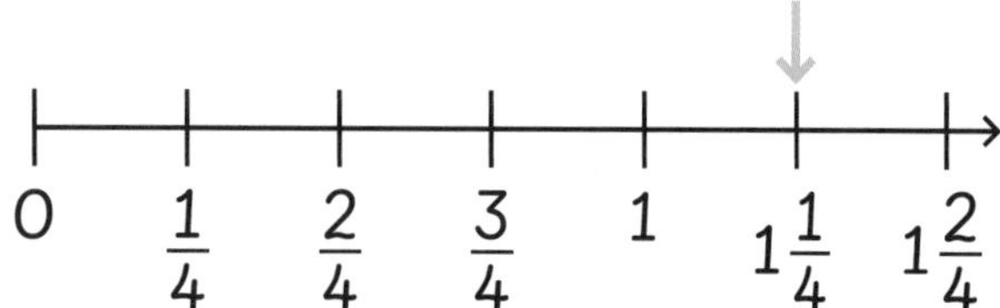

We can show $1\frac{1}{4}$ on a number line like this.

The shopkeeper has $1\frac{1}{4}$ watermelons left at the end of the day.

Practice

1 How many pieces are there? Fill in the blanks.

(a)

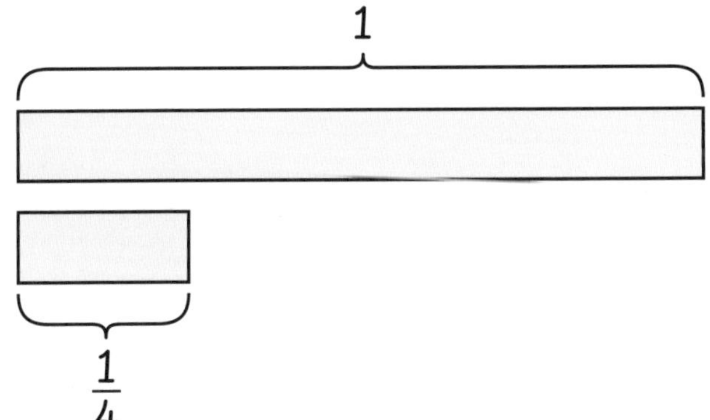

(b)

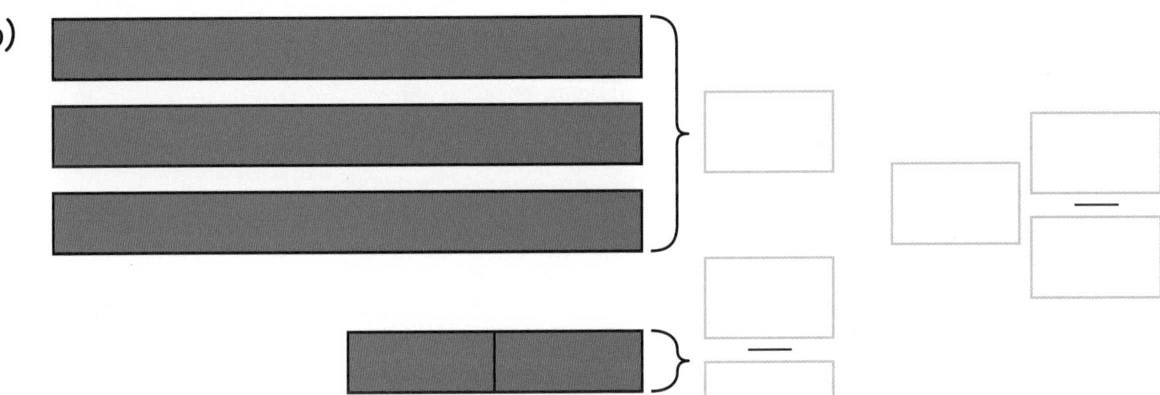

(c)

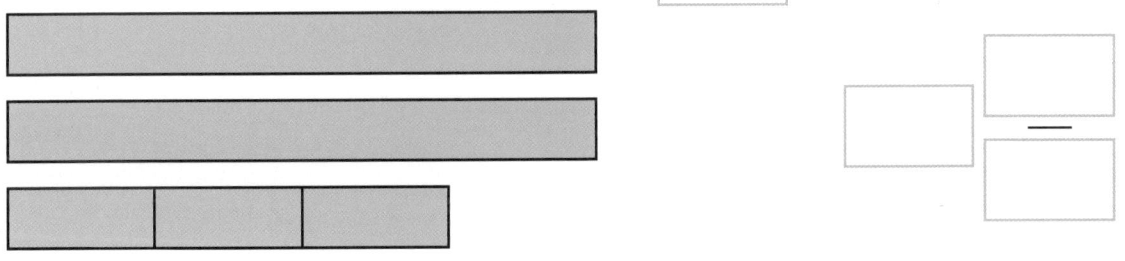

2 Fill in the blanks.

(a)

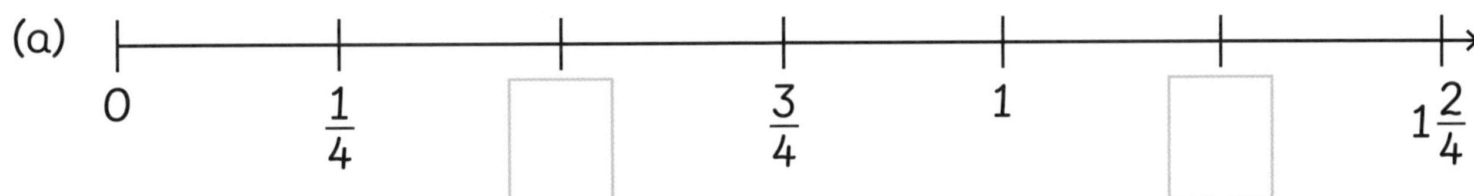

(b)

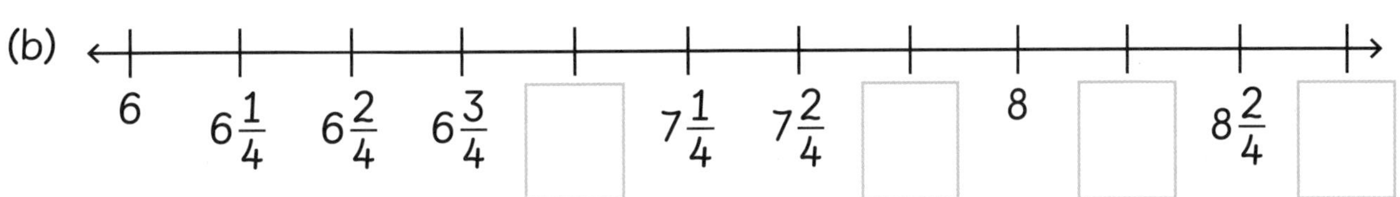

Counting in thirds

Lesson
11

Starter

The pizza chef uses this many blocks of cheese to make pizzas.

How many blocks of cheese does the chef use?

Example

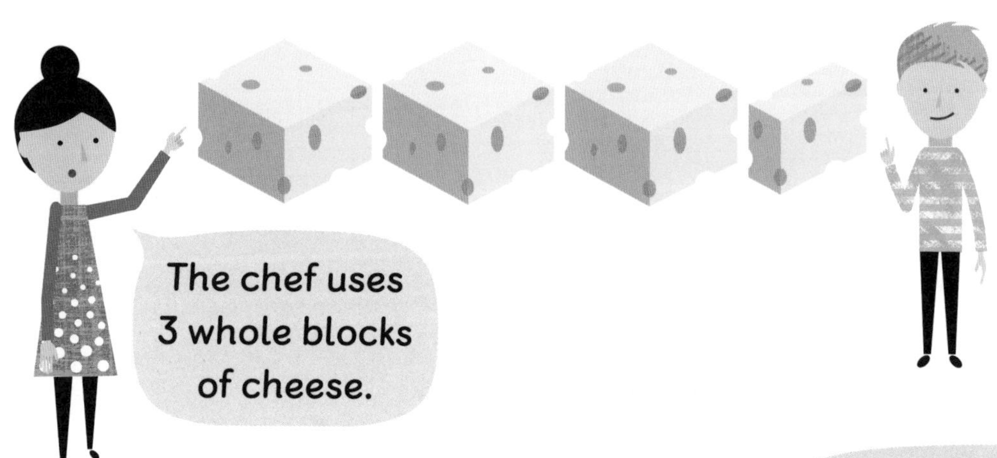

The chef uses 3 whole blocks of cheese.
This piece is 1 third of a block of cheese. We can write it as $\frac{1}{3}$.

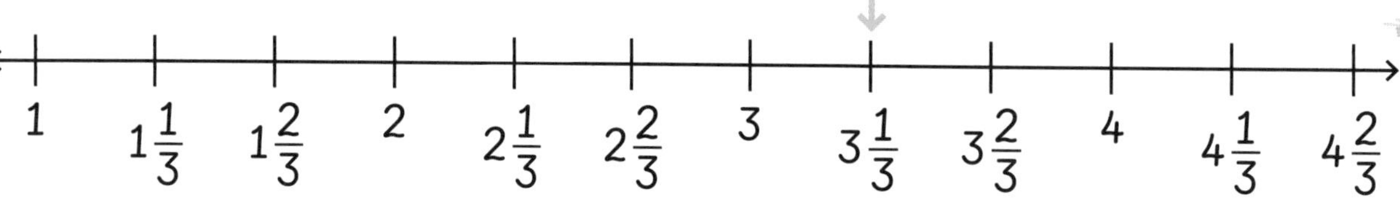

The chef uses $3\frac{1}{3}$ blocks of cheese to make pizzas.

Practice

1 How many pieces are there? Fill in the blanks.

(a)

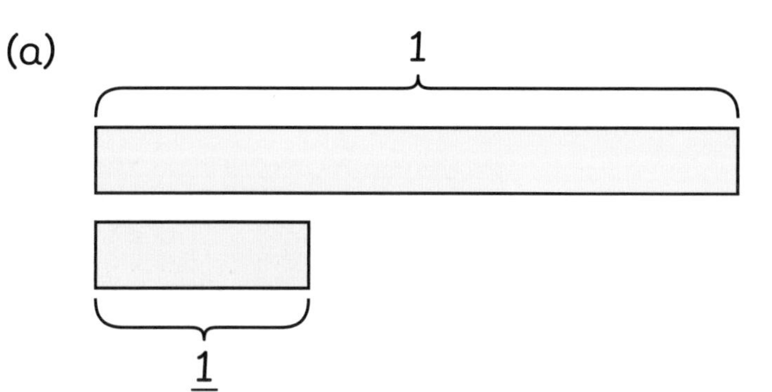

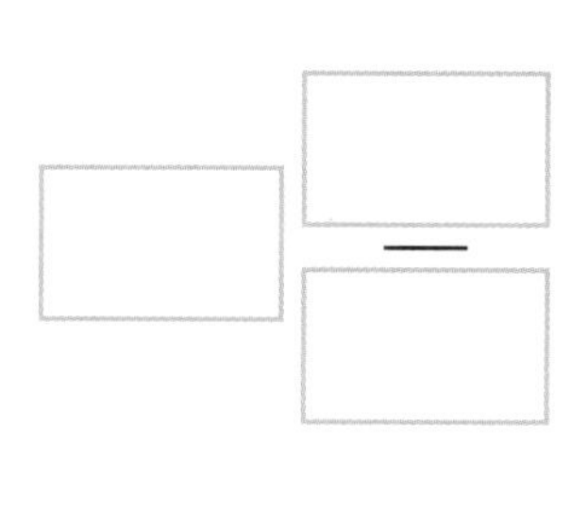

(b)

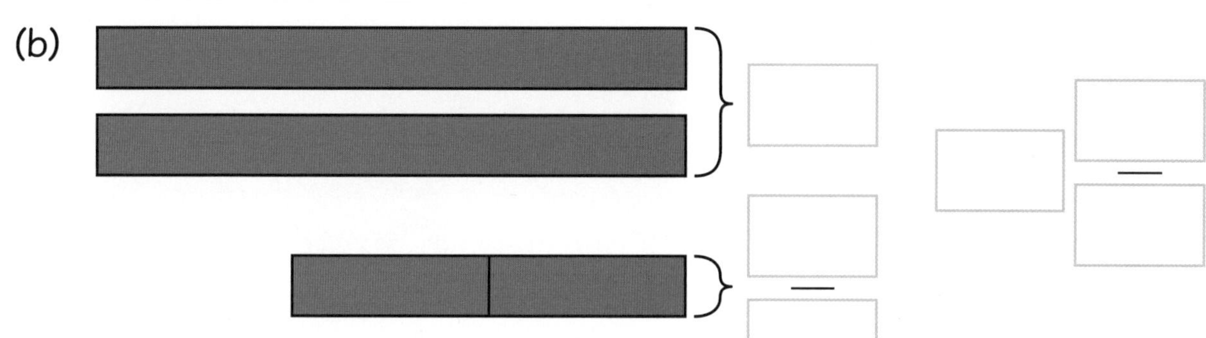

(c)

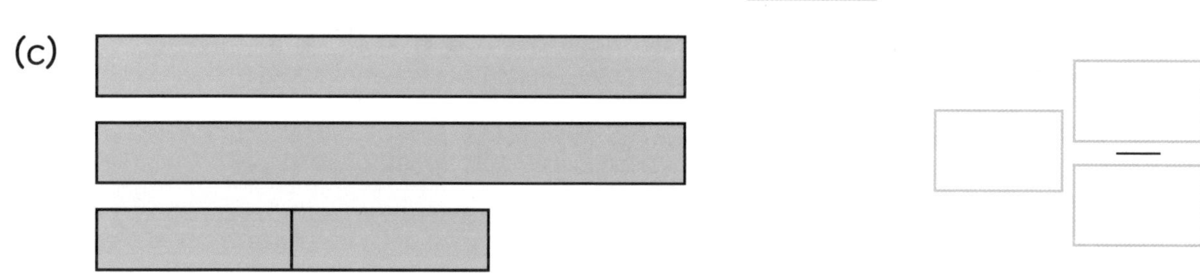

2 Fill in the blanks.

(a)

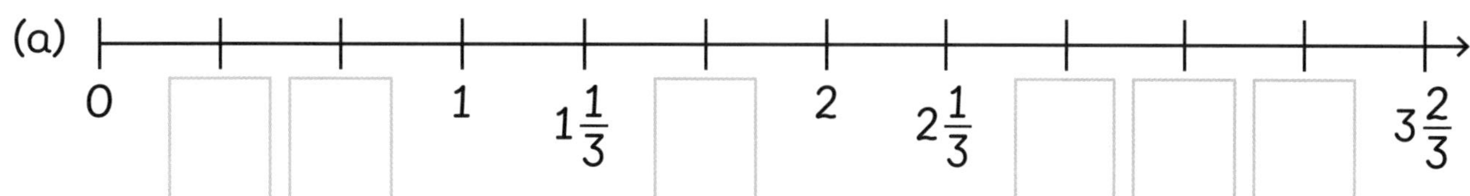

(b)

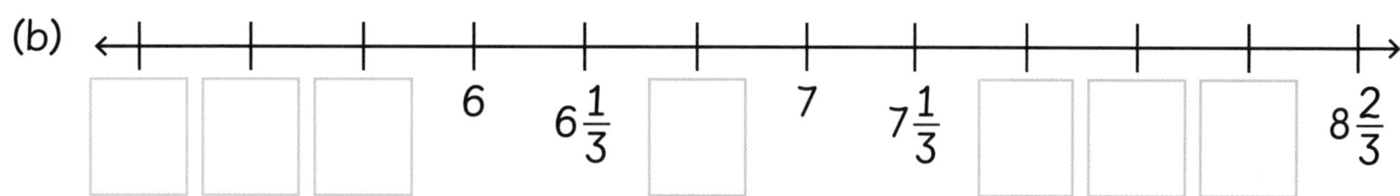

Half of a set

Lesson 12

Starter

How many pieces does half of the chocolate bar have?

Example

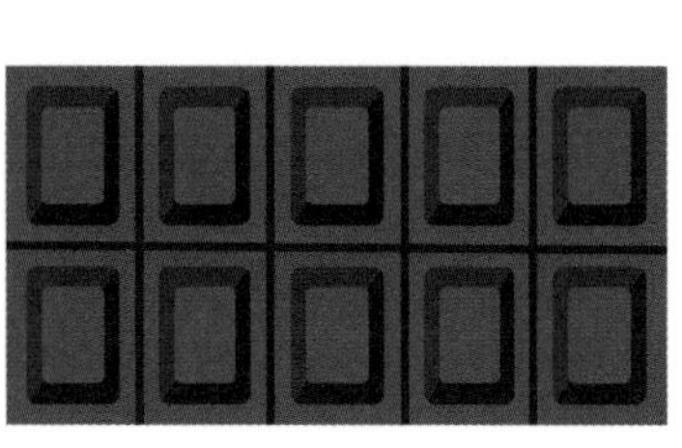

The whole chocolate bar has 10 pieces.

Half of the chocolate bar has half of the number of pieces.

$\frac{1}{2}$ of 10 is 5.

Half of the chocolate bar has 5 pieces.

Practice

Fill in the blanks.

1 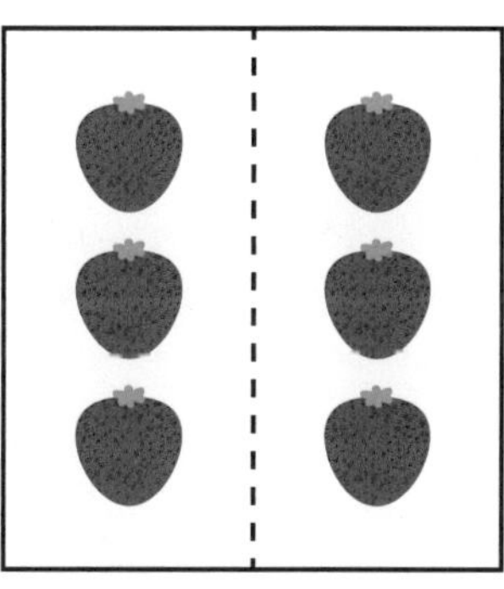

$\frac{1}{2}$ of 6 = ☐

2 

$\frac{1}{2}$ of 12 = ☐

3    

$\frac{1}{2}$ of 4 = ☐

4 

$\frac{1}{2}$ of 30 = ☐

Third of a set

Lesson 13

Starter

The children each get $\frac{1}{3}$ of the strawberry cake.

How many strawberries will each of them get?

Example

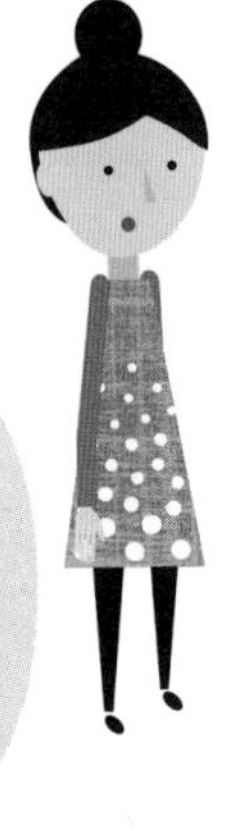

There are 9 strawberries on the whole cake. Each third has 3 strawberries.

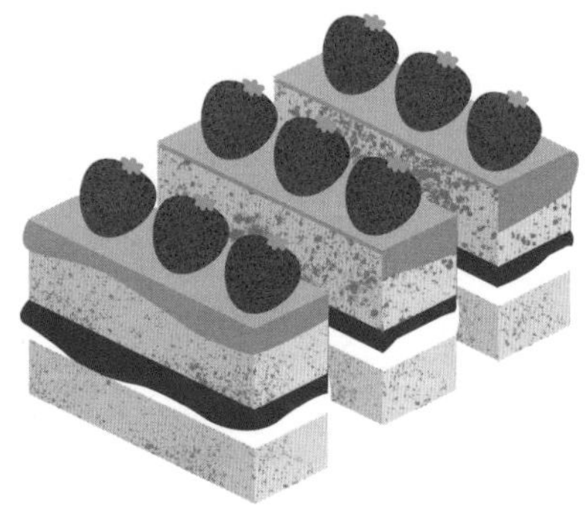

$\frac{1}{3}$ of 9 is 3.

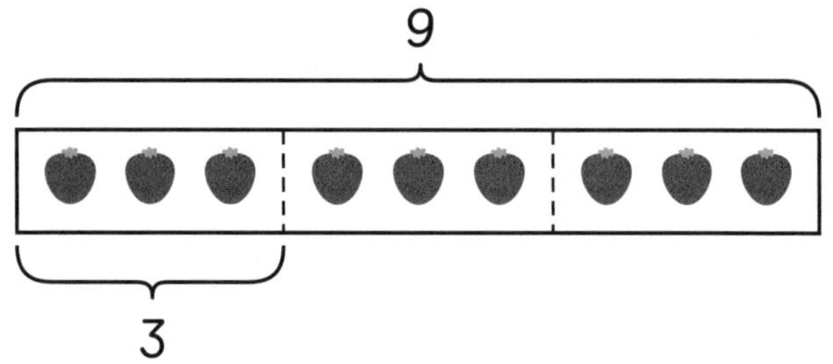

Each child will get 3 strawberries.

Practice

Fill in the blanks.

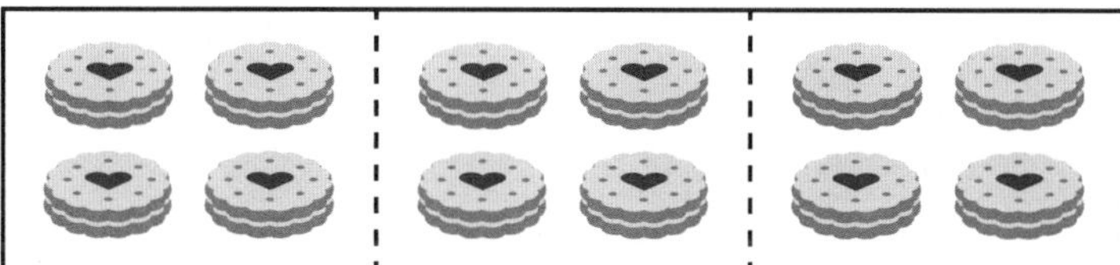

$\frac{1}{3}$ of 12 = ☐

    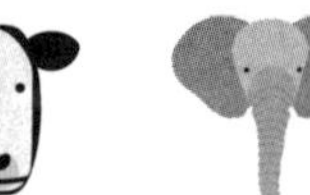

$\frac{1}{3}$ of 15 = ☐

$\frac{1}{3}$ of 12 = ☐

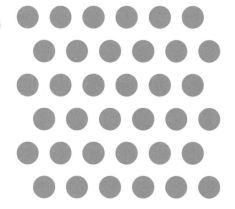

$\frac{1}{3}$ of 36 = ☐

Quarter of a set

Starter

There are 36 counters in total. Each stack is $\frac{1}{4}$ of the total amount.

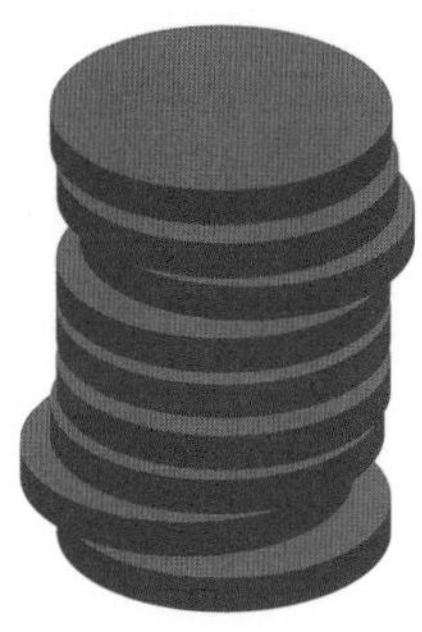

How many yellow counters are there?

Example

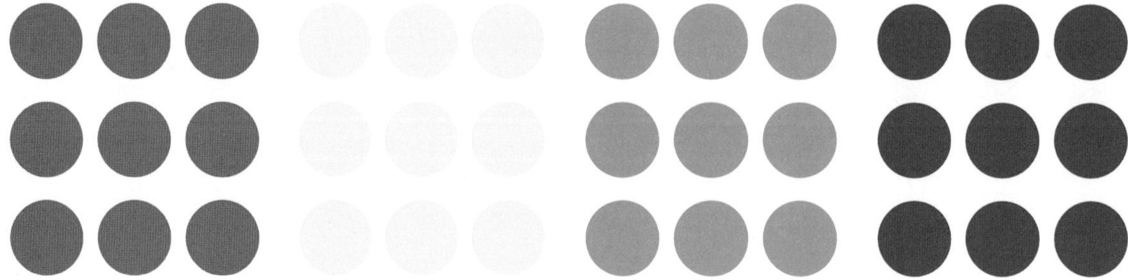

There are 36 counters in total.
1 quarter of the counters are yellow.

$\frac{1}{4}$ of 36 is 9.

There are 9 yellow counters.

Practice

Match.

$\frac{1}{4}$ of 12	10
$\frac{1}{4}$ of 8	2
$\frac{1}{4}$ of 4	3
$\frac{1}{4}$ of 40	8
$\frac{1}{4}$ of 32	1

Fractions of a quantity

Starter

Amira's 3-year-old sister is half as tall as her dad. Her dad is 2 m tall.

How tall is Amira's sister?

Example

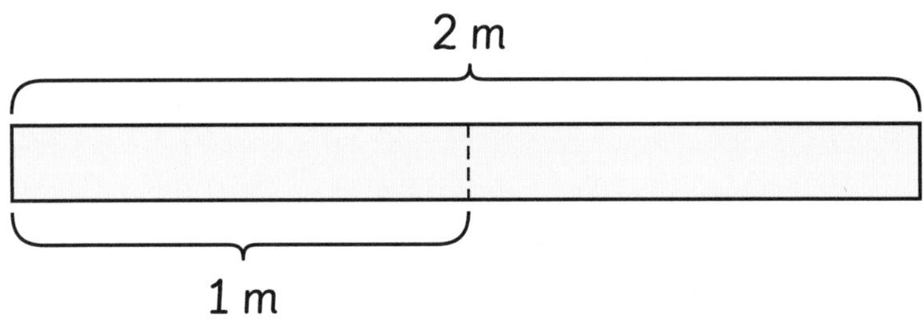

Amira's dad is 2 m tall.
One half of 2 m is 1 m.

$\frac{1}{2}$ of 2 m = 1 m

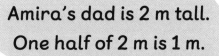

Practice

Fill in the blanks to solve the word problems.

1. The length of a car is $\frac{1}{4}$ of the length of a lorry. The lorry is 16 m. How long is the car?

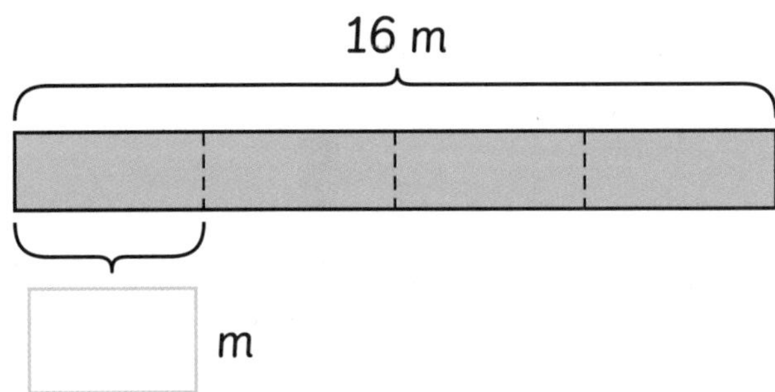

$\frac{1}{4}$ of 16 m = ☐ m

The car is ☐ m long.

2. Jacob went shopping with his dad. They bought a jacket, a pair of trousers and a T-shirt.

(a) The jacket cost £48 and the trousers cost half of the price of the jacket. How much did the trousers cost?

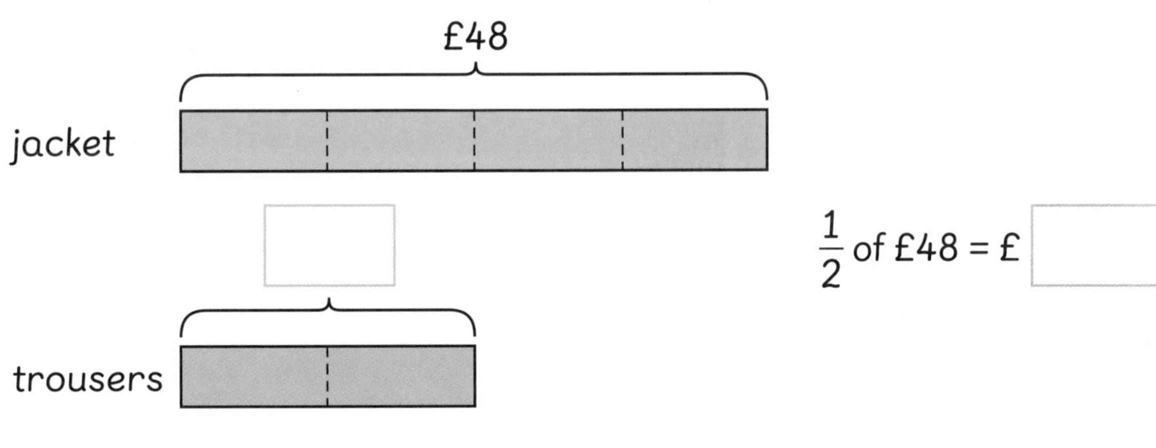

$\frac{1}{2}$ of £48 = £ ☐

The trousers cost £ ☐ .

(b) The T-shirt cost half as much as the trousers. How much did the T-shirt cost?

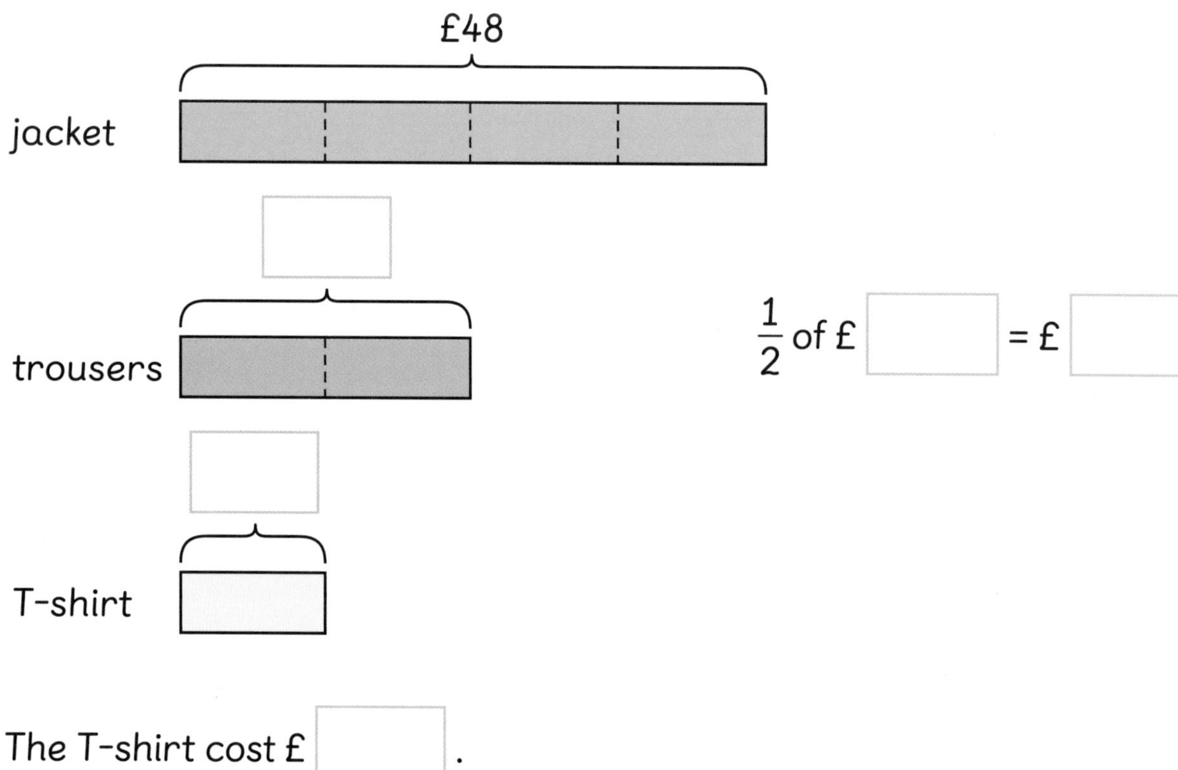

The T-shirt cost £ [ ] .

3 Lulu started her homework at 4 o'clock and finished at half past four. She took half as long to finish her homework as her older sister did.

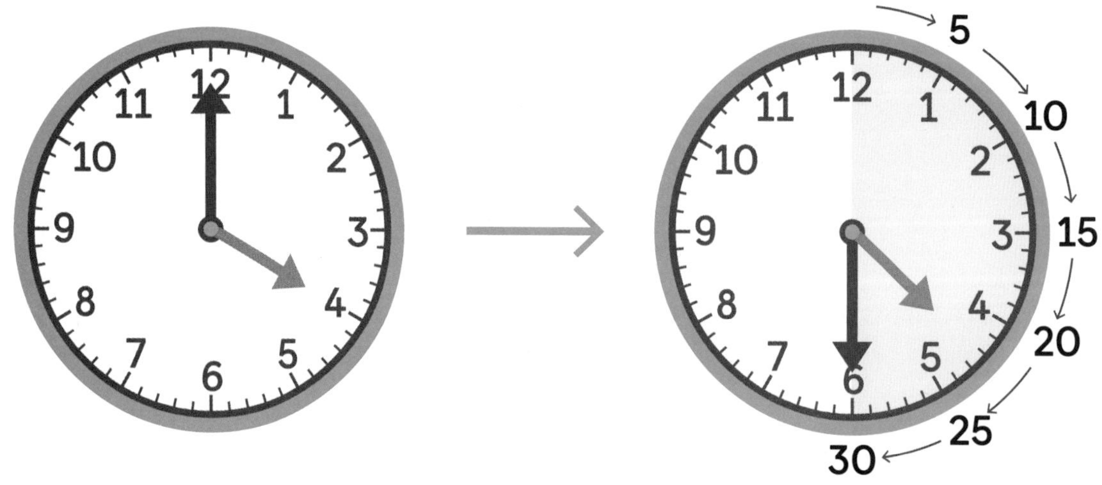

How long did it take Lulu's older sister to do her homework?

Lulu's older sister took [ ] to do her homework.

4 Look at the pictures and fill in the blanks.

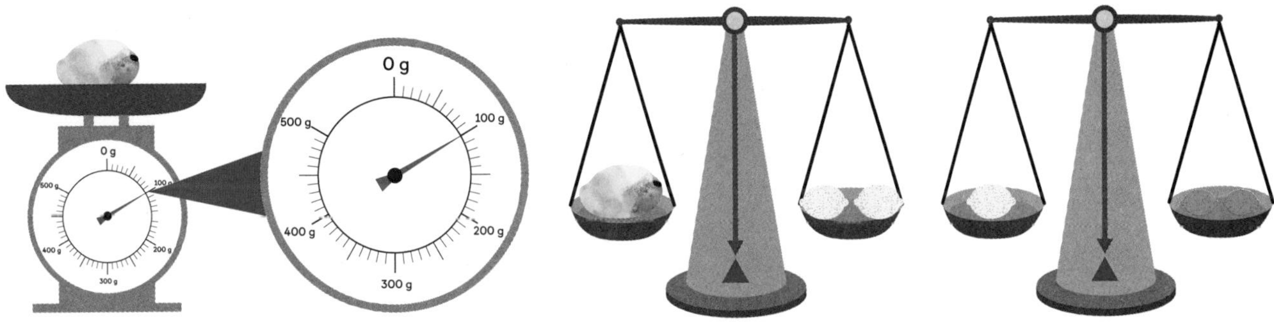

(a) The [potato] weighs ☐ g.

(b) One [lemon] weighs $\frac{☐}{☐}$ as much as one [potato].

(c) One [lemon] weighs ☐ g.

(d) One [plum] weighs $\frac{☐}{☐}$ as much as one [lemon].

(e) One [plum] weighs $\frac{☐}{☐}$ as much as one [potato].

(f) One [plum] weighs ☐ g.

Review and challenge

1 Circle the shapes that show equal parts.

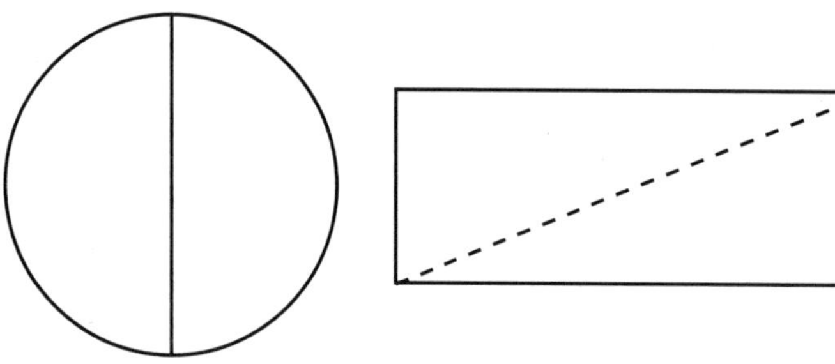
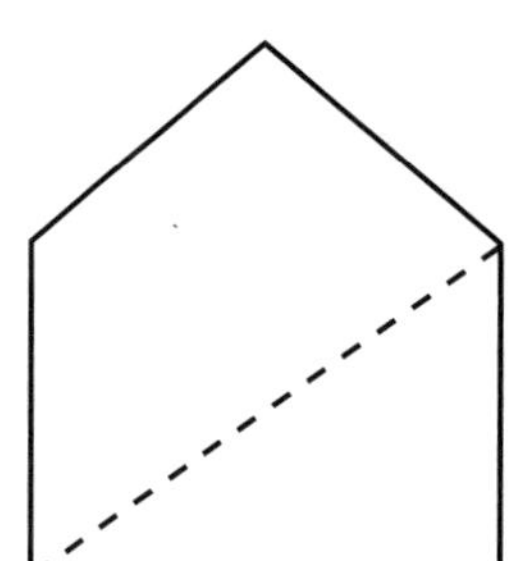
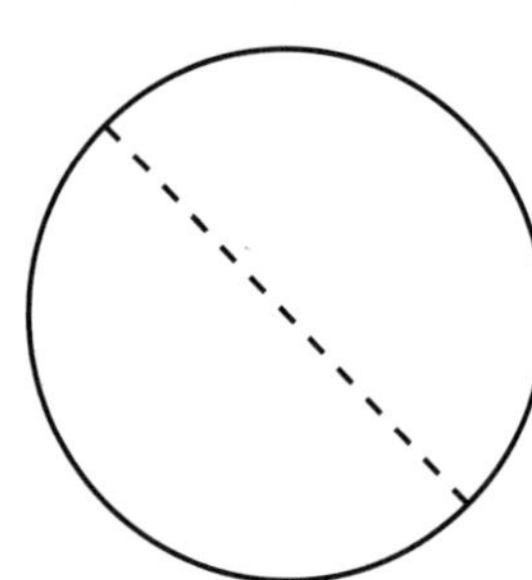

2 Draw lines on each shape to show:

(a) $\frac{1}{2}$

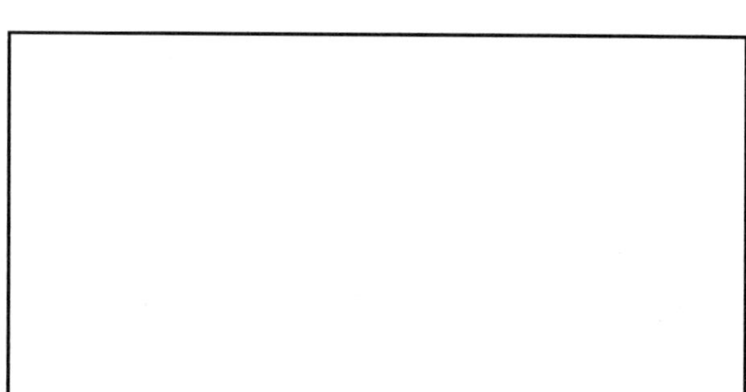

(b) $\frac{1}{4}$

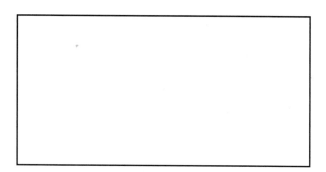

(c) $\frac{1}{3}$

3 What fraction of the shape is shaded?

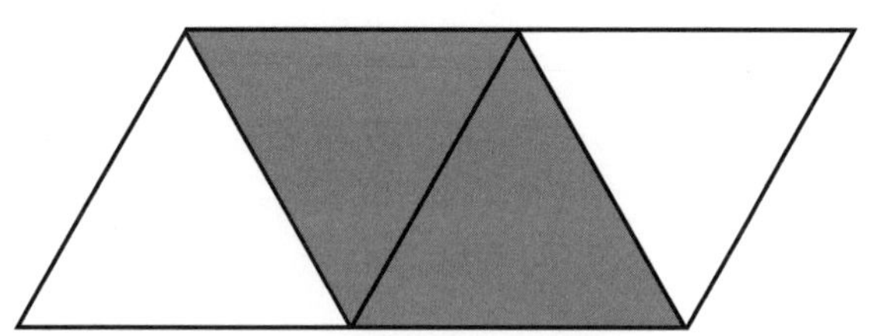

☐ out of ☐ parts is shaded.

☐ is the numerator.

☐ is the denominator.

4 Fill in the blanks.

(a) $\frac{2}{\square} = 1$

(b) $\frac{\square}{3} = 1$

(c) $\frac{\square}{2} = \frac{2}{4}$

(d) $\frac{2}{4} = \frac{1}{\square}$

(e) $\frac{3}{\square} = 1$

(f) $\frac{\square}{4} = 1$

5 Shade and fill in the blanks.

(a) $\frac{3}{4}$

$\frac{1}{2}$

$\frac{\square}{\square}$ is greater than $\frac{\square}{\square}$.

$\frac{\square}{\square}$ is smaller than $\frac{\square}{\square}$.

(b) $\frac{2}{3}$

$\frac{3}{4}$

$\frac{\square}{\square}$ is greater than $\frac{\square}{\square}$.

$\frac{\square}{\square}$ is smaller than $\frac{\square}{\square}$.

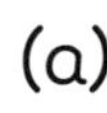

Fill in the blanks.

(a)

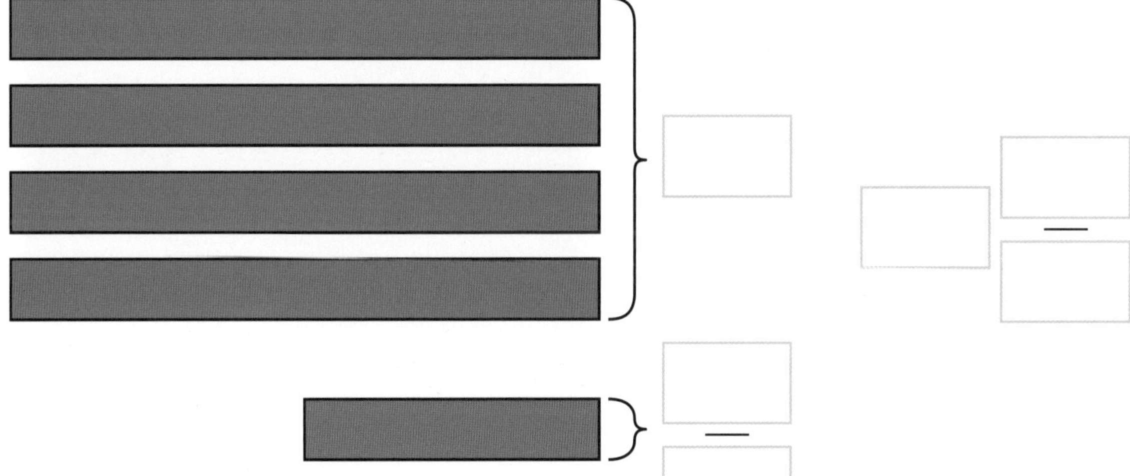

(b)

(c)

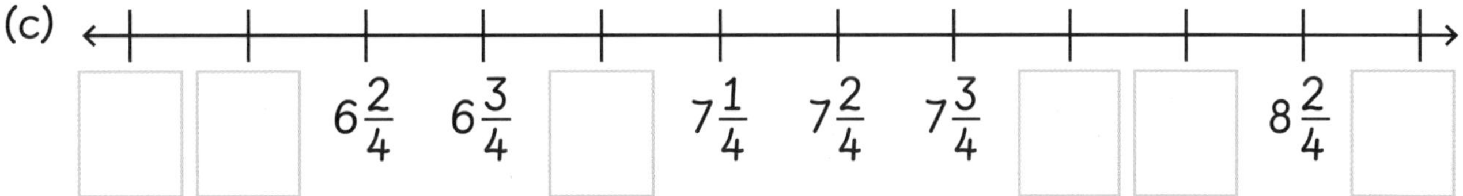

7 Draw an arrow where $8\frac{3}{4}$ is on the number line.

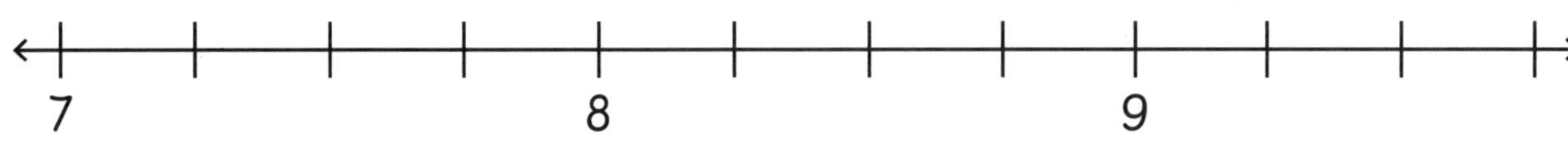

8 Draw an arrow where $5\frac{1}{3}$ is on the number line.

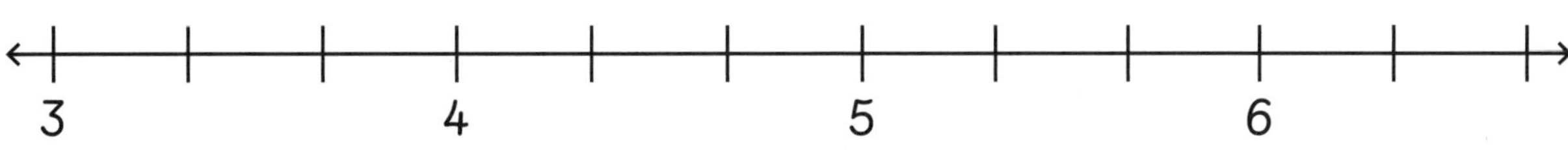

9 Fill in the blanks.

(a)

$\frac{1}{3}$ of 27 = ☐

(b)

$\frac{1}{4}$ of 36 = ☐

(c)

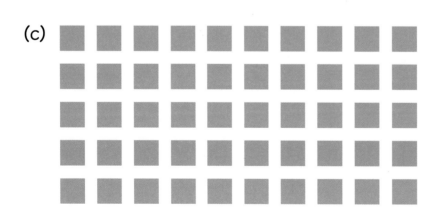

$\frac{1}{2}$ of 50 = ☐

10  weighs 20 kg.

Her dog weighs $\frac{1}{2}$ as much as .

Her cat weighs $\frac{1}{4}$ as much as .

How much do the dog and the cat weigh altogether?

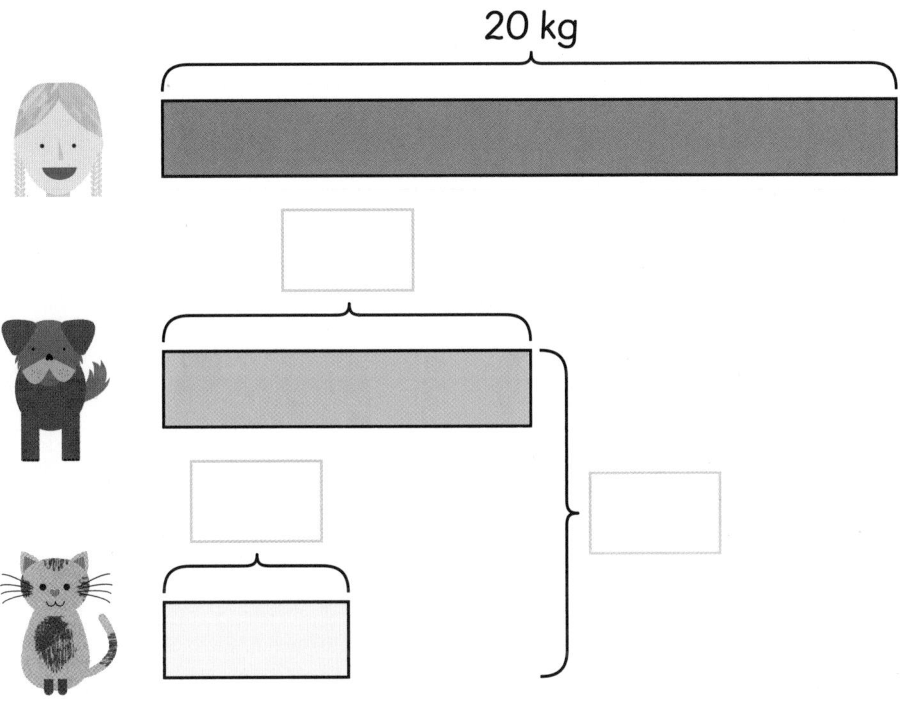

The dog and the cat weigh  kg altogether.

Answers

Page 6 **1 (a)** Possible answers: 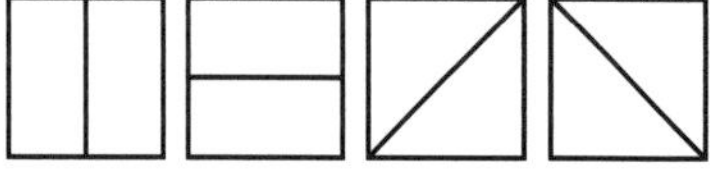

(b) Possible answers: 

2 (a) Possible answers: 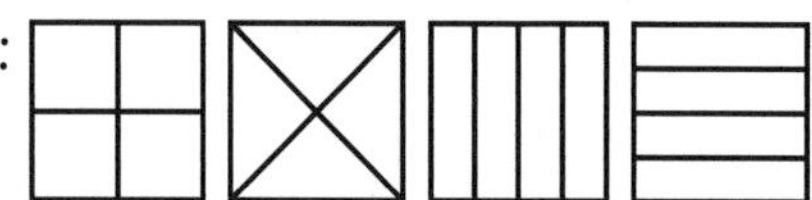

(b) Possible answers: 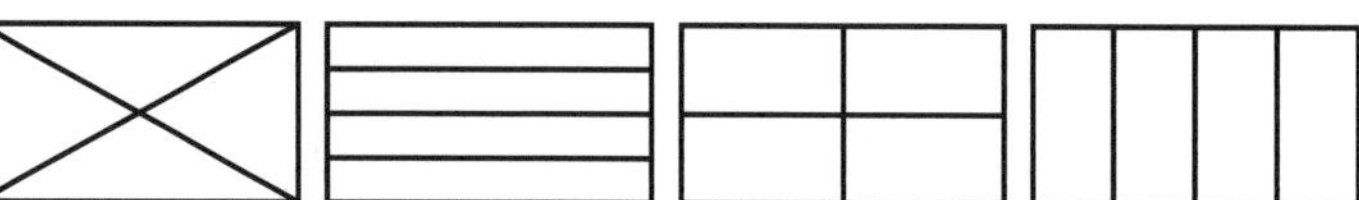

Page 7 **3** 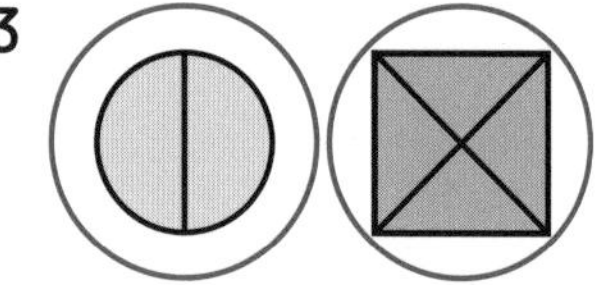 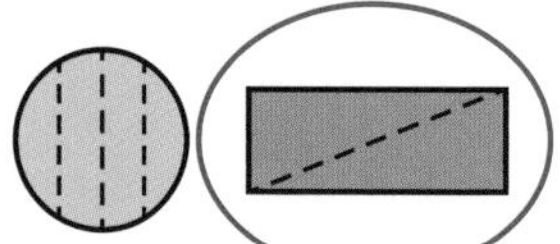 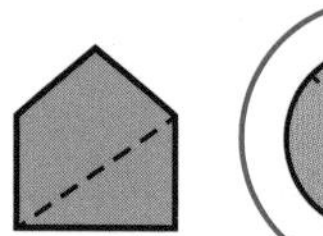 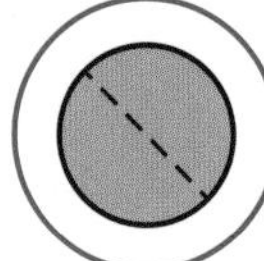

Page 9

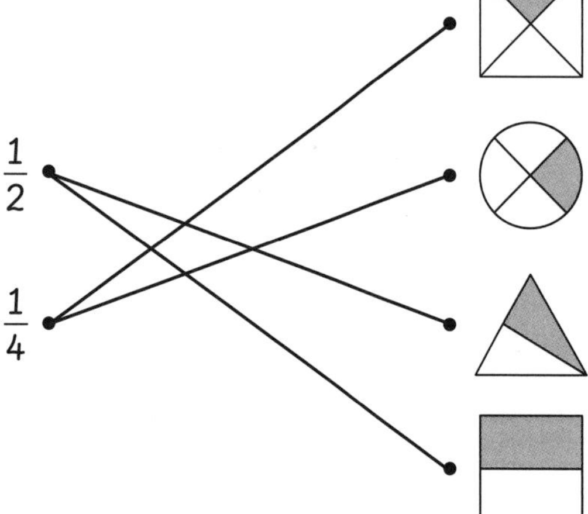

Page 11 **1** $\frac{2}{3}$, 2 thirds **2** $\frac{1}{3}$, 1 third **3** $\frac{3}{3}$, 3 thirds

Page 13 **1 (a)** 2 parts out of 4 parts are shaded. 2 is the numerator. 4 is the denominator.
(b) 1 part out of 4 parts is shaded. 1 is the numerator. 4 is the denominator.
(c) 1 part out of 2 parts is shaded. 1 is the numerator. 2 is the denominator. **2** $\frac{2}{4}$, $\frac{2}{4}$

Page 16 **1**

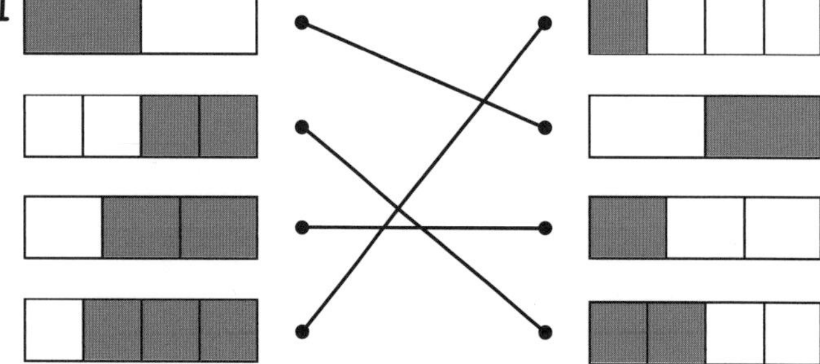

Page 17 **2 (a)** $\frac{2}{2} = 1$ **(b)** $\frac{3}{3} = 1$ **(c)** $\frac{3}{3} = 1$ **(d)** $\frac{4}{4} = 1$ **(e)** $\frac{1}{2} = \frac{2}{4}$ **(f)** $\frac{2}{4} = \frac{1}{2}$

Page 19 **1** Any 1 part shaded, for example:
Any 3 parts shaded, for example: , $\frac{3}{4}$ is greater than $\frac{1}{4}$. $\frac{1}{4}$ is smaller than $\frac{3}{4}$.
2 (a) $\frac{3}{4}, \frac{2}{4}, \frac{1}{4}$ **(b)** $\frac{1}{3}, \frac{2}{3}, \frac{3}{3}$

Page 21 **1 (a)** $\frac{1}{4} < \frac{1}{2}$ **(b)** $\frac{1}{3} > \frac{1}{4}$ **(c)** $\frac{1}{3} < \frac{1}{2}$ **2** $\frac{1}{4}, \frac{1}{3}, \frac{1}{2}$

Page 23 **1** 2, $\frac{3}{4}$, $2\frac{3}{4}$ **2** 1, $\frac{1}{3}$, $1\frac{1}{3}$ **3** 2, $\frac{1}{2}$, $2\frac{1}{2}$ **4** 3, $\frac{1}{4}$, $3\frac{1}{4}$

Page 25 **1 (a)** $1\frac{1}{2}$ **(b)** 4, $\frac{1}{2}$, $4\frac{1}{2}$ **(c)** $3\frac{1}{2}$ **2** 2, $3\frac{1}{2}$, $4\frac{1}{2}$, $5\frac{1}{2}$

Page 27 **1 (a)** $1\frac{1}{4}$ **(b)** 3, $\frac{2}{4}$, $3\frac{2}{4}$ **(c)** $2\frac{3}{4}$ **2 (a)** $\frac{2}{4}$, $1\frac{1}{4}$ **(b)** 7, $7\frac{3}{4}$, $8\frac{1}{4}$, $8\frac{3}{4}$

Page 29 **1 (a)** $1\frac{1}{3}$ **(b)** 2, $\frac{2}{3}$, $2\frac{2}{3}$ **(c)** $2\frac{2}{3}$ **2 (a)** $\frac{1}{3}$, $\frac{2}{3}$, $1\frac{2}{3}$, $2\frac{2}{3}$, 3, $3\frac{1}{3}$ **(b)** 5, $5\frac{1}{3}$, $5\frac{2}{3}$, $6\frac{2}{3}$, $7\frac{2}{3}$, 8, $8\frac{1}{3}$

Page 31 **1** 3 **2** 6 **3** 2 **4** 15

Page 33 **1** 4 **2** 5 **3** 4 **4** 12

Page 35

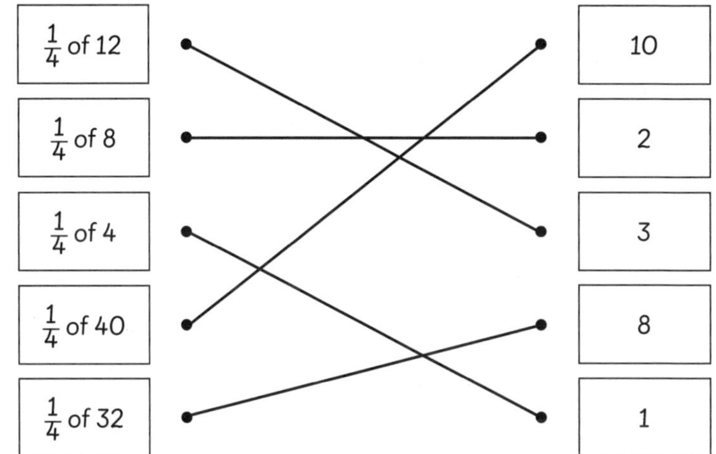

Page 37 **1** 4 m, $\frac{1}{4}$ of 16 m = 4 m. The car is 4 m long. **2 (a)** £24, $\frac{1}{2}$ of £48 = £24. The trousers cost £24.

Page 38 **(b)** £24 (trousers) , $\frac{1}{2}$ of £24 is £12. £12 (T-shirt) . The T-shirt cost £12. **3** Lulu's older sister took 60 minutes OR 1 hour to do her homework.

Page 39 **4 (a)** The mango weighs 100 g. **(b)** One lemon weighs $\frac{1}{2}$ as much as one mango.
(c) One lemon weighs 50 g. **(d)** One lime weighs $\frac{1}{2}$ as much as one lemon.
(e) One lime weighs $\frac{1}{4}$ as much as one mango. **(f)** One lime weighs 25 g.

Answers continued

Page 40 **1** Possible answers:

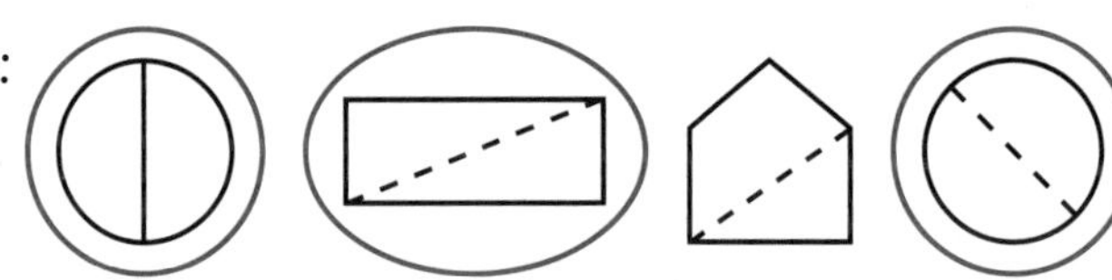

2 (a) Possible answers:

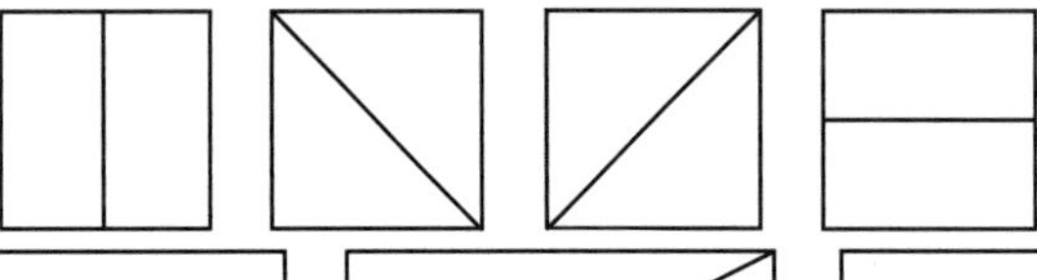

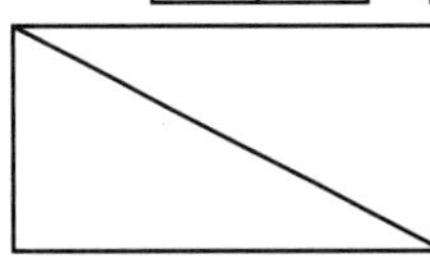

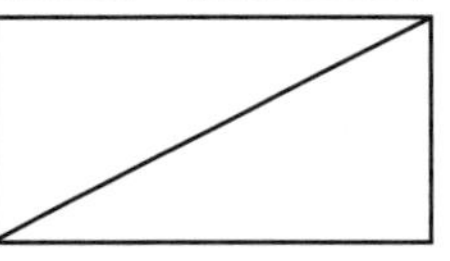

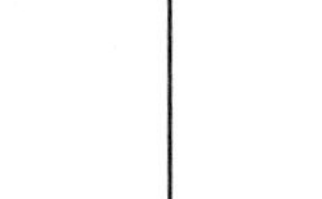

(b) Possible answers:

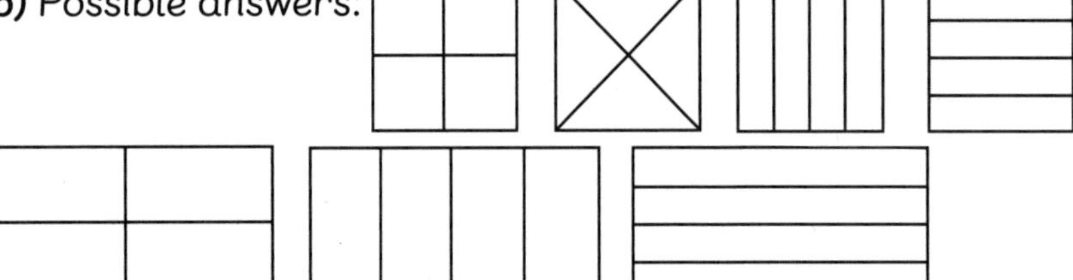

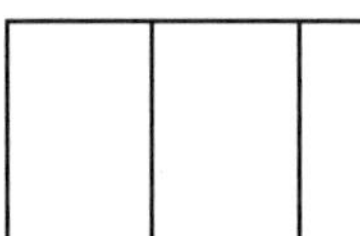

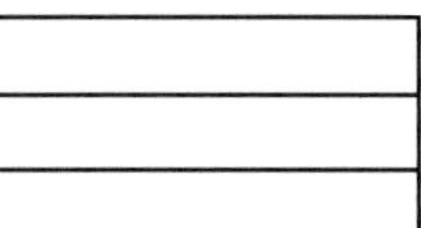

Page 41 **(c)** Possible answers:

3 2 out of 4 parts is shaded. 2 is the numerator. 4 is the denominator.

4 (a) $\frac{2}{2} = 1$ **(b)** $\frac{3}{3} = 1$ **(c)** $\frac{1}{2} = \frac{2}{4}$ **(d)** $\frac{2}{4} = \frac{1}{2}$ **(e)** $\frac{3}{3} = 1$ **(f)** $\frac{4}{4} = 1$

Page 42 **5 (a)** Any 3 parts shaded, for example: $\frac{3}{4}$

Any 2 parts shaded, for example: $\frac{1}{2}$ $\frac{3}{4}$ is greater than $\frac{1}{2}$.

$\frac{1}{2}$ is smaller than $\frac{3}{4}$.

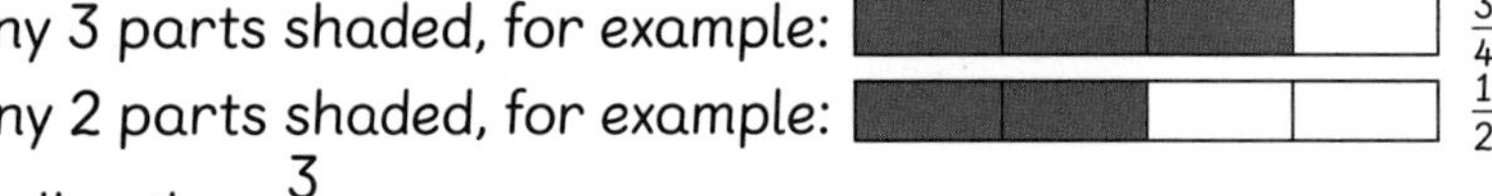

(b) Any 2 parts shaded, for example: $\frac{2}{3}$

Any 3 parts shaded, for example: $\frac{3}{4}$ $\frac{3}{4}$ is greater than $\frac{2}{3}$.

$\frac{2}{3}$ is smaller than $\frac{3}{4}$.

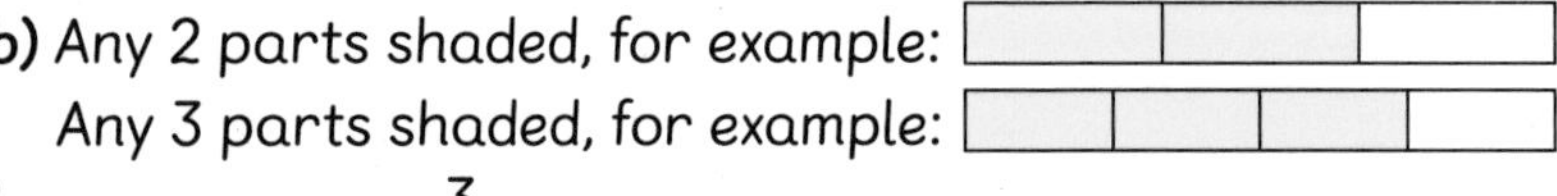

Page 43 **6 (a)** 4, $\frac{1}{2}$, $4\frac{1}{2}$ **(b)** $2\frac{2}{3}$ **(c)** 6, $6\frac{1}{4}$, 7, 8, $8\frac{1}{4}$, $8\frac{3}{4}$

7 **8**

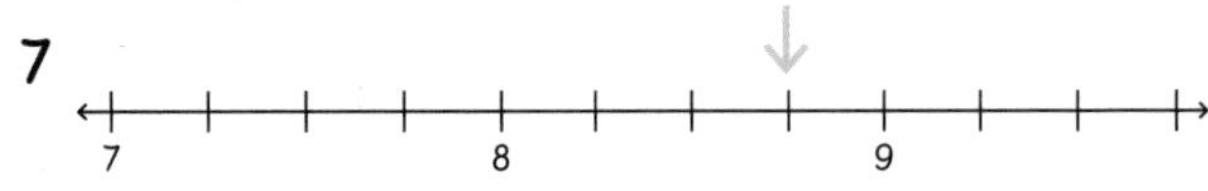

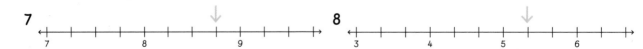

Page 44 **9 (a)** 9 **(b)** 9 **(c)** 25

Page 45 **10** 10 kg (dog), 5 kg (cat), 15 kg. The dog and cat weigh 15 kg altogether.

KS1
5–7
Years

Master Maths at Home

Extra Challenges

Scan the QR code to help your child's learning at home.

mastermathsathome.com

How to use this book

Maths — No Problem! created **Master Maths at Home** to help children develop fluency in the subject and a rich understanding of core concepts.

Key features of the Master Maths at Home books include:

- Carefully designed lessons that provide structure but also allow flexibility in how they're used. For example, some children may want to write numbers, while others might want to trace.
- Speech bubbles containing content designed to spark diverse conversations, with many discussion points that don't have obvious 'right' or 'wrong' answers.
- Rich illustrations that will guide children to a discussion of shapes and units of measurement, allowing them to make connections to the wider world around them.
- Exercises that allow a flexible approach and can be adapted to suit any child's cognitive or functional ability.
- Clearly laid out pages that encourage children to practise a range of higher-order skills.
- A community of friendly and relatable characters who introduce each lesson and come along as your child progresses through the series.

You can see more guidance on how to use these books at **mastermathsathome.com**.

We're excited to share all the ways you can learn maths!

Maths — No Problem!
masternmathsathome.com
www.mathsnoproblem.com
hello@mathsnoproblem.com

First published in Great Britain in 2022 by
Dorling Kindersley Limited
One Embassy Gardens, 8 Viaduct Gardens, London SW11 7BW
A Penguin Random House Company

The authorised representative in the EEA is Dorling Kindersley Verlag GmbH. Amulfstr. 124, 80636 Munich, Germany

10 9 8 7 6 5 4 3 2 1
001–327072–Jan/22

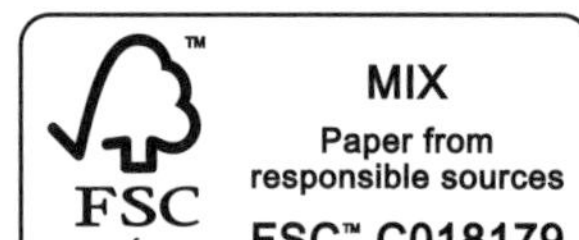

This book was made with Forest Stewardship Council™ certified paper - one small step in DK's commitment to a sustainable future. For more information go to www.dk.com/our-green-pledge

A CIP catalogue record for this book is available from the British Library.

ISBN: 978-0-24153-915-6
Printed and bound in China

For the curious
www.dk.com

Acknowledgements
The publisher would like to thank the authors and consultants Andy Psarianos, Judy Hornigold, Adam Gifford and Dr Anne Hermanson.

The Castledown typeface has been used with permission from the Colophon Foundry.

Contents

Ruby
Elliott
Amira
Charles
Lulu
Sam
Oak
Holly
Ravi
Emma
Jacob
Hannah

Comparing numbers

Lesson 1

Starter

Emma uses 2, 1 and 3 to write three 2-digit numbers.

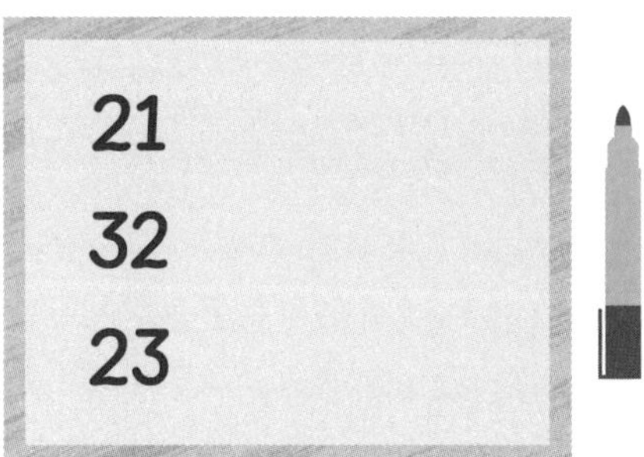

Which is the smallest number?

Example

tens	ones
2	1

tens	ones
3	2

tens	ones
2	3

3 tens is more than 2 tens.

32 is greater than 21. 32 > 21

32 is greater than 23. 32 > 23

32 is the greatest number.

23 is greater than 21. 23 > 21
21 is the smallest number.

The tens are the same, compare the ones next.

Practice

1. Use 4, 3 and 5 to write:

   (a) the greatest 2-digit number ☐

   (b) the smallest 2-digit number ☐

2. Use 8, 4 and 6 to write two different 2-digit numbers.

   Use the numbers to fill in the blanks.

   ☐ < ☐

   Is there more than one answer?

3. Use 7, 5 and 6 to write six different 2-digit numbers.

   Put the numbers in order, starting with the greatest.

   ☐, ☐, ☐, ☐, ☐, ☐

4. (a) Fill in the blanks on the number line using the following numbers.

   59, 72, 63, 54, 85, 77

   ☐ ☐ ☐ ☐ ☐ ☐

   50 60 70 80 90

   (b) Compare the numbers using > or <.

   63 ☐ 59   77 ☐ 85

   54 ☐ 72   72 ☐ 77

Solving addition problems

Lesson 2

Starter

There are 26 children in the sports club.
There are 37 children in the arts club.
How many children are in the clubs altogether?

Example

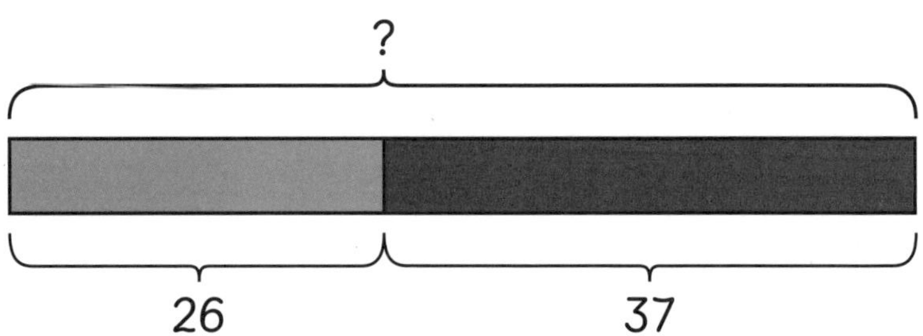

$$\begin{array}{rrr} & {}^{1}2 & 6 \\ + & 3 & 7 \\ \hline & & 3 \\ \hline \end{array} \qquad \begin{array}{rrr} & {}^{1}2 & 6 \\ + & 3 & 7 \\ \hline & 6 & 3 \\ \hline \end{array}$$

Add the ones.

Then add the tens.

26 + 37 = 63

There are 63 children in the clubs altogether.

Practice

1 Charles read 37 pages of a book on Monday.
He read 45 pages of the book on Tuesday.
How many pages did he read over the two days?

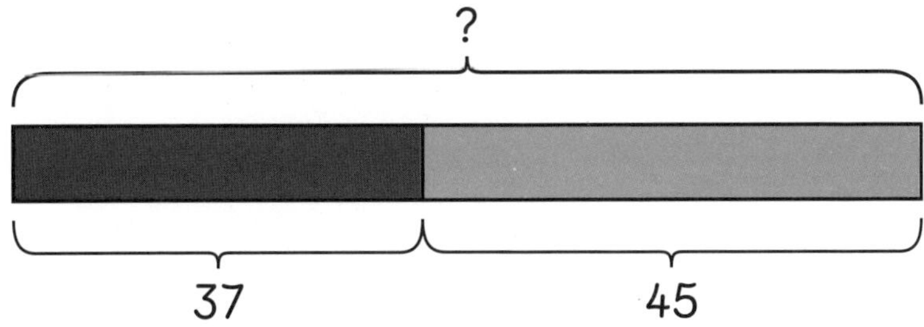

Charles read [ ] pages over the two days.

2 Class 2A has 56 books in their class library.
Class 2B has 39 books in their class library.
How many books do the two classes have altogether?

The two classes have [ ] books altogether.

Solving subtraction problems

Lesson 3

Starter

There are 53 passengers on a train.
When the train stops, 28 passengers get off.
How many passengers are left on the train?

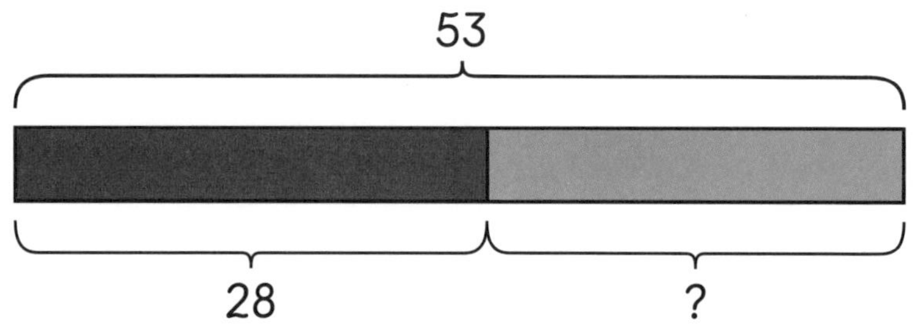

Example

$$\begin{array}{rrr} & {}^{4}\cancel{5} & {}^{13}\cancel{3} \\ - & 2 & 8 \\ \hline & & 5 \\ \hline \end{array} \qquad \begin{array}{rrr} & {}^{4}\cancel{5} & {}^{13}\cancel{3} \\ - & 2 & 8 \\ \hline & 2 & 5 \\ \hline \end{array}$$

Rename 1 ten as 10 ones, then subtract the ones.

Subtract the tens.

53 – 28 = 25

There are 25 passengers left on the train.

Practice

1 There are 63 children in the school hall.
37 children leave to go back to their classrooms.
How many children are still in the hall?

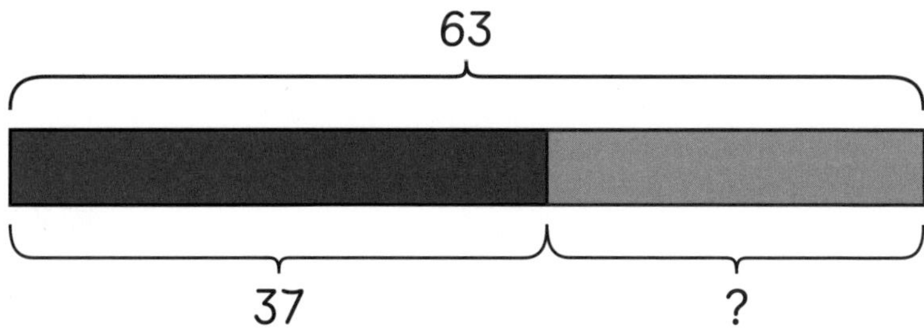

There are [ ] children still in the hall.

2 82 children start a sponsored run.
After an hour, 48 children have finished the run.
How many children have not yet finished the run?

[ ] children have not yet finished the run.

Solving multiplication problems

Lesson 4

Starter

Holly uses 15 cm of ribbon to make a flower. How much ribbon does she need to make 3 flowers?

Example

Each flower needs 15 cm of ribbon.
There are 3 flowers.

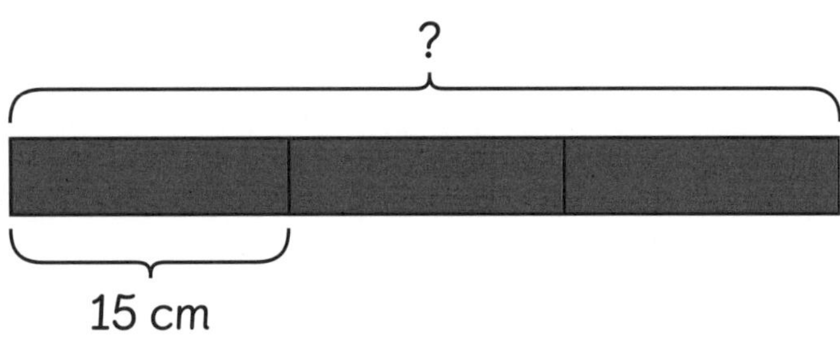

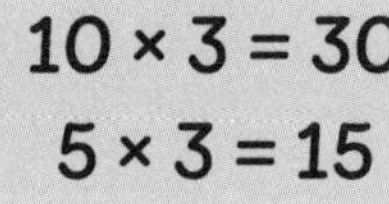

's method:

15 + 15 + 15 = 45

's method:

15 × 3 = 45

Holly needs 45 cm of ribbon to make 3 flowers.

Which method do you prefer?
Which method would be better to find out how much ribbon is needed to make 10 flowers?

Practice

1. Ruby places 10 identical straws in a straight line. Each straw is 8 cm long. What is the total length of the 10 straws?

?

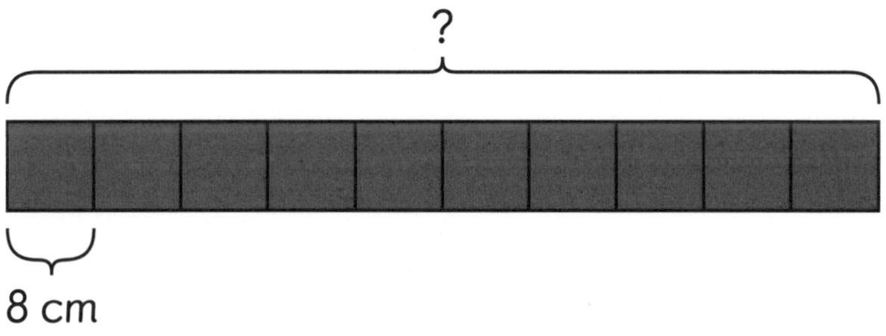

8 cm

The total length of the 10 straws is ☐ cm.

2. Emma stacks 9 identical books. Each book is 5 cm thick. What is the height of the stack of 9 books?

?

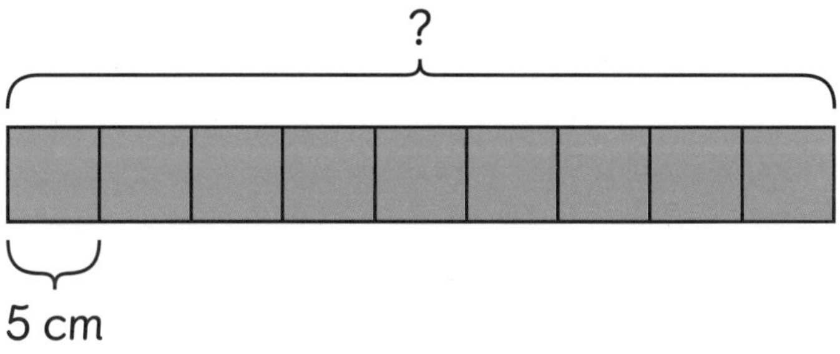

5 cm

The height of the stack of 9 books is ☐ cm.

3. Sam cuts a strip of paper into 5 equal pieces. Each piece is 7 cm long. What was the length of the strip of paper to begin with?

The length of the strip of paper was ☐ cm to begin with.

Solving division problems

Lesson 5

Starter

A farmer is building a fence that is 10 m long. He uses 5 identical fence panels. How long is each fence panel?

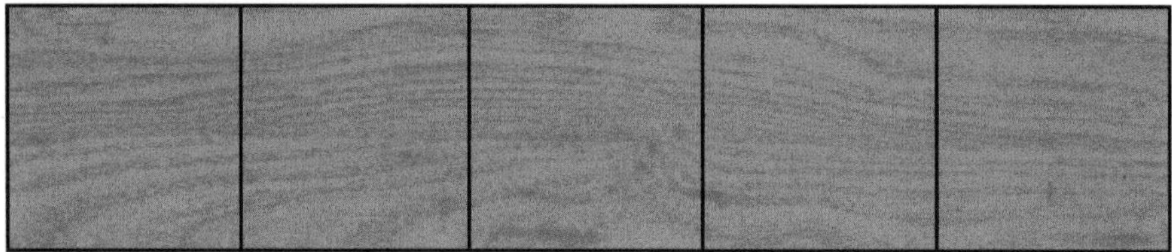

Example

Do we multiply or divide?

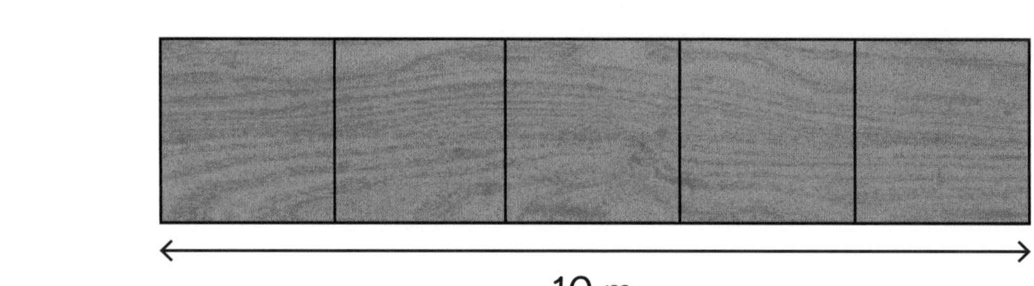

10 ÷ 5 = 2

Each fence panel is 2 m long.

2 + 2 + 2 + 2 + 2 = 10

Check your answer using multiplication. 2 × 5 = 10

Practice

Solve.

1. Ruby needs 2 m of fabric to make a skirt. How many skirts can she make from 14 m of fabric?

Ruby can make ☐ skirts.

2. A stack of 10 identical packages is 40 cm tall. What is the height of each package?

The height of each package is  ☐ cm.

height ↕

3. Lulu makes a triangle from a pipe cleaner that is 15 cm long. The triangle has 3 sides of equal length. How long is each side?

Each side is ☐ cm.

Pictograms and tables

Lesson 6

Starter

The pictogram shows the number of each type of animal in a Wildlife Rescue Centre.

How many of each type of animal are there?

Animals in a Wildlife Rescue Centre

▲▲▲▲	▲▲▲▲▲	▲	▲▲▲
tiger	monkey	elephant	giraffe
Each ▲ stands for 2 animals			

Example

We can use ▲ to show more than 1 animal.

▲▲▲▲	▲▲▲▲▲	▲	▲▲▲
tiger	monkey	elephant	giraffe

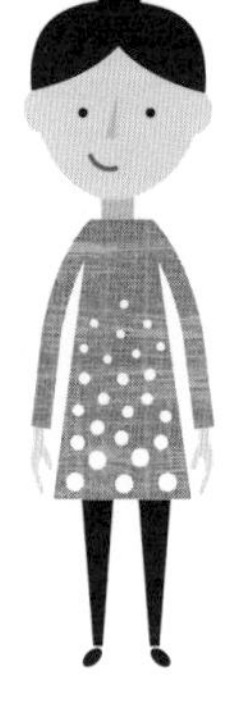
Each ▲ stands for 2 animals.

Animal	Number of animals
tiger	8
monkey	10
elephant	2
giraffe	6

Practice

1 The pictogram shows the number of prizes won by some children during a game. Look at the pictogram and fill in the blanks.

(a) Ravi won [ ] prizes.

(b) [ ] won the greatest number of prizes.

(c) [ ] won the fewest number of prizes.

Number of Prizes Won

● ● ● ● ● ●	● ● ●	● ● ● ● ●
Ravi	Lulu	Charles
Each ● stands for 2 prizes.		

(d) The three children won [ ] prizes altogether.

2 A group of children were asked to vote for their favourite food. The results are shown in this pictogram.

Children's Favourite Food

roast chicken	⬭ ⬭ ⬭ ⬭ ⬭ ⬭
cheese sandwich	⬭ ⬭ ⬭
beans on toast	⬭ ⬭ ⬭ ⬭ ⬭
fish fingers	⬭ ⬭ ⬭ ⬭ ⬭ ⬭ ⬭ ⬭
lasagne	⬭ ⬭ ⬭ ⬭ ⬭ ⬭ ⬭ ⬭ ⬭
Each ⬭ stands for 2 children	

(a) The most popular food is [ ].

(b) The least popular food is a [ ].

(c) [ ] more children voted for lasagne than beans on toast.

(d) [ ] children voted altogether.

Pictograms, tally charts and tables

Lesson 7

Starter

Amira made a tally chart to show the number of different coloured marbles in the jars.

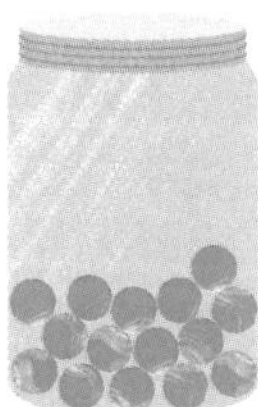

Tally Chart

yellow marbles	𝍸 𝍸
green marbles	𝍸 𝍸 𝍸
blue marbles	𝍸 𝍸 𝍸 𝍸 𝍸
red marbles	𝍸 𝍸 𝍸 𝍸 𝍸 𝍸 𝍸

Is there another way to show the number of different coloured marbles?

Example

Jacob made this pictogram using the information from the tally chart.

yellow marbles	🟫 🟫
green marbles	🟫 🟫 🟫
blue marbles	🟫 🟫 🟫 🟫 🟫
red marbles	🟫 🟫 🟫 🟫 🟫 🟫 🟫
Each 🟫 stands for 5 marbles.	

I used 🟫 to stand for 5 marbles.

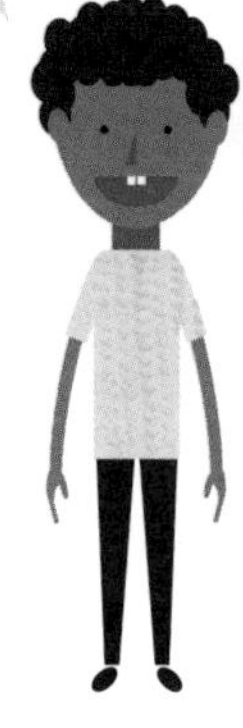

Practice

1 A sports shop sells footballs, volleyballs and basketballs. The pictogram shows the number of each type of ball sold in one week.
Look at the pictogram and fill in the blanks.

(a) The sports shop sold ☐ footballs in one week.

(b) The sports shop sold ☐ fewer volleyballs than basketballs.

(c) The sports shop sold ☐ balls altogether.

Number of Balls Sold

● ● ● ● ● ● ● ● ● ●	● ● ● ● ● ●	● ● ● ● ●
footballs	basketballs	volleyballs
Each ● stands for 5 balls.		

2 Four children collect marbles. The pictogram shows the number of marbles they each have. Look at the pictogram and fill in the blanks.

Number of Marbles

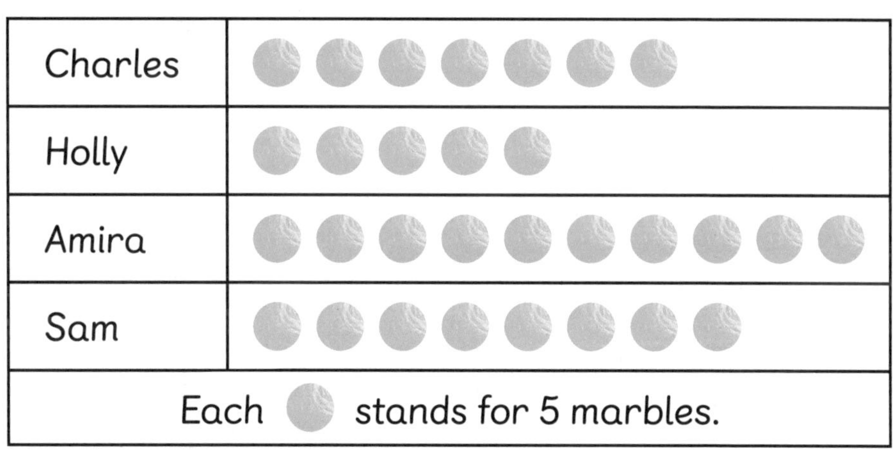

(a) ☐ has the greatest number of marbles.

(b) Amira has ☐ more marbles than Sam has.

(c) Holly has ☐ fewer marbles than Charles has.

(d) Charles and Sam have ☐ marbles altogether.

More pictograms and tables

Lesson 8

Starter

This pictogram shows the number of books each child read last year.

Sam	📘📘📘📘📘
Charles	📘📘📘📘📘📘📘📘
Ravi	📘📘📘📘
Elliott	📘📘📘📘📘📘📘
Each 📘 stands for 10 books	

What questions can we ask?

Example

Compare the number of books each child read.

How many books did Elliott read?
$7 \times 10 = 70$
Elliott read 70 books.

Who read the greatest number of books?
Charles read 80 books.
He read the greatest number of books.

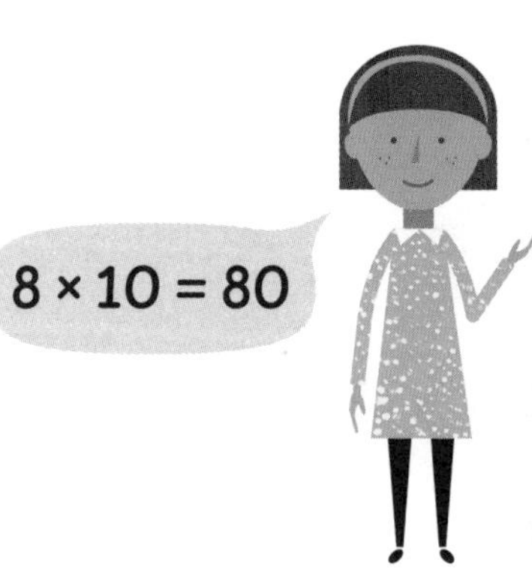

How many more books than Elliott did Charles read?
$80 - 70 = 10$
Charles read 10 more books than Elliott read.

What is the difference between the greatest number of books read and the fewest number of books read?

Charles read the greatest number of books.
Ravi read the fewest books.

80 − 40 = 40

The difference in the number of books Charles and Ravi read is 40. Charles read 40 more books than Ravi read.

How many books did the children read in total?

5 + 8 + 4 + 7 = 24
24 × 10 = 240

The children read 240 books in total.

Practice

The pictogram shows the number of pupils in each year group who have a pet. Look at the pictogram and answer the questions below.

Pupils Who Have Pets

Year 1	Year 2	Year 3	Year 4	Year 5	Year 6
Each ▪ stands for 10 pupils.					

1. How many pupils in Year 3 have pets?
2. Which year has the fewest number of pupils who have pets?
3. What is the difference between the year with the greatest number of pupils with pets and the year with the fewest number of pupils with pets?
4. How many pupils have pets in all year groups altogether?

Comparing fractions

Lesson 9

Starter

Ravi and Hannah are eating pancakes.

I cut mine into
3 equal pieces.

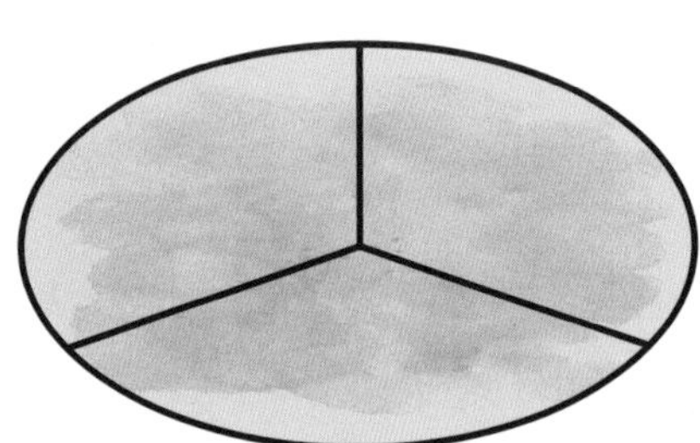
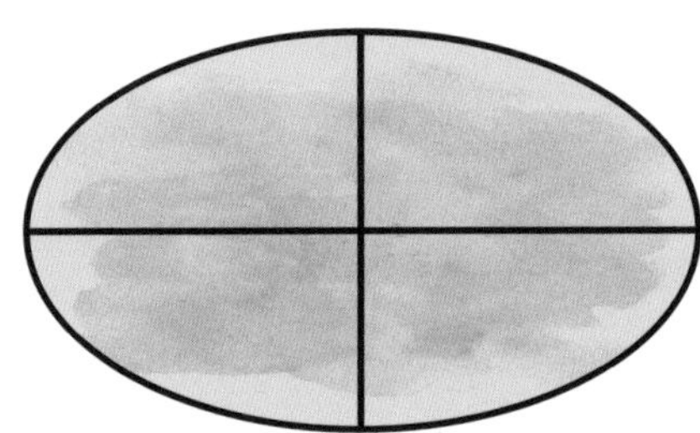

I cut mine into
4 equal pieces.

Ravi and Hannah each take 1 piece of their pancakes.
Have they each taken the same amount?

Example

$\frac{1}{3}$

$\frac{1}{4}$

$\frac{1}{3}$ is greater than $\frac{1}{4}$.

$\frac{1}{3} > \frac{1}{4}$

Ravi has taken more pancake than Hannah has.

Practice

1 Fill in the blanks. Use > or <.

(a) $\frac{1}{3}$ ☐ $\frac{1}{5}$

(b) $\frac{1}{5}$ ☐ $\frac{1}{4}$

(c) $\frac{3}{4}$ ☐ $\frac{2}{3}$

(d) $\frac{2}{3}$ ☐ $\frac{4}{5}$

2 Arrange the fractions in order.
Start with the smallest.

$\frac{3}{4}$, $\frac{1}{3}$, $\frac{3}{5}$, $\frac{2}{3}$

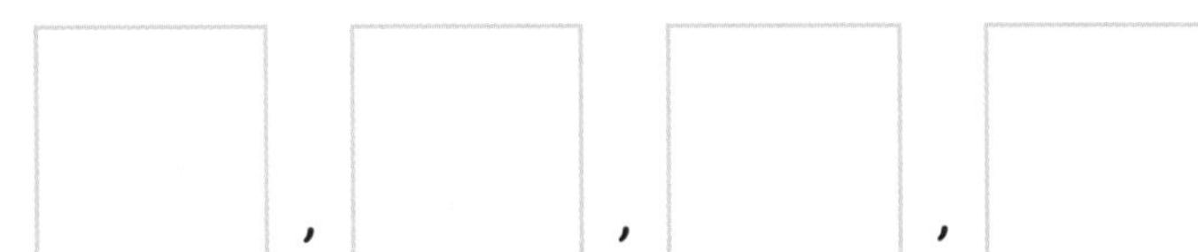

☐ , ☐ , ☐ , ☐

smallest

Finding a fraction of a set

Lesson 10

Starter

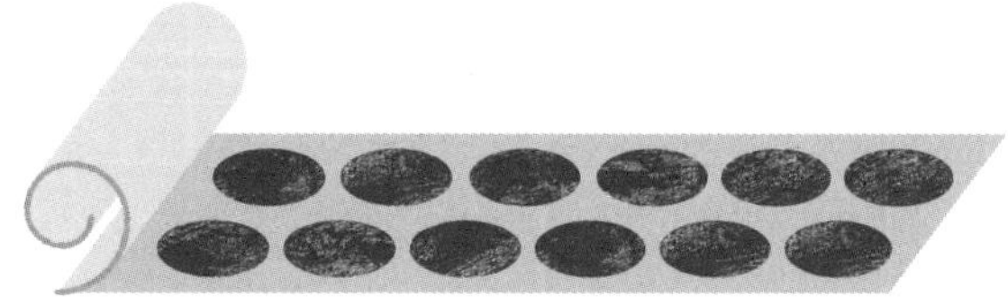

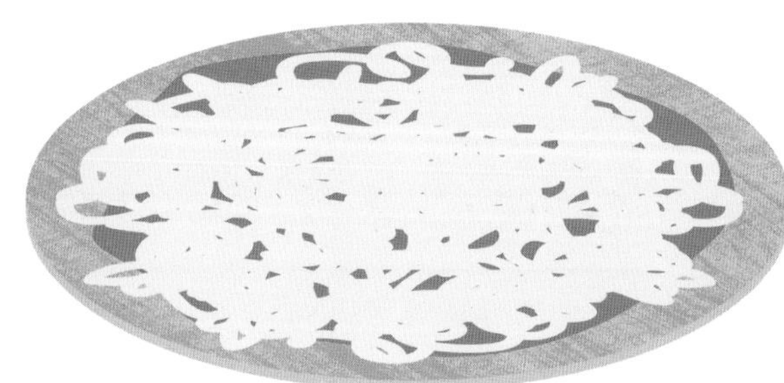

Lulu puts $\frac{1}{4}$ of the 12 salami slices on a pizza.

How many salami slices does she put on the pizza?

Example

$\frac{1}{4}$ of 12 is 3.

Lulu puts 3 salami slices on the pizza.

Practice

1 Elliott has 20 packets of football cards. He opens $\frac{1}{4}$ of them.

How many packets of football cards does Elliott open?

$\frac{1}{4}$ of 20 is ☐.

Elliott opens ☐ packets of football cards.

2 18 children are reading books.

$\frac{1}{3}$ of them are reading non-fiction books.

How many children are reading non-fiction books?

☐ children are reading non-fiction books.

3 Emma bakes a batch of 24 cookies.

$\frac{1}{4}$ of the cookies have chocolate chips.

$\frac{1}{3}$ of the cookies have walnuts.

The rest of the cookies are plain.

(a) How many cookies have chocolate chips? ☐

(b) How many cookies have walnuts? ☐

(c) How many cookies are plain? ☐

Finding a fraction of a quantity

Lesson 11

Starter

Ravi uses $\frac{1}{4}$ of the wrapping paper on a present.

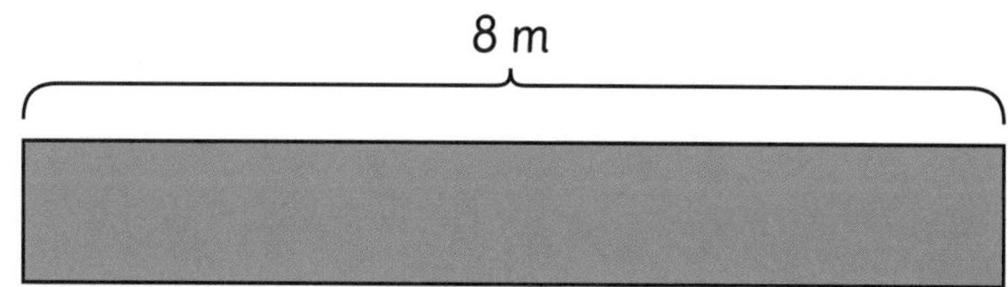

How many metres of wrapping paper does Ravi use?

Example

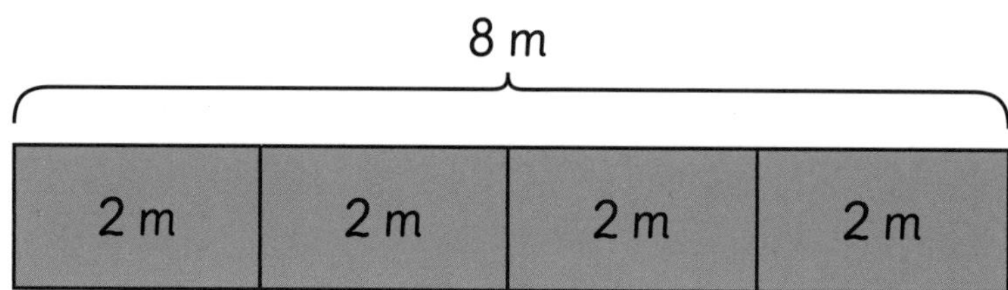

$\frac{1}{4}$ of 8 m = 2 m

Ravi uses 2 m of wrapping paper.

Practice

1 Ruby puts a $\frac{1}{4}$ of a 40 m piece of fishing line on her fishing rod.

What is the length of the line Ruby puts on her fishing rod?

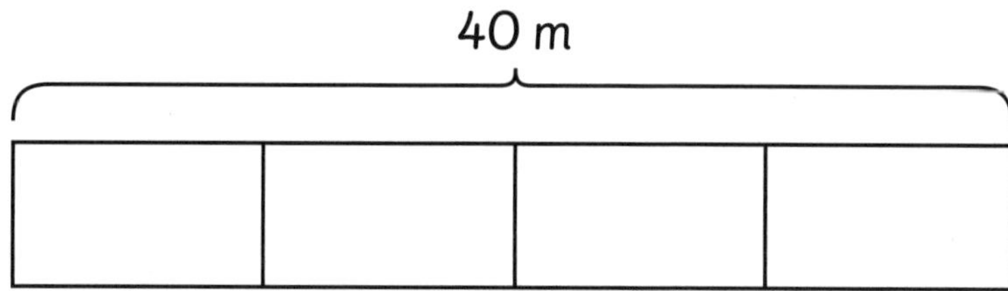

$\frac{1}{4}$ of 40 m = ☐ m

Ruby puts ☐ m of line on her fishing rod.

2 Elliott's mum used $\frac{1}{3}$ of a 15 m roll of wallpaper on a wall.

How many metres of wallpaper did Elliott's mum use?

$\frac{1}{3}$ of 15 m = ☐ m

Elliott's mum used ☐ m of wallpaper.

Solving mass problems

Lesson 12

Starter

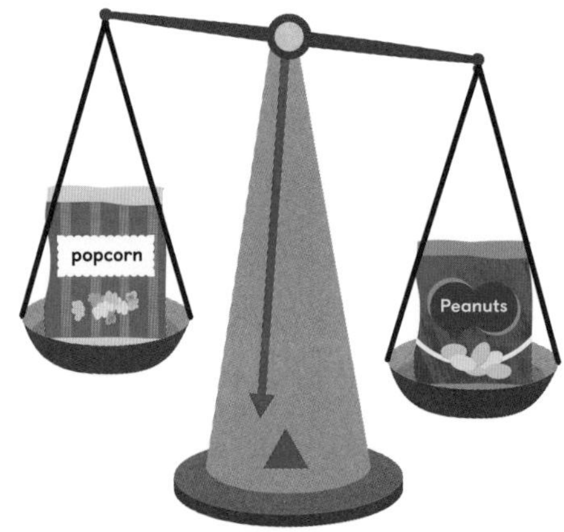

The mass of the packet of popcorn is 32 g.
The packet of peanuts is 68 g heavier than the packet of popcorn.
What is the mass of the packet of peanuts?

Example

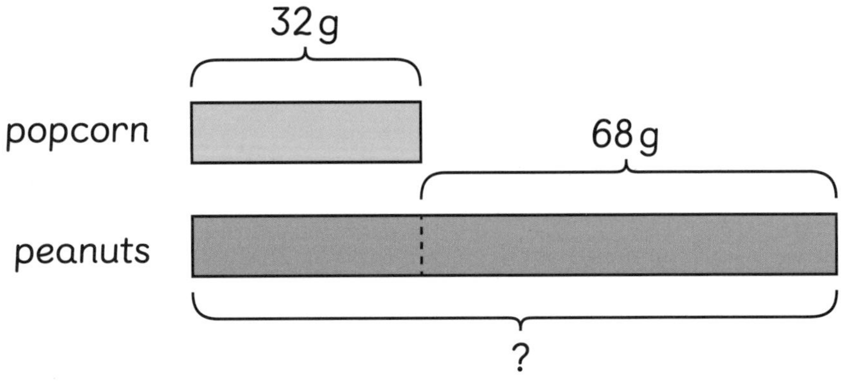

32 + 68 = 100

The mass of the packet of peanuts is 100 g.

Practice

Solve.

1 The mass of a cupcake is 85 g. It is 27 g heavier than a cookie. What is the mass of the cookie?

The mass of the cookie is  g.

2 Look at the scales below. Find the mass of the pineapple.

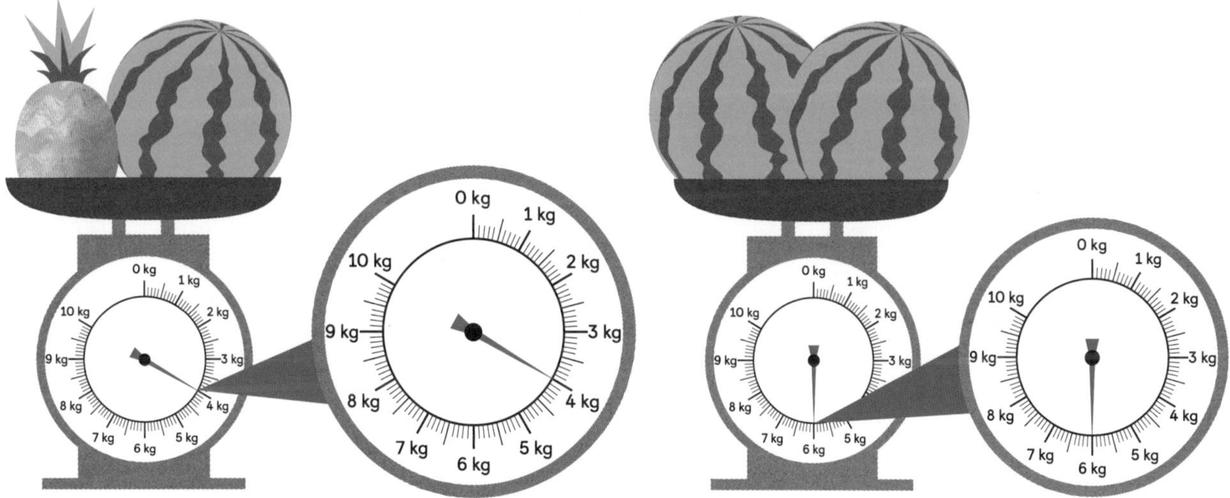

The mass of the pineapple is  kg.

Comparing three masses

Lesson 13

Starter

Compare the masses of these different animals.
What questions can we ask?

34 kg

28 kg

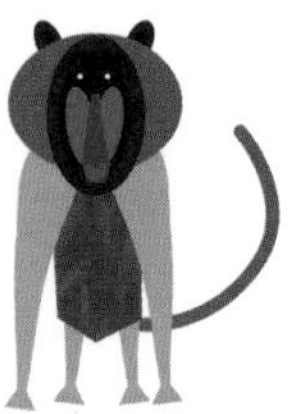
32 kg

Example

How much heavier is the  than the  ?

The  has a mass of 34 kg. The  has a mass of 32 kg.

34 − 32 = 2

The  is 2 kg heavier than the  .

How much lighter is the  than the  ?

The  has a mass of 28 kg. The  has a mass of 32 kg.

32 − 28 = 4

The  is 4 kg lighter than the  .

Which animal is the lightest? Which animal is the heaviest?

 28 kg  32 kg  34 kg

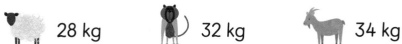

The  is the lightest. The  is the heaviest.

Practice

Look at the pictures and fill in the blanks.

1 (a) The  has a mass of  kg.

(b) The  has a mass of  kg.

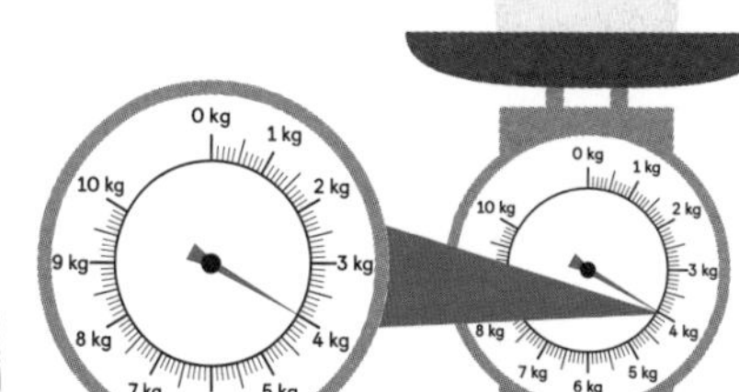

(c) The  has a mass of  kg.

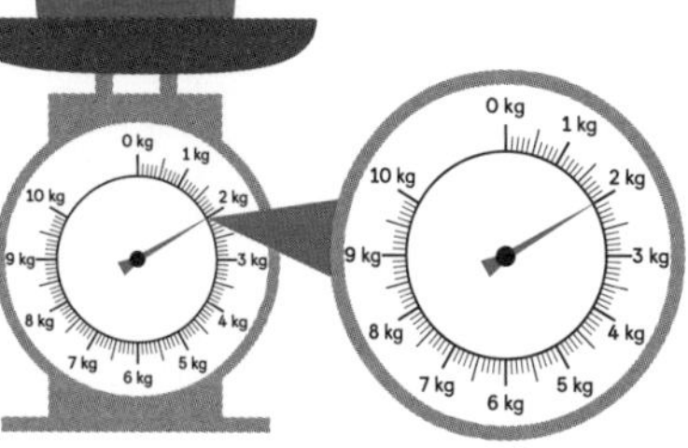

(d) The ☐ is the lightest.

(e) The ☐ is the heaviest.

2

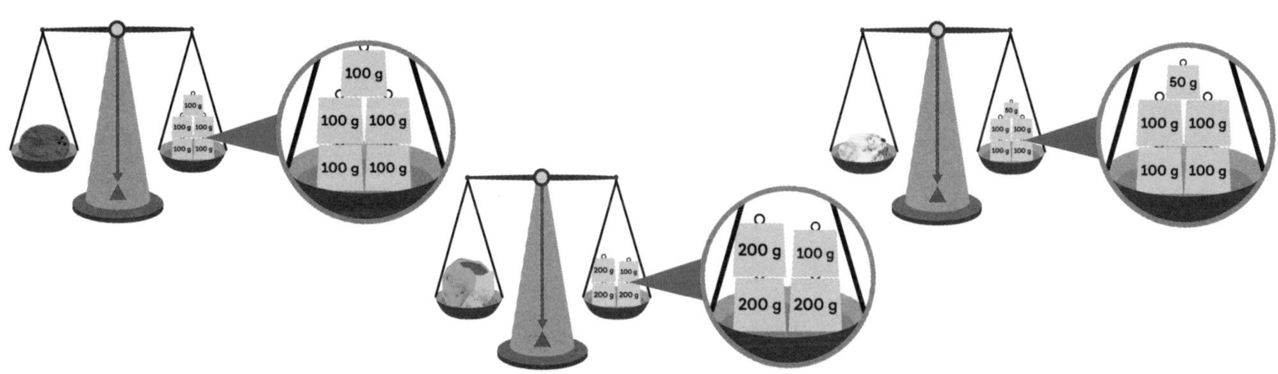

(a) The mass of the coconut is  g.

(b) The mass of the mango is  g.

(c) The mass of the cabbage is  g.

(d) The  is the lightest.

(e) The  is the heaviest.

Lines of symmetry

Lesson 14

Starter

Elliott draws the following shape.

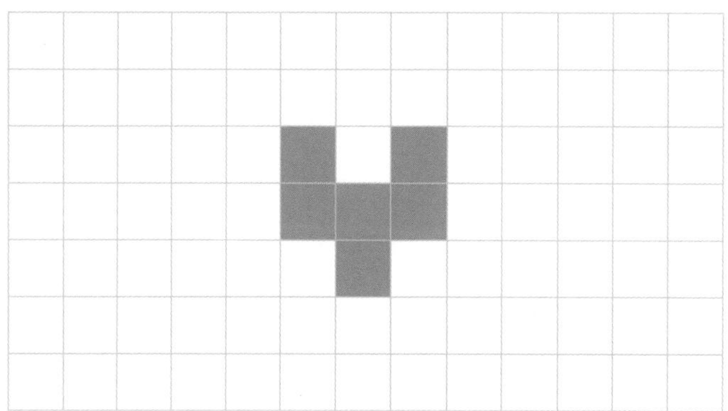

Is this shape symmetrical?

Example

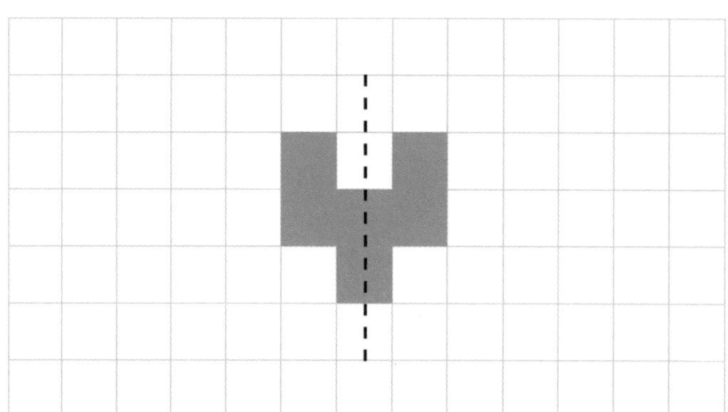

This shape is symmetrical. It has a line of symmetry.
If we fold the shape on the line of symmetry, one half overlaps the other half.

Practice

1. Draw the line of symmetry on each shape.

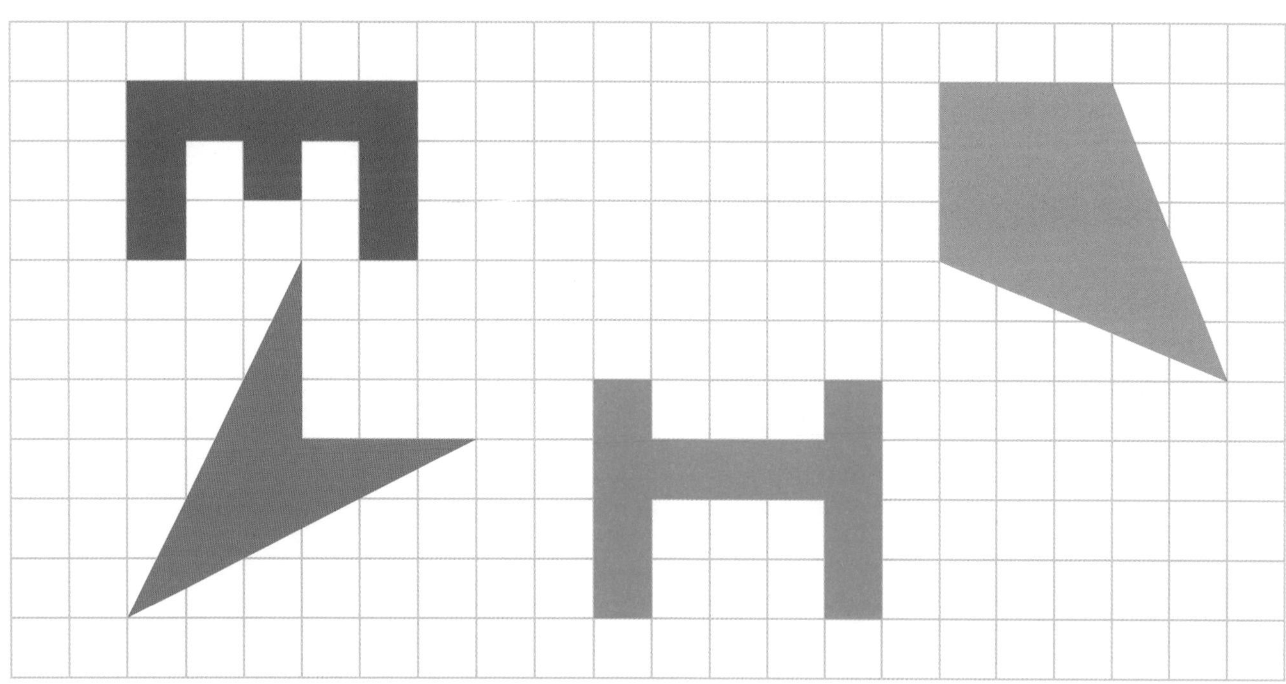

2. Draw 2 shapes. Each shape should have 6 sides and at least 1 line of symmetry.

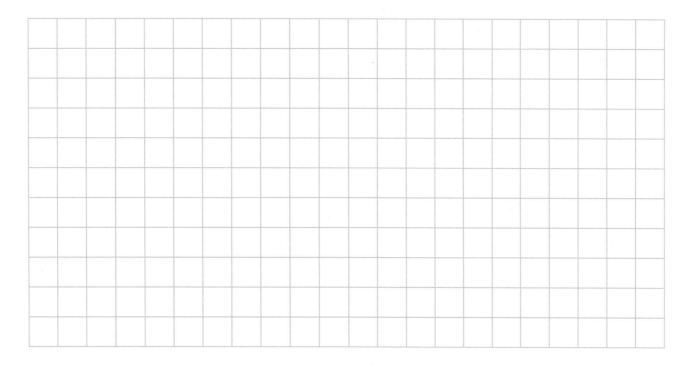

Solving money problems (part 1)

Lesson 15

Starter

 saved £49.

 saved £6 less than  saved.

How much have they saved altogether?

Example

£49 – £6 = £43

 saved £43.

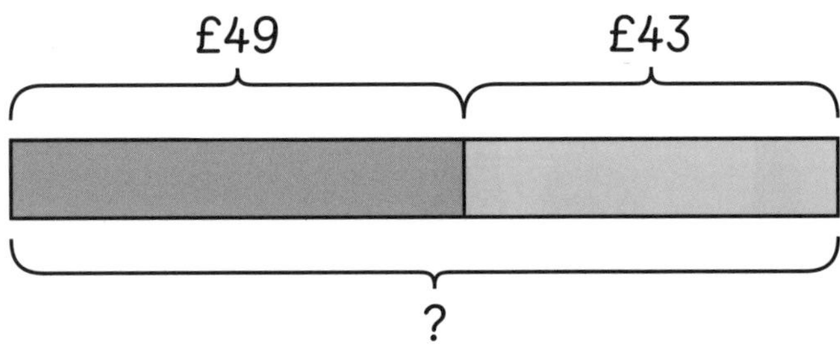

£43 + £49 = £92

 and  have saved £92 altogether.

Practice

1 A robot costs £18. A doll costs £15 more than the robot. How much does the doll cost?

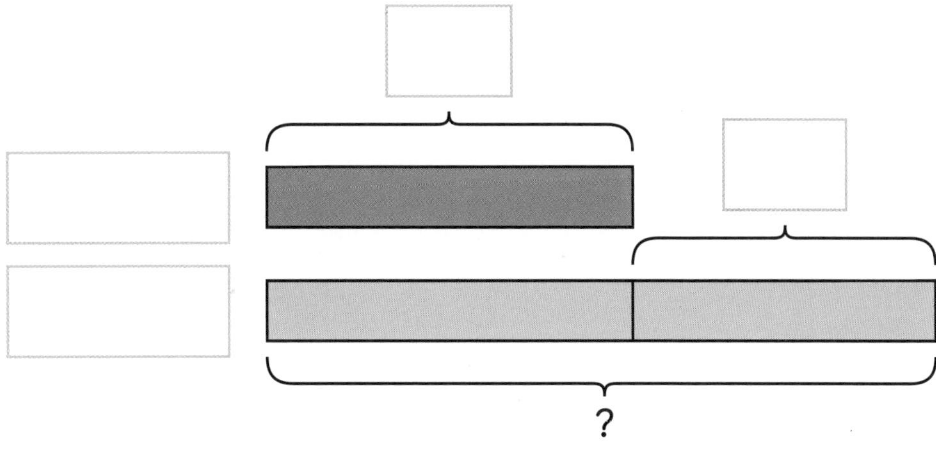

The doll costs £ ☐.

2 A dress costs £39. It costs £10 more than a hat.

(a) How much does the hat cost?

The hat costs £ ☐.

(b) How much do the dress and the hat cost altogether?

The dress and the hat cost £ ☐ altogether.

Solving money problems (part 2)

Lesson 16

Starter

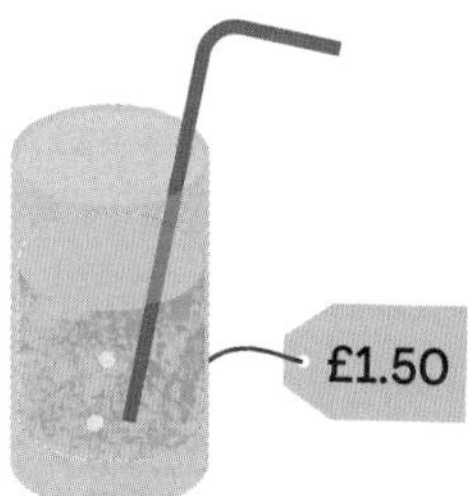

What is the total cost of 2 burgers and 2 milkshakes?

Example

The total cost of the burgers is £6.

The total cost of the milkshakes is £3.

The total cost of 2 burgers and 2 milkshakes is £9.

£3	£3	£1.50	£1.50

?

Practice

1 Elliott saves 50p on Monday. He saves 25p on Tuesday and 35p on Wednesday.

(a) How much in total does Elliott save on Monday and Tuesday?

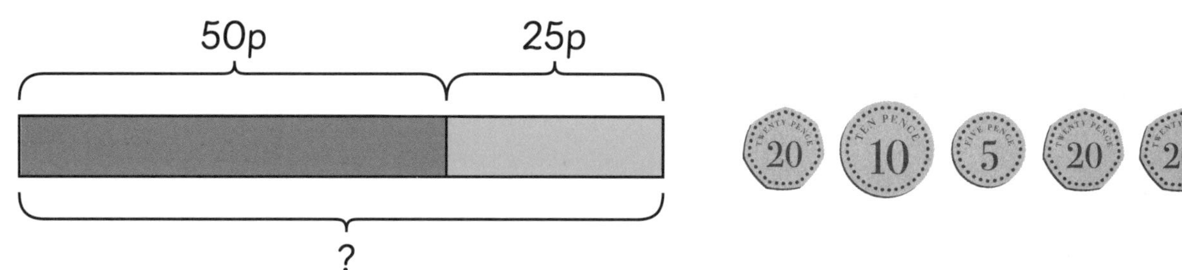

50p + 25p = ☐ p

Elliott saves ☐ p on Monday and Tuesday.

(b) How much in total does Elliott save over the three days?

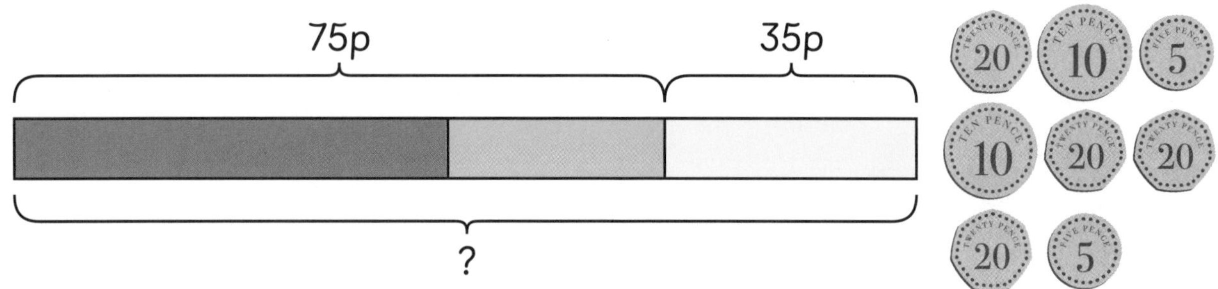

75p + 35p = [ ]

[ ] p = £ [ ] and [ ] p

Elliott saves £ [ ] and [ ] p over the three days.

2 Lulu has £52.
Amira has £19 less than Lulu has.
How much money do Lulu and Amira have altogether?

Lulu and Amira have £ [ ] altogether.

Finding change

Lesson 17

Starter

How much change does Sam get after he buys the two items?

Example

Sam has four  .

I have £80.

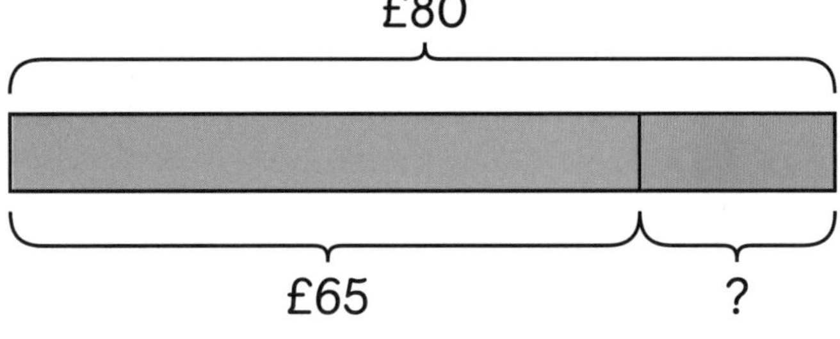

Sam spends £65.

80 – 65 = 15

Practice

1 Amira has £100.
She buys a coat for £42, a necklace for £13 and a bag for £22.
How much money does Amira have left?

Amira has £ ☐ left.

2 Charles buys a and a .

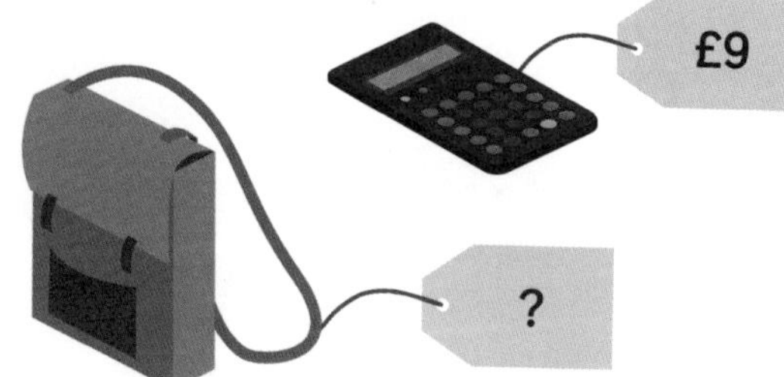

After paying the cashier 

, he receives 

change.

What is the price of the 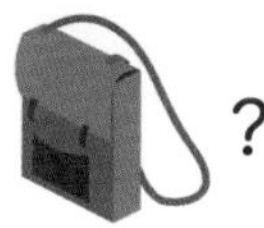 ?

The price of the  is £ ☐ .

Finding duration of time

Lesson 18

Starter

How long did the journey take?

Example

2 h

30 min

2 h + 30 min

The journey took 2 h 30 min.

Add the hours and minutes.

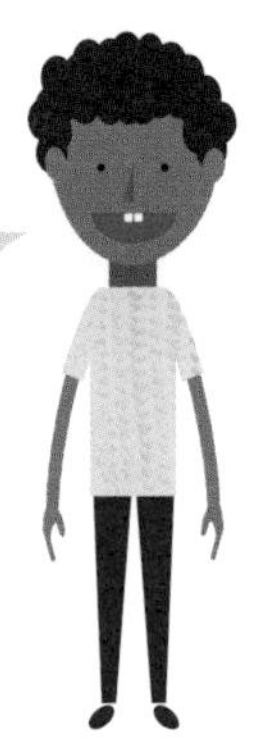

Practice

1 Lulu did two activities in an afternoon.

(a) Look at the clocks and fill in the blanks.

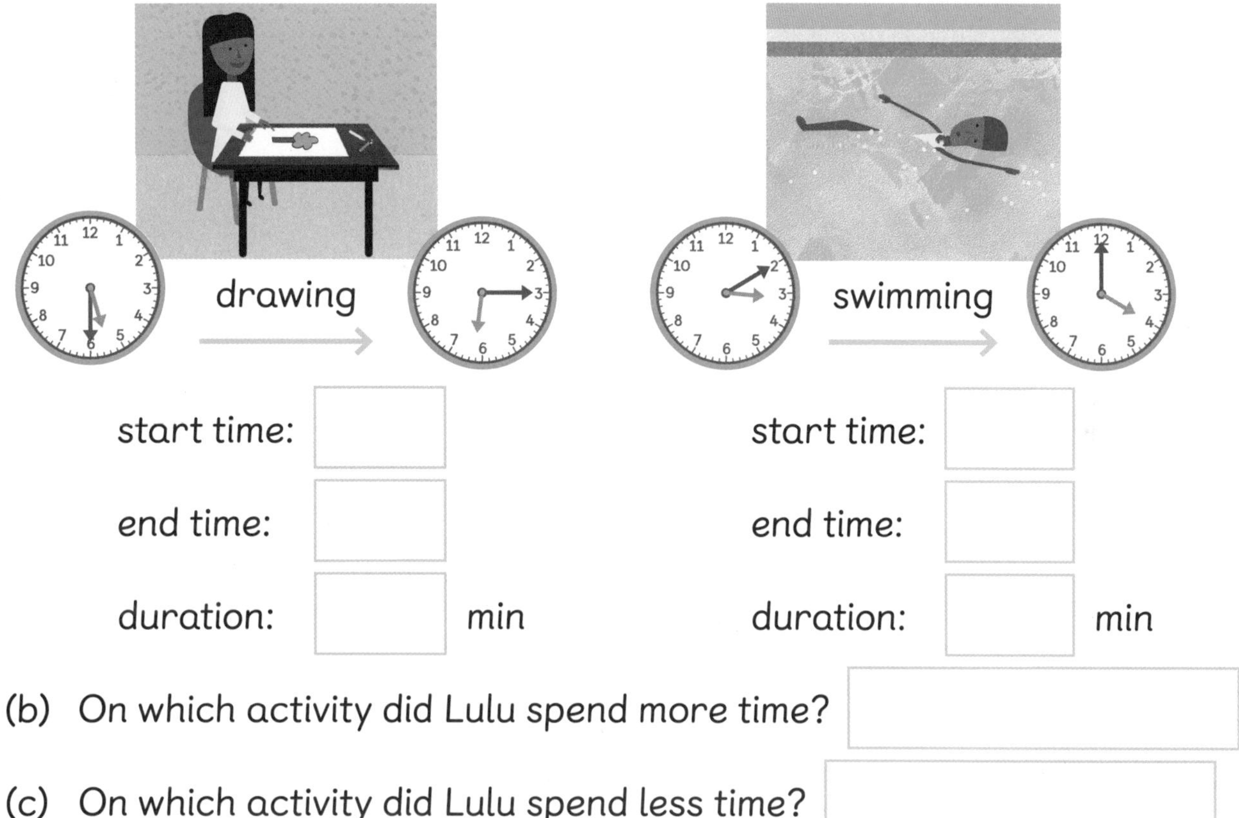

start time: ☐

end time: ☐

duration: ☐ min

start time: ☐

end time: ☐

duration: ☐ min

(b) On which activity did Lulu spend more time? ☐

(c) On which activity did Lulu spend less time? ☐

2 These are the times that three friends finished their homework yesterday afternoon.

Lulu

Emma

Charles

(a) Lulu spent 40 minutes on her homework. She started at ☐ .

(b) Emma worked for 20 minutes longer than Lulu. She started at ☐ .

(c) Charles started at 5:50. How long did he spend on his homework?

He spent ☐ on his homework.

Reading and comparing temperature

Lesson 19

Starter

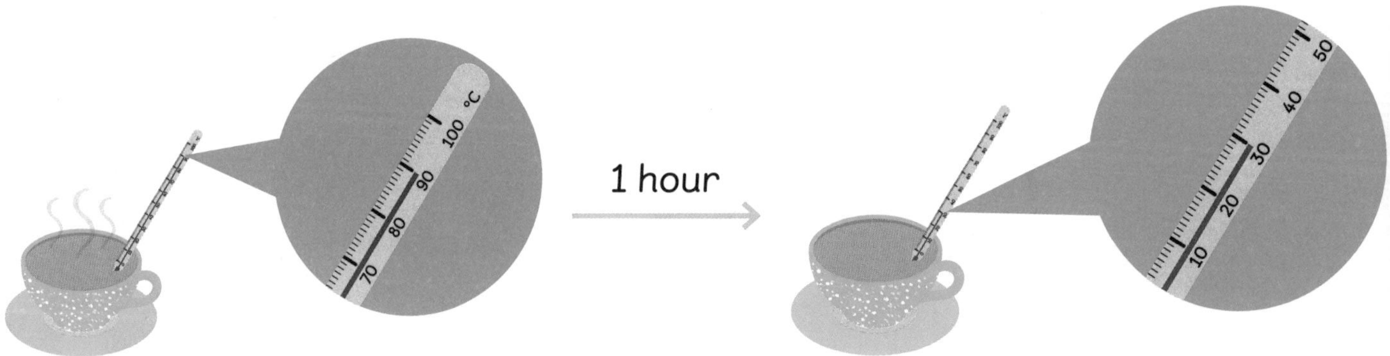

Hannah measured the temperature of a cup of tea when it was made.
She measured the temperature an hour later.
What is the difference between the two temperatures?

Example

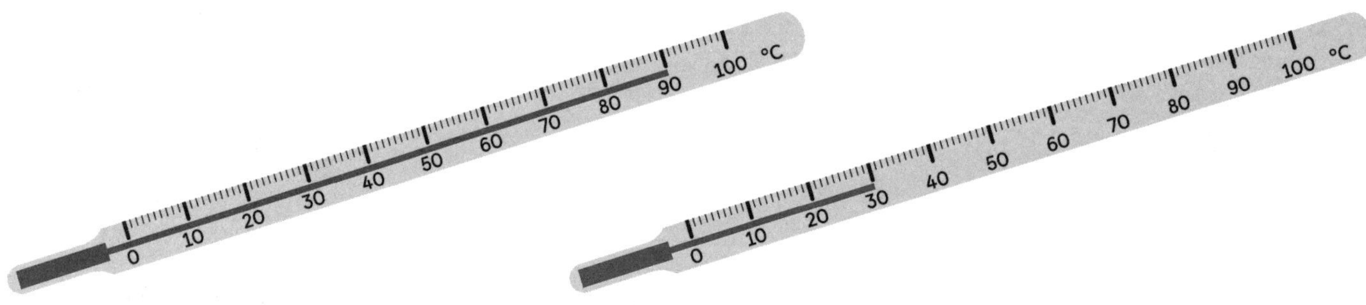

At the start, the tea was 90 °C.
After an hour, the tea was 30 °C.

90 – 30 = 60

The difference between the two temperatures is 60 °C.

Practice

Read the thermometers to find the temperature of the liquids.
Find the difference between the two temperatures.

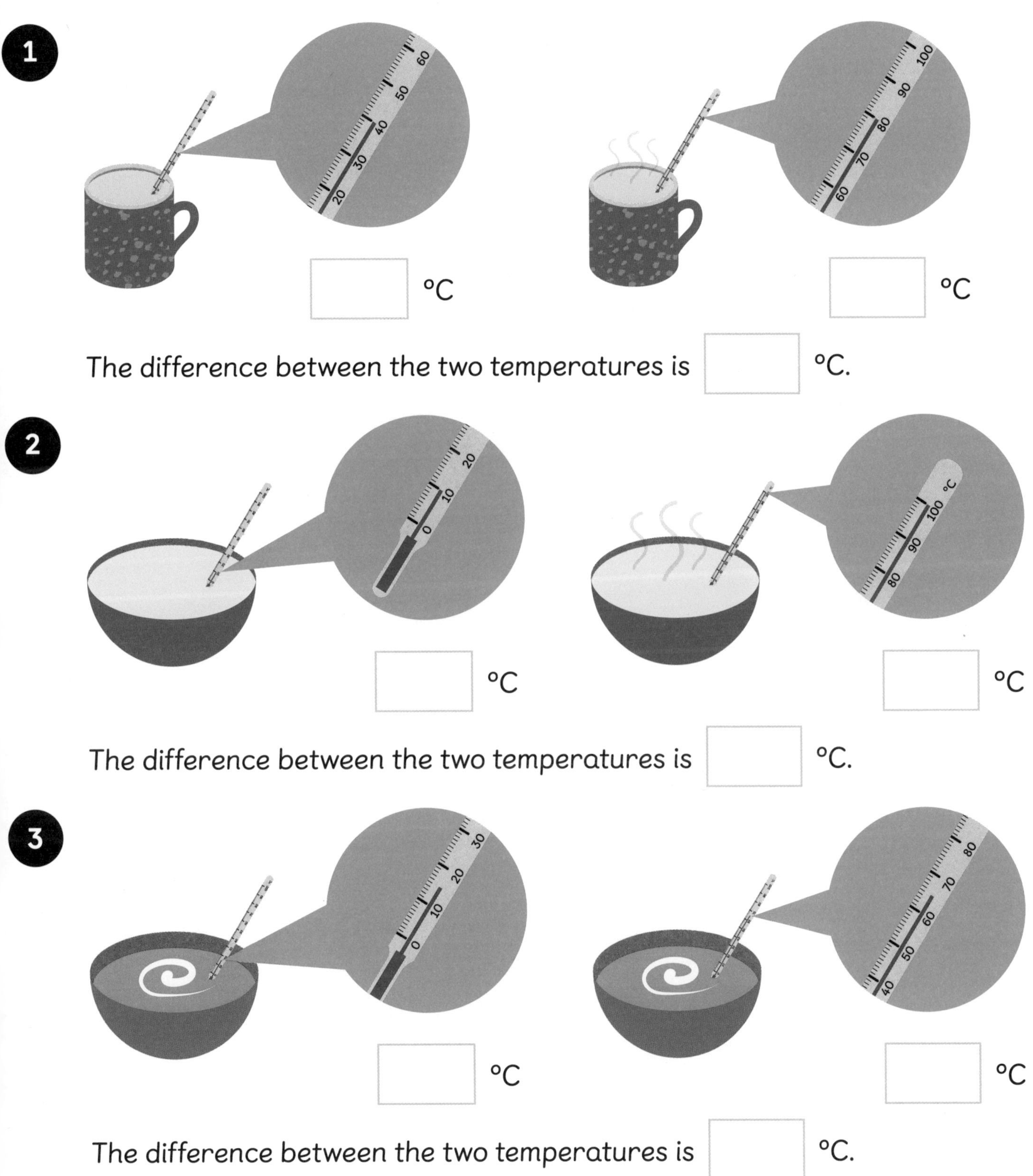

1. ☐ °C ☐ °C

The difference between the two temperatures is ☐ °C.

2. ☐ °C ☐ °C

The difference between the two temperatures is ☐ °C.

3. ☐ °C ☐ °C

The difference between the two temperatures is ☐ °C.

Word problems

Lesson 20

Starter

Ruby has some football cards. She gives 15 away and then buys another 20 football cards.
She now has 80 football cards. How many football cards did she have to begin with?

Example

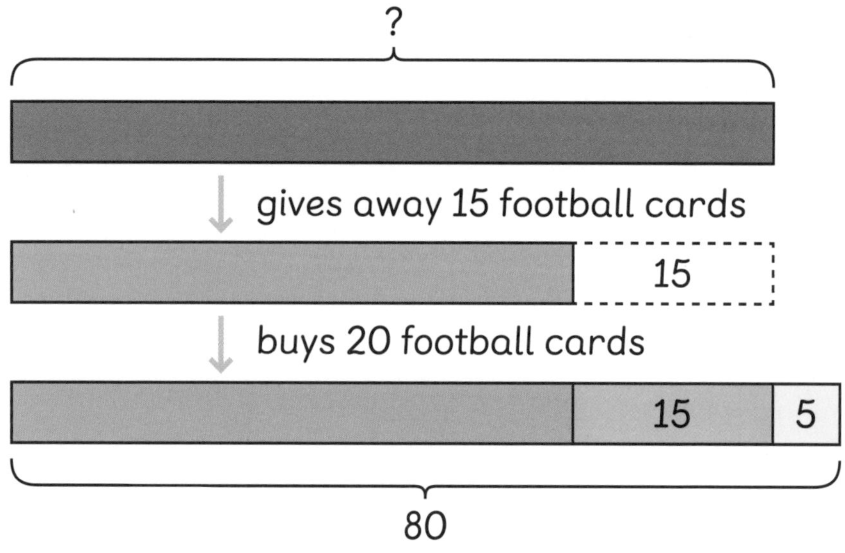

80 – 5 = 75

Ruby had 75 football cards to begin with.

Practice

1 The total mass of a sack of potatoes and a sack of carrots is 18 kg.
The sack of potatoes is 8 kg heavier than the sack of carrots.
What is the mass of the sack of carrots?

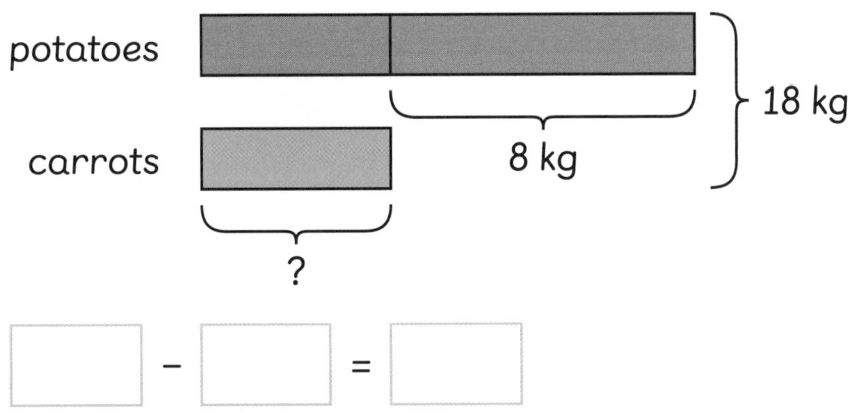

☐ − ☐ = ☐

The mass of the sack of carrots is  ☐ kg.

2

The skateboard and the scooter have a total mass of 14 kg.
The scooter and the bike have a total mass of 18 kg.
The skateboard weighs 2 kg less than the scooter.
Find the mass of each item.

  kg  ☐ kg   kg

Measuring and comparing volume

Starter

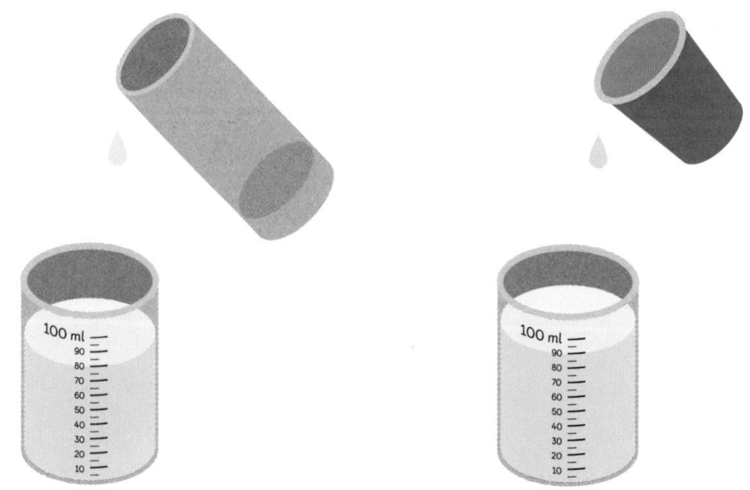

Sam compares the volume of water in a glass and in a paper cup.

Example

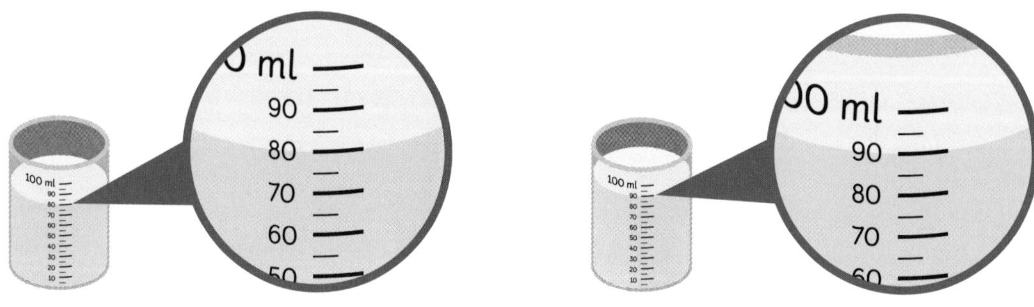

90 − 80 = 10

The volume of water in the glass is 80 ml.
The volume of water in the paper cup is 90 ml.

The difference between the volume of water in the glass and the paper cup is 10 ml.

Practice

Find the volume of water in each beaker.

Find the difference between the two volumes of water.

1

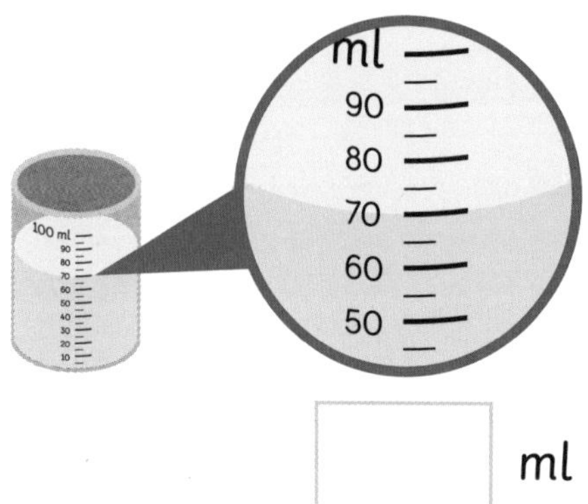

☐ ml ☐ ml

The difference between the two volumes of water is ☐ ml.

2

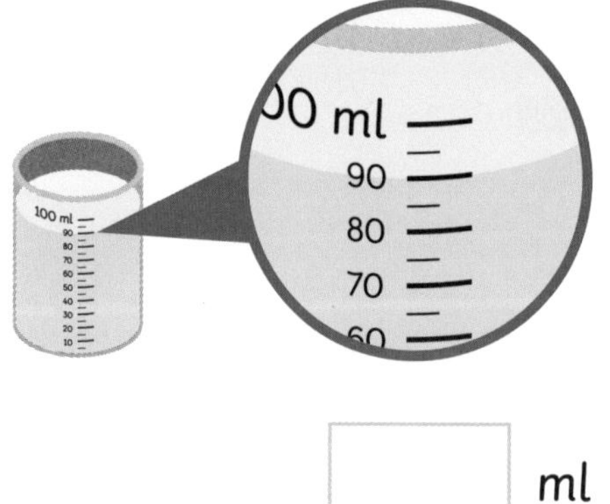

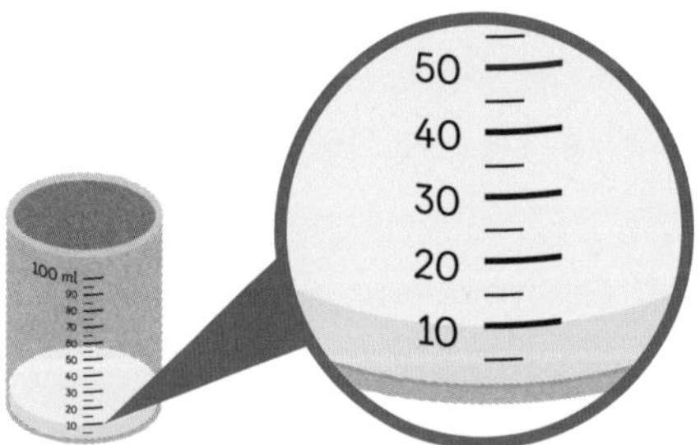

☐ ml ☐ ml

The difference between the two volumes of water is ☐ ml.

3

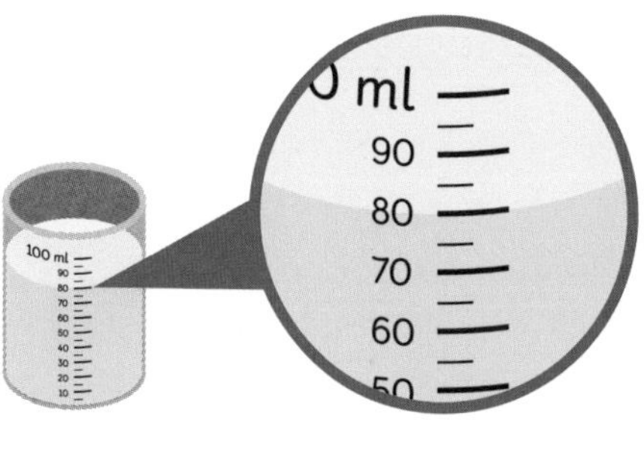

☐ ml ☐ ml

The difference between the two volumes of water is ☐ ml.

Answers

Page 5 **1 (a)** 54 **(b)** 34 **2** Answers will vary. **3** 76, 75, 67, 65, 57, 56
4 (a) 54, 59, 63, 72, 77, 85 **(b)** 63 > 59, 77 < 85, 54 < 72, 72 < 77

Page 7 **1 (a)** 37 + 45 = 82. Charles read 82 pages over the two days.

2 56 + 39 = 95. The two classes have 95 books altogether.

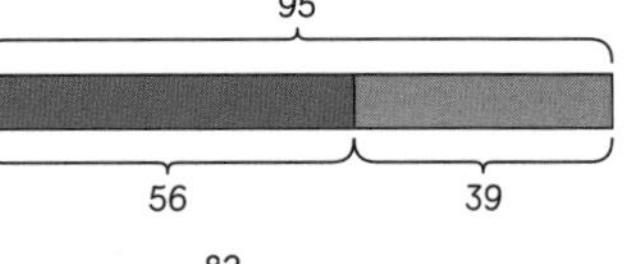

Page 9 **1** 63 − 37 = 26. There are 26 children still in the hall.

2 82 − 48 = 34. 34 children have not yet finished the run.

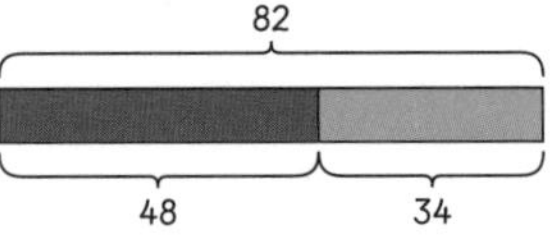

Page 11 **2** 8 × 10 = 80. The total length of the 10 straws is 80 cm. **2** 5 × 9 = 45. The height of the stack of 9 books is 45 cm. **3** 5 × 7 = 35. The length of the strip of paper was 35 cm to begin with.

Page 13 **1** 14 ÷ 2 = 7. Ruby can make 7 skirts.
2 40 ÷ 10 = 4. The height of each package is 4 cm.

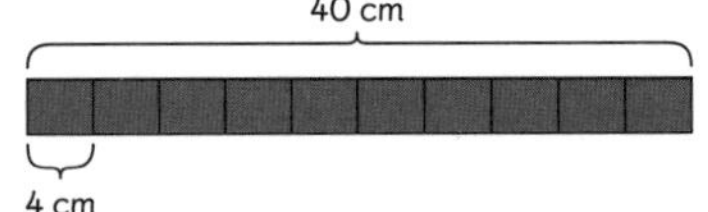

3 15 ÷ 3 = 5. Each side is 5 cm.

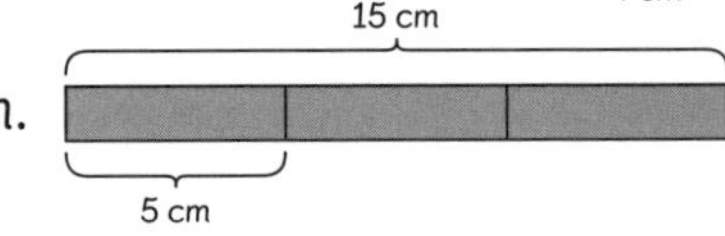

Page 15 **1 (a)** Ravi won 12 prizes. **(b)** Ravi won the greatest number of prizes. **(c)** Lulu won the fewest number of prizes. **(d)** The three children won 28 prizes altogether. **2 (a)** The most popular food is lasagne. **(b)** The least popular food is a cheese sandwich. **(c)** 8 more children liked lasagne better than beans on toast. **(d)** 62 children voted altogether.

Page 17 **1 (a)** The sports shop sold 50 footballs in one week. **(b)** The sports shop sold 5 fewer volleyballs than basketballs. **(c)** The sports shop sold 105 balls altogether. **2 (a)** Amira has the greatest number of marbles. **(b)** Amira has 10 more marbles than Sam has. **(c)** Holly has 10 fewer marbles than Charles has. **(d)** Charles and Sam have 75 marbles altogether.

Page 19 **1** 40 **2** Year 2 **3** 40 **4** 240

Page 21 **1 (a)** $\frac{1}{3} > \frac{1}{5}$ **(b)** $\frac{1}{5} < \frac{1}{4}$ **(c)** $\frac{3}{4} > \frac{2}{3}$ **(d)** $\frac{2}{3} < \frac{4}{5}$ **2** $\frac{1}{3}, \frac{3}{5}, \frac{2}{3}, \frac{3}{4}$

Page 23 **1**

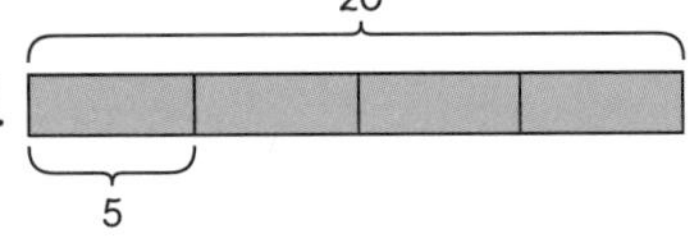

20 ÷ 4 = 5

$\frac{1}{4}$ of 20 is 5

Elliott opens 5 packets of football cards.

2 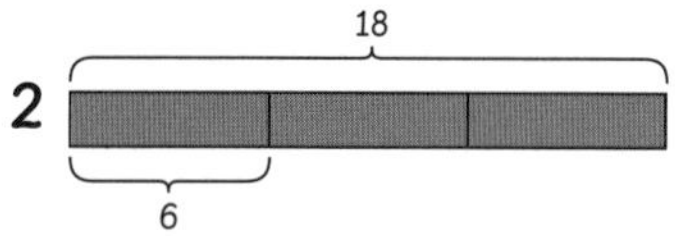

18 ÷ 3 = 6
6 children are reading non-fiction books.

3 (a) 24 ÷ 4 = 6 $\frac{1}{4}$ of 24 = 6 6 cookies share chocolate chips.

(b) 24 ÷ 3 = 8 $\frac{1}{3}$ of 24 = 8 8 cookies have walnuts.

(c) 6 + 8 = 14 24 − 14 = 10 10 cookies are plain.

Page 25 **1 (a)** $\frac{1}{4}$ of 40 m = 10 m. Ruby puts 10 m of line on her fishing rod.

2 $\frac{1}{3}$ of 15 m = 5 m. Elliott's mum used 5 m of wallpaper.

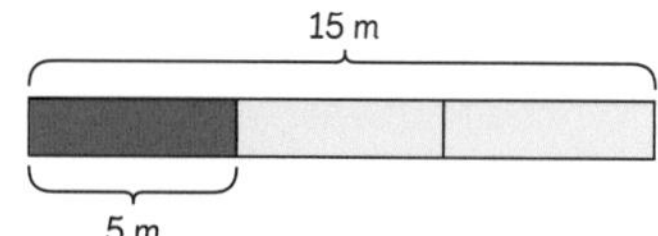

Page 27 **1** 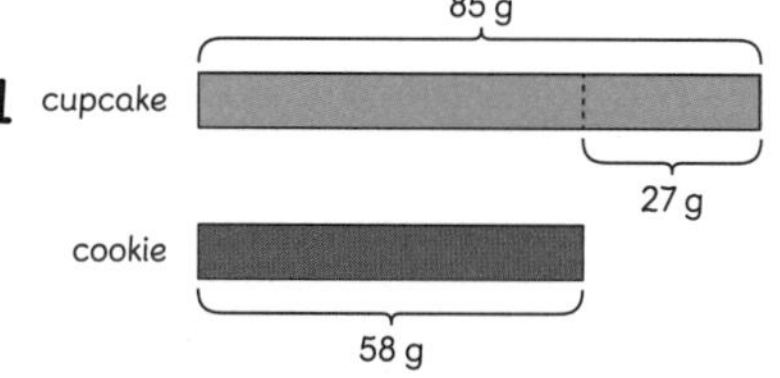

85 - 27 = 58
The mass of the cookie is 58 g.

2 6 ÷ 2 = 3, 4 − 3 = 1. The mass of the pineapple is 1 kg.

Page 29 **1 (a)** The Flour has a mass of 1 kg. **(b)** The  has a mass of 4 kg. **(c)** The  has a mass of 2 kg. **(d)** The flour is the lightest. **(e)** The rice is the heaviest. **2 (a)** The mass of the coconut is 500 g. **(b)** The mass of the mango is 450 g. **(c)** The mass of the cabbage is 700 g. **(d)** The mango is the lightest. **(e)** The cabbage is the heaviest.

Page 31 **1** 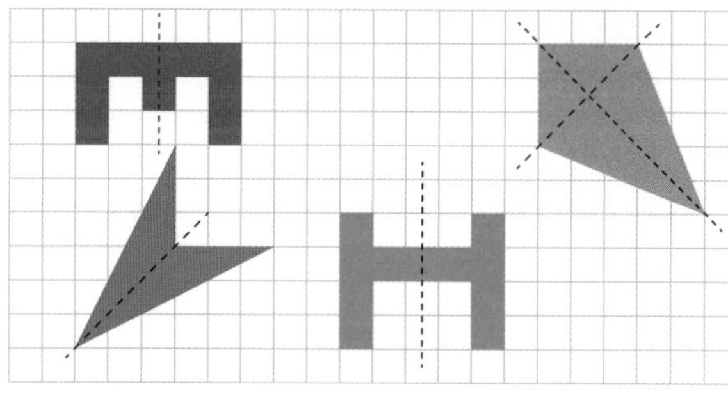

2 Answers will vary.

Page 33 **1** 18 + 15 = 33. The doll costs £33.

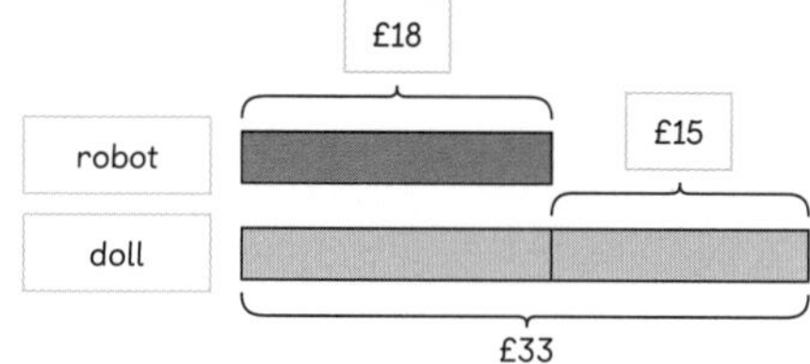

Answers continued

2 (a)

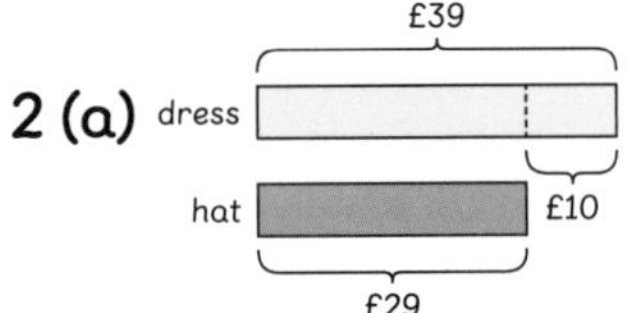

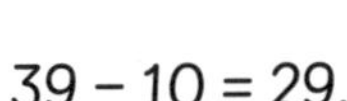

39 – 10 = 29.
The hat costs £29.

(b)

£68
£39 £29

39 + 29 = 68
The dress and the hat cost £68 altogether.

Page 34 **1 (a)** 50p + 25p = 75p. Elliott saves 75p on Monday and Tuesday.

Page 35 **(b)** 75p + 35p = 110p, 110p = £1 and 10p. Elliott saves £1 and 10p over the three days.

2

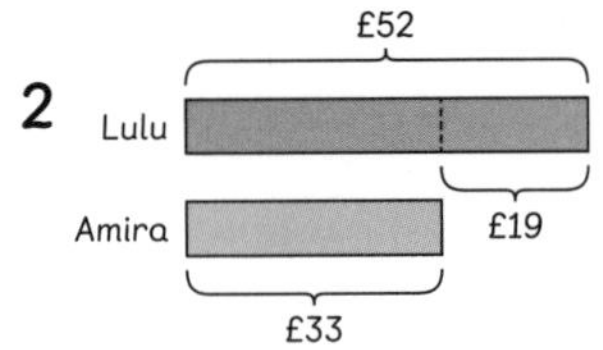

52 – 19 = 33

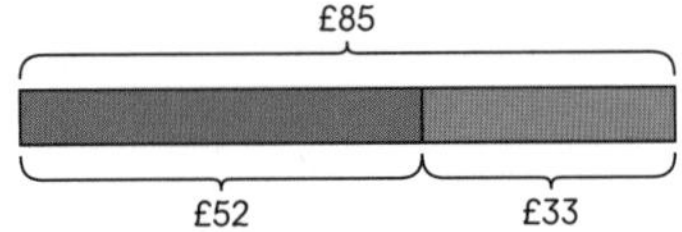

52 + 33 = 85. Lulu and Amira have £85 altogether.

Page 37 **1** 42 + 13 + 22 = 77

£100
£77 £23

100 – 77 = 23
Amira has £23 left.

2

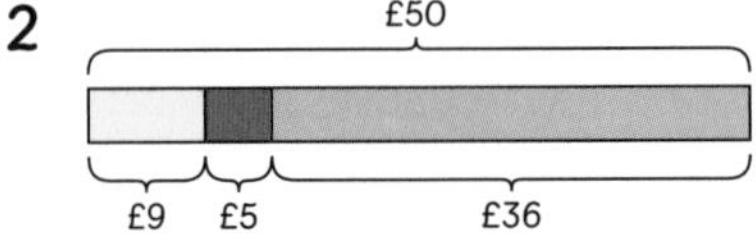

9 + 5 = 14
50 – 14 = 36
The price of the satchel is £36.

Page 39 **1 (a)** (drawing) start time: 5:30, end time: 6:15, duration: 45 min, (swimming) start time: 3:10, end time: 4:00, duration: 50 min **(b)** swimming **(c)** drawing **2 (a)** Lulu started at 4:05. **(b)** Emma started at 4:15. **(c)** Charles spent 55 minutes on his homework.

Page 41 **1** 40 °C, 80 °C, 80 – 40 = 40. The difference between the two temperatures is 40 °C.
2 10 °C, 100 °C, 100 – 10 = 90. The difference between the two temperatures is 90 °C.
3 15 °C, 65 °C, 65 – 15 = 50. The difference between the two temperatures is 50 °C.

Page 43 **1** 18 – 8 = 10. The mass of the sack of carrots is 5 kg.

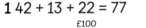

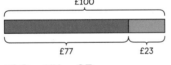

2

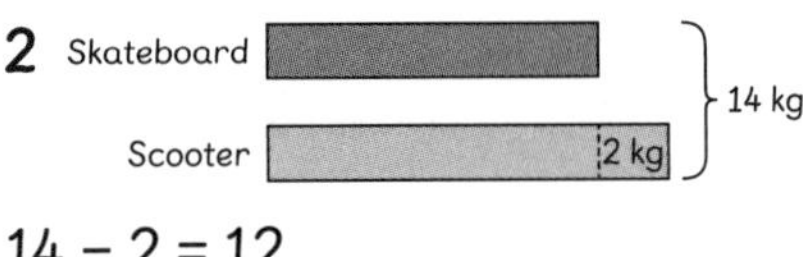

14 – 2 = 12
12 ÷ 2 = 6
skateboard: 6 kg
scooter: 8 kg

18 kg
8 kg 10 kg

18 – 8 = 10
bike: 10 kg

Page 45 **1** 70 – 30 = 40. The difference between the two volumes of water is 40 ml. **2** 90 – 10 = 80. The difference between the two volumes of water is 80 ml. **3** 80 – 20 = 60. The difference between the two volumes of water is 60 ml.

KS1
5–7
Years

Master Maths at Home

Multiplication and Division

Scan the QR code to help your child's learning at home.

mastermathsathome.com

How to use this book

Maths — No Problem! created **Master Maths at Home** to help children develop fluency in the subject and a rich understanding of core concepts.

Key features of the Master Maths at Home books include:

- Carefully designed lessons that provide structure but also allow flexibility in how they're used. For example, some children may want to write numbers, while others might want to trace.
- Speech bubbles containing content designed to spark diverse conversations, with many discussion points that don't have obvious 'right' or 'wrong' answers.
- Rich illustrations that will guide children to a discussion of shapes and units of measurement, allowing them to make connections to the wider world around them.
- Exercises that allow a flexible approach and can be adapted to suit any child's cognitive or functional ability.
- Clearly laid out pages that encourage children to practise a range of higher-order skills.
- A community of friendly and relatable characters who introduce each lesson and come along as your child progresses through the series.

You can see more guidance on how to use these books at **mastermathsathome.com**.

We're excited to share all the ways you can learn maths!

Maths — No Problem!
mastermathsathome.com
www.mathsnoproblem.com
hello@mathsnoproblem.com

First published in Great Britain in 2022 by
Dorling Kindersley Limited
One Embassy Gardens, 8 Viaduct Gardens, London SW11 7BW
A Penguin Random House Company

The authorised representative in the EEA is Dorling Kindersley Verlag GmbH. Amulfstr. 124, 80636 Munich, Germany

10 9 8 7 6 5 4 3 2 1
001-327073-Jan/22

This book was made with Forest Stewardship Council™ certified paper - one small step in DK's commitment to a sustainable future. For more information go to www.dk.com/our-green-pledge

A CIP catalogue record for this book is available from the British Library.

ISBN: 978-0-24153-916-3
Printed and bound in China

For the curious
www.dk.com

Acknowledgements
The publisher would like to thank the authors and consultants Andy Psarianos, Judy Hornigold, Adam Gifford and Dr Anne Hermanson.

The Castledown typeface has been used with permission from the Colophon Foundry.

Contents

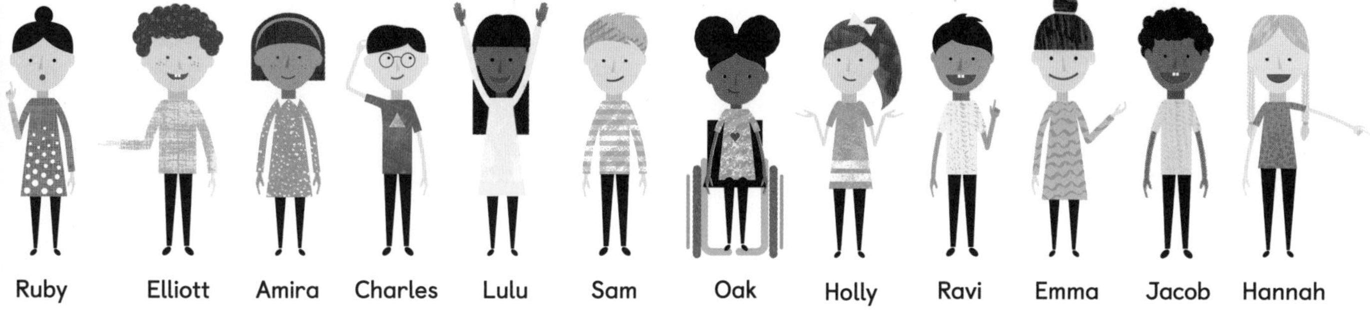

Ruby
Elliott
Amira
Charles
Lulu
Sam
Oak
Holly
Ravi
Emma
Jacob
Hannah

Groups

Starter

How many children are there on the teacup ride?

Example

$3 + 3 + 3 + 3 = 12$

There are 4 teacups on the ride. Each teacup has 3 children. There are 4 threes.

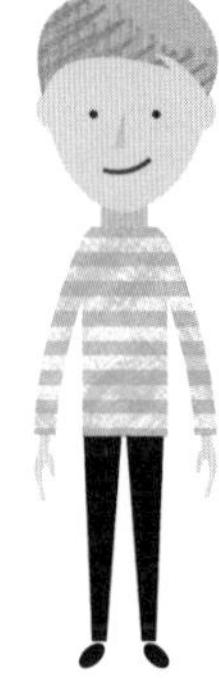

$4 \times 3 = 12$
We say 4 times 3 equals 12.

There are 12 children on the teacup ride.

Practice

Fill in the blanks.

1

☐ + ☐ + ☐ = ☐

☐ groups of ☐ = ☐

☐ × ☐ = ☐

2

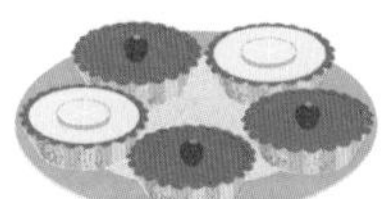  

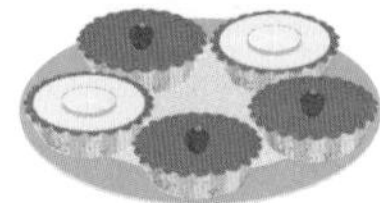 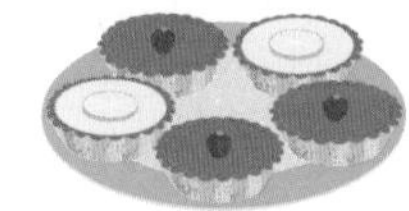 

☐ + ☐ + ☐ + ☐ + ☐ + ☐ = ☐

☐ groups of ☐ = ☐

☐ × ☐ = ☐

2 times table

Lesson 2

Starter

How many chocolates are there?

Example

1 box of 2 chocolates

1 box of 2 chocolates

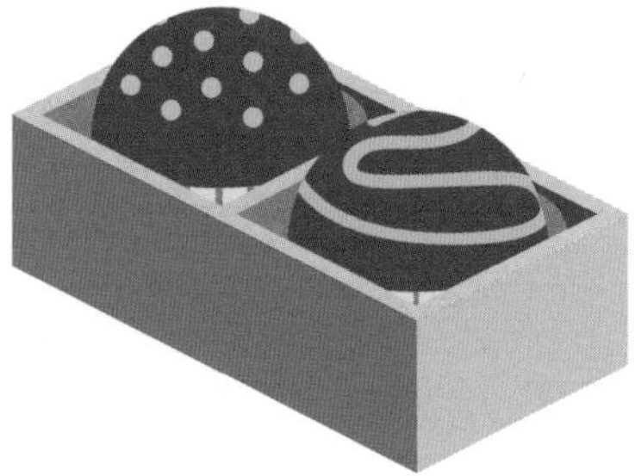
1 box of 2 chocolates

There are 3 boxes. Each box has 2 chocolates.

There are 3 groups of 2.
$3 \times 2 = 6$

There are 6 chocolates.

Practice

Fill in the blanks.

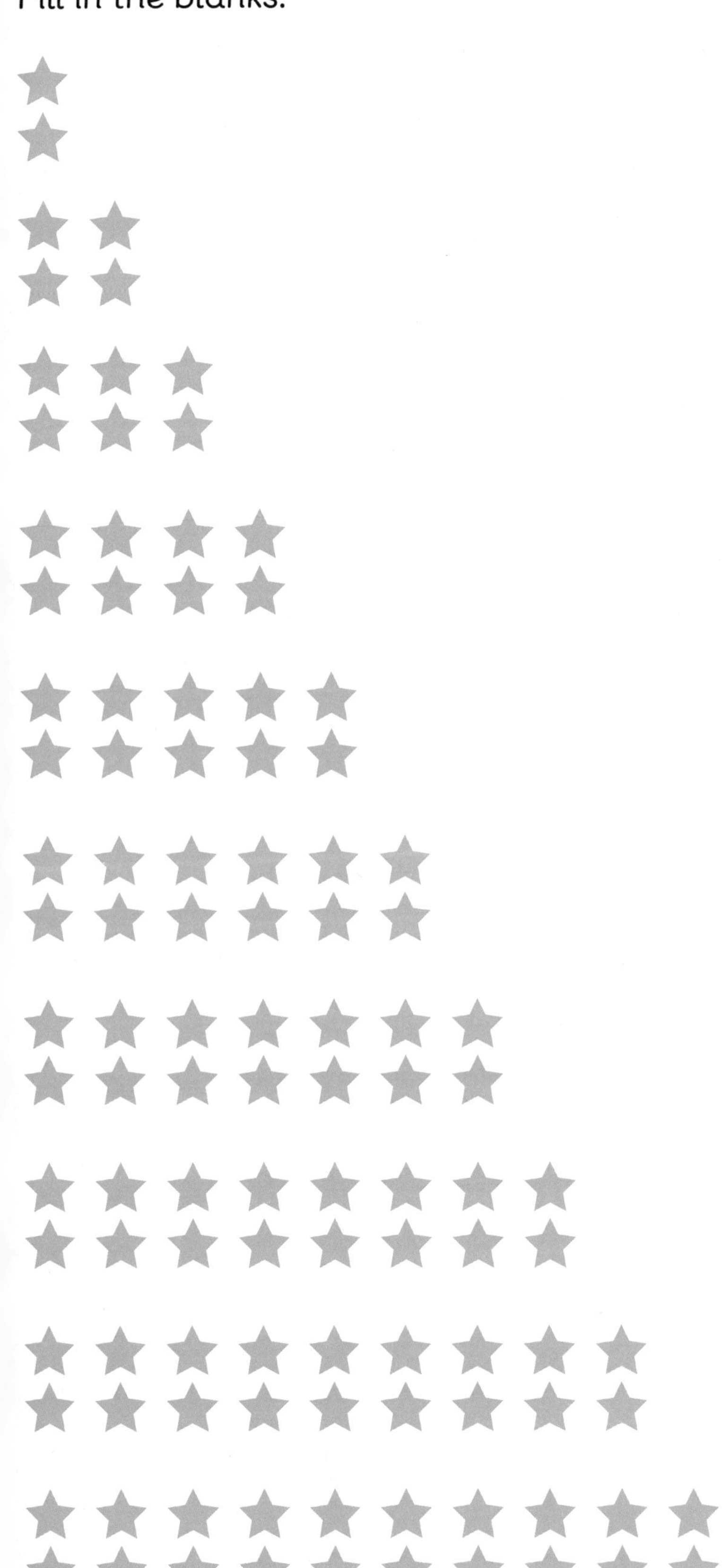

1 group of 2 = 2
1 × 2 = 2

2 groups of 2 = 4
☐ × ☐ = ☐

☐ groups of ☐ = ☐
☐ × ☐ = ☐

☐ groups of ☐ = ☐
☐ × ☐ = ☐

☐ groups of ☐ = ☐
☐ × ☐ = ☐

☐ groups of ☐ = ☐
☐ × ☐ = ☐

☐ groups of ☐ = ☐
☐ × ☐ = ☐

☐ groups of ☐ = ☐
☐ × ☐ = ☐

☐ groups of ☐ = ☐
☐ × ☐ = ☐

☐ groups of ☐ = ☐
☐ × ☐ = ☐

5 times table

Lesson 3

Starter

How many hotdogs did Charles prepare for the party?

Example

1	2	3	4	5	6	7	8	9	10
11	12	13	14	15	16	17	18	19	20
21	22	23	24	25	26	27	28	29	30

I can count in fives using the number chart.

Can you see a pattern in the number chart?

There are 6 fives.
$6 \times 5 = 30$
Charles prepared 30 hotdogs for the party.

Practice

Count the stickers and fill in the blanks.

1 group of 5 = 5

1 × 5 = 5

2 groups of 5 = 10

☐ × ☐ = ☐

☐ groups of ☐ = ☐

☐ × ☐ = ☐

☐ groups of ☐ = ☐

☐ × ☐ = ☐

☐ groups of ☐ = ☐

☐ × ☐ = ☐

☐ groups of ☐ = ☐

☐ × ☐ = ☐

☐ groups of ☐ = ☐

☐ × ☐ = ☐

☐ groups of ☐ = ☐

☐ × ☐ = ☐

☐ groups of ☐ = ☐

☐ × ☐ = ☐

☐ groups of ☐ = ☐

☐ × ☐ = ☐

10 times table

Lesson 4

Starter

How many crayons are there on the table?

Example

There are 6 boxes.
Each box has 10 crayons.
6 × 10 = 60

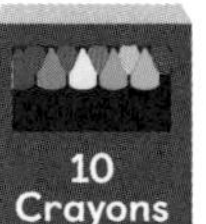

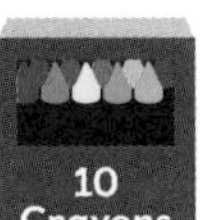

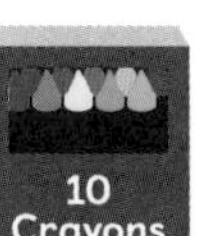

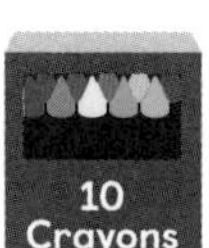

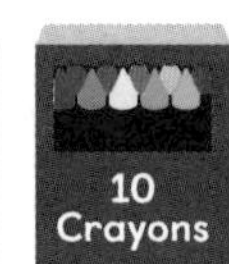

There are 60 crayons on the table.

Practice

1 Count and fill in the blanks.

(a)

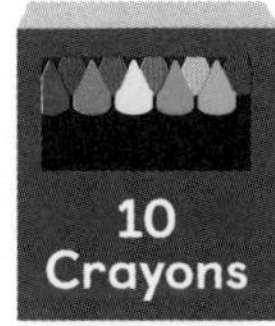

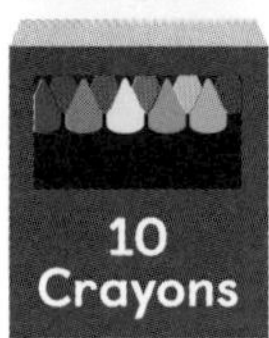

☐ groups of ☐ = ☐

☐ × 10 = ☐

(b)

☐ groups of ☐ = ☐

☐ × ☐ = ☐

(c)

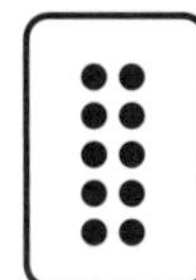

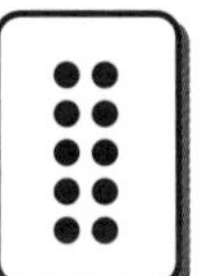
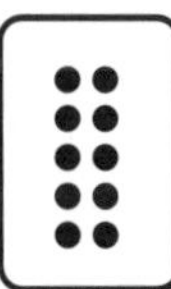
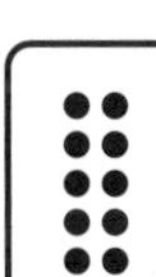

☐ groups of ☐ = ☐

☐ × ☐ = ☐

2 Fill in the blanks.

(a) 2 × 10 = ☐

(b) 6 × 10 = ☐

(c) 5 × 10 = ☐

(d) 10 × 5 = ☐

More multiplying

Lesson 5

Starter

How can we work out how many stickers there are?

Example

There are 2 groups of 10 stickers.
$2 \times 10 = 20$
There are 20 stickers.

There are 10 groups of 2 stickers.
$10 \times 2 = 20$
I agree, there are 20 stickers.

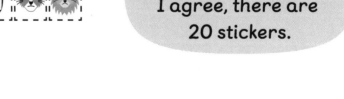

$2 \times 10 = 10 \times 2$
They are both equal to 20.

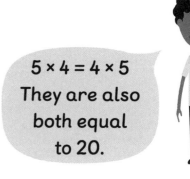

$5 \times 4 = 4 \times 5$
They are also both equal to 20.

Practice

1 Fill in the blanks.

(a)

5 × ☐ = ☐ × 5

5 × ☐ = 15

☐ × 5 = 15

(b) $2 \times 4 = 4 \times 2$

2 × ☐ = ☐

☐ × 2 = ☐

(c)

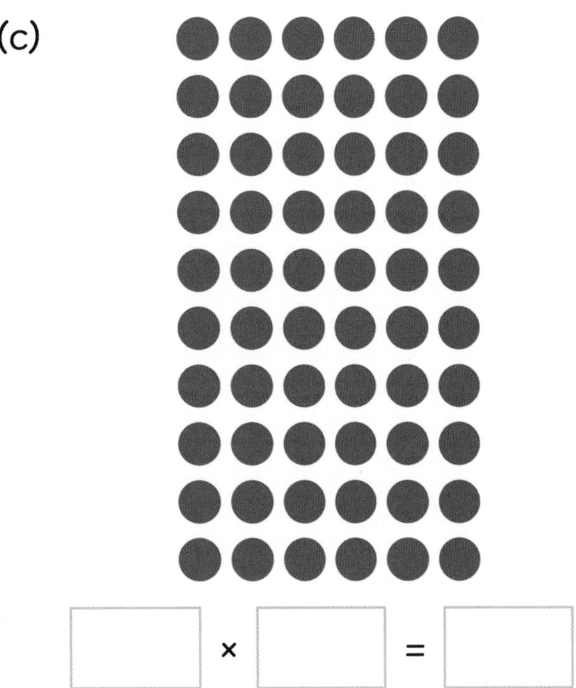

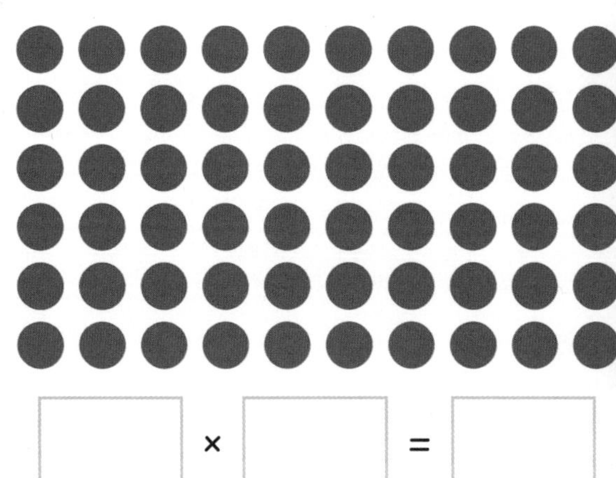

$\square \times \square = \square$ $\square \times \square = \square$

2 Draw lines to match.

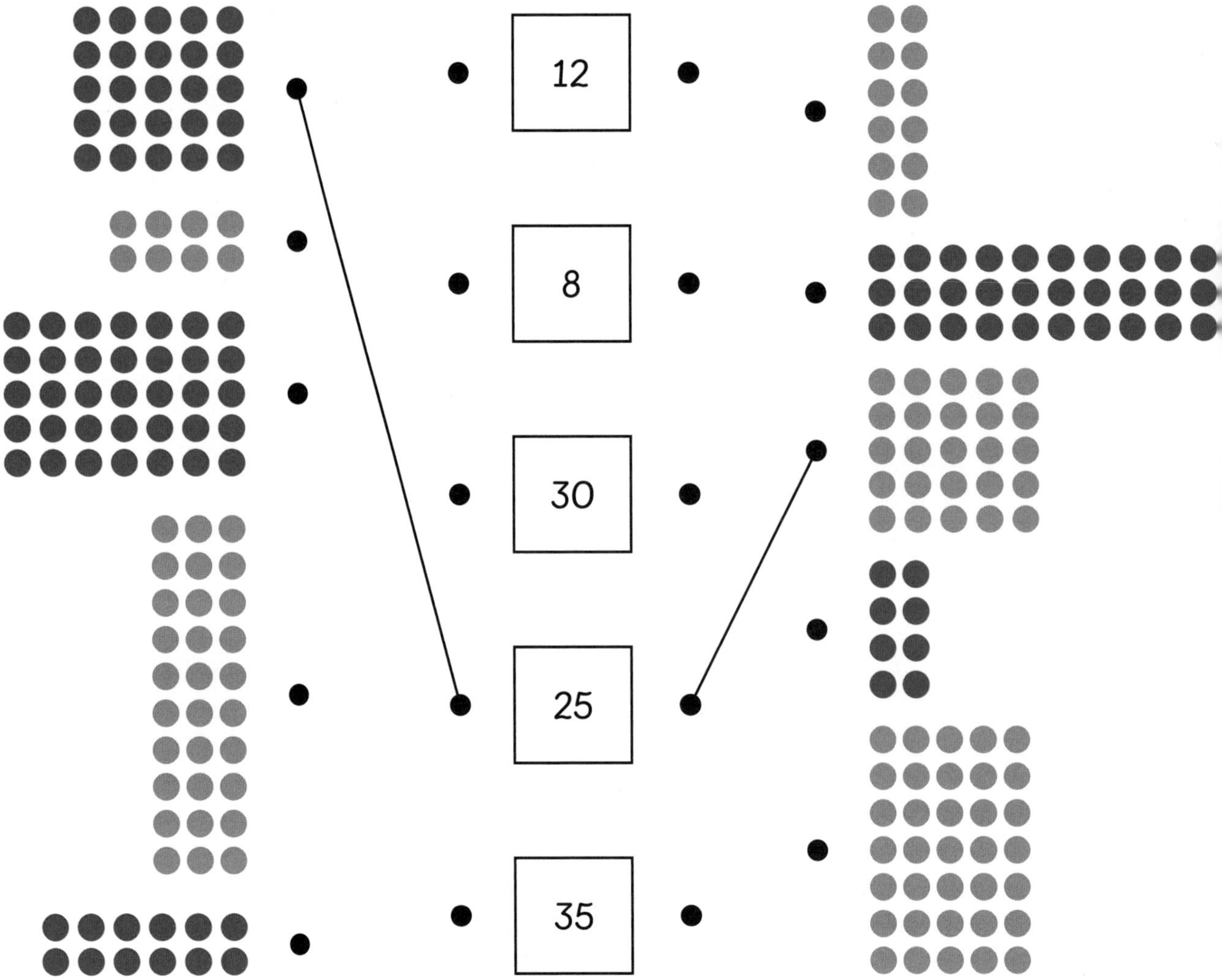

12

8

30

25

35

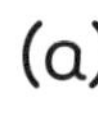

3 Write 2 equations for each picture.

(a)

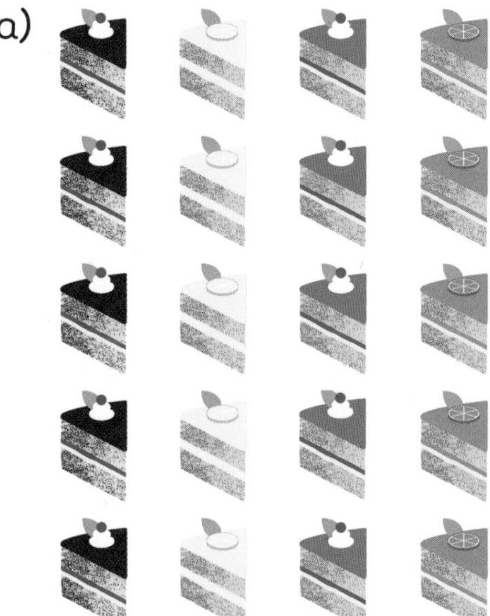

$\square \times \square = \square$

$\square \times \square = \square$

(b)

$\square \times \square = \square$

$\square \times \square = \square$

(c)

$\square \times \square = \square$

$\square \times \square = \square$

Word problems

Lesson 6

Starter

Sam prints 7 sheets of invitations for the school play.
Each sheet has 5 invitations.
How many invitations does Sam print?

Example

Sam prints 7 sheets.
Each sheet has 5 invitations.

$7 \times 5 = 35$

Sam prints 35 invitations.

Practice

Solve.

1. A farmer has 5 horses in his stable that need new horseshoes.
Each horse needs 4 horseshoes.
How many horseshoes does the farmer need?

2. 10 children go the theme park. Each child gets 8 ride tickets.
How many rides can the children take altogether?

3. An ice cream parlour sells 9 ice cream cones at lunchtime.
Each ice cream cone has 2 scoops of ice cream.
How many scoops of ice cream does the parlour use at lunchtime?

Grouping

Lesson 7

Starter

How many baskets of 5 apples can Hannah make?

Example

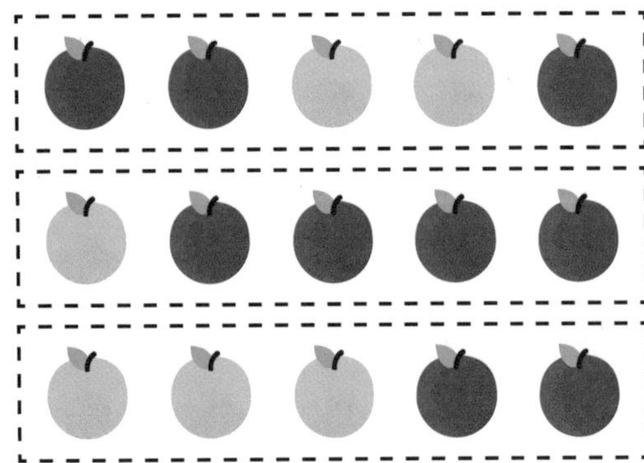

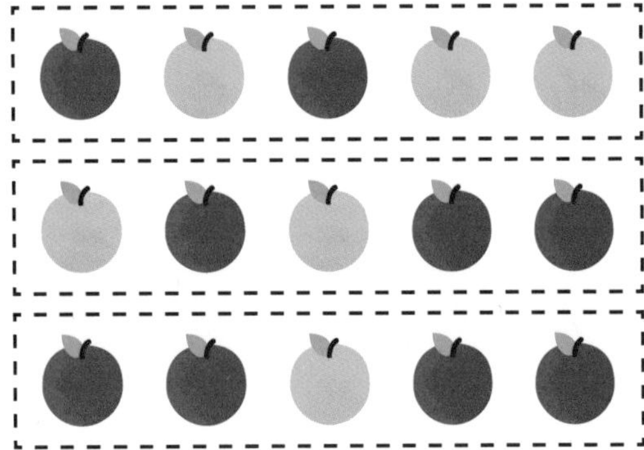

There are 30 apples in total. When I make groups of 5, I get 6 groups. $30 \div 5 = 6$

$\div$ means to divide. $30 \div 5 = 6$ is a division equation. We say 30 divided by 5 is equal to 6.

Hannah can make 6 baskets of 5 apples.

Practice

1 Circle to make groups of 5.
How many groups are there?

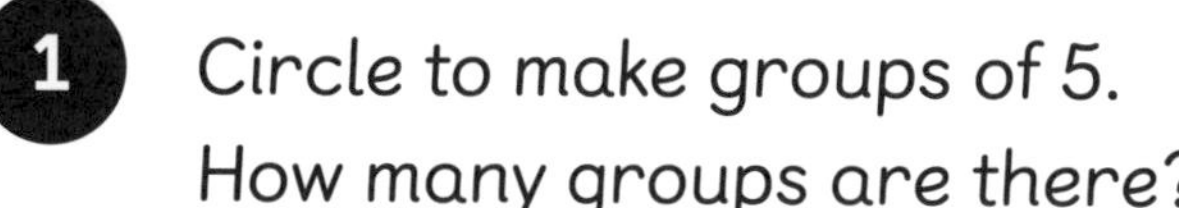

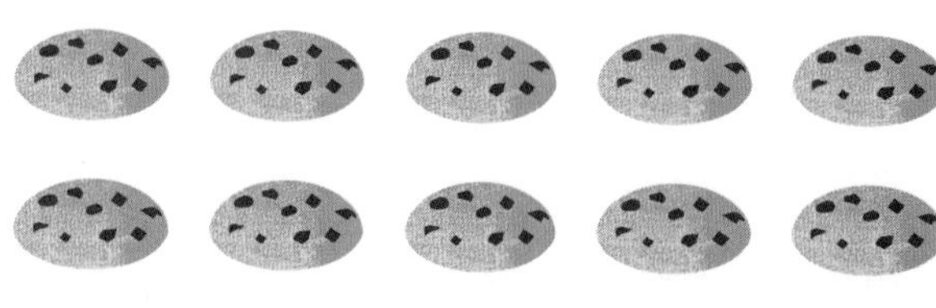

$\square \div \square = \square$

There are $\square$ groups.

2 Circle to make groups of 2.
How many groups are there?

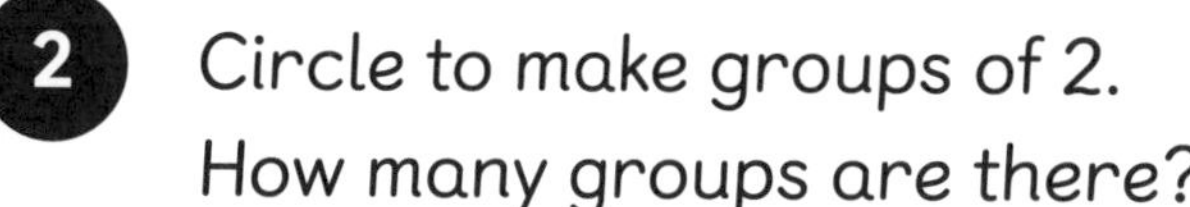

$\square \div \square = \square$

There are $\square$ groups.

3 Fill in the blanks.

(a) Group the mugs in twos.

$\square \div \square = \square$

(b) Group the cupcakes in fives.

$\square \div \square = \square$

Sharing

Lesson
8

Starter

How many cards does each player get?

Example

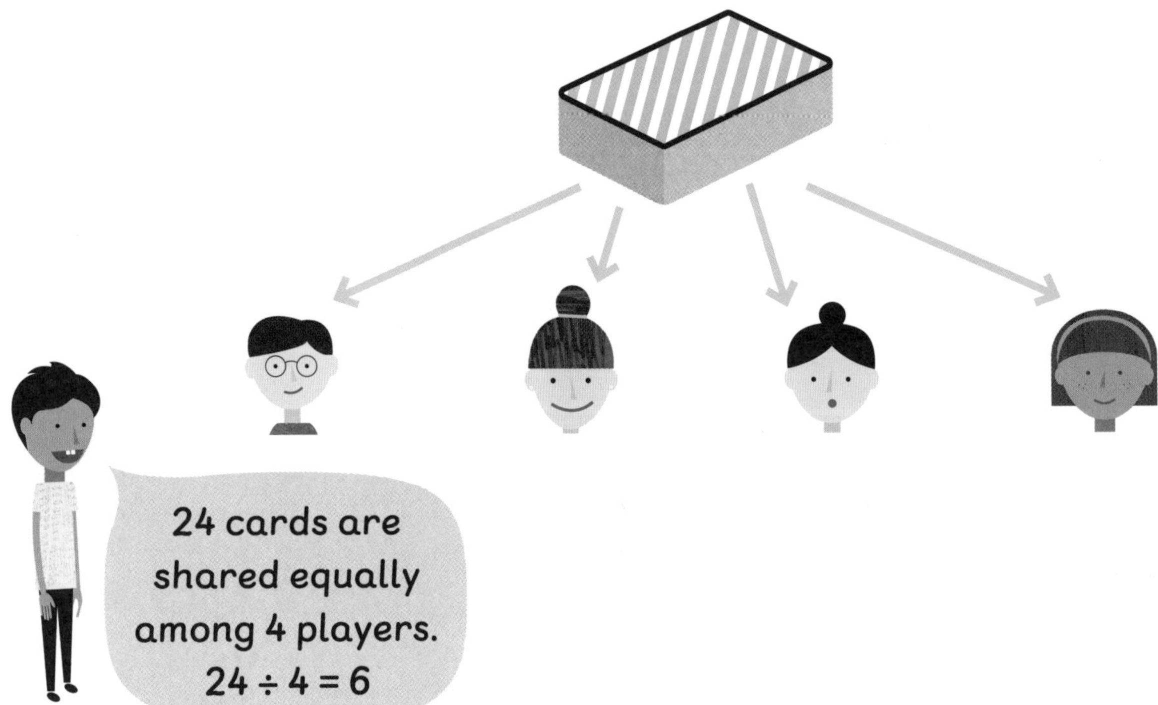

Each player gets 6 cards.

Practice

Fill in the blanks.

1 Elliott has 12 doughnuts.

I put the doughnuts equally on 2 plates.

☐ ÷  = ☐

There are  doughnuts on each plate.

2 Share 20 cards equally among 5 players.

 ÷  = 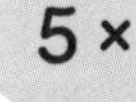

5 × 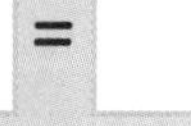 = ☐

3 Put 30 counters equally into 3 groups.

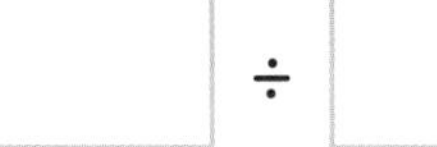 ÷ 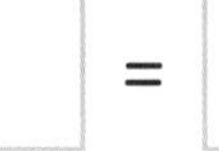  = 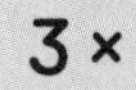

3 ×  = ☐

Dividing by 2

Lesson 9

Starter

Lulu needs to put the dice into groups of 2 for a game.
How many equal groups can Lulu make?

Example

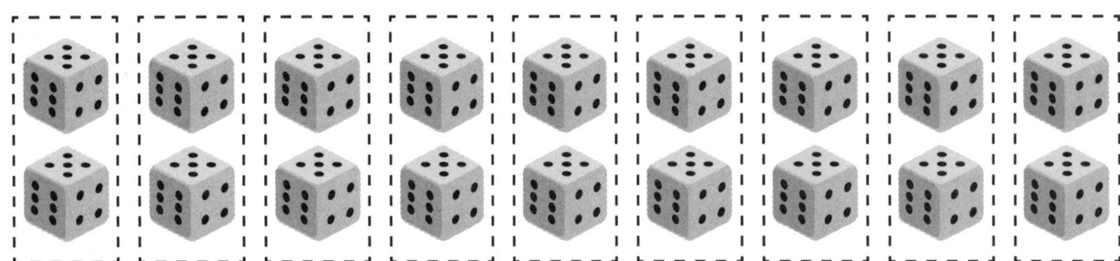

18 ÷ 2 = 9
Lulu can make 9 equal groups.

I put 18 dice into groups of 2. I made 9 groups.

Practice

1 Sam puts the biscuits into boxes.
Each box has 2 biscuits.

☐ ÷ 2 = ☐

There are ☐ boxes of 2 biscuits.

2 Ruby puts the grapes equally onto 2 plates.

☐ ÷ 2 = ☐

There are ☐ grapes on each plate.

3 Fill in the blanks.

(a) 8 ÷ 2 = ☐

(b) 16 ÷ 2 = ☐

(c) 40 ÷ 2 = ☐

(d) ☐ ÷ 2 = 5

Dividing by 5

Lesson 10

Starter

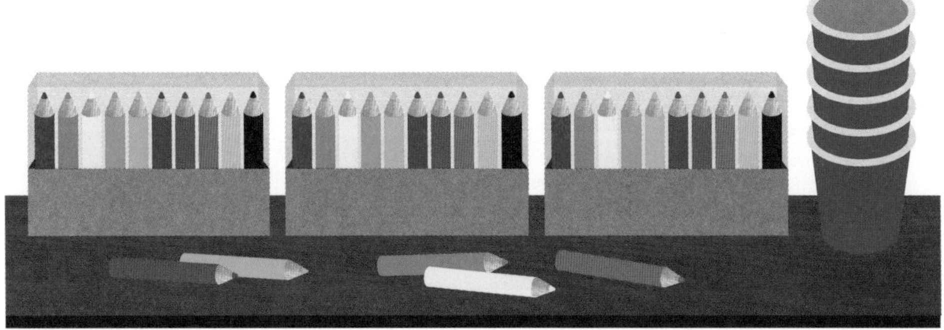

Jacob puts the pencils equally into 5 pots.
How many pencils does he put in each pot?

Example

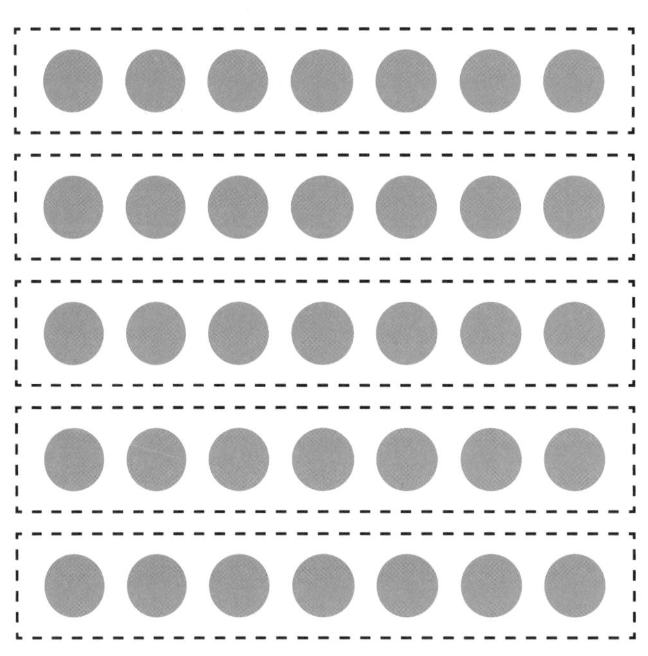

$35 \div 5 = 7$
Jacob puts 7 pencils in each pot.

There are 35 pencils in total. There are 5 pots.

Practice

1 Hannah puts the drinks into boxes. Each box has 5 drinks.

☐ ÷ 5 = ☐

There are ☐ boxes of 5 drinks.

2 Charles puts the cakes equally onto 5 plates.

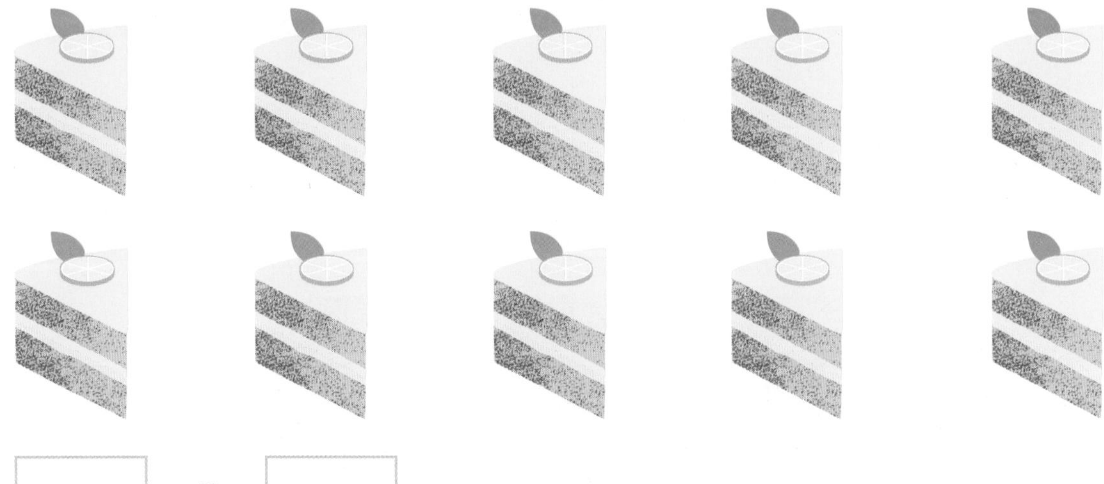

☐ ÷ 5 = ☐

There are ☐ cakes on each plate.

3 Fill in the blanks.

(a) 20 ÷ 5 = ☐

(b) 50 ÷ 5 = ☐

(c) 35 ÷ 5 = ☐

(d) ☐ ÷ 5 = 5

Dividing by 10

Starter

The chef has filled one box of chocolates so far.

How many more boxes can the chef fill?

Example

There are 90 chocolates left in the tray. Each box can hold 10 chocolates. $90 \div 10 = 9$

The chef can fill 9 more boxes with chocolates.

Practice

1 Emma puts the counters into stacks.
Each stack has 10 counters.

☐ ÷ 10 = ☐

There are ☐ stacks of 10 counters.

2 Ravi puts the biscuits equally onto 10 plates.

☐ ÷ 10 = ☐

There are ☐ biscuits on each plate.

3 Fill in the blanks.

(a) 20 ÷ 10 = ☐

(b) 60 ÷ 10 = ☐

(c) ☐ ÷ 10 = 8

(d) ☐ ÷ 10 = 10

Multiplication and division

Lesson 12

Starter

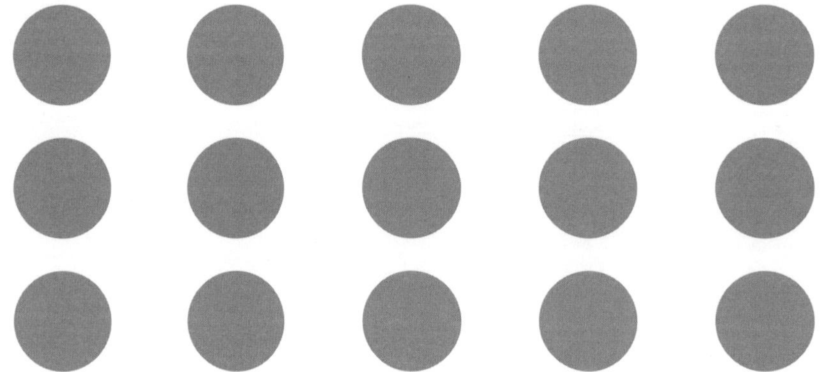

Can you write multiplication and division equations for this image?

Example

There are 3 groups of 5.
$3 \times 5 = 15$

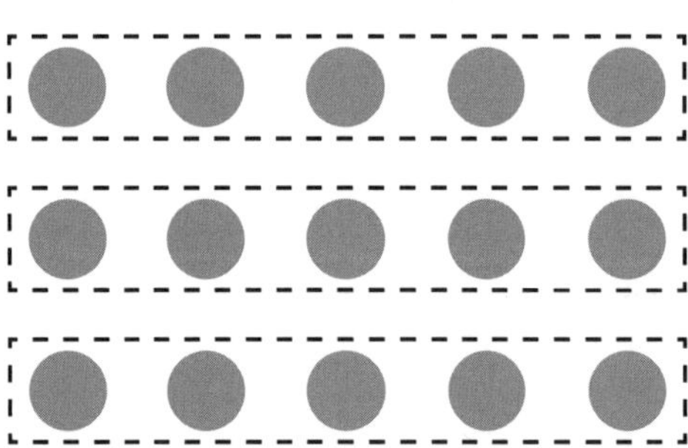

I can make groups of 5.
$15 \div 5 = 3$
There are 3 groups of 5.

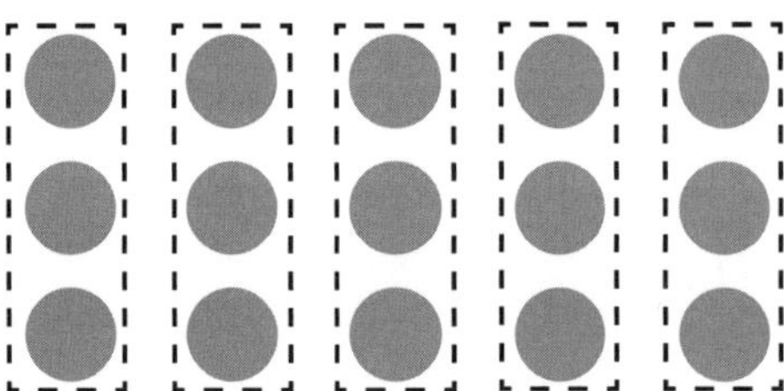

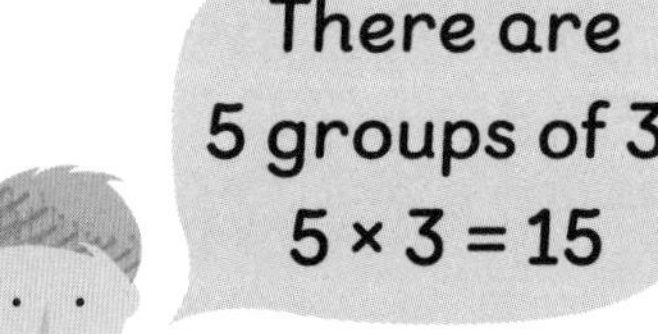

I can see groups of 3.
$15 \div 3 = 5$
There are 5 groups of 3.

$3 \times 5 = 15$　　$15 \div 5 = 3$

$5 \times 3 = 15$　　$15 \div 3 = 5$

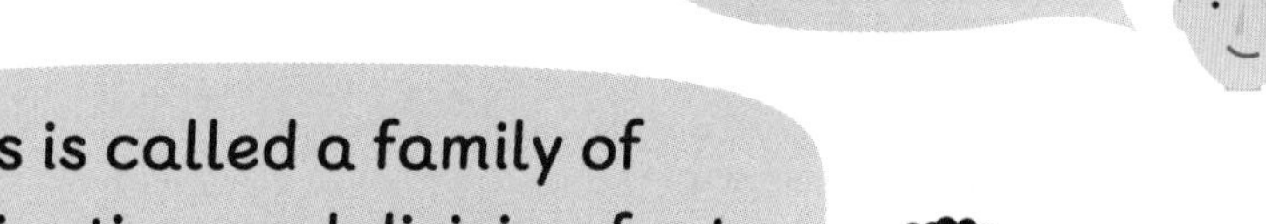

This is called a family of
multiplication and division facts.

Practice

Complete the families of multiplication and division facts.

1

2 × 4 = ____   8 ÷ 4 = ____

4 × 2 = ____   8 ÷ 2 = ____

2

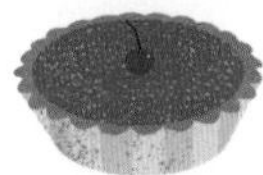   

3 × 4 = ____   12 ÷ ____ = 4

4 × 3 = ____   ____ ÷ 4 = ____

3

 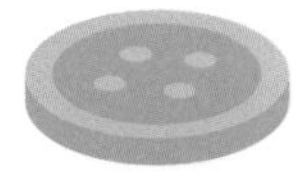 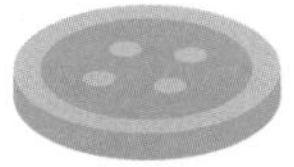 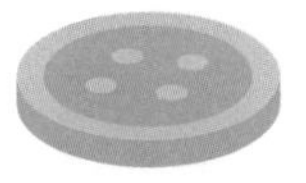 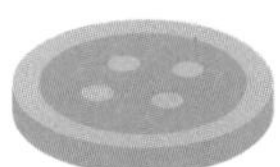

 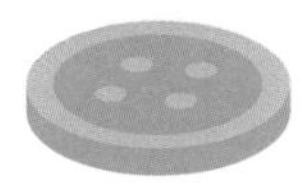   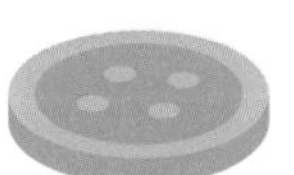

____ × ____ = ____   ____  ____

____ × ____ = ____    ÷  = ____

More word problems

Lesson 13

Starter

Can the 3 children share the cookies equally?

Example

There are 18 cookies.
3 children share the cookies equally.
How many cookies does each child get?

Try Ravi's method to find how many cookies each child gets.

Ravi's method  uses  to stand for  and  to stand for each child.

Emma's method  draws a picture to show how many cookies each child gets.

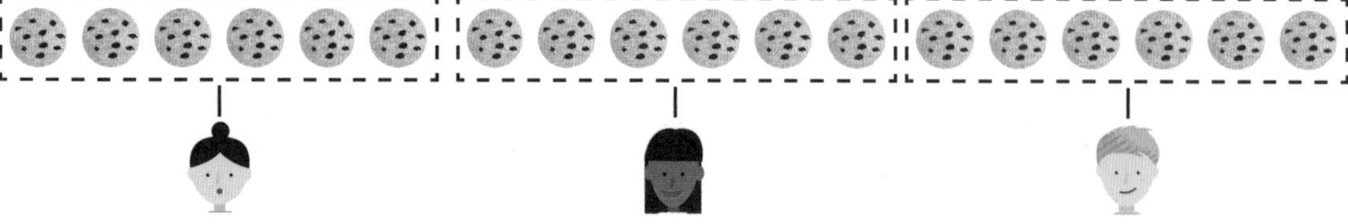

Holly's method  uses a division equation.

$18 \div 3 = 6$

Each child gets 6 cookies.

Practice

1 Charles has 30 apples.
He wants to put the apples into bags.
Each bag should have 5 apples.
How many bags will he need?

Ravi's method

 uses  to stand for  and  to stand for each bag.

Emma's method

 draws a picture to show how many bags Charles will need.

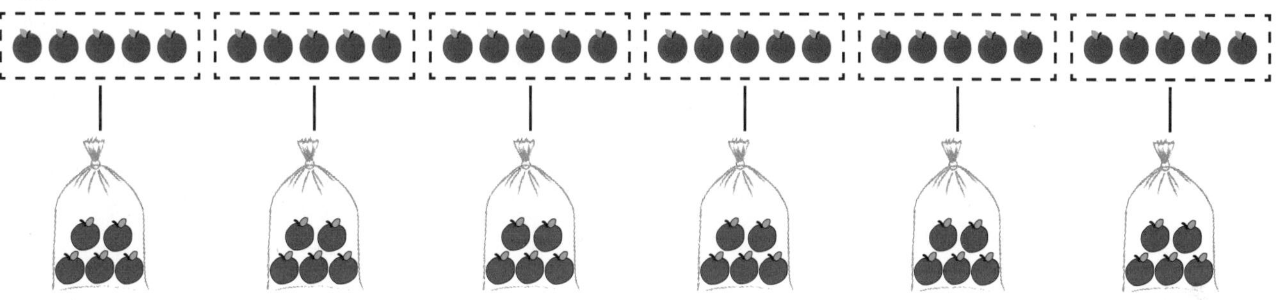

Holly's method

 uses a division equation.

☐ ÷ ☐ = ☐

Charles will need  bags.

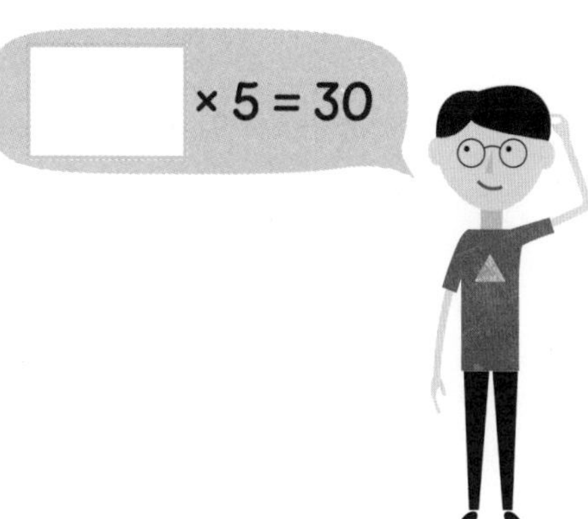

2 The P. E. teacher has 12 footballs.
He gives some children 2 footballs each.
How many children get 2 footballs?

Ravi's method

 uses  to stand for  and  to stand for each child.

Emma's method

 draws a picture to show how many children get 2 footballs.

Holly's method

 uses a division equation.

 ÷  =

 children get 2 footballs.

3 Solve and fill in the blanks.

(a) Elliott and Ravi make 16 paper planes.
They share them equally.
How many paper planes does each of them get?

$\square \div \square = \square$

Elliott and Ravi each get $\square$ paper planes.

(b) A baker has 100 muffins. She puts them into boxes of 10.
How many boxes does she fill?

The baker fills $\square$ boxes.

Odd and even numbers

Lesson 14

Starter

Can you help Hannah put the apples into bags of 2 and the pears into bags of 2?

Example

Even numbers can be put into groups of 2.

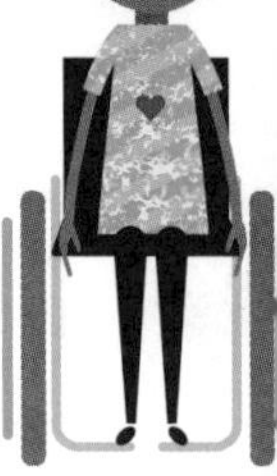

I can put all the apples into groups of 2. That means 8 is an even number.

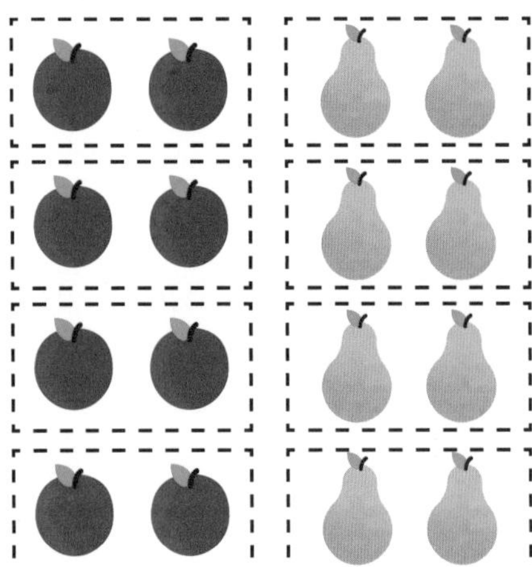

I can't put all the pears into groups of 2. That means 9 is an odd number.

Odd numbers are whole numbers that can't be divided exactly into groups of 2.

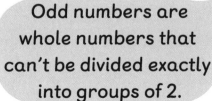

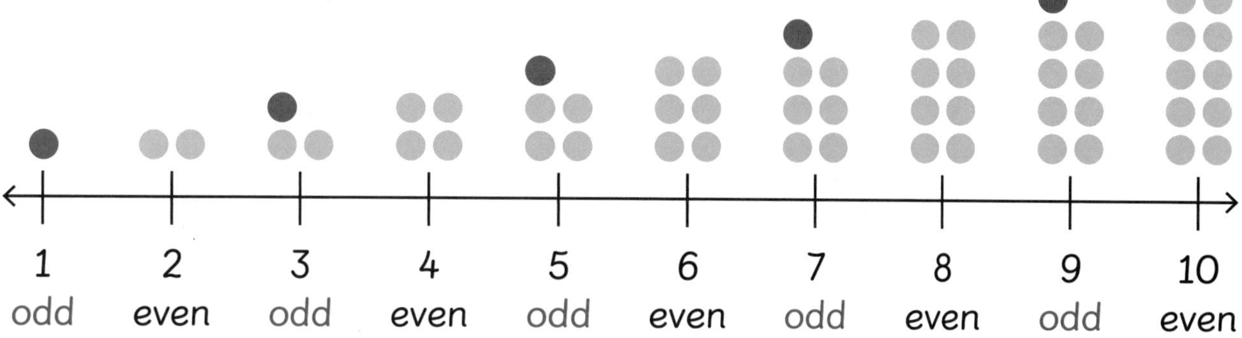

Practice

1 Look at the numbers below.
Sort the numbers into odd numbers and even numbers.

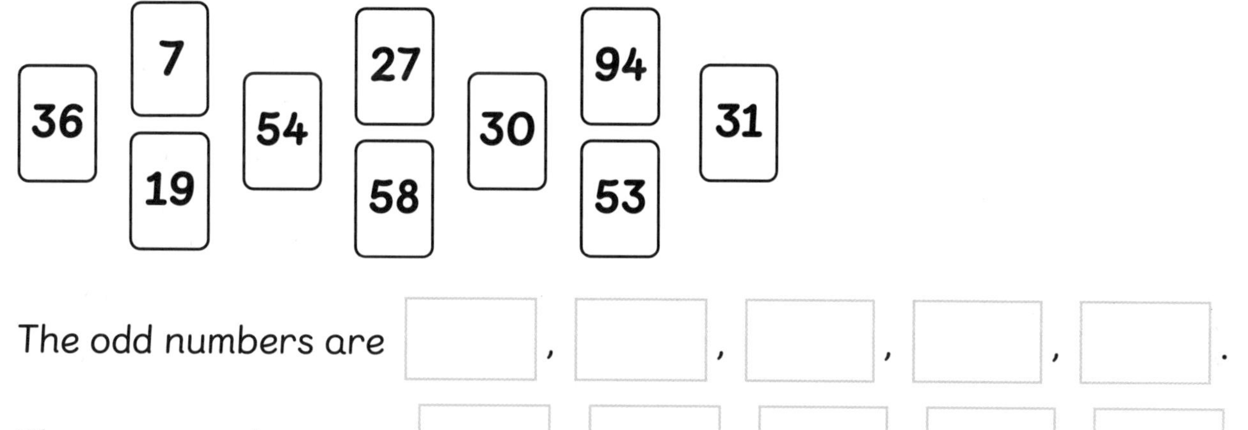

The odd numbers are ☐, ☐, ☐, ☐, ☐.

The even numbers are ☐, ☐, ☐, ☐, ☐.

2 4 6 5

Use the 3 digits to form:

(a) the greatest 2-digit even number. ☐

(b) the smallest 2-digit even number. ☐

(c) the greatest 2-digit odd number. ☐

(d) the smallest 2-digit odd number. ☐

Review and challenge

1 Fill in the blanks.

☐ + ☐ +  +  +   + ☐ = ☐

☐ groups of  = ☐

☐ × ☐ = ☐

2 Fill in the blanks.

(a) $1 \times 2 =$ ☐

(b) $2 \times 2 =$ ☐

(c) $2 \times 5 =$ ☐

(d) $5 \times 6 =$ ☐

(e) $10 \times 2 =$ ☐

(f) $2 \times 7 =$ ☐

(g) $7 \times 2 =$ ☐

(h) $8 \times 2 =$ ☐

(i) $5 \times 5 =$ ☐

(j) $8 \times 10 =$ ☐

3. Count in fives and highlight the numbers on the number chart. The first one is done for you.

1	2	3	4	5	6	7	8	9	10
11	12	13	14	15	16	17	18	19	20
21	22	23	24	25	26	27	28	29	30
31	32	33	34	35	36	37	38	39	40
41	42	43	44	45	46	47	48	49	50

4. Count in tens and highlight the numbers on the number chart.

1	2	3	4	5	6	7	8	9	10
11	12	13	14	15	16	17	18	19	20
21	22	23	24	25	26	27	28	29	30
31	32	33	34	35	36	37	38	39	40
41	42	43	44	45	46	47	48	49	50
51	52	53	54	55	56	57	58	59	60
61	62	63	64	65	66	67	68	69	70
71	72	73	74	75	76	77	78	79	80
81	82	83	84	85	86	87	88	89	90
91	92	93	94	95	96	97	98	99	100

5 Fill in the blanks.

(a)

(b)

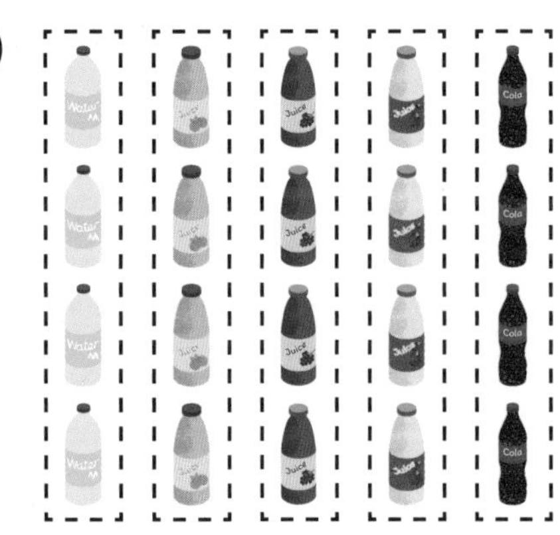

(a) ___ groups of ___ = ___ 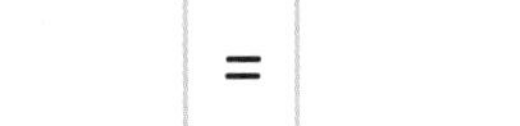

___ × ___ = ___

(b) ___ groups of ___ = ___ 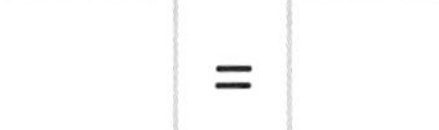

___ × ___ = ___

6 Fill in the blanks.

(a) 0, 5, ___, 15, 20, ___, ___, ___, ___, 45, ___

(b) 0, ___, 4, ___, 8, 10, 12, ___, 16, 18, ___, ___

(c) 0, ___, 20, ___, ___, ___, ___, ___, ___, ___, 100

7 Fill in the blanks.

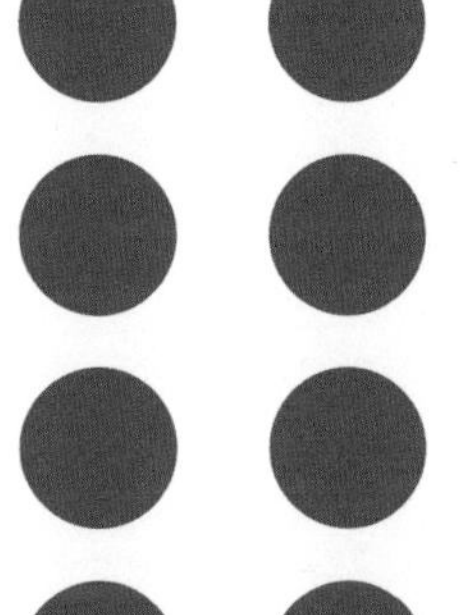
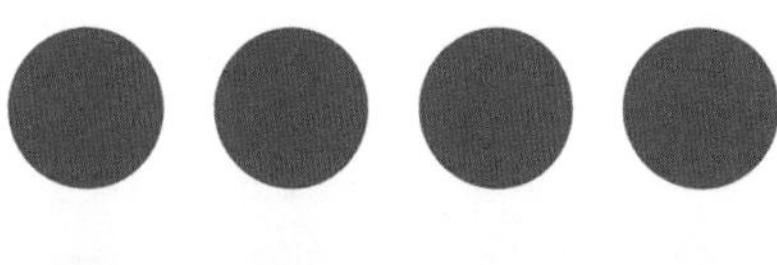
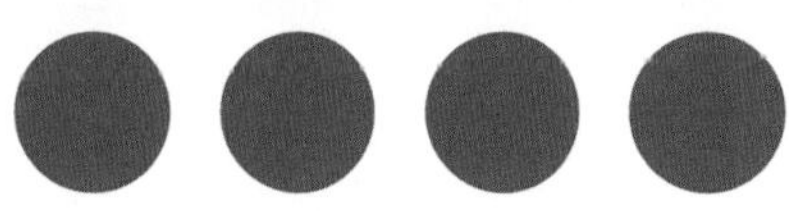

2 × ☐ = ☐ × 2

8 Fill in the blanks. Draw pictures to help you.
A florist has 6 vases. He puts 5 flowers in each vase.
How many flowers does he put in the vases in total?

☐ × ☐ = ☐

9 Solve and fill in the blanks.

Lulu and her friends are playing a game.

Lulu shares 50 playing cards with her friends.

How many cards does each friend get?

___ ÷ ___ = ___

Each friend gets ___ playing cards.

10 Solve and fill in the blanks.

Jacob needs to fill baskets with 5 lemons each.

He has 45 lemons.

How many baskets can he fill?

45 lemons

÷ =

Jacob can fill 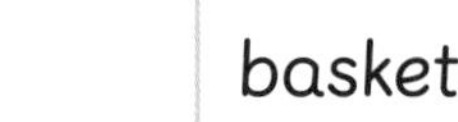 baskets.

11 Fill in the blanks.

(a) $30 \div 5 =$ ☐ (b) $30 \div 10 =$ ☐

(c) $8 \div 2 =$ ☐ (d) $90 \div 10 =$ ☐

(e) $10 \div 5 =$ ☐ (f) $10 \div 2 =$ ☐

(g) $35 \div 5 =$ ☐ (h) $100 \div 10 =$ ☐

12 Complete the family of multiplication and division facts.

$5 \times 4 =$ ☐ $20 \div$ ☐ $= 4$

$4 \times 5 =$ ☐ ☐ $\div 4 =$ ☐

13 Complete the family of multiplication and division facts.

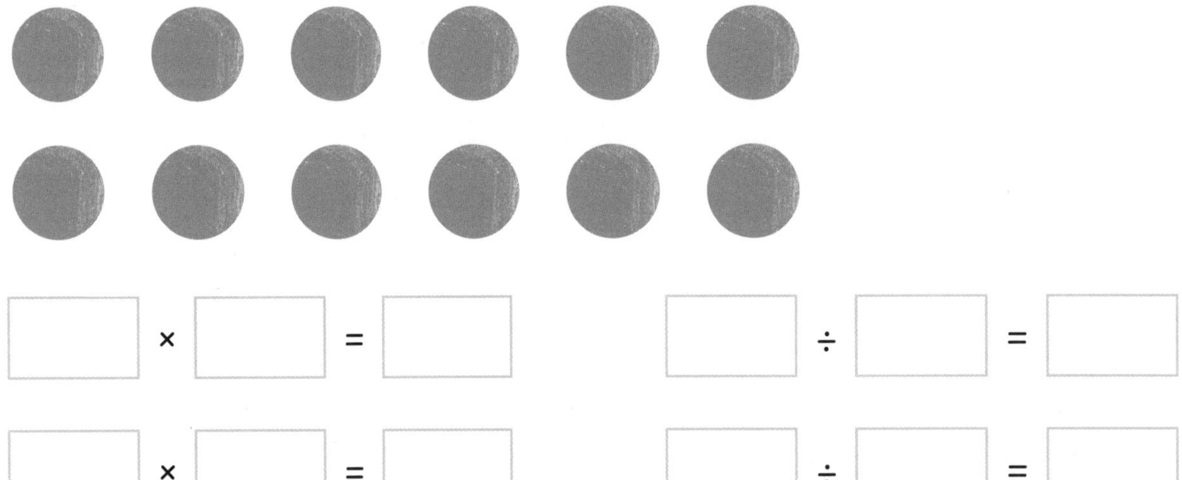

☐ × ☐ = ☐ ☐ ÷ ☐ = ☐

☐ × ☐ = ☐ ☐ ÷ ☐ = ☐

14 Solve and fill in the blanks.
Emma and her mum need to make 60 muffins for the school bake sale.
They can bake 10 muffins in one batch.
How many batches do they need to bake?

☐ ÷ ☐ = ☐

They need to bake ☐ batches.

15 (a) Highlight all the even numbers.
The first one is done for you.

1	2	3	4	5	6	7	8	9	10
11	12	13	14	15	16	17	18	19	20
21	22	23	24	25	26	27	28	29	30
31	32	33	34	35	36	37	38	39	40

(b) Highlight all the odd numbers.

1	2	3	4	5	6	7	8	9	10
11	12	13	14	15	16	17	18	19	20
21	22	23	24	25	26	27	28	29	30
31	32	33	34	35	36	37	38	39	40

16 8 7 6

Use the 3 digits to form:

(a) the greatest 2-digit even number.

(b) the smallest 2-digit even number.

(c) the greatest 2-digit odd number.

(d) the smallest 2-digit odd number.

17 Ravi has 40 counters. He wants to arrange them into equal rows.
The diagram below shows one way Ravi can do this.

Draw to show different ways Ravi can arrange the counters.

Fill in the blanks to show the family of multiplication and subtraction facts.

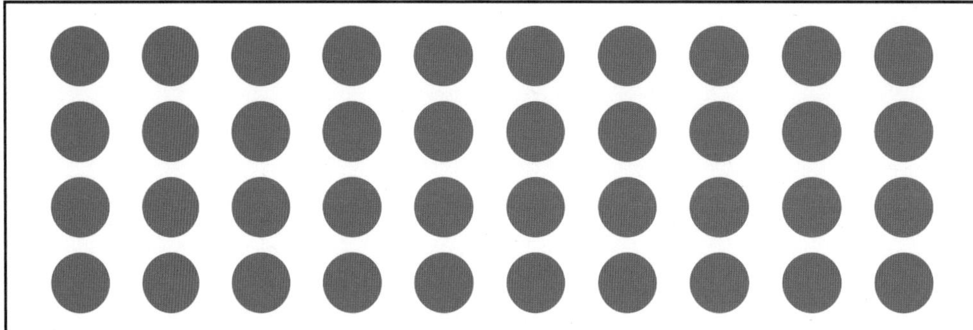

☐ × ☐ = ☐ ☐ ÷ ☐ = ☐

☐ × ☐ = ☐ ☐ ÷ ☐ = ☐

☐ × ☐ = ☐ ☐ ÷ ☐ = ☐

☐ × ☐ = ☐ ☐ ÷ ☐ = ☐

□ × □ = □   □ ÷ □ = □

□ × □ = □   □ ÷ □ = □

18 Oak has 3 packs of 10 football cards. She buys another 4 packs of 10 football cards. She then gives 2 packs to Jacob.

Oak gives Jacob □ cards.

She now has □ cards left.

19 Sam drew the invitations for the school concert so that 10 invitations can fit on each sheet of paper. He needs 35 invitations for the families and 15 invitations for the teachers.
How many sheets of invitations does Sam need to print?

Sam needs to print □ sheets of invitations.

Answers

Page 5 **1** 5 + 5 + 5 = 15, 3 groups of 5 = 15, 3 × 5 = 15
2 5 + 5 + 5 + 5 + 5 + 5 = 30, 6 groups of 5 = 30, 6 × 5 = 30

Page 7 2 × 2 = 4, 3 groups of 2 = 6, 3 × 2 = 6, 4 groups of 2 = 8, 4 × 2 = 8, 5 groups of 2 = 10, 5 × 2 = 10, 6 groups of 2 = 12, 6 × 2 = 12, 7 groups of 2 = 14, 7 × 2 = 14, 8 groups of 2 = 16, 8 × 2 = 16, 9 groups of 2 = 18, 9 × 2 = 18, 10 groups of 2 = 20, 10 × 2 = 20

Page 9 2 × 5 = 10, 3 groups of 5 = 15, 3 × 5 = 15, 4 groups of 5 = 20, 4 × 5 = 20, 5 groups of 5 = 25, 5 × 5 = 25, 6 groups of 5 = 30, 6 × 5 = 30, 7 groups of 5 = 35, 7 × 5 = 35, 8 groups of 5 = 40, 8 × 5 = 40, 9 groups of 5 = 45, 9 × 5 = 45, 10 groups of 5 = 50, 10 × 5 = 50

Page 11 **1 (a)** 4 groups of 10 = 40, 4 × 10 = 40 **(b)** 3 groups of 10 = 30, 3 × 10 = 30 **(c)** 7 groups of 10 = 70, 7 × 10 = 70 **2 (a)** 20 **(b)** 60 **(c)** 50 **(d)** 50

Page 13 **1 (a)** 5 × 3 = 3 × 5, 5 × 3 = 15, 3 × 5 = 15 **(b)** 2 × 4 = 8, 4 × 2 = 8

Page 14 **(c)** 6 × 10 = 60, 10 × 6 = 60

2

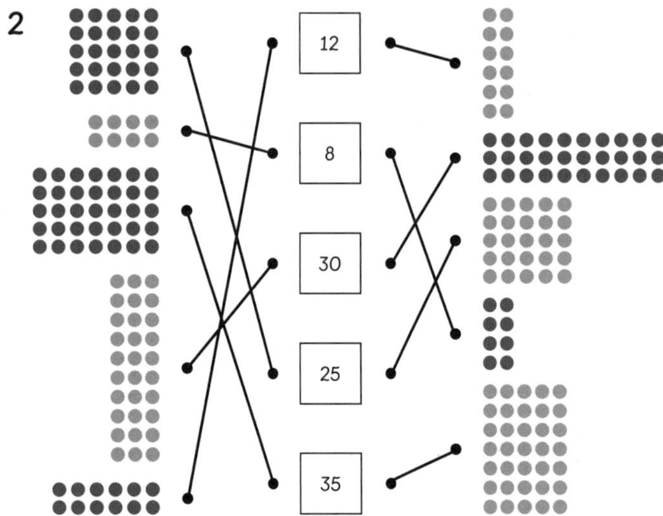

Page 15 **3 (a)** 4 × 5 = 20, 5 × 4 = 20 **(b)** 8 × 5 = 40, 5 × 8 = 40 **(c)** 2 × 6 = 12, 6 × 2 = 12

Page 17 **1** 5 × 4 = 20. The farmer needs 20 horseshoes. **2** 10 × 8 = 80. The children can take 80 rides altogether. **3** 9 × 2 = 18. The parlour uses 18 scoops of ice cream at lunchtime.

Page 19 **1** 15 ÷ 5 = 3. There are 3 groups. **2** 8 ÷ 2 = 4. There are 4 groups. **3 (a)** 8 ÷ 2 = 4 **(b)** 20 ÷ 5 = 4

Page 21 **1** 12 ÷ 2 = 6. There are 6 doughnuts on each plate. **2** 20 ÷ 5 = 4, 5 × 4 = 20 **3** 30 ÷ 3 = 10, 3 × 10 = 30

Page 23 **1** 20 ÷ 2 = 10. There are 10 boxes of 2 biscuits. **2** 16 ÷ 2 = 8. There are 8 grapes on each plate. **3 (a)** 4 **(b)** 8 **(c)** 20 **(d)** 10

Page 25 **1** 20 ÷ 5 = 4. There are 4 boxes of 5 drinks. **2** 10 ÷ 5 = 2. There are 2 cakes on each plate. **3 (a)** 4 **(b)** 10 **(c)** 7 **(d)** 25

Page 27 **1** 40 ÷ 10 = 4. There are 4 stacks of 10 counters. **2** 30 ÷ 10 = 3. There are 3 biscuits on each plate. **3 (a)** 2 **(b)** 6 **(c)** 80 **(d)** 100

Page 29 **1** 2 × 4 = 8, 8 ÷ 4 = 2, 4 × 2 = 8, 8 ÷ 2 = 4 **2** 3 × 4 = 12, 12 ÷ 3 = 4, 4 × 3 = 12, 12 ÷ 4 = 3 **3** 2 × 5 = 10, 10 ÷ 5 = 2, 5 × 2 = 10, 10 ÷ 2 = 5

Page 31 **1** 30 ÷ 5 = 6. Charles will need 6 bags. 6 × 5 = 30

Page 32 **2** 12 ÷ 2 = 6. 6 children get 2 footballs.

Page 33 **3 (a)** 16 ÷ 2 = 8. Elliott and Ravi each get 8 paper planes. **(b)** 100 ÷ 10 = 10. The baker fills 10 boxes.

Page 35 **1** The odd numbers are 7, 19, 27, 31, 53. The even numbers are 30, 36, 54, 58, 94. **2 (a)** 64 **(b)** 46 **(c)** 65 **(d)** 45

Page 36 **1** 5 + 5 + 5 + 5 + 5 + 5 = 30, 6 groups of 5 = 30, 6 × 5 = 30 **2 (a)** 2 **(b)** 4 **(c)** 10 **(d)** 30 **(e)** 20 **(f)** 14 **(g)** 14 **(h)** 16 **(i)** 25 **(j)** 80

Page 37 **3**

1	2	3	4	5	6	7	8	9	10
11	12	13	14	15	16	17	18	19	20
21	22	23	24	25	26	27	28	29	30
31	32	33	34	35	36	37	38	39	40
41	42	43	44	45	46	47	48	49	50

4

1	2	3	4	5	6	7	8	9	10
11	12	13	14	15	16	17	18	19	20
21	22	23	24	25	26	27	28	29	30
31	32	33	34	35	36	37	38	39	40
41	42	43	44	45	46	47	48	49	50
51	52	53	54	55	56	57	58	59	60
61	62	63	64	65	66	67	68	69	70
71	72	73	74	75	76	77	78	79	80
81	82	83	84	85	86	87	88	89	90
91	92	93	94	95	96	97	98	99	100

Page 38 **5 (a)** 4 groups of 5 = 20, 4 × 5 = 20 **(b)** 5 groups of 4 = 20, 5 × 4 = 20 **6 (a)** 10, 25, 30, 35, 40, 50 **(b)** 2, 6, 14, 20, 22 **(c)** 10, 30, 40, 50, 60, 70, 80, 90

Page 39 **7** 2 × 4 = 4 × 2 **8** 6 × 5 = 30. He puts 30 flowers in the vases in total.

Page 40 **9** 50 ÷ 5 = 10. Each friend gets 10 playing cards. **10** 45 ÷ 5 = 9. Jacob can fill 9 baskets.

Page 41 **11 (a)** 6 **(b)** 3 **(c)** 4 **(d)** 9 **(e)** 2 **(f)** 5 **(g)** 7 **(h)** 10 **12** 5 × 4 = 20, 20 ÷ 5 = 4, 4 × 5 = 20, 20 ÷ 4 = 5

Page 42 **13 (a)** 6 × 2 = 12, 12 ÷ 6 = 2, 2 × 6 = 12, 12 ÷ 2 = 6 **14** 60 ÷ 10 = 6. They need to bake 6 batches.
15 (a)

1	2	3	4	5	6	7	8	9	10
11	12	13	14	15	16	17	18	19	20
21	22	23	24	25	26	27	28	29	30
31	32	33	34	35	36	37	38	39	40

Page 43 **(b)**

1	2	3	4	5	6	7	8	9	10
11	12	13	14	15	16	17	18	19	20
21	22	23	24	25	26	27	28	29	30
31	32	33	34	35	36	37	38	39	40

16 (a) 86 **(b)** 68 **(c)** 87 **(d)** 67

Answers continued

Page 44–45 **17** $10 \times 4 = 40$, $4 \times 10 = 40$, $40 \div 4 = 10$, $40 \div 10 = 4$

Possible answers include: $8 \times 5 = 40$, $5 \times 8 = 40$, $40 \div 5 = 8$, $40 \div 8 = 5$

The next family of equations as follows: $20 \times 2 = 40$, $2 \times 20 = 40$, $40 \div 2 = 20$, $40 \div 20 = 2$

$40 \times 1 = 40$, $1 \times 40 = 40$, $40 \div 1 = 40$, $40 \div 40 = 1$

Page 45 **18** Oak gives Jacob 20 cards. She has 50 cards left. **19** Sam needs to print 5 sheets of invitations.

KS1
5–7
Years

Master Maths at Home

Measuring

Scan the QR code to help your child's learning at home.

MATHS NO PROBLEM!

mastermathsathome.com

How to use this book

Maths — No Problem! created **Master Maths at Home** to help children develop fluency in the subject and a rich understanding of core concepts.

Key features of the Master Maths at Home books include:

- Carefully designed lessons that provide structure but also allow flexibility in how they're used. For example, some children may want to write numbers, while others might want to trace.
- Speech bubbles containing content designed to spark diverse conversations, with many discussion points that don't have obvious 'right' or 'wrong' answers.
- Rich illustrations that will guide children to a discussion of shapes and units of measurement, allowing them to make connections to the wider world around them.
- Exercises that allow a flexible approach and can be adapted to suit any child's cognitive or functional ability.
- Clearly laid out pages that encourage children to practise a range of higher-order skills.
- A community of friendly and relatable characters who introduce each lesson and come along as your child progresses through the series.

You can see more guidance on how to use these books at **mastermathsathome.com.**

We're excited to share all the ways you can learn maths!

Maths — No Problem!
mastermathsathome.com
www.mathsnoproblem.com
hello@mathsnoproblem.com

First published in Great Britain in 2022 by
Dorling Kindersley Limited
One Embassy Gardens, 8 Viaduct Gardens, London SW11 7BW
A Penguin Random House Company

The authorised representative in the EEA is Dorling Kindersley Verlag GmbH. Amulfstr. 124, 80636 Munich, Germany

10 9 8 7 6 5 4 3 2 1
001–327074–Jan/22

This book was made with Forest Stewardship Council™ certified paper - one small step in DK's commitment to a sustainable future. For more information go to www.dk.com/our-green-pledge

A CIP catalogue record for this book is available from the British Library.

ISBN: 978-0-24153-917-0
Printed and bound in China

For the curious
www.dk.com

Acknowledgements
The publisher would like to thank the authors and consultants Andy Psarianos, Judy Hornigold, Adam Gifford and Dr Anne Hermanson.

The Castledown typeface has been used with permission from the Colophon Foundry.

Contents

Ruby
Elliott
Amira
Charles
Lulu
Sam
Oak
Holly
Ravi
Emma
Jacob
Hannah

Measuring length in metres

Lesson
1

Starter

How is Ravi measuring the table?

Example

Ravi is using a metre stick to measure the table.

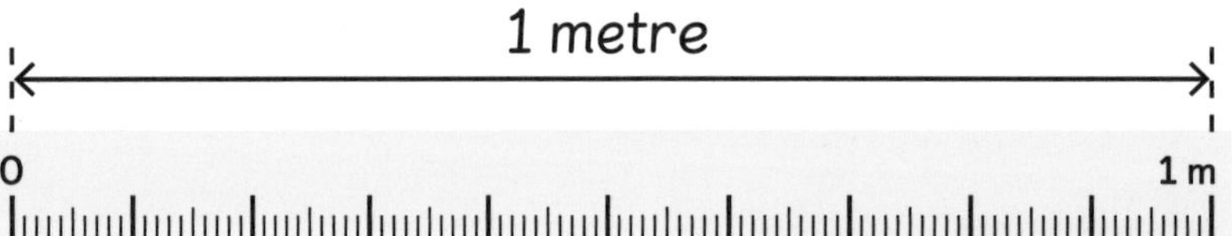

This is a metre stick. It is 1 metre long. The width of the table is exactly 1 m. We can measure the lengths of objects around us.

A metre is a unit of length. We write this as 1 m.

coffee table

dining table

Practice

1 Ask an adult at home if they have a tape measure.
Look for objects at home that measure more than 1 m and less than 1 m.
Try and guess the length of each object before measuring it.

Record your results in a table.

Less than 1 m	More than 1 m

2 Ask an adult to help you measure your own height.

I am [ ] (less / more) than a metre tall.

3 How tall do you think a two-storey house is in metres?

I think a two-storey house is about [ ] m tall.

Measuring length in centimetres

Lesson
2

Starter

What can we use to measure shorter things?

Example

We can use a ruler to measure shorter things.

This is a centimetre ruler.
It is about 15 cm long.

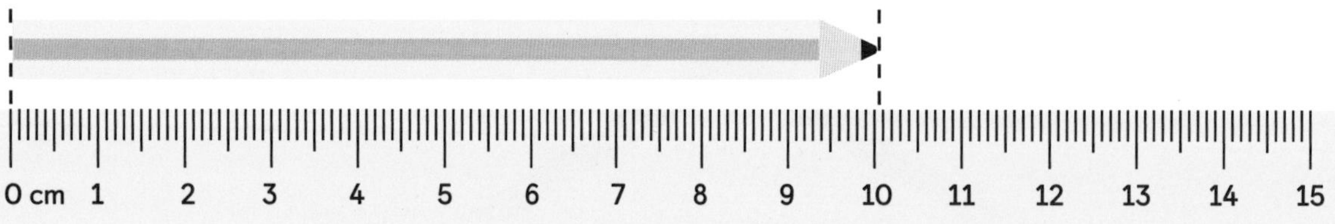

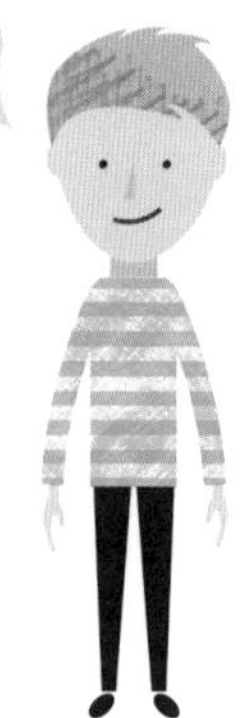

The pencil is 10 cm long.

We must line up the item
with 0 cm on the ruler

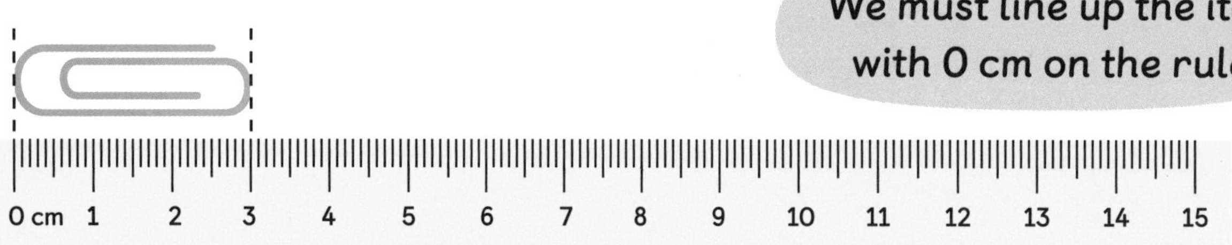

The paper clip is 3 cm long.

Practice

1 Find these items in your home and use a centimetre ruler to measure them. Record your results in a table.

Item	Length in cm
spoon	
toothbrush	
crayon	
book	
mobile phone	
envelope	
hairbrush	

2 Measure the length of these items using a centimetre ruler.

(a)

?

about ☐ cm

(b)

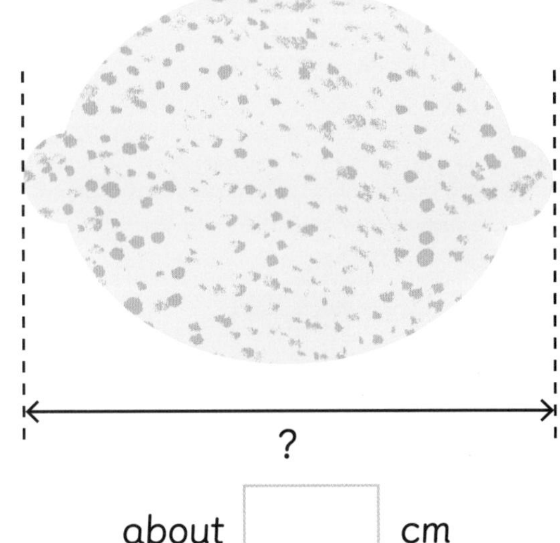

?

about ☐ cm

Comparing lengths

Lesson 3

Starter

Which item is the longest?

Example

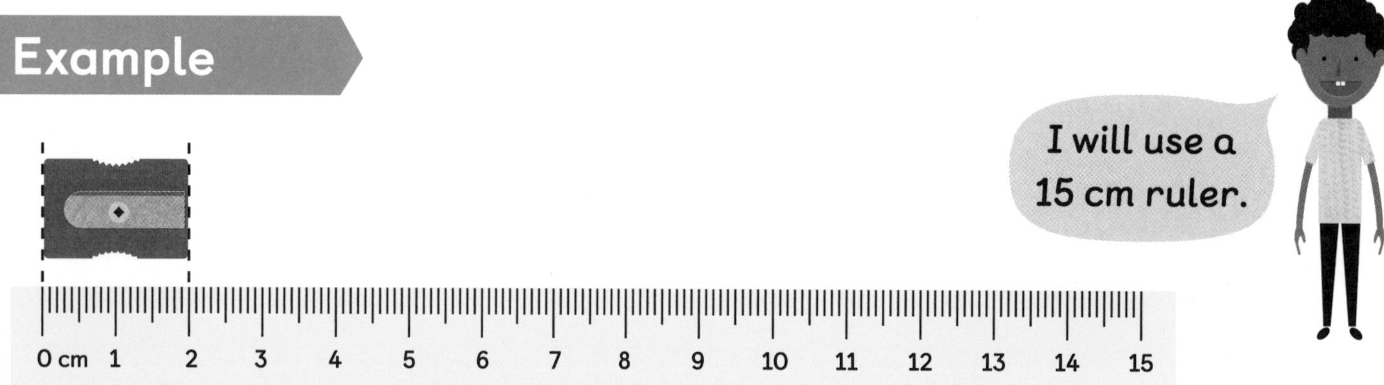

The pencil sharpener is 2 cm long. It is the shortest item.

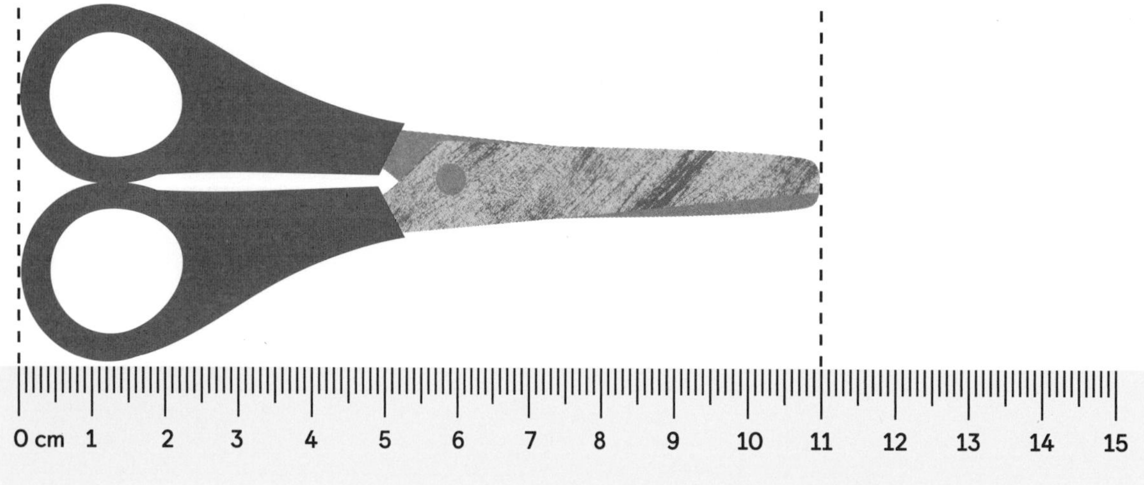

The scissors are 11 cm long. They are the longest item.

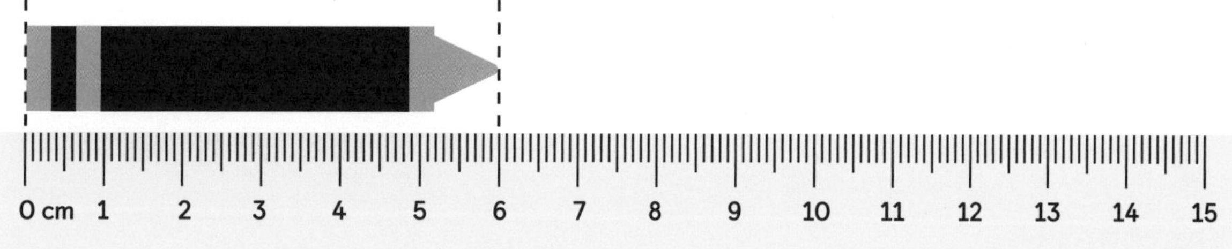

The crayon is 6 cm long. The crayon is longer than the pencil sharpener and shorter than the scissors.

Practice

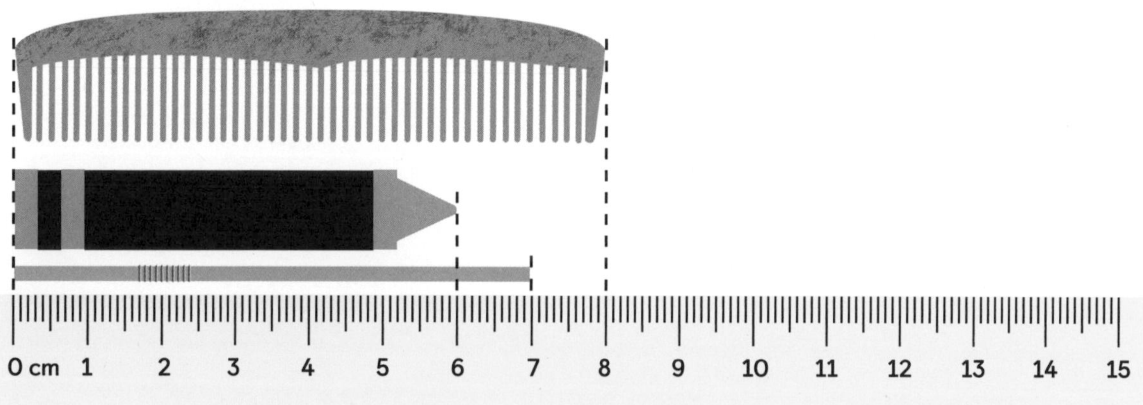

Compare the lengths and fill in the blanks.

1. The is cm long.
2. The is cm long.
3. The is cm long.
4. The is cm longer than the .
5. The is cm shorter than the .
6. The is the longest.
7. The is the shortest.

Measuring mass in kilograms

Lesson 4

Starter

How can we find out how heavy the vegetables are?

Example

We can measure mass by using a weighing scale.

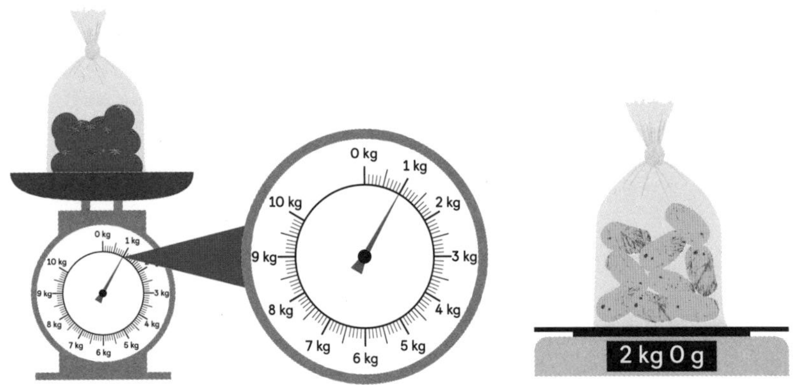

The mass of something tells us how heavy it is.

The tomatoes have a mass of 1 kg.
The potatoes have a mass of 2 kg.

We can also use balance scales and a weight to find out how heavy something is.

This is a one-kilogram mass.
A **kilogram** is a unit of mass.
We write **kg** for kilogram.

The bag of rice balances with the 1 kg mass.
The bag of rice has a mass of 1 kg.

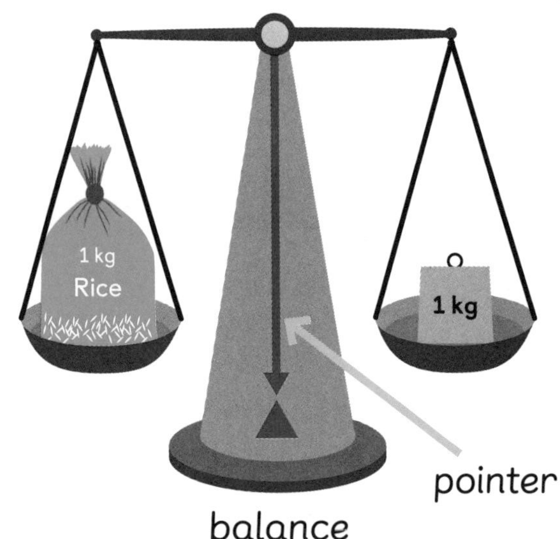

The bag of oranges is **lighter than** 1 kg.
The mass of the bag of oranges is **less than** 1 kg.

The bag of onions is **heavier** than 1 kg.
The mass of the bag of onions is **more than** 1 kg.

Practice

1 Find something in your kitchen that has a mass of 1 kg, such as a bag of flour or sugar.
Find an item that you think is heavier than this.
Find an item that you think is lighter than this.
If you have a weighing scale, find the mass of your items to see if you are correct.

2 Find the mass of the watermelon.

The mass of the watermelon is about ☐ kg.

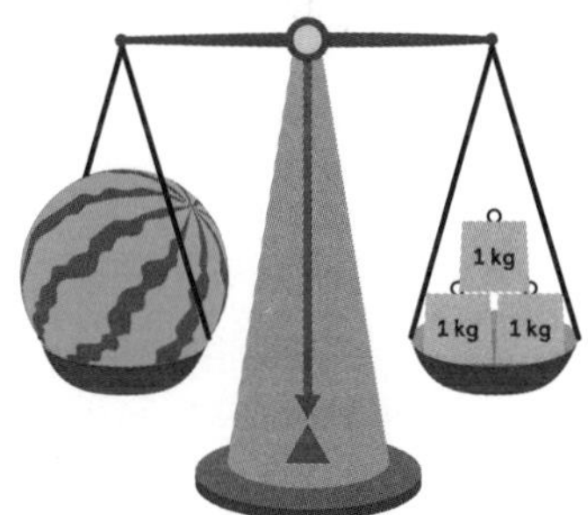

3 What is the mass of each item?

(a)

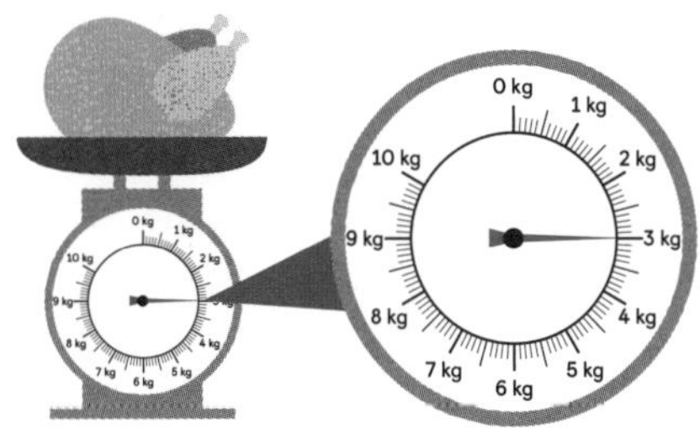

☐ kg

(b)

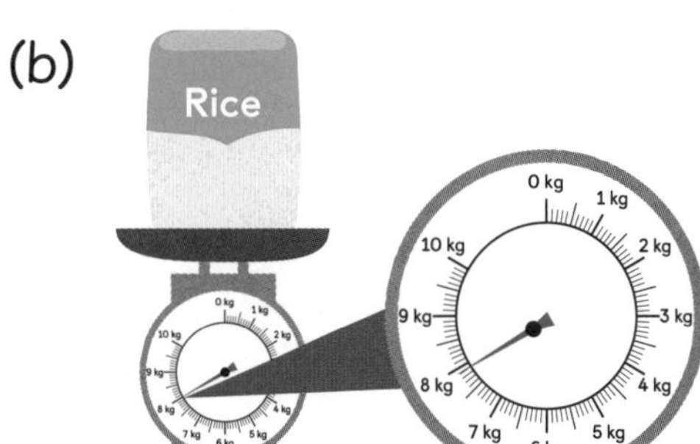

☐ kg

Measuring mass in grams

Lesson 5

Starter

These items are light.
How can we find the mass of these items?

Example

We can't measure these items in kilograms. We need a smaller unit of mass.

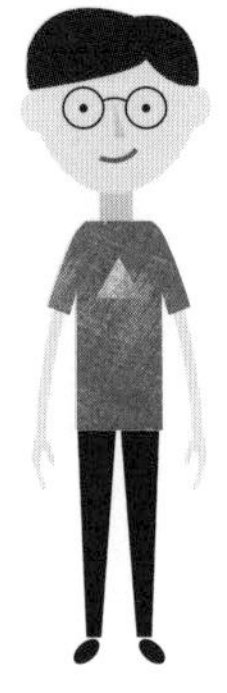

We can measure lighter objects using grams. We write g for gram.

These are some things that have a mass of 1 g.

The paper clip has a mass of 1 g.

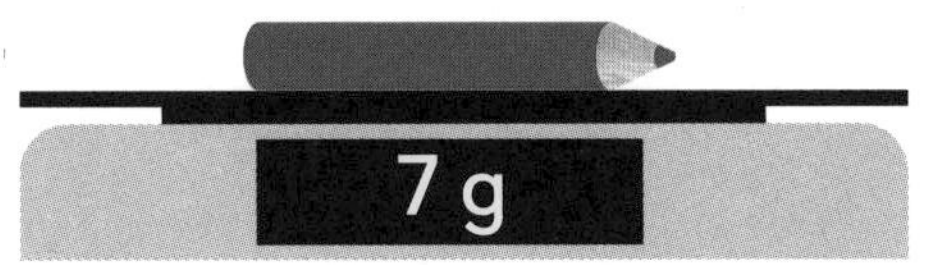

The pencil has a mass of 7 g.

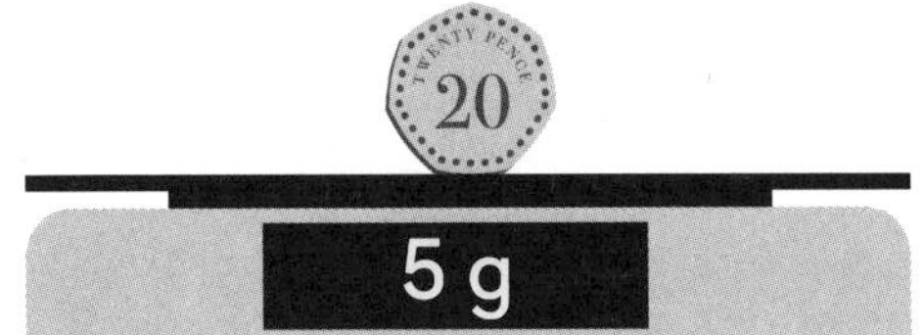

The 20p coin has a mass of 5 g.

The rubber has a mass of 10 g.

The rubber is the heaviest and the paper clip is the lightest.

Practice

1 Look at some items in your home that are measured in grams. List them in order from lightest to heaviest in the table.

Item	Mass in grams

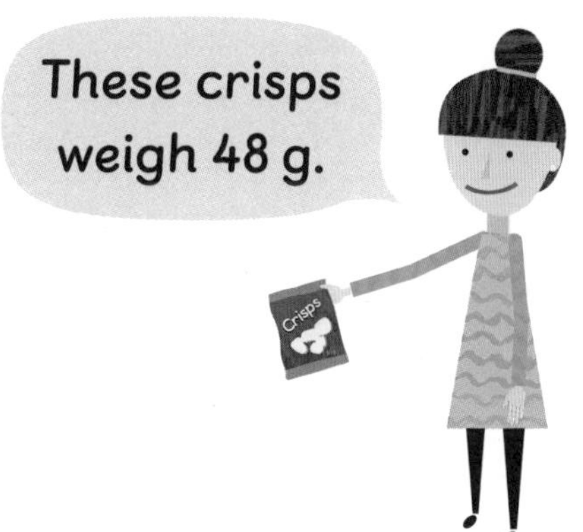

2 Find the mass of each item below.

(a)

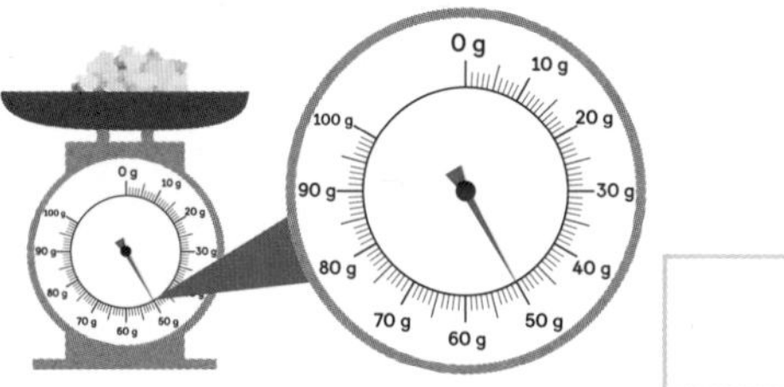

☐ g

(b)

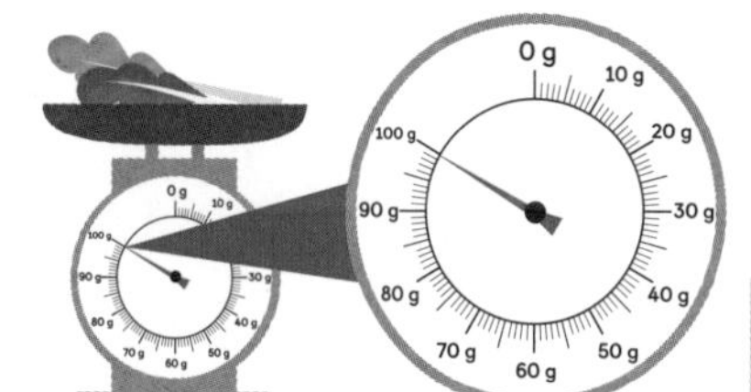

☐ g

(c)

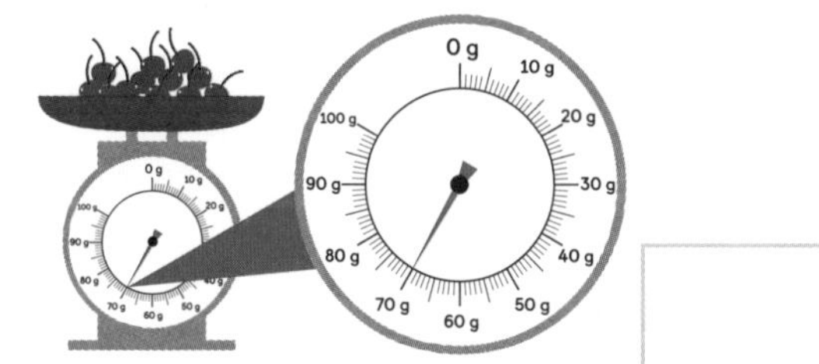

☐ g

(d)

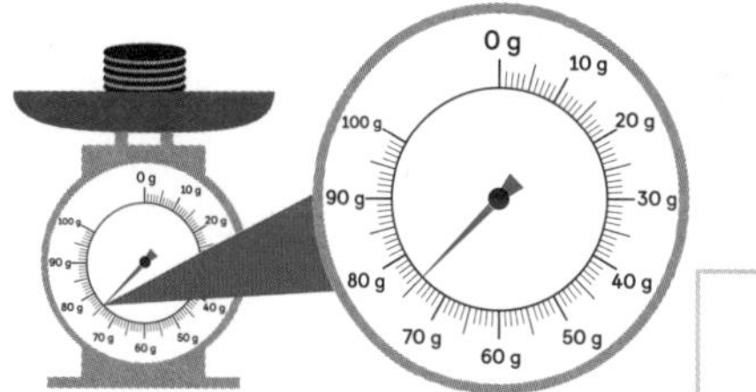

☐ g

3 Find the mass of each item below.

(a)

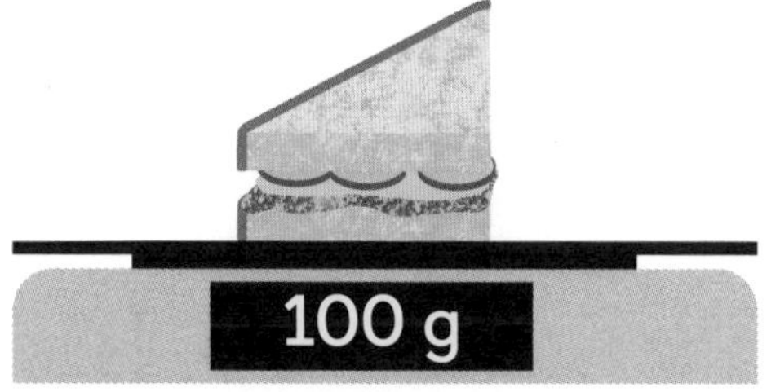

The sandwich weighs about ☐ g.

(b)

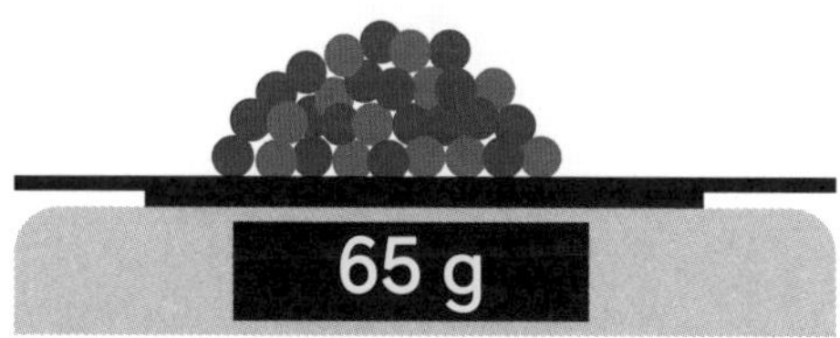

The mass of the blueberries is about ☐ g.

Comparing masses

Lesson 6

Starter

How can we find out which is heavier?

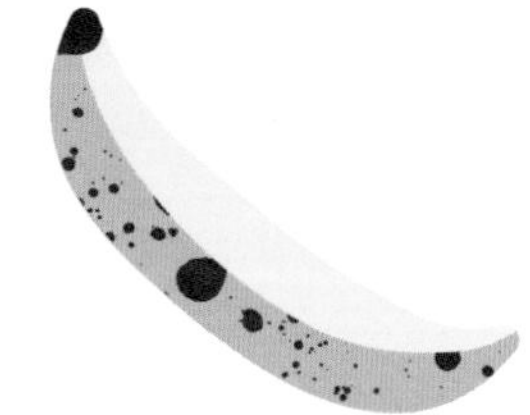

Example

There are 10 spaces between 100 and 200.
Each space stands for 10 g. This scale shows 120 g.

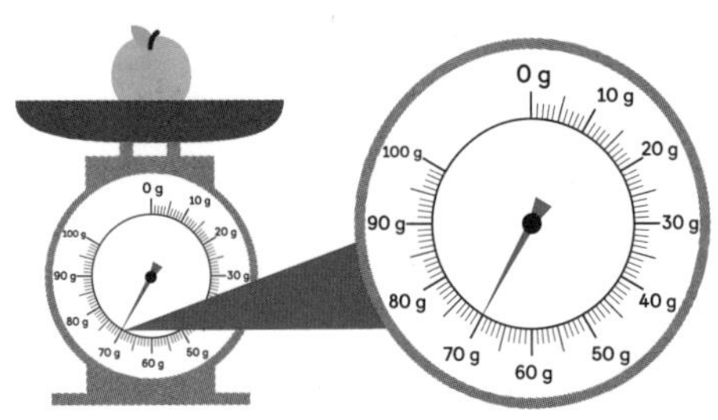

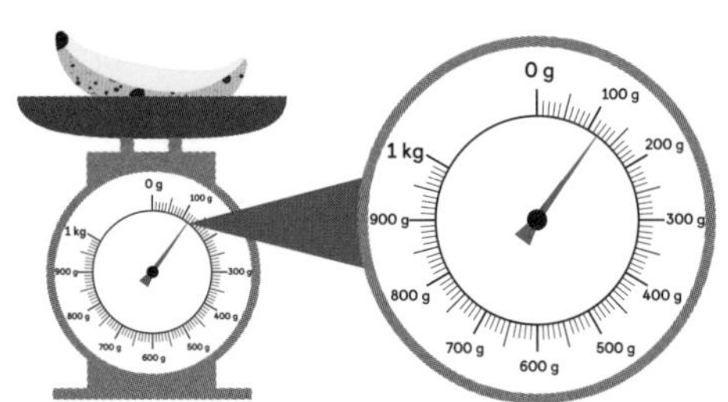

 has a mass of 70 g.

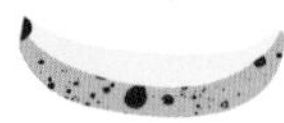 has a mass of 120 g.

 is heavier than .

 is lighter than .

Practice

1 Read the scales, then fill in the blanks.

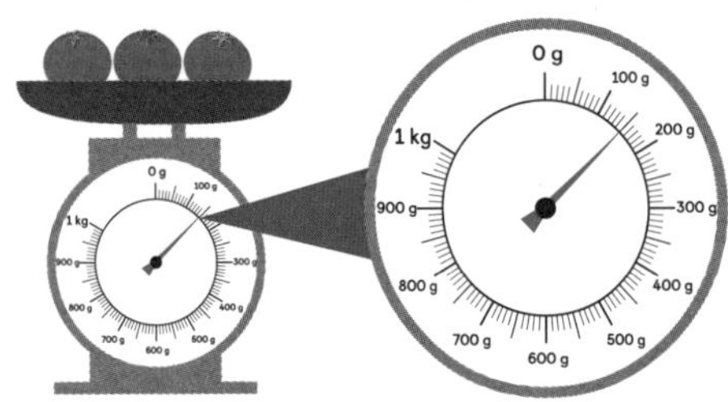

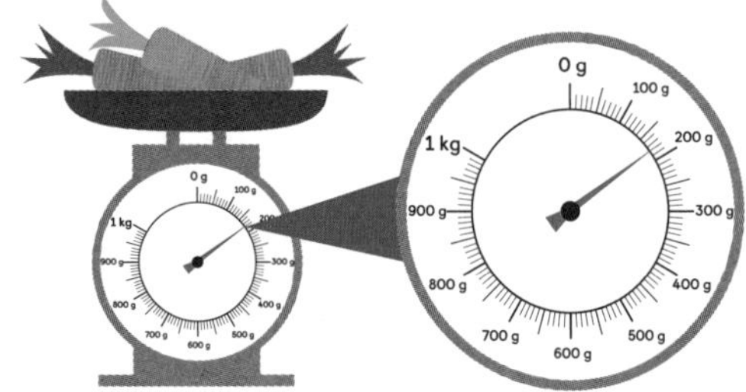

(a) The ______ are heavier.

(b) The ______ are lighter.

(c) The mass of the tomatoes is about ______ g.

(d) The mass of the carrots is about ______ g.

(e) The carrots are ______ g ______ (heavier / lighter) than the tomatoes.

(f) The tomatoes are ______ g ______ (heavier / lighter) than the carrots.

2 Read the scales, then fill in the blanks.

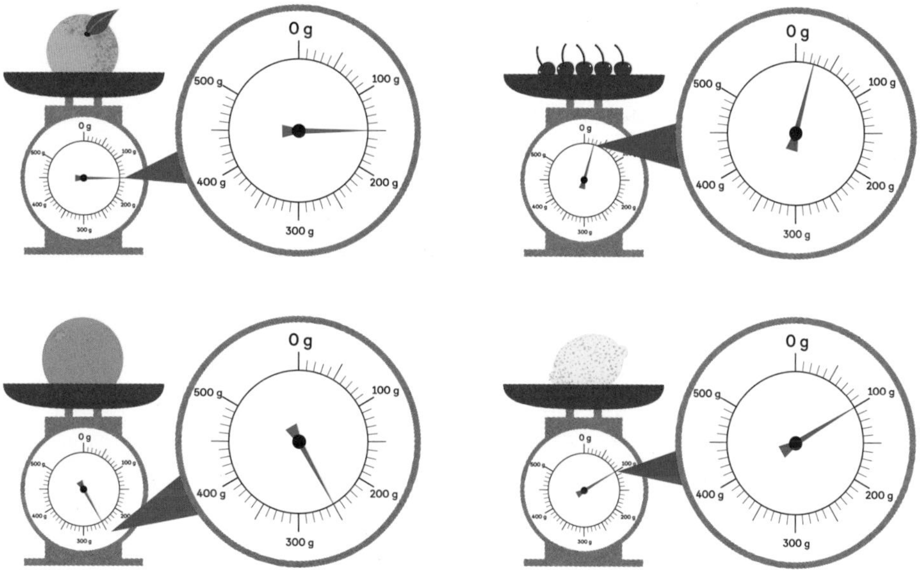

(a) The mass of the ______ is ______ g more than the mass of the ______.

(b) The ______ have the lightest mass.

(c) The ______ and ______ together have the same mass as the ______.

Temperature

Lesson 7

Starter

How do we measure temperature?

I have a digital thermometer.

I have a glass thermometer.

Example

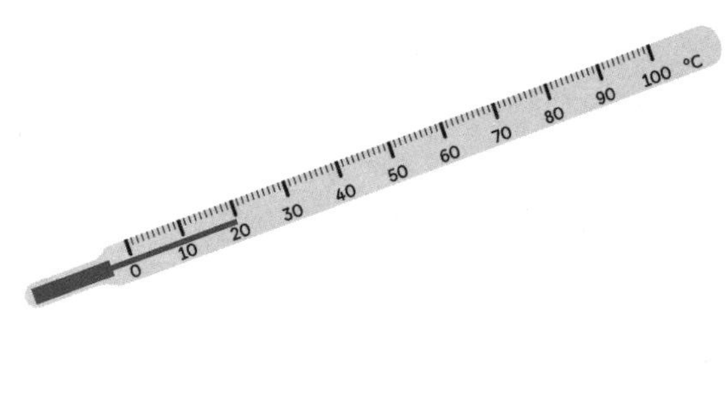

This is a **thermometer**. It measures how cold or hot something is.

We use a thermometer to measure temperature.
Temperature is measured in **degrees Celsius**.
This thermometer shows a temperature of 20 °C.
We read this as 20 degrees Celsius.

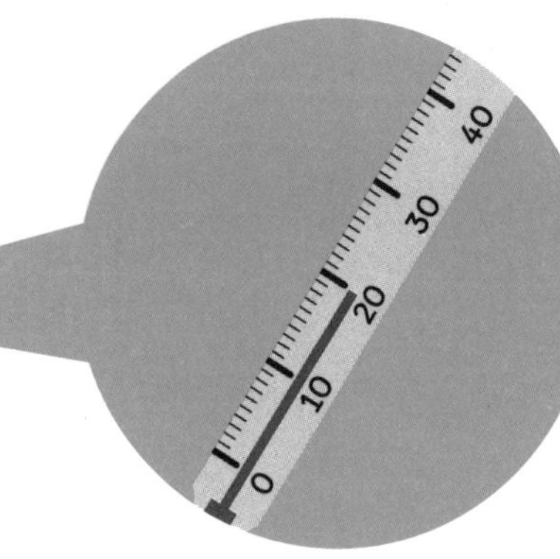

Practice

1 Ask an adult in your home if they have a thermometer.
Use the thermometer to find the temperature of everyone in your family.
Record your results in a table.

Family member	Body temperature

2 Fill in the blanks.

(a)

The body temperature of Charles is about ☐ °C.

(b)

The temperature of the tea is about ☐ °C.

(c)

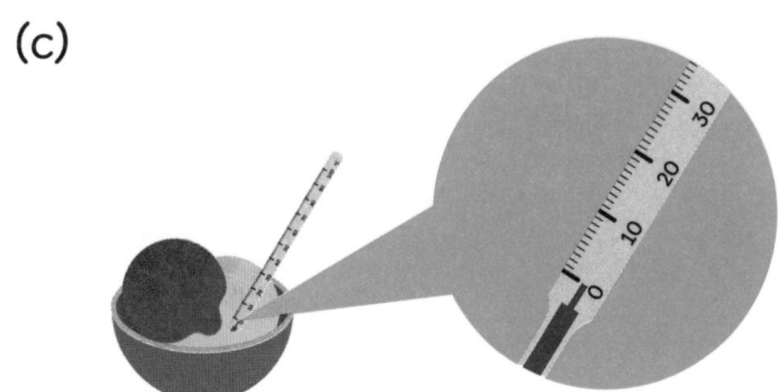

The temperature of the ice cream is about ☐ °C.

Writing and counting notes

Lesson 8

Starter

Who has more money?

Charles

Lulu

Example

This is a **five pound note**. We write it as **£5**.

This is a **ten pound note**. We write it as **£10**.

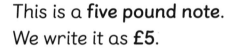

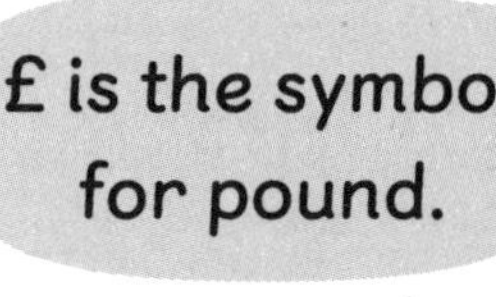

 has  +  +  .

He has £25.

 has  +  +  +  .

She has £20.

Practice

1 Write the amount of money shown.

(a) £ [ ]

(b) £ [ ]

(c) £ [ ]

(d)  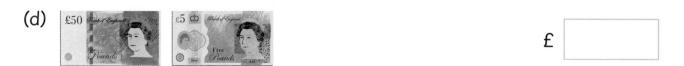 £ [ ]

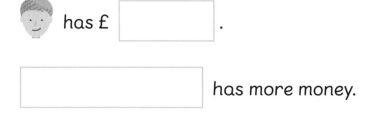

2 Who has more money?

has £ [ ] .

has £ [ ] .

[ ] has more money.

Writing and counting coins

Lesson 9

Starter

Does Elliott have enough money to buy the 

?

Example

These are the coins that we use in the UK.

These coins are in pence.
1p, 2p, 5p, 10p, 20p and 50p.

These coins are in pounds.
£1 and £2.

Elliott has £2 + 50p + 20p + 10p + 5p + 5p.
Elliott has £2 and 90 pence. We write this as £2.90.
The chocolate costs £3.
Elliott does not have enough money.

Practice

1 Match.

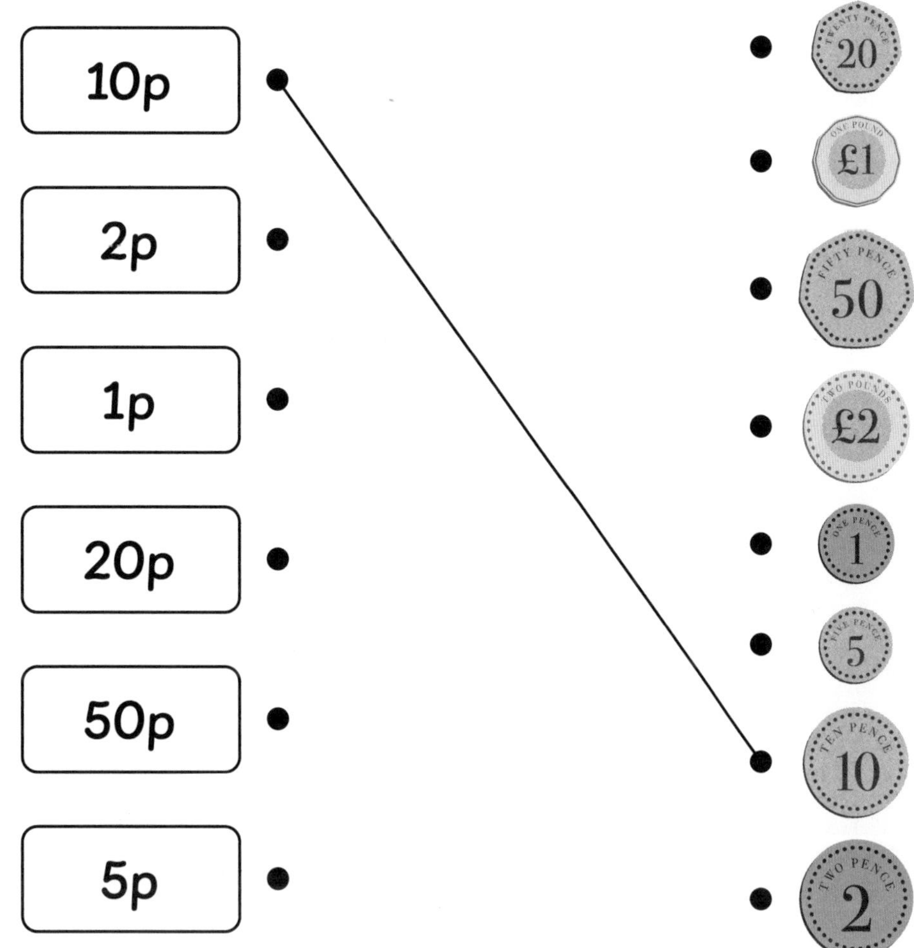

2 How much money is shown?

(a)

(b)

Showing equal amounts of money

Lesson
10

Starter

I have six coins.

I have more money.
I have seven coins.

Who has more money?

Example

1

Add the value of the coins, not the number of coins.

2, 3
3 pounds

50, 60, 65, 70
70 pence

Jacob has £2 + £1 + 50p + 10p + 5p + 5p
= £3 + 70p = £3.70

1, 2, 3
3 pounds

20, 40, 60, 70
70 pence

Emma has £1 + £1 + £1 + 20p + 20p + 20p + 10p
= £3 + 70p = £3.70

Emma is wrong. Jacob and Emma have the same amount of money.

Practice

1 Match equal amounts of money.

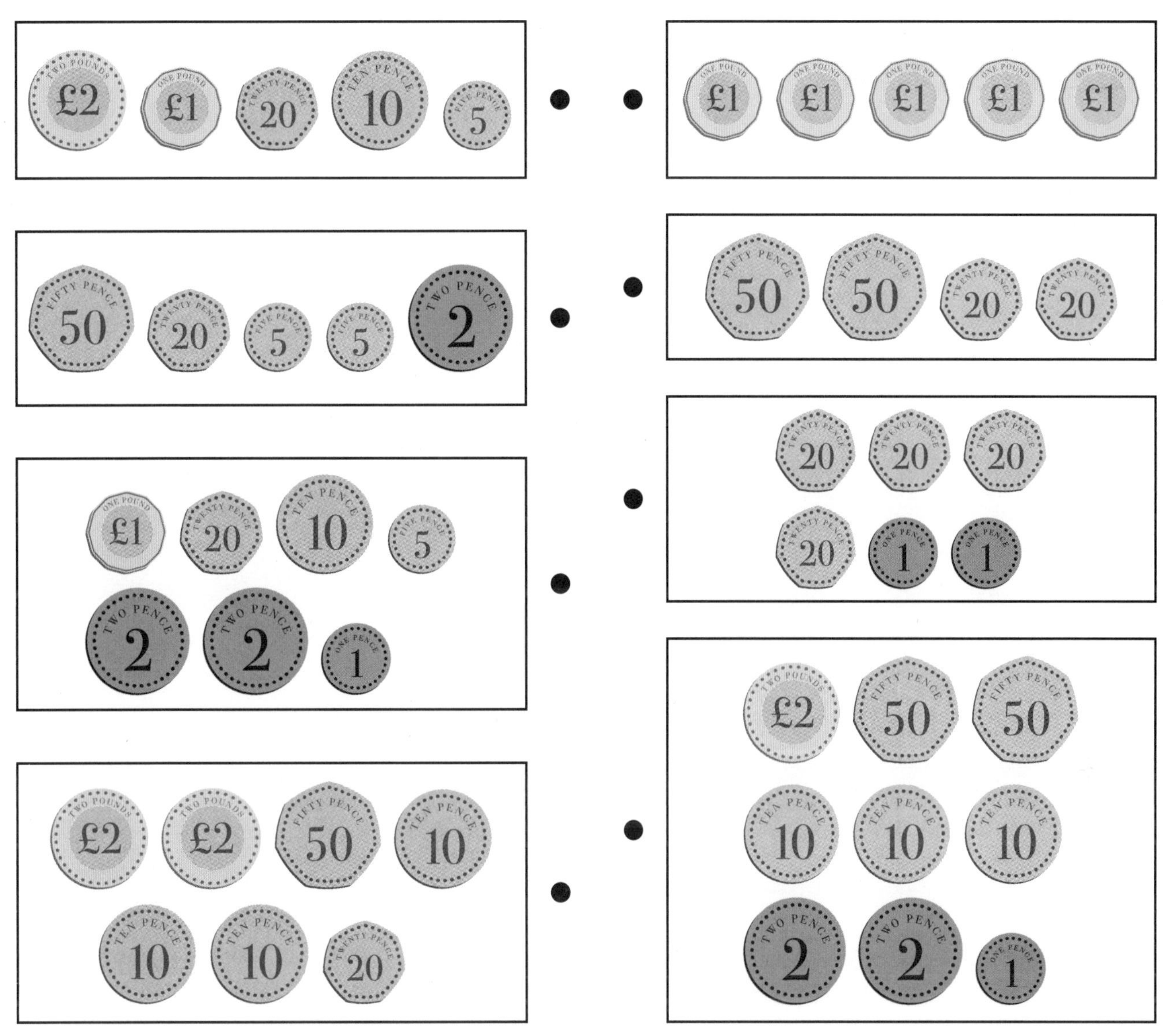

2 Can you make £1 using 50, 20 and 10?

Try to find 4 different ways.

Exchanging money

Lesson 11

Starter

Amira wants to exchange one £2 coin for different coins.
What coins can she get for £2?

Example

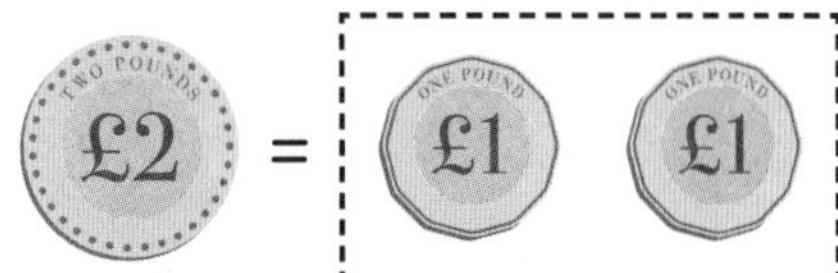

Amira can exchange £2 for 2 £1.

Amira can exchange £2 for 4 50.

Amira can exchange £2 for 10 20.

Practice

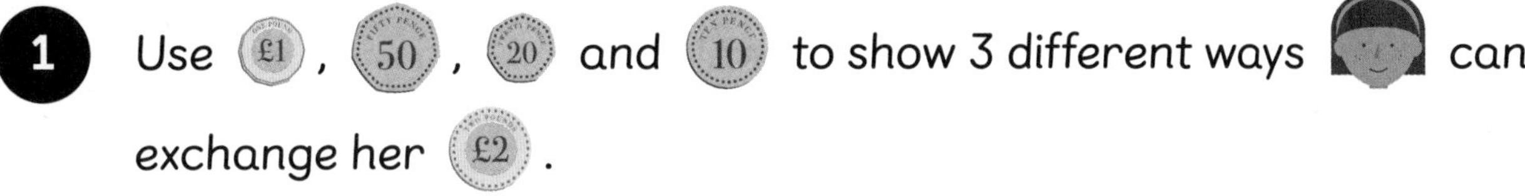

1 Use £1, 50, 20 and 10 to show 3 different ways can exchange her £2.

2 Fill in the blanks.

(a)

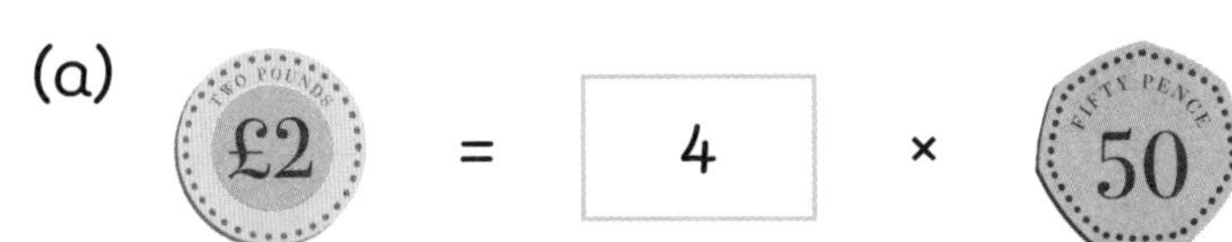

£2 = 4 × 50

(b) £1 = ☐ × 20

(c) £1 = ☐ × 10

(d) 50 = ☐ × 5

(e) 20 = ☐ × 5

(f) 20 = ☐ × 2

Comparing amounts of money

Starter

Which toy costs more?

Example

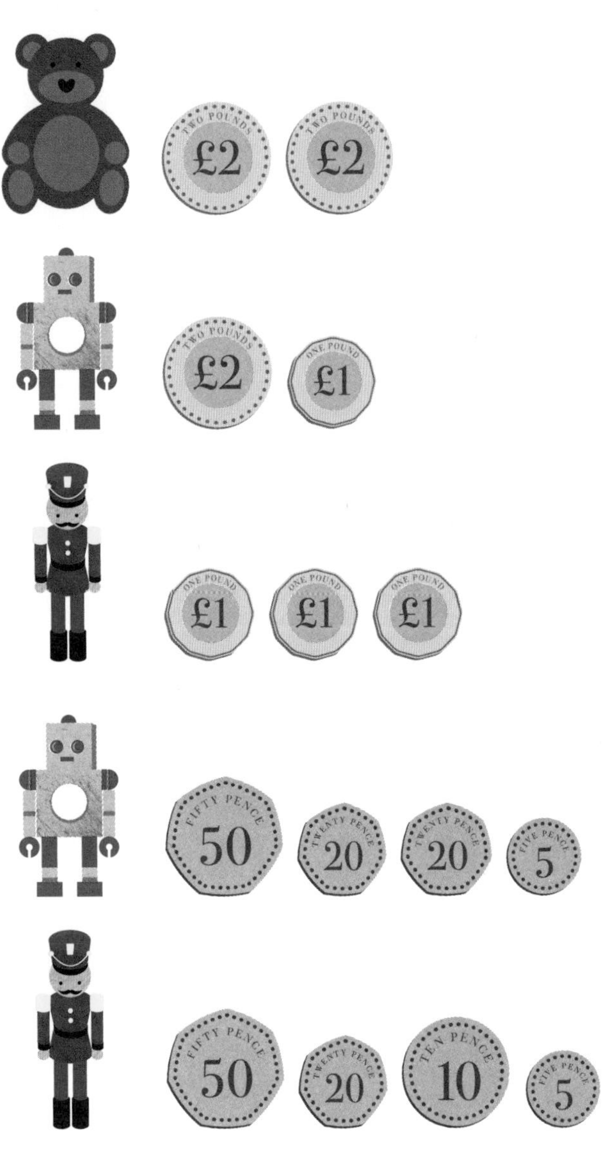

First, we compare the pounds.

£4 is more than £3. The costs more than the and the .

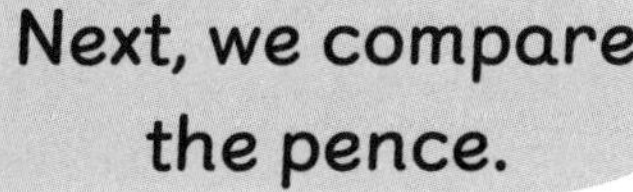

Next, we compare the pence.

95p is more than 85p. The costs more than the .

 costs more than  and .

Practice

1 Compare the two boxes and circle the one with the largest amount of money.

(a)

(b)

(c)

(d)

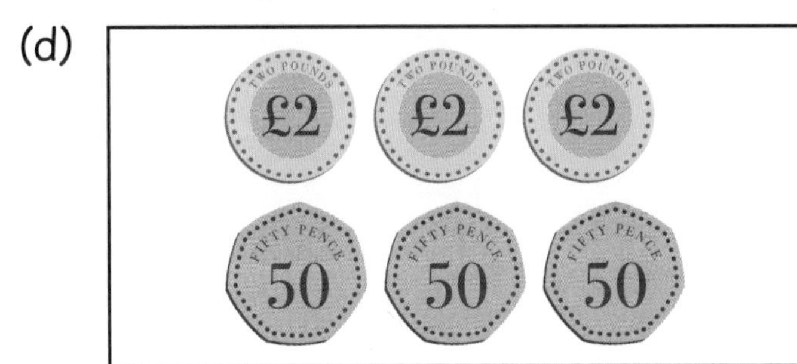

2 Compare the amounts of money and fill in the blanks.

Ruby

Amira

Sam

(a) Who has the most amount of money?

(b) Who has the least amount of money?

(c) How much more money does Amira have than Ruby?

Telling the time to 5 minutes

Lesson 13

Starter

What time do these clocks show?

Example

The time is 3 o'clock.
The hour hand is on 3 and the minute hand is on 12.

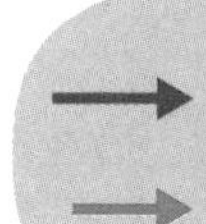

The minute hand is always longer than the hour hand.

The time is 5 minutes after 3 o'clock.
The minute hand has moved from 12 to 1.
It takes 5 minutes for the minute hand to move from 12 to 1.

We write this as 3:05 and we read it as 5 past three.

3:10

3:10 is 10 past 3.

3:25

3:25 is 25 past 3.

Practice

1 What is the time shown?

(a)

(b)

(c)

(d)

2 Write the time shown. Think about what you might be doing at that time.

(a)

in the morning

(b)

in the afternoon

(c)

in the evening

3 Show the correct time by drawing the hour and minute hands.

(a)

3:35

(b)

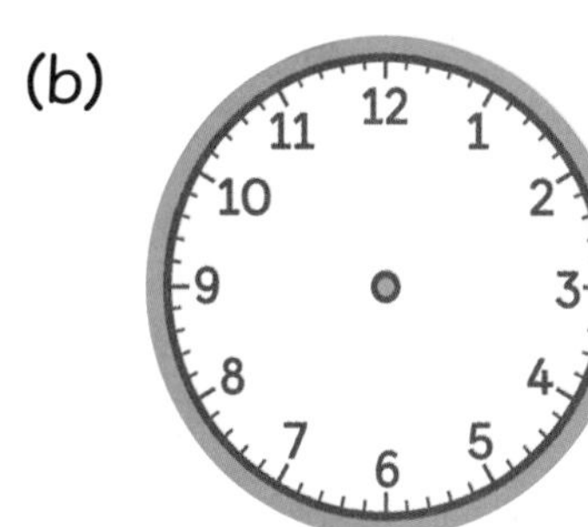

9:45

Telling and writing the time

Lesson 14

Starter

What time does this clock show?

Example

It is 15 minutes past 8 or 8:15.
The minute hand is a quarter of the way around the clock.

We can also say the time is quarter past 8.

After 15 more minutes, the minute hand is halfway around the clock.

It is half past 8.

Now the minute hand is three quarters of the way around the clock. It has a quarter turn until it reaches 12 again.

We say the time is 8:45 or quarter to 9.

Practice

1 Fill in the blanks using **quarter past, half past** or **quarter to.**

(a)

The time is

[ ] 3.

(b)

The time is

 10.

(c)

The time is

[ ] 12.

2 Draw the missing hour and minute hands on the clocks to show:

(a) 1 o'clock

(b) quarter past 4

(c) half past 10

(d) quarter to 5

Finding durations of time

Lesson 15

Starter

Lulu started reading at 3:30 and finished at 4:00.
For how long did she read?

start

end

Example

Count in fives from 3:30 to 4:00.

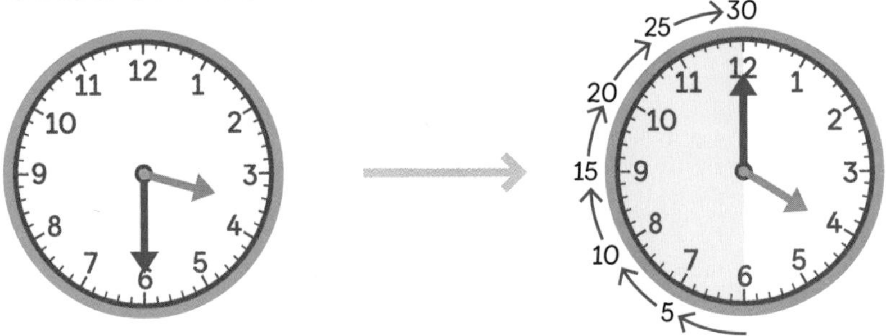

Lulu read for 30 minutes.

Practice

1 Write the time shown on each clock. Draw the missing hour and minute hands on the clocks to show the new time.

(a)

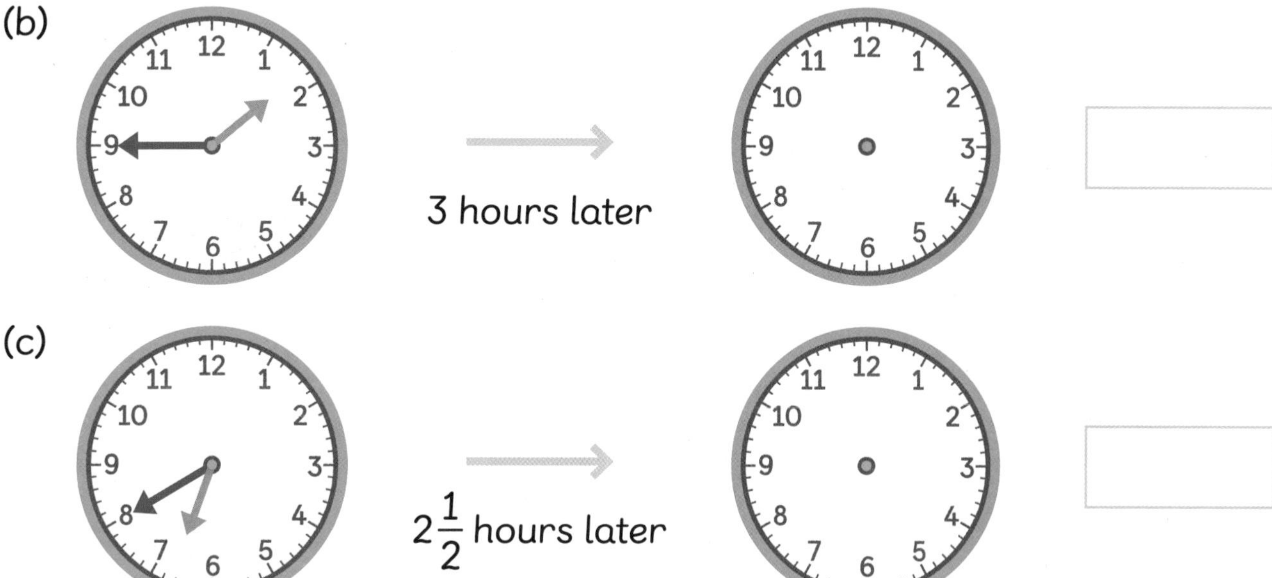

2 Complete the table.

Start time	What time will it be in half an hour?	What time will it be in 2 hours?

Finding ending times

Lesson 16

Starter

School assembly starts in 15 minutes.
The assembly lasts for 35 minutes.
At what time does assembly end?

Example

In 15 minutes, the time will be 9:00.

This is the time assembly starts.

School assembly lasts for 35 minutes.

35 minutes later

Assembly finishes at 9:35.

Practice

1 Write the time shown on each clock. Draw the missing hour and minute hands on the clocks to show the new time.

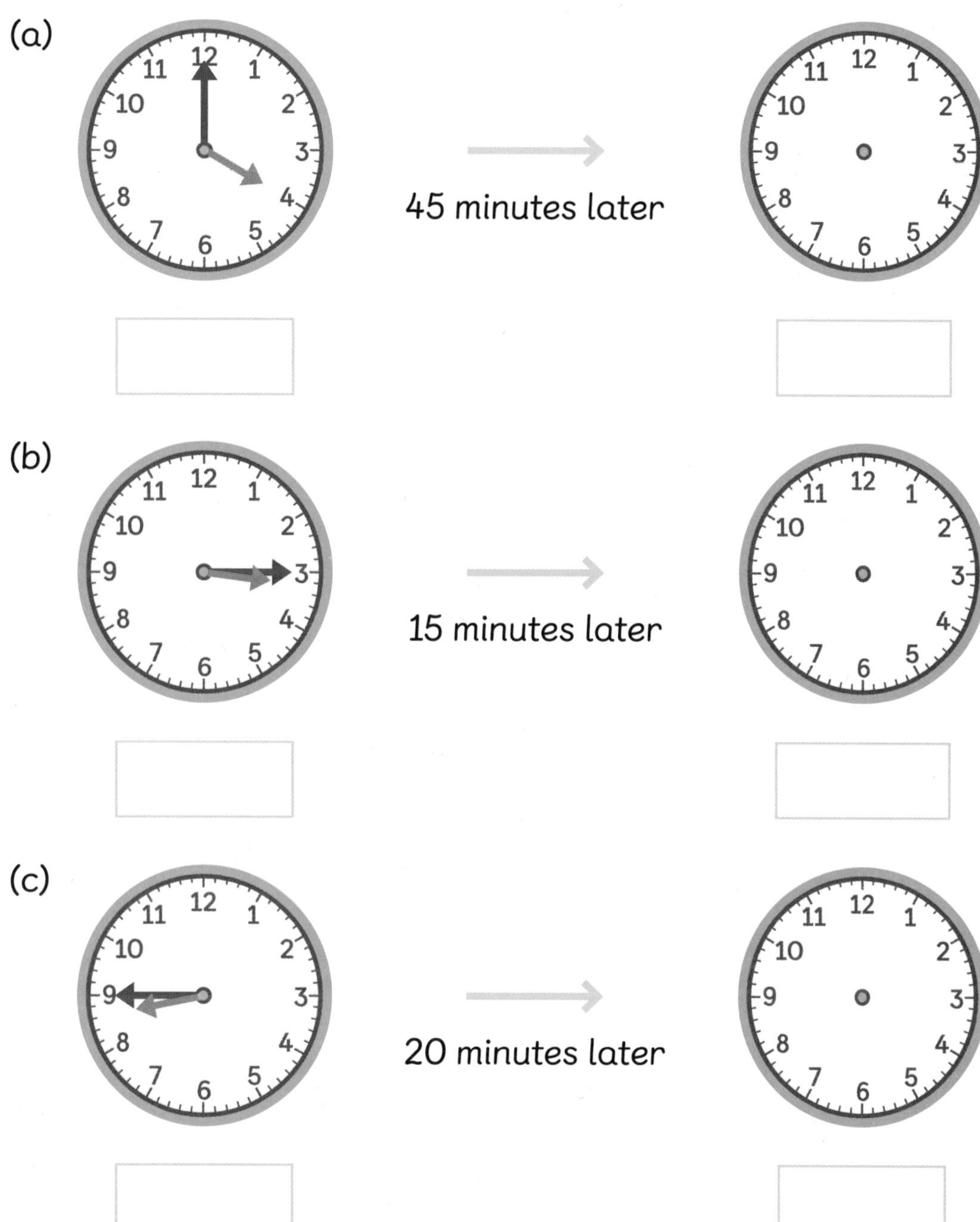

Finding starting times

Lesson 17

Starter

Lulu has been swimming for 30 minutes.
The time now is:

At what time did Lulu start swimming?

Example

What was the time 30 minutes ago?

It was half past 4.
Lulu started swimming at 4:30.

Practice

1 Draw the clock hands to show the start times.

(a)

30 minutes later

(b)

15 minutes later

(c)

1 hour later

(d)

45 minutes later

2 A TV programme ended at 6:30. The programme was an hour long. At what time did the programme start?

The TV programme started at  .

Measuring volume in litres

Lesson 18

Starter

How can we find the volume of liquid in each container?

Example

We can measure volume using a 1-litre beaker.

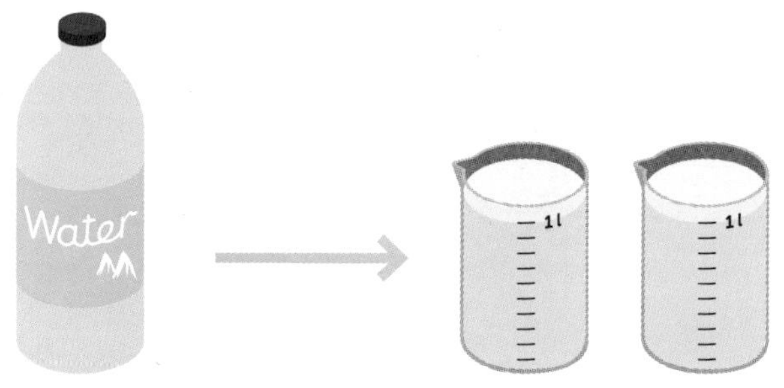

Volume is the amount of liquid in a container.

The volume of water is about 2 **litres**.
We can write this as 2 l.

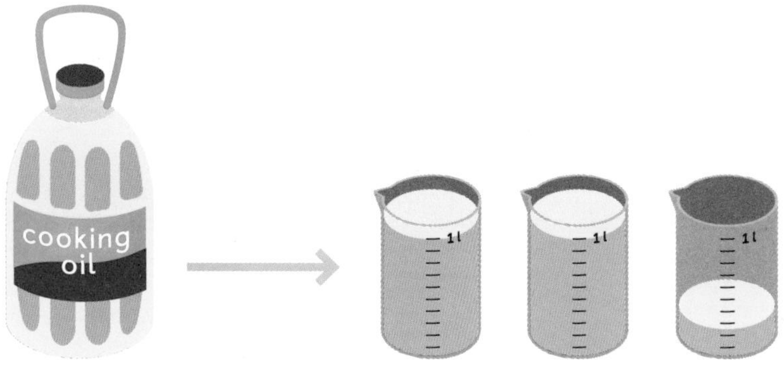

The volume of cooking oil is more than 2 litres.

Practice

1 Find some containers with liquid in your kitchen. Guess the volume of liquid in each container and then measure the actual volume using a measuring jug. Record your results in a table.

Item	Guessed volume (in l)	Measured volume (in l)

2 What is the volume of liquid in each container?

(a)

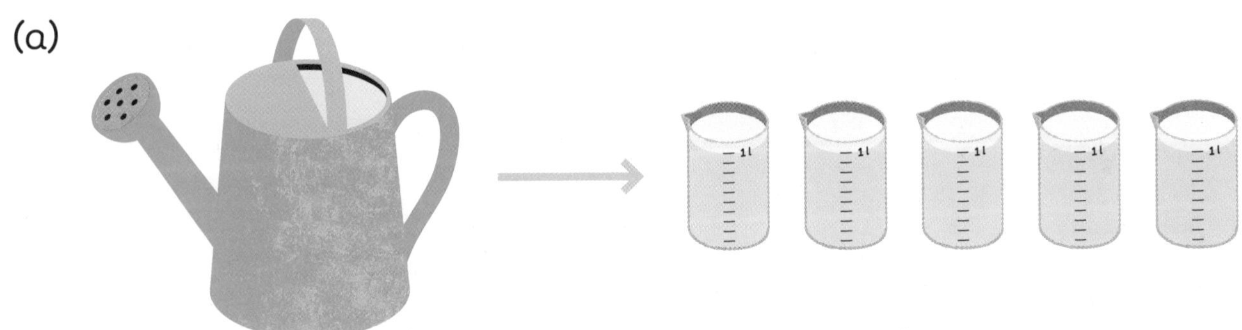

The volume of water in the watering can is ☐ l.

(b)

The volume of chocolate milk in the carton is ☐ l.

Measuring volume in millilitres

Lesson 19

Starter

How can we measure smaller volumes of liquid?

Example

We can measure smaller volumes of liquid in **millilitres**. We write this as **ml**.

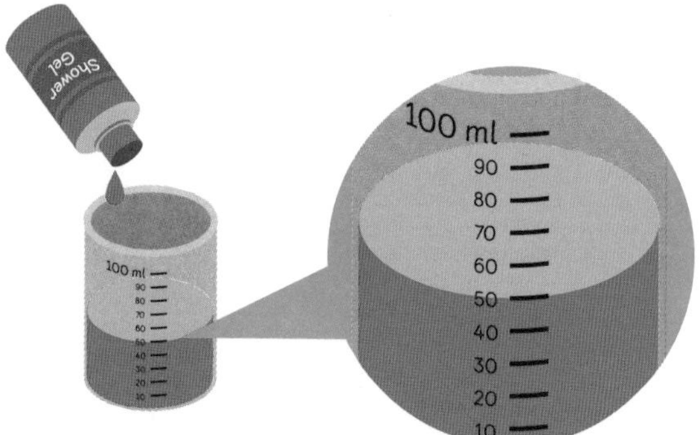

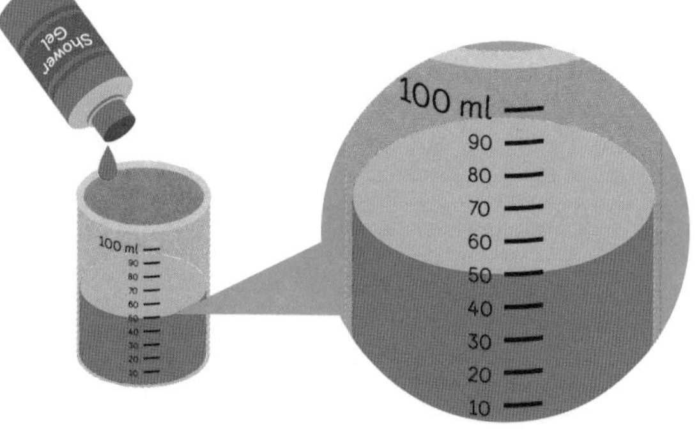

Volume of shower gel = 50 ml

Volume of shower gel = 70 ml

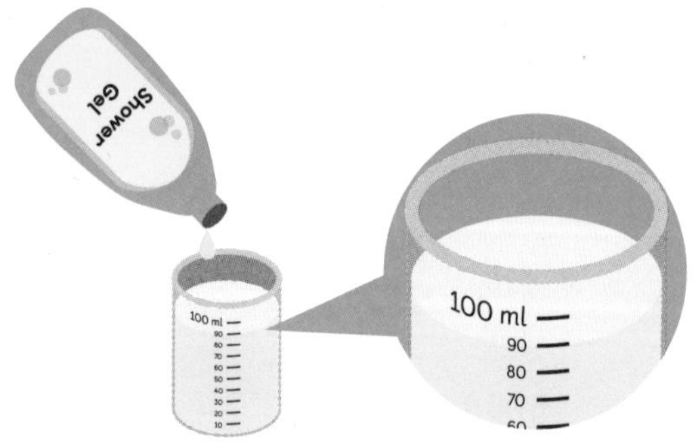

Volume of shower gel = 90 ml

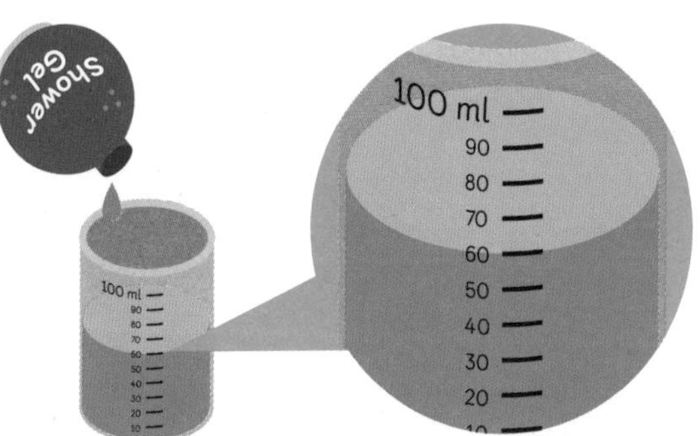

Volume of shower gel = 60 ml

The [Shower Gel] contains the least volume of shower gel. The  contains the greatest volume of shower gel.

Practice

Fill in the blanks.

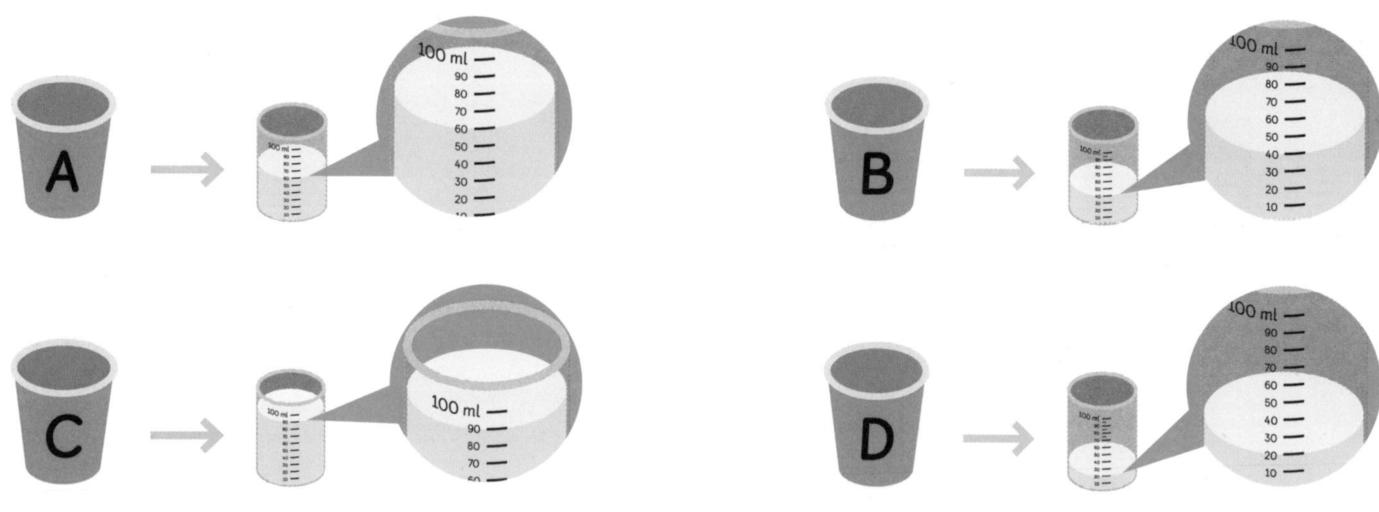

1 The volume of water in cup A is [ ] ml.

2 The volume of water in cup C is [ ] ml.

3 The volume of water in cup A is less than the volume of water in cup [ ].

4 The volume of water in cup B is more than the volume of water in cup [ ].

5 Cup [ ] has the greatest volume of water.

6 Cup [ ] has the smallest volume of water.

Review and challenge

1 Find the length of each item.

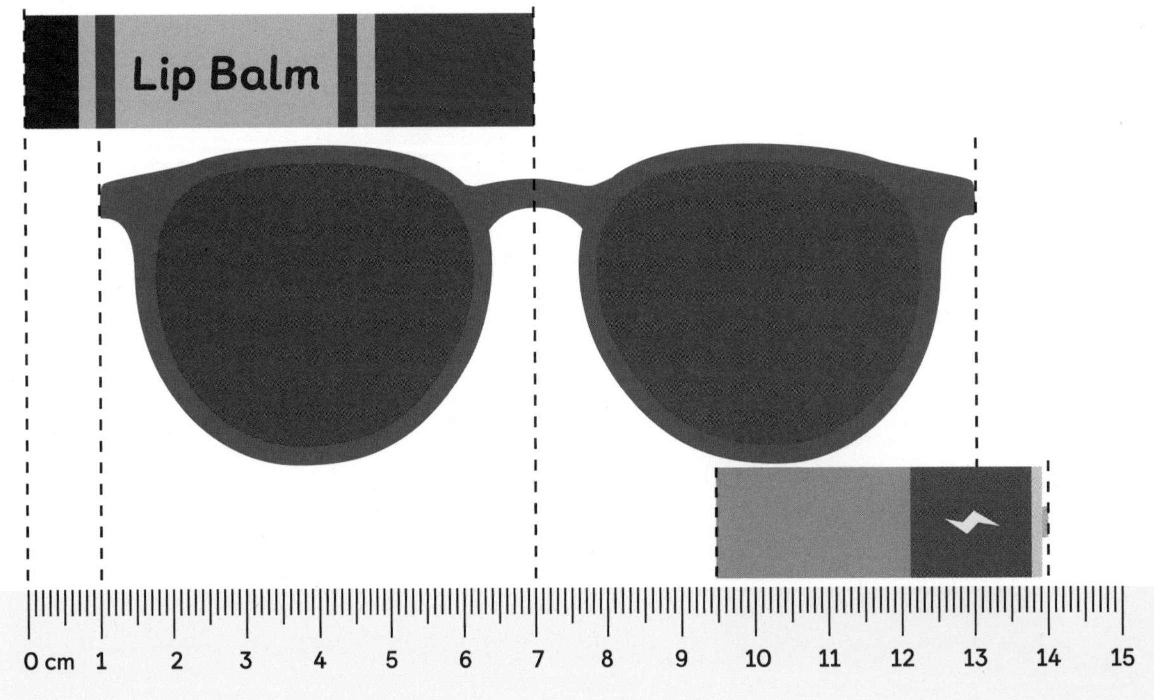

(a) The lip balm is ☐ cm long.

(b) The sunglasses are ☐ cm long.

(c) The battery is ☐ cm long.

(d) The ☐ is shorter than the lip balm.

2 What is the mass of the mango?

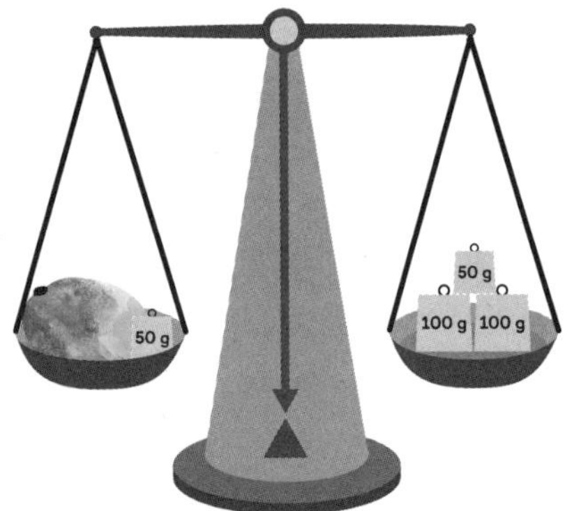

☐ g

3 The temperature in the fridge is 4 °C.
The temperature in the kitchen is 18 °C warmer.
What is the temperature in the kitchen?

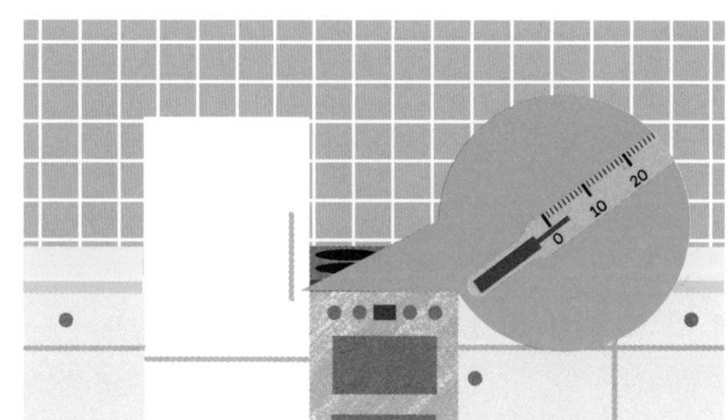

☐ °C

4 Draw different coins to show the same value as the coins below.

(a) 

(b) 

(c) 

5

Purse A

Purse B

Purse C

(a) Which purse contains the most amount of money. ☐

(b) Which purse contains the least amount of money. ☐

(c) Is there enough money in Purse C to buy £9 ? ☐

(d) Put the purses in order, starting with the purse containing the least amount of money.

☐ , ☐ , ☐

6 The clocks show the time Ruby starts each activity.

watches TV | goes to bed | plays football

(a) [   ] is the time that Ruby starts to watch TV.

(b) Ruby starts playing football at [   ].

(c) The last activity of the day is at [   ], when Ruby goes to bed.

(d) Put the activities in order from earliest to latest start time.

[   ], [   ], [   ]

7 What is the volume of water in each container?

(a)

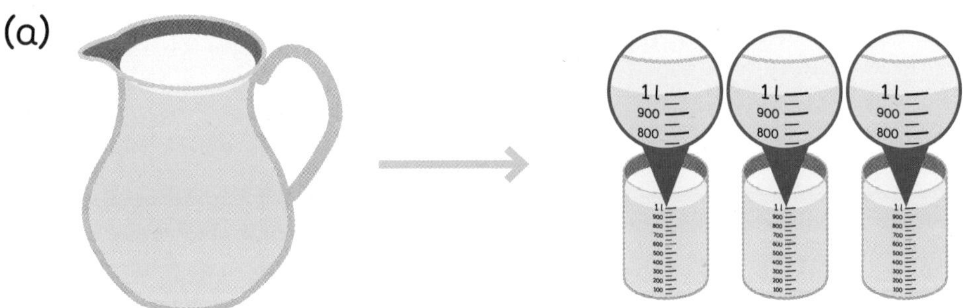

The volume of water in the jug is [   ] l.

(b)

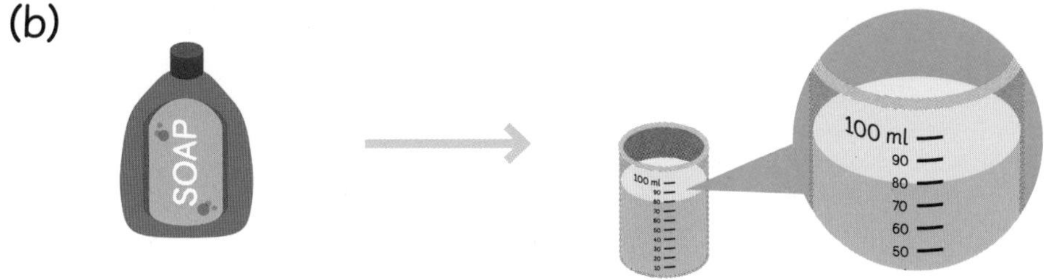

The volume of soap in the bottle is [   ] ml.

Answers

Page 5 **3** Answers will vary.

Page 7 **2 (a)** 4 cm **(b)** 7 cm.

Page 9 **1** The comb is 8 cm long. **2** The crayon is 6 cm long. **3** The straw is 7 cm long. **4** The comb is 1 cm longer than the straw. **5** The crayon is 2 cm shorter than the comb. **6** The comb is the longest. **7** The crayon is the shortest.

Page 11 **2** The mass of the watermelon is about 3 kg. **3 (a)** 3 kg **(b)** 8 kg.

Page 13 **2 (a)** 50 g **(b)** 100 g **(c)** 70 g **(d)** 75 g
3 (a) The sandwich weighs about 100g. **(b)** The mass of the blueberries is about 65 g.

Page 15 **1 (a)** The carrots are heavier. **(b)** The tomatoes are lighter. **(c)** The mass of the tomatoes is about 150 g. **(d)** The mass of the carrots is about 180 g. **(e)** The carrots are 30 g heavier than the tomatoes. **(f)** The tomatoes are 30 g lighter than the carrots.
2 (a) The mass of the orange is 100 g more than the mass of the peach. **(b)** The cherries have the lightest mass. **(c)** The lemon and the peach together have the same mass as the orange.

Page 17 **2 (a)** 37 °C **(b)** 90 °C **(c)** 0 °C.

Page 19 **1 (a)** £15 **(b)** £25 **(c)** £55 **(d)** £55 **2** Amira has £40. Sam has £50. Sam has more money.

Page 21 **1**

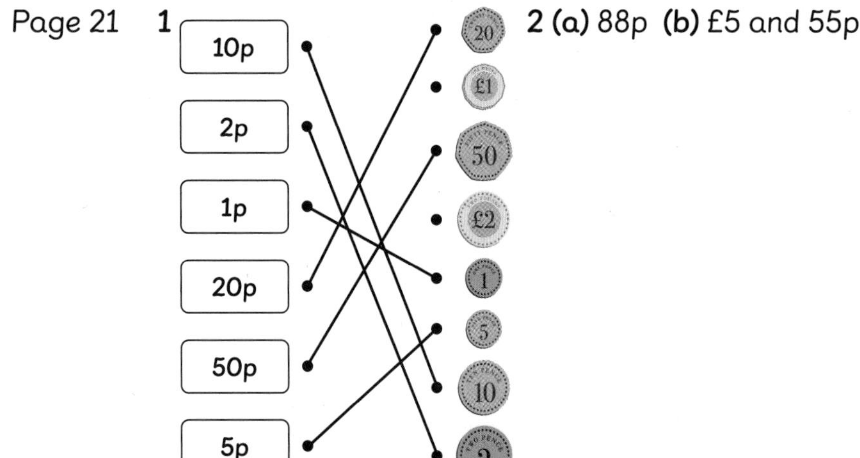

2 (a) 88p **(b)** £5 and 55p

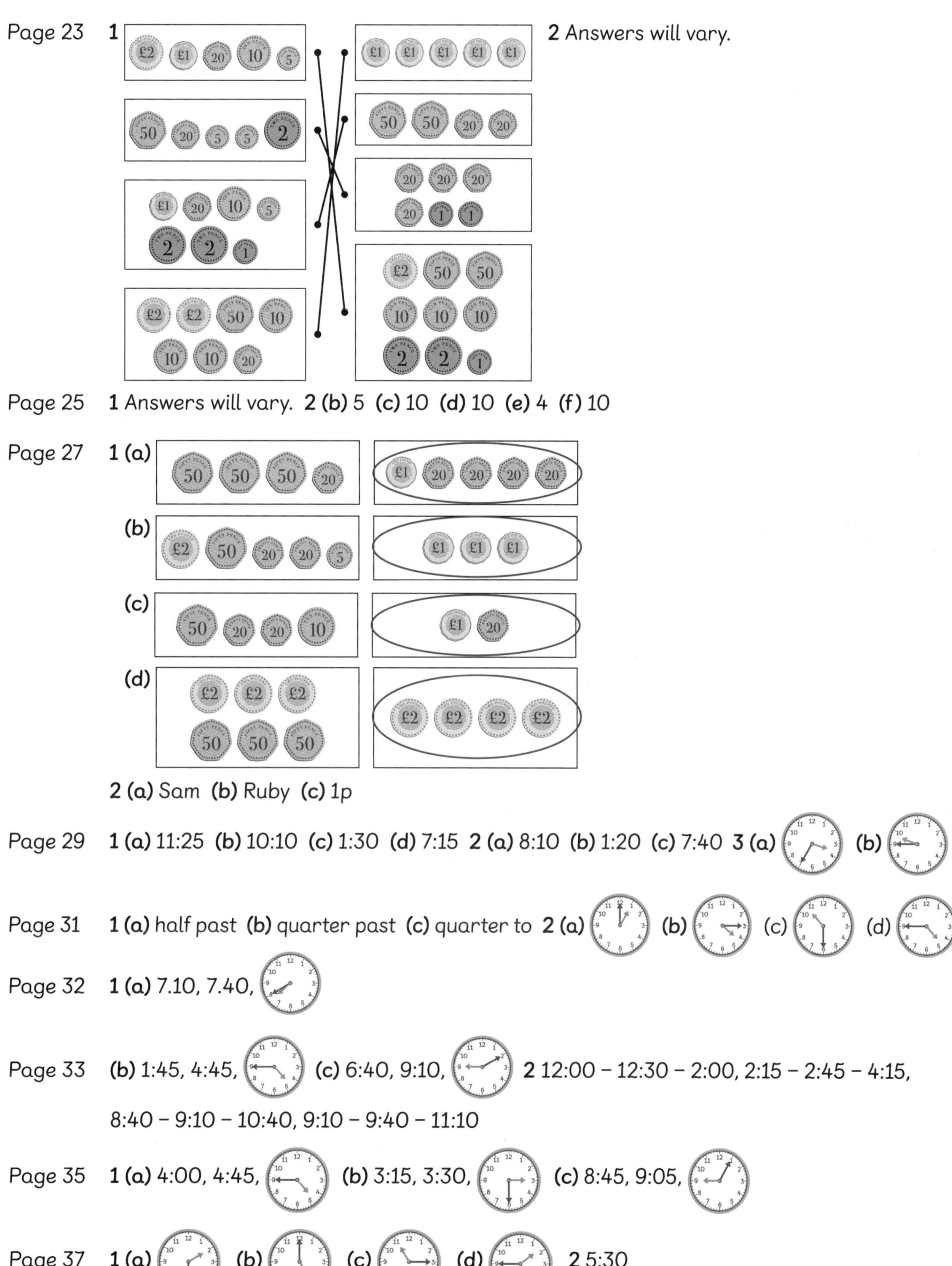

Page 23 **1** **2** Answers will vary.

Page 25 **1** Answers will vary. **2 (b)** 5 **(c)** 10 **(d)** 10 **(e)** 4 **(f)** 10

Page 27 **1 (a)**

(b)

(c)

(d)

2 (a) Sam **(b)** Ruby **(c)** 1p

Page 29 **1 (a)** 11:25 **(b)** 10:10 **(c)** 1:30 **(d)** 7:15 **2 (a)** 8:10 **(b)** 1:20 **(c)** 7:40 **3 (a)** **(b)**

Page 31 **1 (a)** half past **(b)** quarter past **(c)** quarter to **2 (a)** **(b)** **(c)** **(d)**

Page 32 **1 (a)** 7.10, 7.40,

Page 33 **(b)** 1:45, 4:45, **(c)** 6:40, 9:10, **2** 12:00 – 12:30 – 2:00, 2:15 – 2:45 – 4:15, 8:40 – 9:10 – 10:40, 9:10 – 9:40 – 11:10

Page 35 **1 (a)** 4:00, 4:45, **(b)** 3:15, 3:30, **(c)** 8:45, 9:05,

Page 37 **1 (a)** **(b)** **(c)** **(d)** **2** 5:30

Answers continued

Page 39 **2 (a)** 5 l **(b)** 1 l

Page 41 **1** The volume of water in cup A is 60 ml. **2** The volume of water in cup C is 90 ml. **3** The volume of water in cup A is less than the volume of water in cup C. **4** The volume of water in cup B is more than the volume of water in cup D. **5** Cup C has the greatest volume of water. **6** Cup D has the smallest volume of water.

Page 42 **1 (a)** The lip balm is 7 cm long. **(b)** The sunglasses are 12 cm long. **(c)** The battery is 4.5 cm long. **(d)** The battery is shorter than the lip balm. **2** 200 g

Page 43 **3** 22 °C **4 (a–c)** Answers will vary.

Page 44 **5 (a)** Purse A **(b)** Purse B **(c)** no **(d)** Purse B, Purse C, Purse A.

Page 45 **6 (a)** 6:15 is the time that Ruby starts to watch TV. **(b)** Ruby starts playing football at 4:45. **(c)** The last activity of the day is at 8:30, when Ruby goes to bed. **(d)** plays football, watches TV, goes to bed **7 (a)** The volume of water in the jug is 3 l. **(b)** The volume of soap in the bottle is 80 ml.

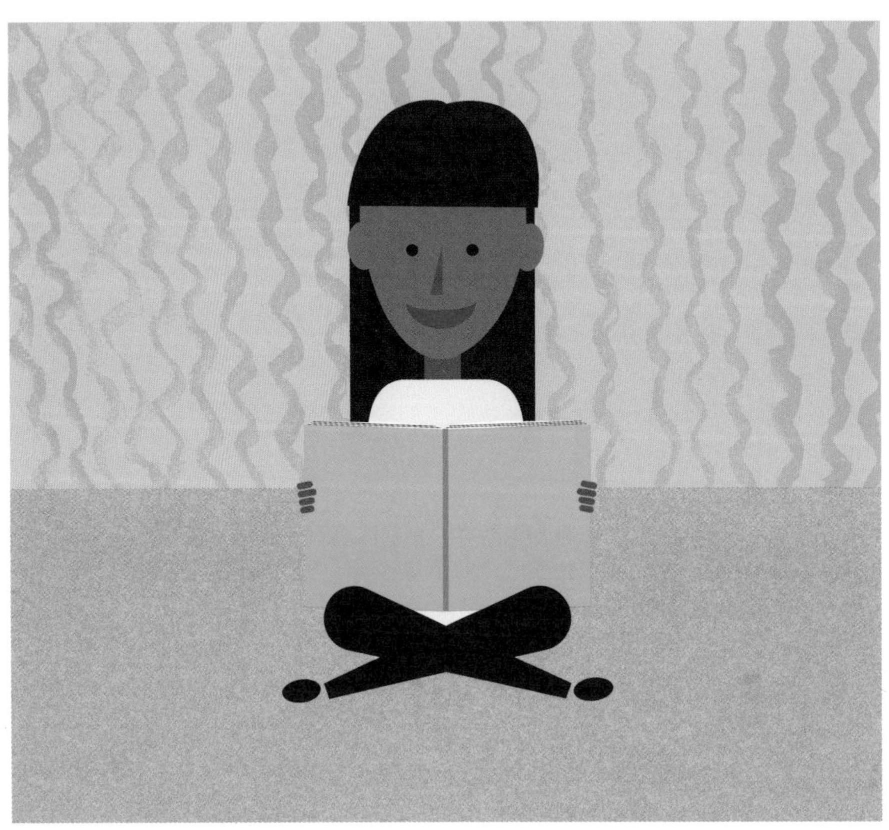

KS1
5–7
Years

Master Maths at Home

Geometry and Shape

Scan the QR code to help your child's learning at home.

mastermathsathome.com

How to use this book

Maths — No Problem! created **Master Maths at Home** to help children develop fluency in the subject and a rich understanding of core concepts.

Key features of the Master Maths at Home books include:

- Carefully designed lessons that provide structure but also allow flexibility in how they're used. For example, some children may want to write numbers, while others might want to trace.
- Speech bubbles containing content designed to spark diverse conversations, with many discussion points that don't have obvious 'right' or 'wrong' answers.
- Rich illustrations that will guide children to a discussion of shapes and units of measurement, allowing them to make connections to the wider world around them.
- Exercises that allow a flexible approach and can be adapted to suit any child's cognitive or functional ability.
- Clearly laid out pages that encourage children to practise a range of higher-order skills.
- A community of friendly and relatable characters who introduce each lesson and come along as your child progresses through the series.

You can see more guidance on how to use these books at **mastermathsathome.com**.

We're excited to share all the ways you can learn maths!

Maths — No Problem!
mastermathsathome.com
www.mathsnoproblem.com
hello@mathsnoproblem.com

First published in Great Britain in 2022 by
Dorling Kindersley Limited
One Embassy Gardens, 8 Viaduct Gardens, London SW11 7BW
A Penguin Random House Company

The authorised representative in the EEA is Dorling Kindersley Verlag GmbH. Amulfstr. 124, 80636 Munich, Germany

10 9 8 7 6 5 4 3 2 1
001–327071–Jan/22

This book was made with Forest Stewardship Council™ certified paper – one small step in DK's commitment to a sustainable future. For more information go to www.dk.com/our-green-pledge

A CIP catalogue record for this book is available from the British Library.

ISBN: 978-0-24153-913-2
Printed and bound in China

For the curious
www.dk.com

Acknowledgements
The publisher would like to thank the authors and consultants Andy Psarianos, Judy Hornigold, Adam Gifford and Dr Anne Hermanson.

The Castledown typeface has been used with permission from the Colophon Foundry.

Contents

Ruby
Elliott
Amira
Charles
Lulu
Sam
Oak
Holly
Ravi
Emma
Jacob
Hannah

Identifying sides

Lesson
1

Starter

How many sides do these shapes have?

Example

We can count the number of sides.

1. This is a triangle.

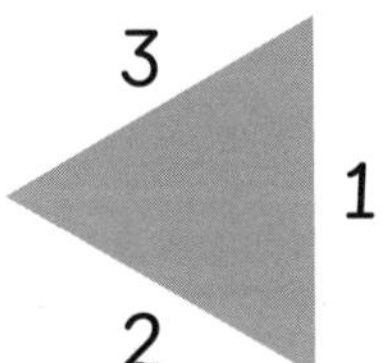

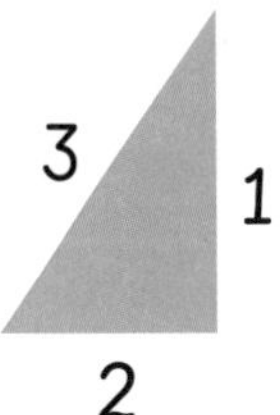

All triangles have 3 sides.

2. These are rectangles.

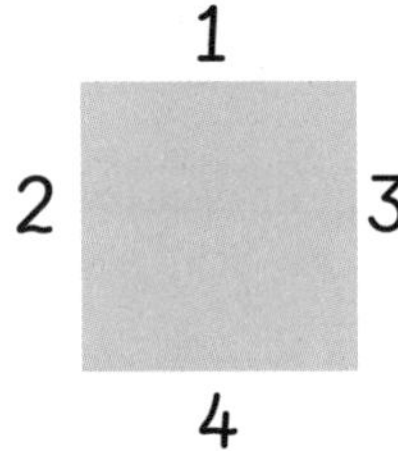

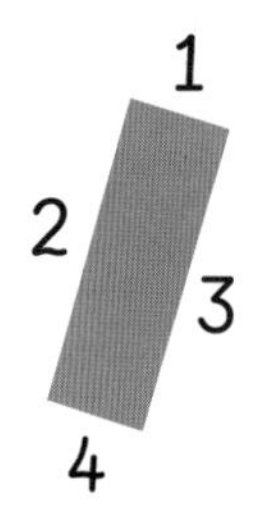

All rectangles have 4 sides.

Practice

1 Write the number of sides that each shape has.

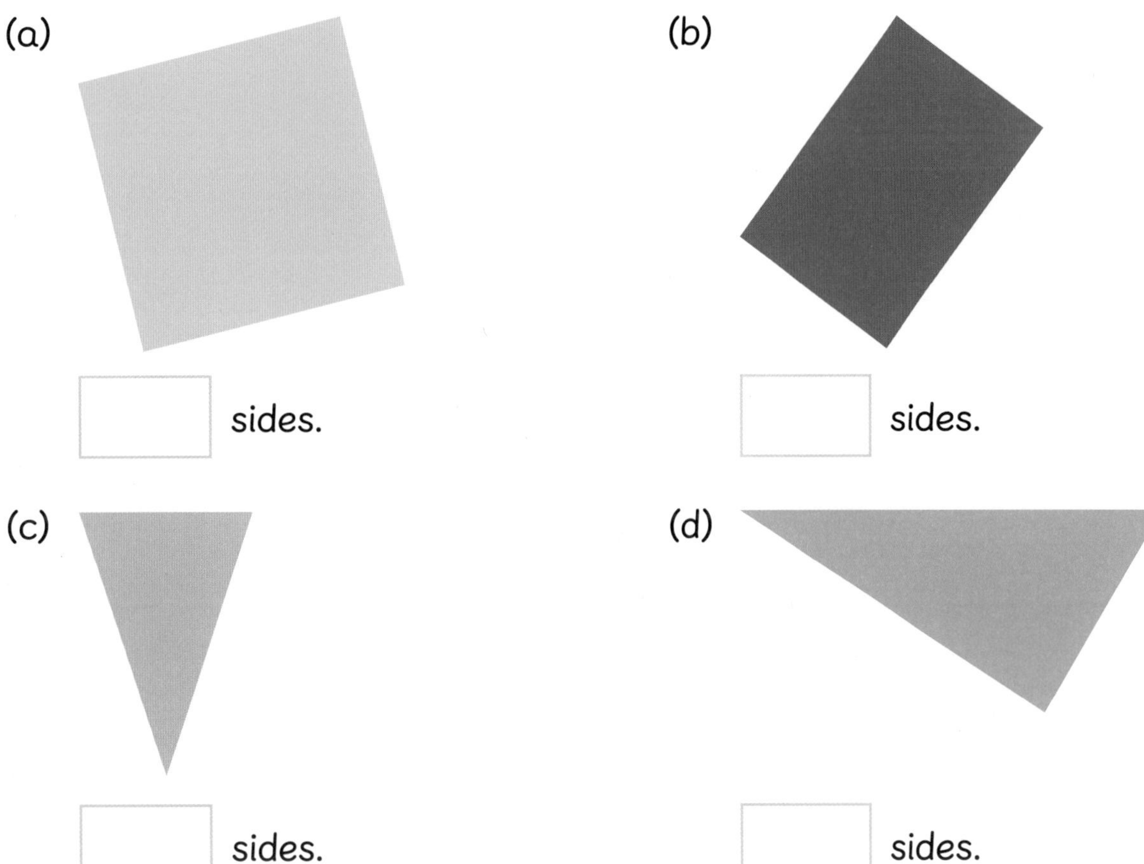

2 Circle the shapes with 4 sides.

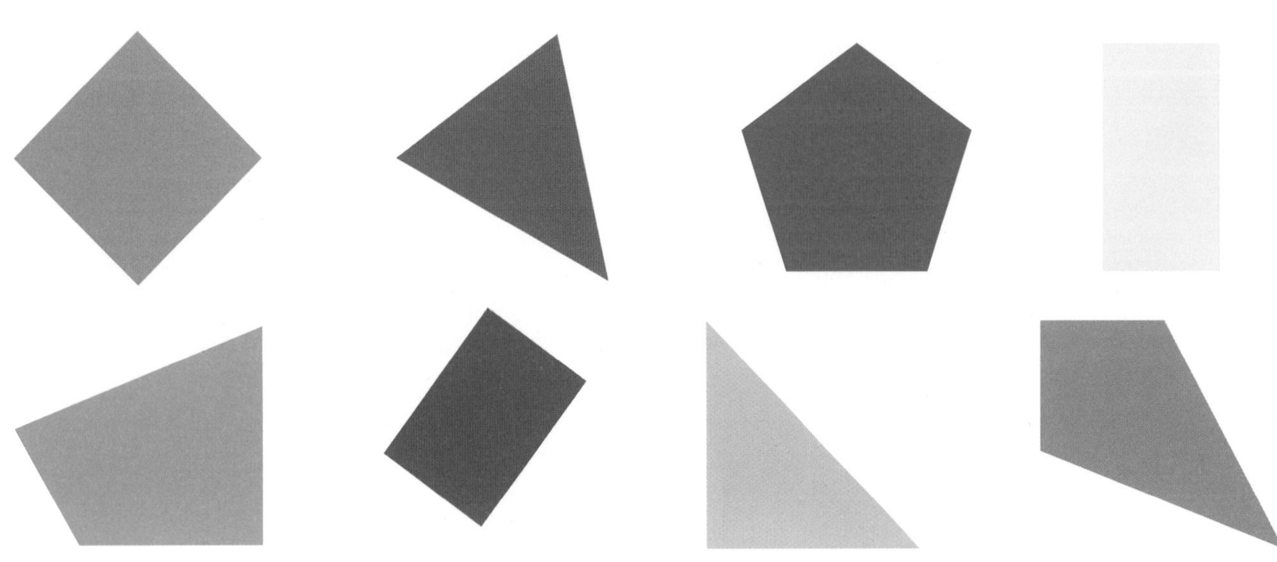

Identifying vertices

Lesson 2

Starter

How can we sort these shapes?

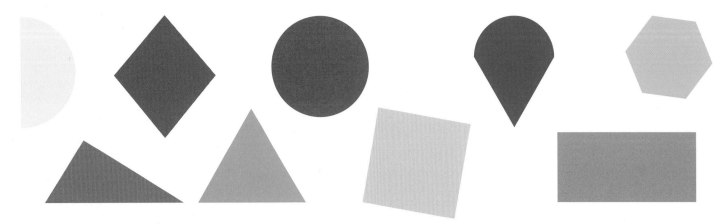

Example

These shapes are all polygons. All the sides of a polygon are straight.

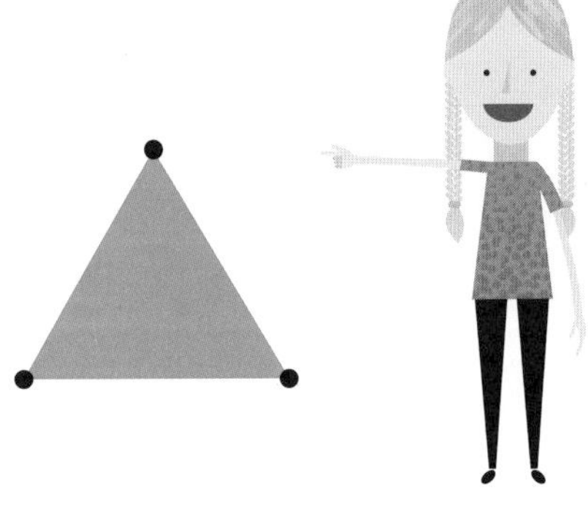

The point where two lines meet is called a **vertex.**

The plural for vertex is **vertices.**

These shapes are not polygons. Not all of their sides are straight.

Practice

Circle the vertices on the shapes and complete the table.

	Polygon	Number of vertices	Number of sides
1			
2			
3			
4			
5			
6			
7			
8			

Identifying lines of symmetry

Lesson 3

Starter

Can we fold these shapes so one half covers the other half exactly?

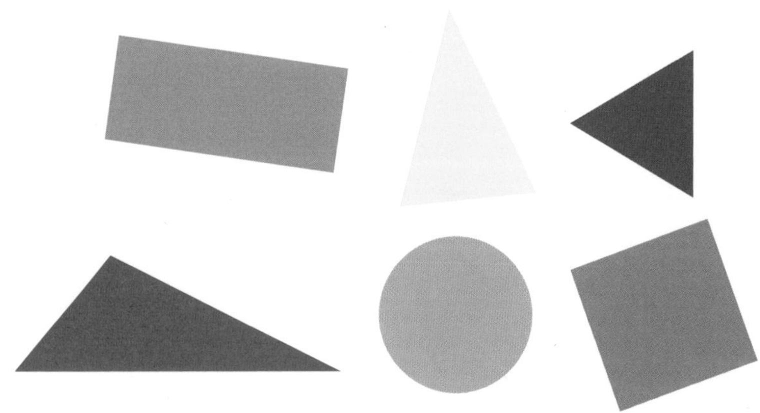

Example

When we fold the square like this, the two halves match exactly.

We can also fold the square like this because each half is the same.

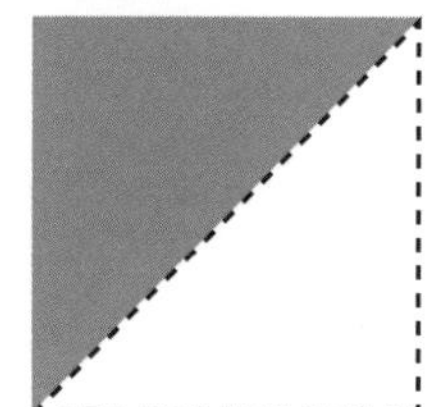

We say that a square is **symmetrical**.

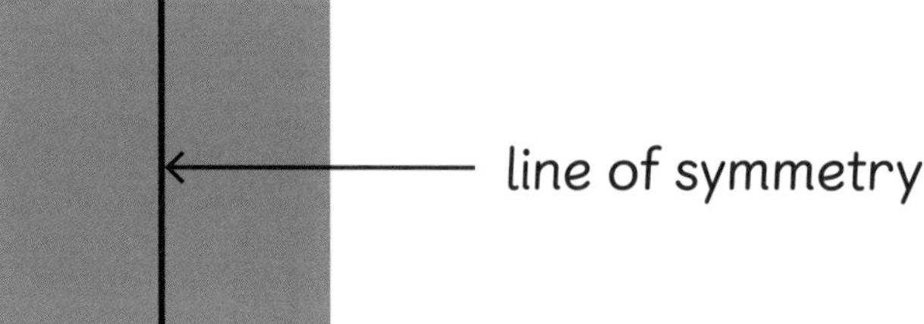

The fold line is called the line of symmetry.

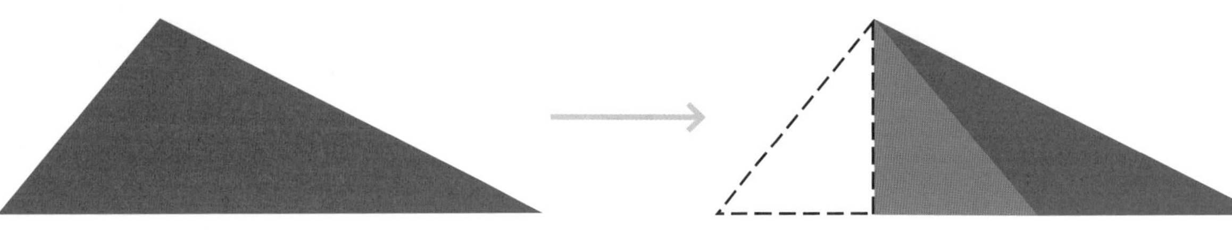

We can't fold this shape exactly in half. It does not have a line of symmetry.

Practice

Which of the following shapes are symmetrical?
Put a tick (✓) or cross (✗) next to each shape.

	Shape	Is it symmetrical?
1		
2		
3		
4		
5	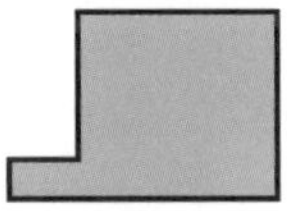	
6		
7	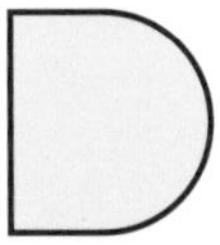	
8	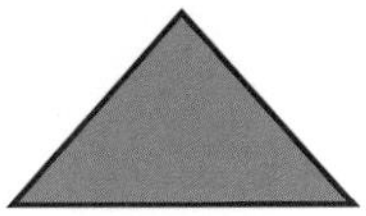	

Making figures

Lesson 4

Starter

Is it possible to arrange 3 of these shapes to make a symmetrical figure?

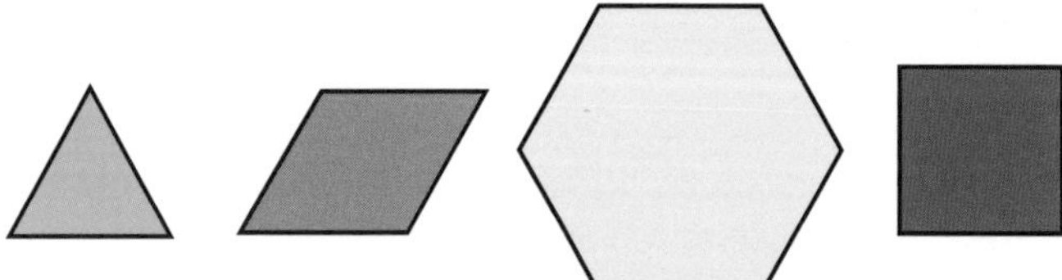

Example

I made this figure. It is not symmetrical. It does not have a line of symmetry.

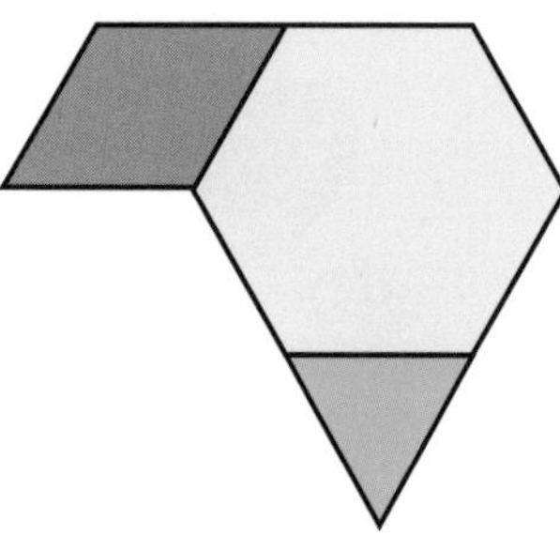

I made this figure. It is symmetrical. It has a line of symmetry.

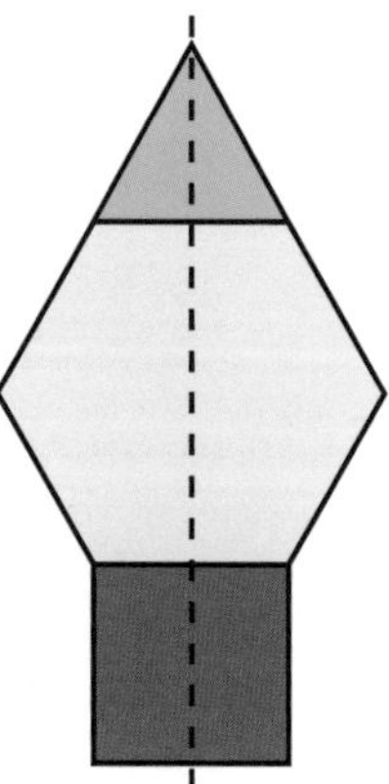

I made this figure. It is also symmetrical.

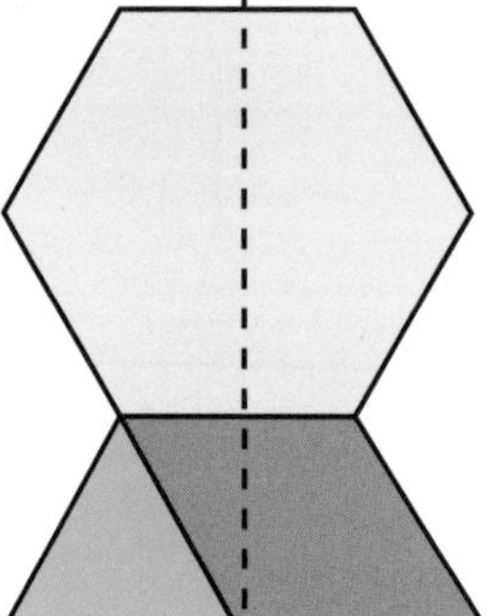

Practice

1. Draw two shapes that are symmetrical. Mark the line of symmetry on each shape.

2. Use [square], [triangle] and [parallelogram] to make two figures, one that is symmetrical and one that is not symmetrical.

Draw them here.

3. Circle the shapes that are symmetrical and draw the lines of symmetry.

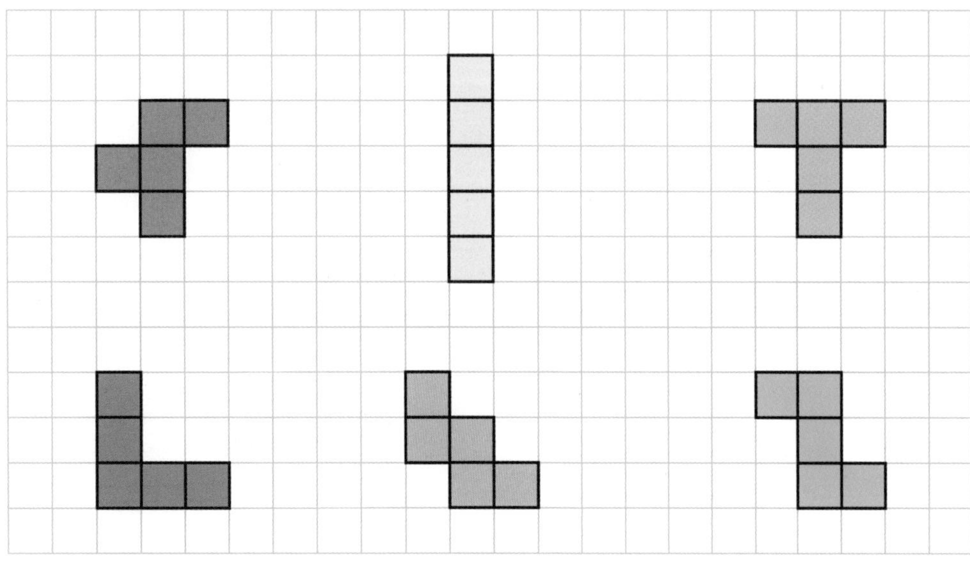

Sorting shapes

Lesson 5

Starter

How can we sort these shapes?

Example

Polygons	Not polygons

I am looking for polygons.

3 straight sides	4 or more straight sides

I am looking at the number of straight sides.

Symmetrical	Not symmetrical

I am looking for symmetrical shapes.

Practice

Look at the shapes below.

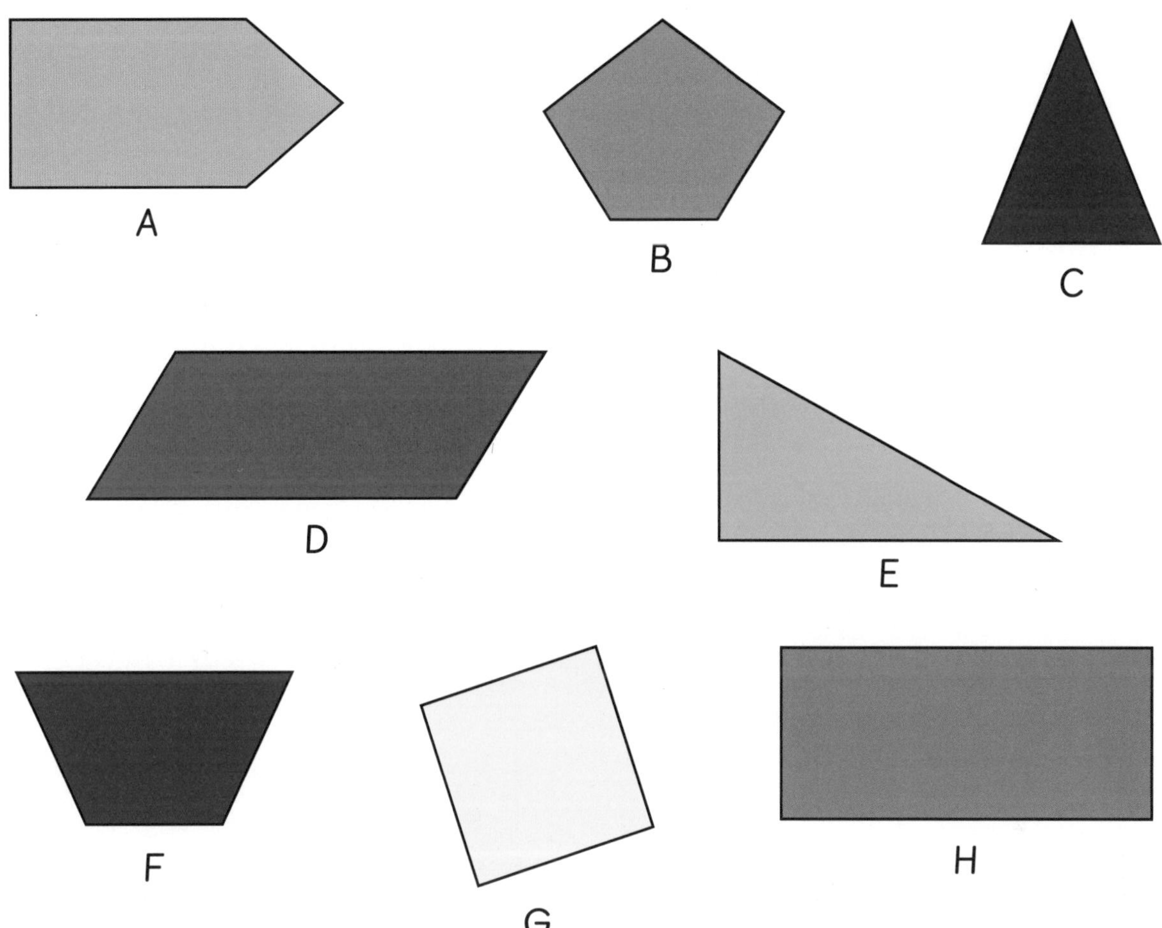

1 Sort the shapes by the number of vertices.

3 vertices	4 vertices	5 vertices

2 Sort the shapes by their lines of symmetry.

No line of symmetry	One line of symmetry	More than one line of symmetry

Drawing shapes

Lesson 6

Starter

What shape can we draw?

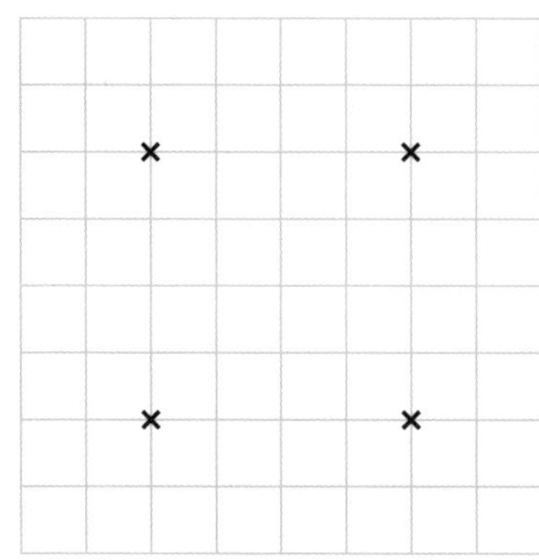

Example

Join up the crosses.

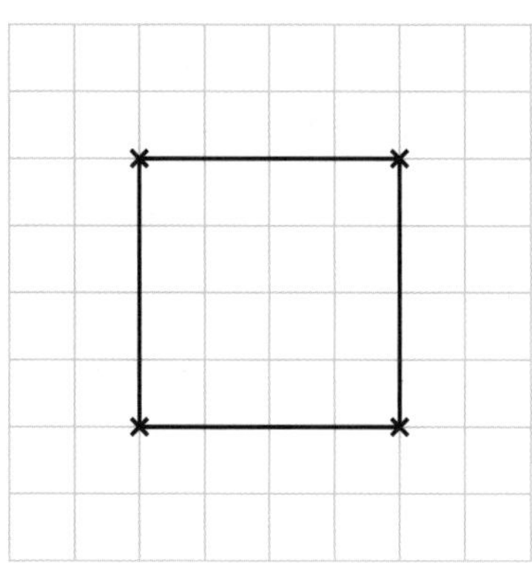

This shape has 4 straight sides and 4 vertices.
All the sides are the same length. It is a square.

We can draw other shapes as well.

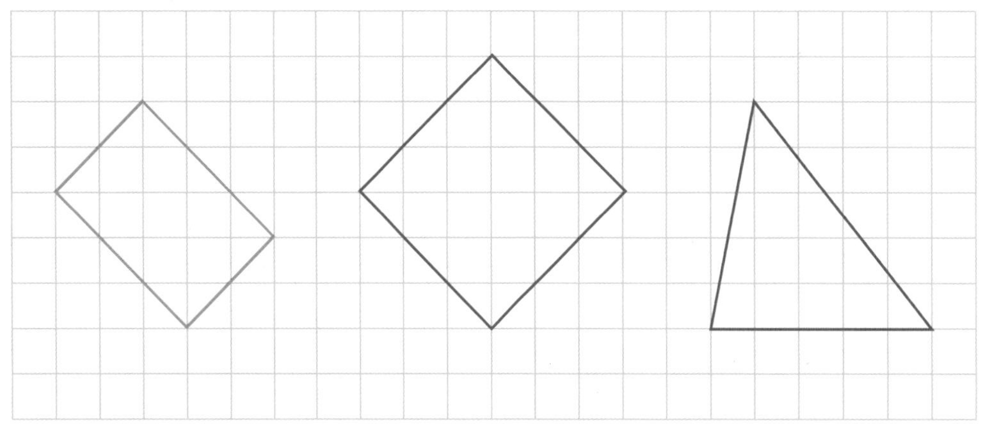

Practice

1 Copy these figures on the square grid below.

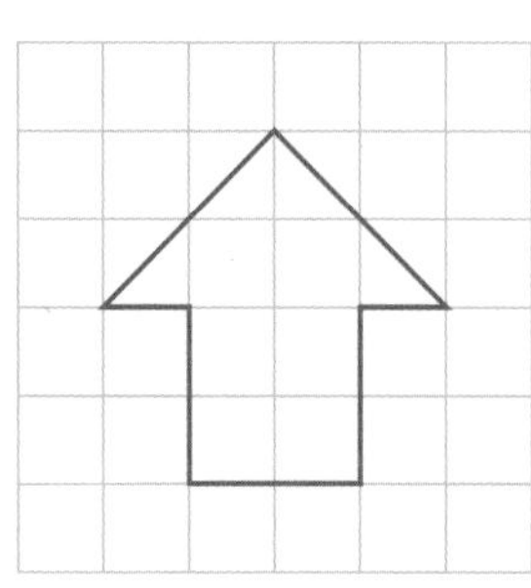
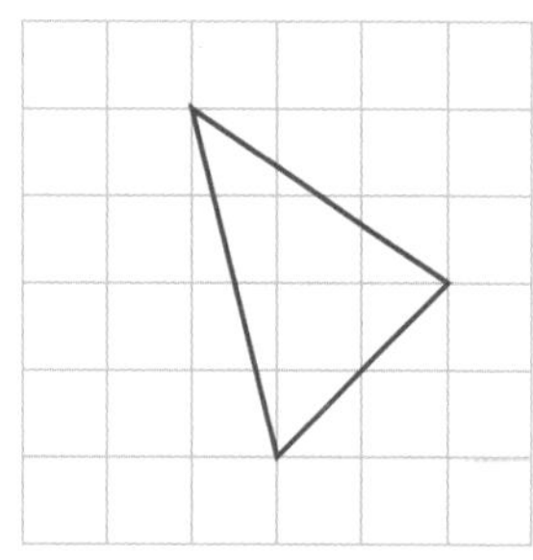
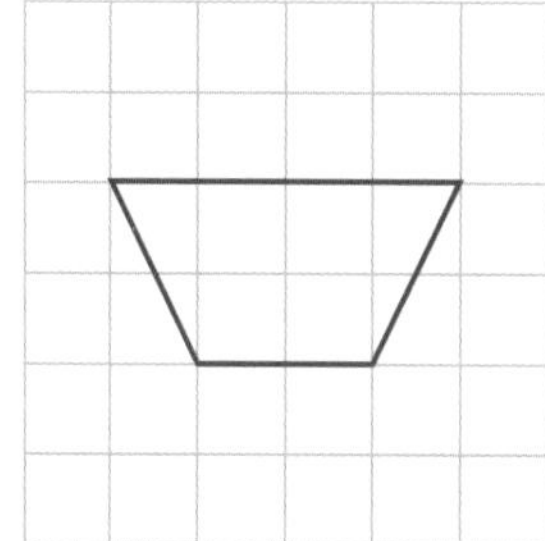

2 Draw a rectangle and a symmetrical triangle on the square grid below.

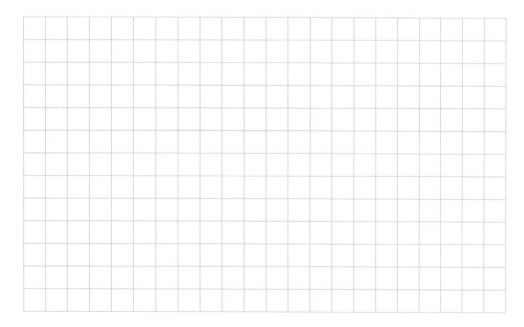

Making patterns (part 1)

Lesson 7

Starter

What repeating patterns can we make with these shapes?

Example

1  made this pattern.

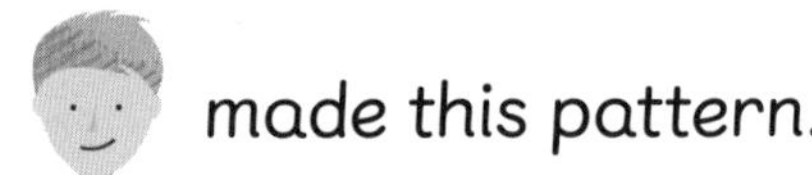 made this pattern.

2 Here are some other repeating patterns.

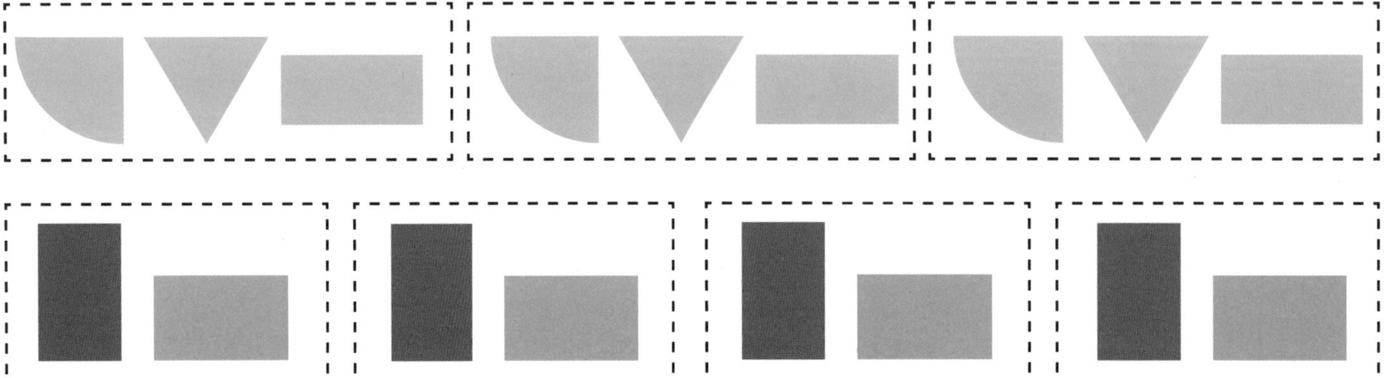

Practice

1 Make some repeating patterns using these shapes.

Draw your patterns here.

2 Draw the missing shapes in the boxes for each of these repeating patterns.

(a) ?

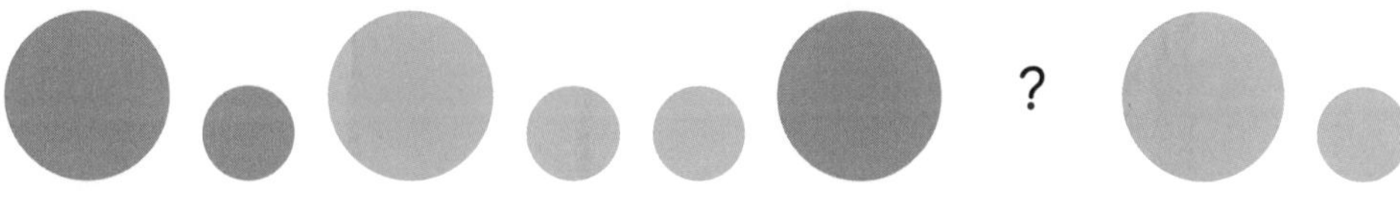

(b) ?

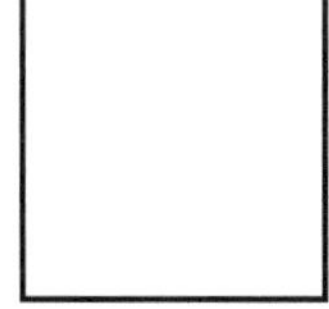

(c) ?

Describing patterns

Starter

How can we describe this pattern?

Example

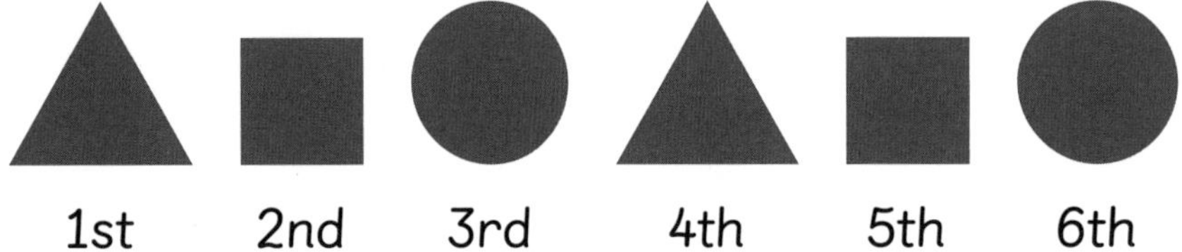

1st 2nd 3rd 4th 5th 6th

The pattern uses three different shapes.

The 1st shape is a blue triangle. 

The 2nd shape is a blue square. 

The 3rd shape is a blue circle. 

Do you know what the 9th shape will be?
What about the 99th shape?

The 9th and 99th shapes will both be .

The 100th shape will start the pattern again. It will be a 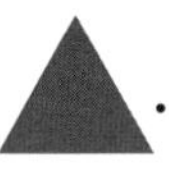.

Practice

1 Draw the 12th shape in these patterns.

(a) ...

1st

12th

(b)

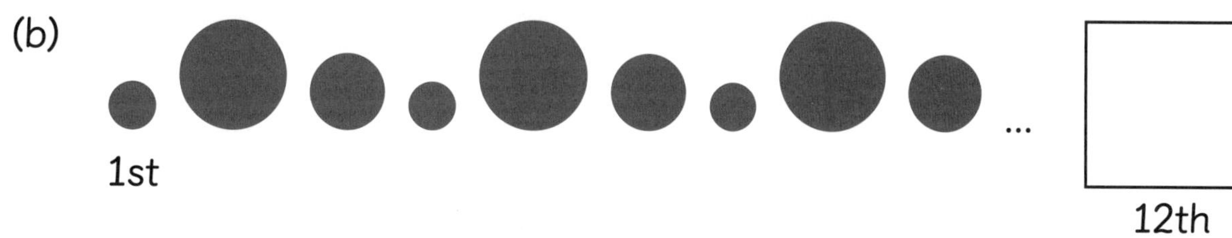

1st

12th

2 Draw the 1st shape in these patterns.

(a)

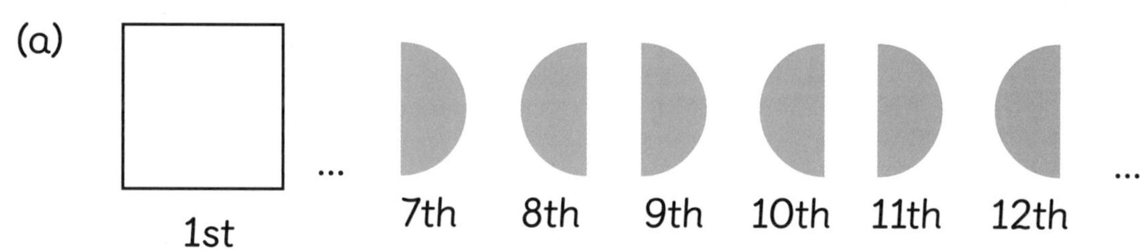

1st

7th 8th 9th 10th 11th 12th

(b)

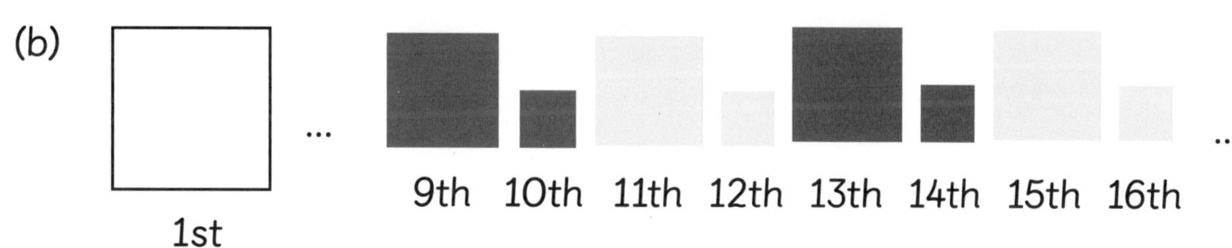

1st

9th 10th 11th 12th 13th 14th 15th 16th

3 Make a pattern using these shapes.

Ask an adult if they can predict what the 10th shape will be.

Moving shapes

Lesson 9

Starter

Describe how to move 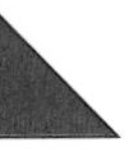 to triangle A and to triangle B.

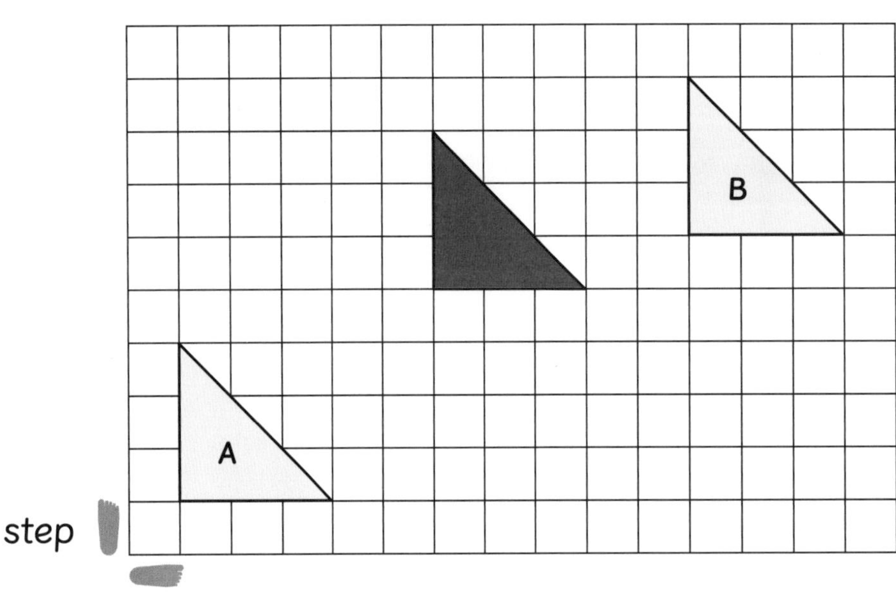

Example

 gave these instructions to move  to triangle A.

Move  5 steps to the left.

Move  4 steps down.

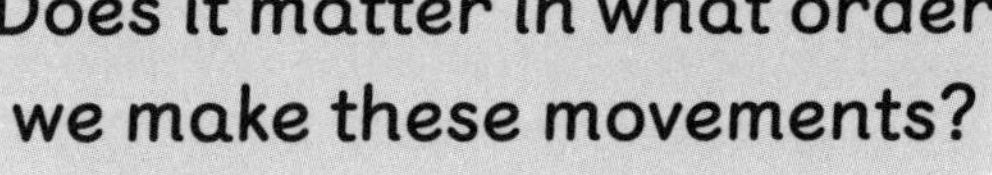

  gave these instructions to move  to triangle B.

Move  5 steps to the right.

Move  1 step up.

Practice

1 Draw the new position of each shape after moving each one 2 steps to the right and 1 step down.

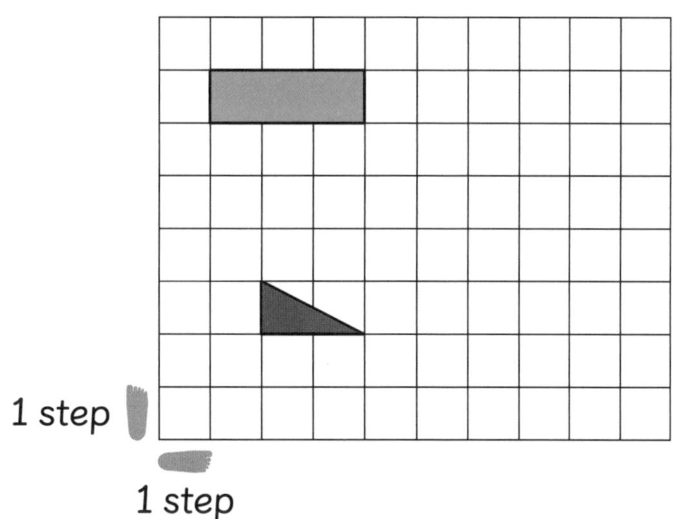

2 Draw the new position of each shape after moving each one 3 steps to the right and 2 steps up.

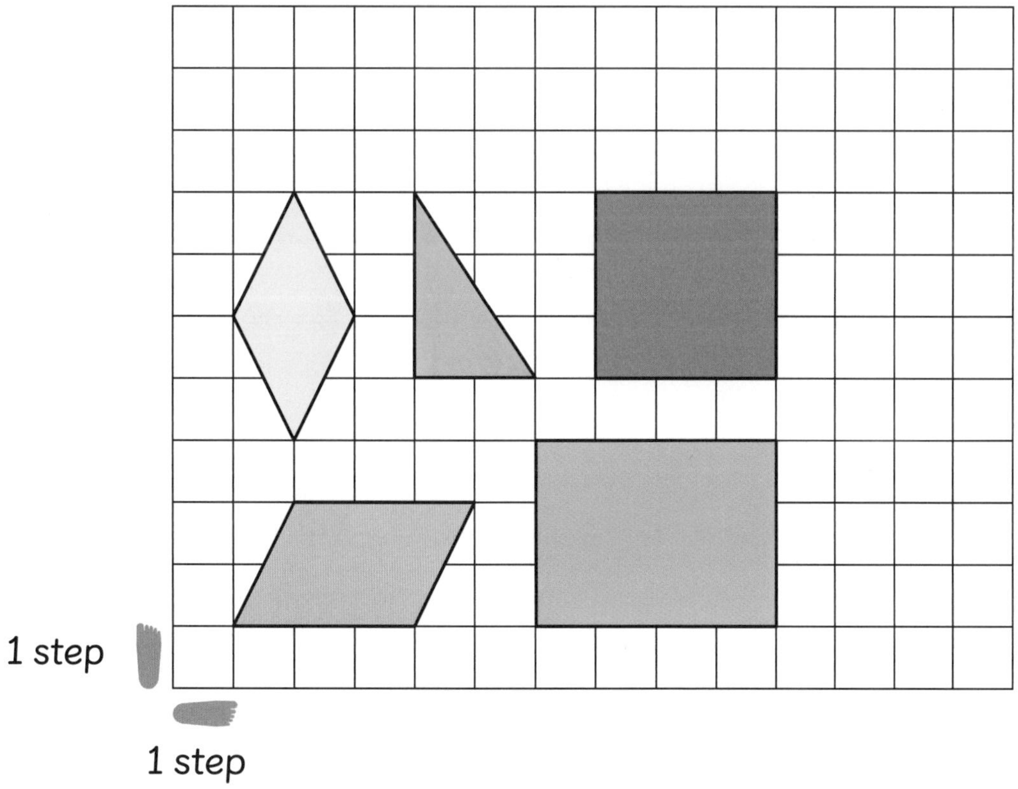

Turning shapes

Lesson 10

Starter

What will be the new position of the after a half turn clockwise?

Example

Turn clockwise by half a turn.

We can also make quarter turns and three-quarter turns.

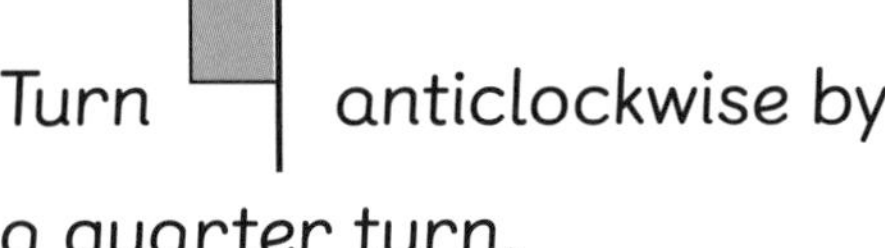

Turn anticlockwise by a quarter turn.

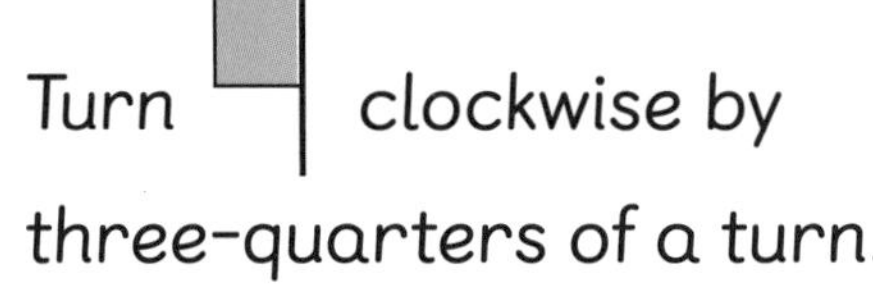

Turn clockwise by three-quarters of a turn.

Practice

1 Draw the new positions of [flag] after:

(a) a quarter turn clockwise

(b) a half turn anticlockwise.

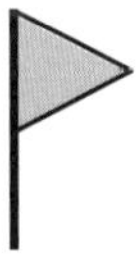

2 Draw the new positions of [triangle] after:

(a) half a turn

(b) three-quarters of a turn anticlockwise.

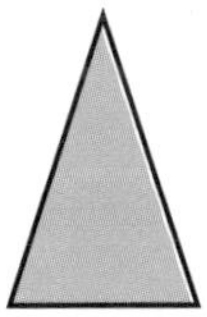

Solving word problems with 2D shapes

Lesson 11

Starter

How many [quarter circle] are needed to make 2 [circle] ?

Example

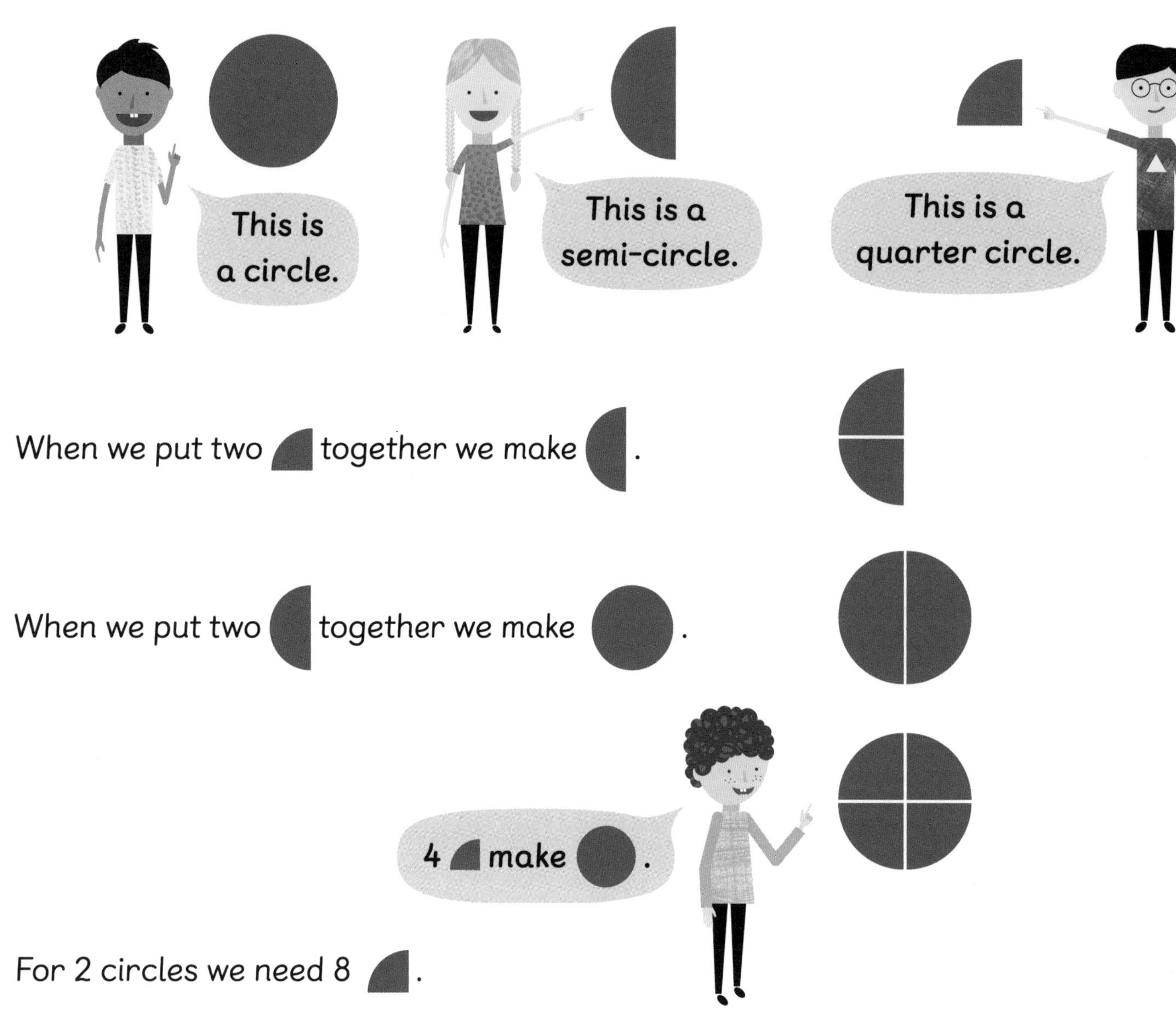

This is a circle.
This is a semi-circle.
This is a quarter circle.
When we put two together we make .
When we put two together we make .
4 make .

For 2 circles we need 8 [quarter circle].

Practice

  cuts a slice of cake like this.

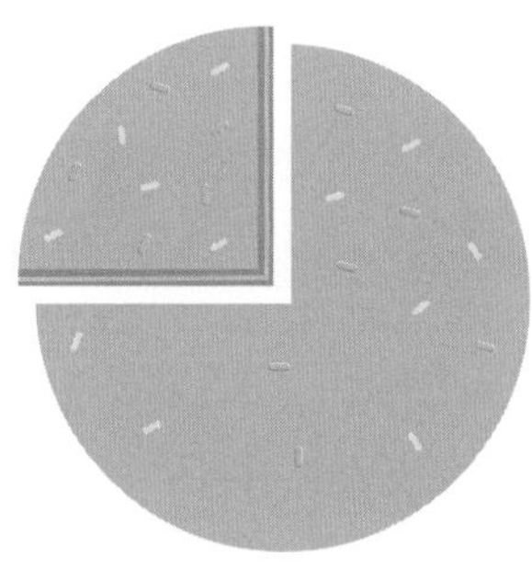

How many people can have a piece the same size as this?

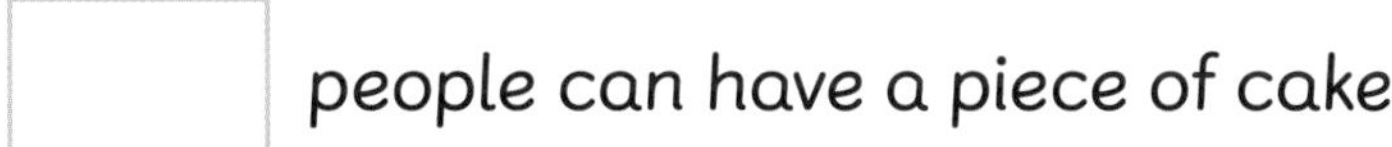 people can have a piece of cake.

2 What time will this clock show when the minute hand has moved a quarter circle from 12 to 3?

The clock will show  .

3 Each friend will eat a  of pizza.

How many friends will these pizzas serve?

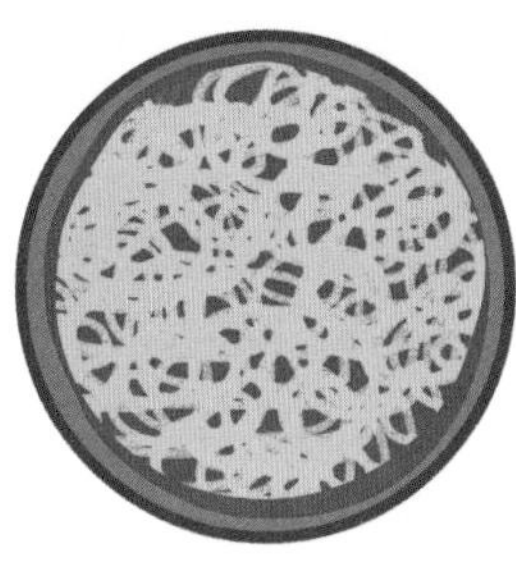 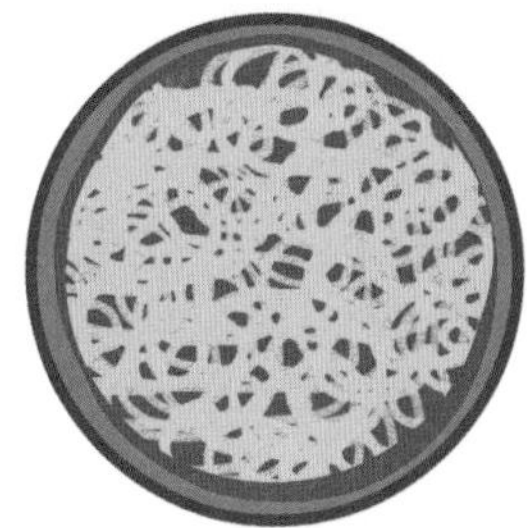 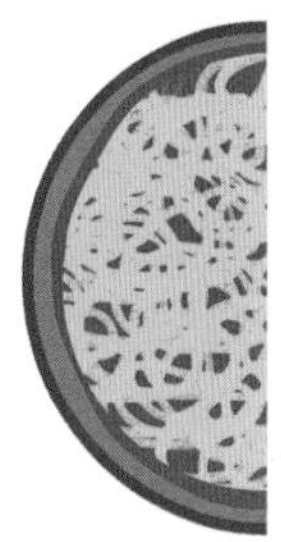

Recognising 3D shapes

Lesson 12

Starter

What are the names of these shapes?

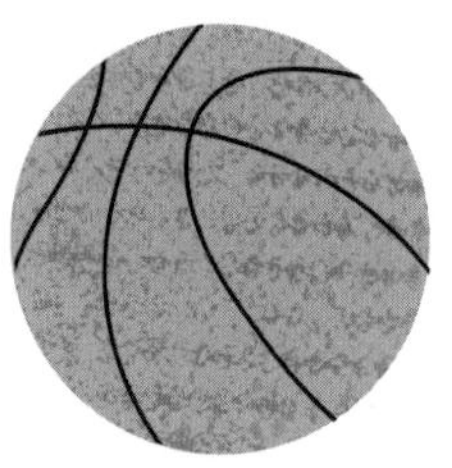

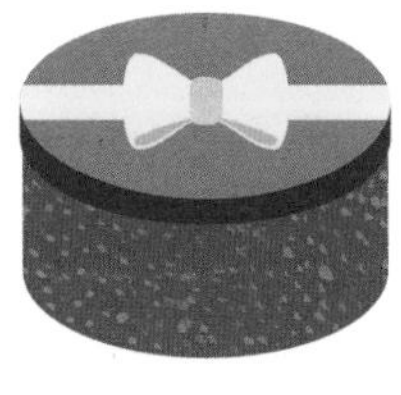

Example

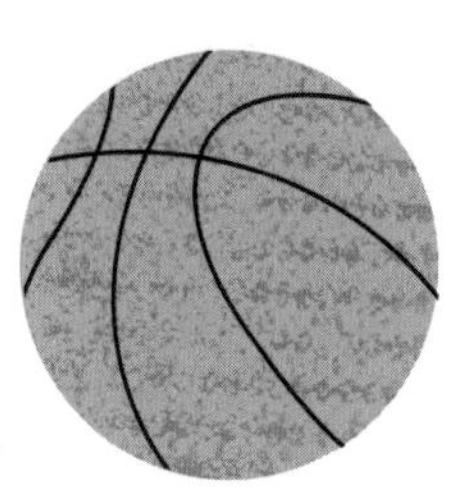

This shape has a curved surface.
It is called a **sphere**.

A sphere can roll.
It has no flat sides.

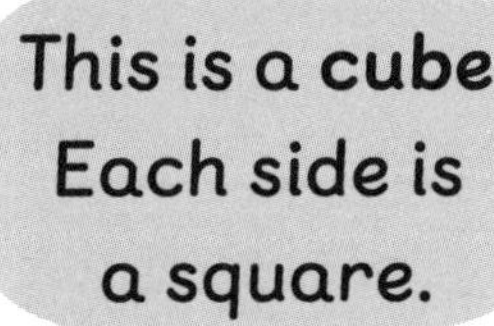

This is a **cube**.
Each side is a square.

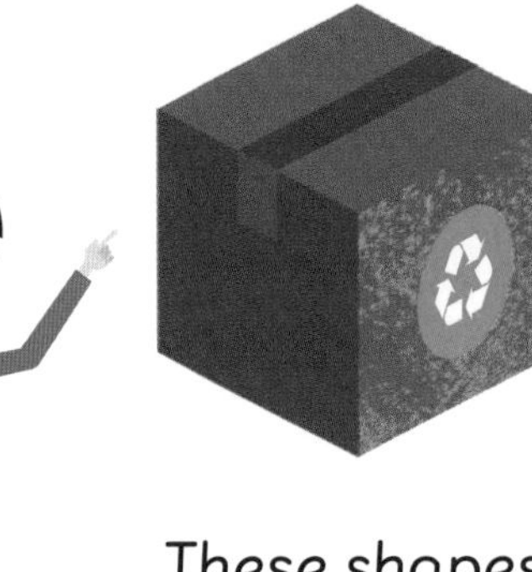

This is a cuboid.

These shapes have flat sides and straight edges.

This shape has both flat and curved sides.
It is called a **cylinder**.

Practice

1 Match the objects with the shapes.

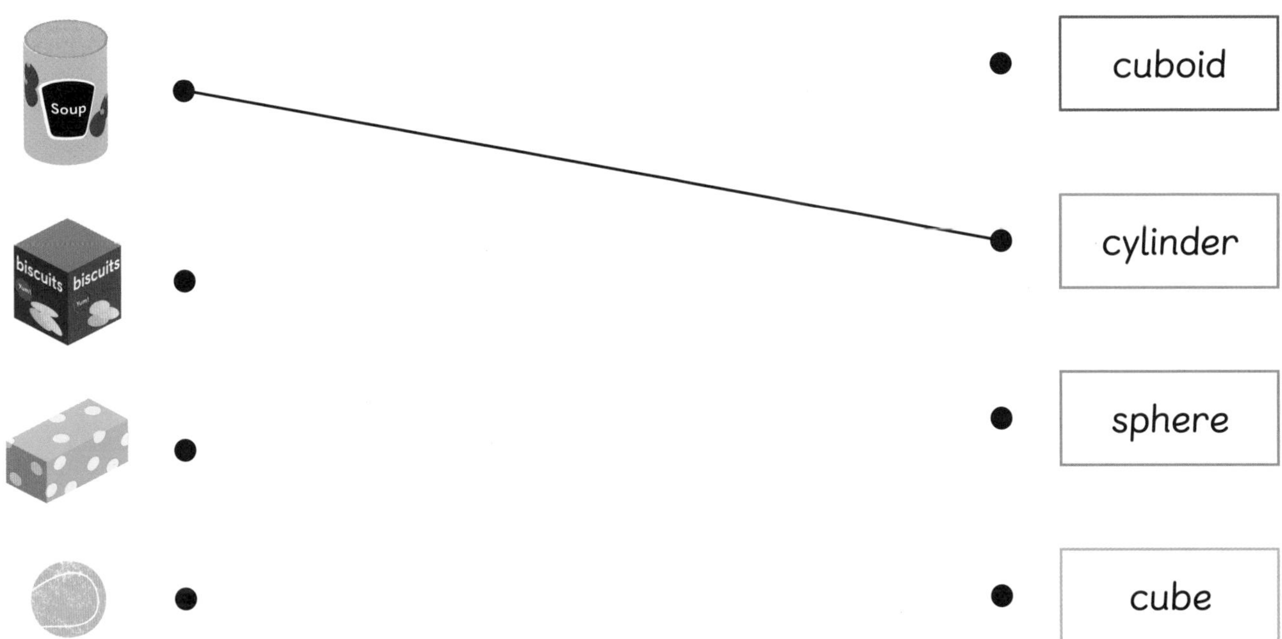

2 Look around your home for different 3D shapes.
Record your findings in a table.

Item	Name of shape

3 Look at the sides of the shapes you find. Are they curved or flat?

Item	Curved	Flat

Describing 3D shapes

Lesson 13

Starter

How can we describe these shapes?

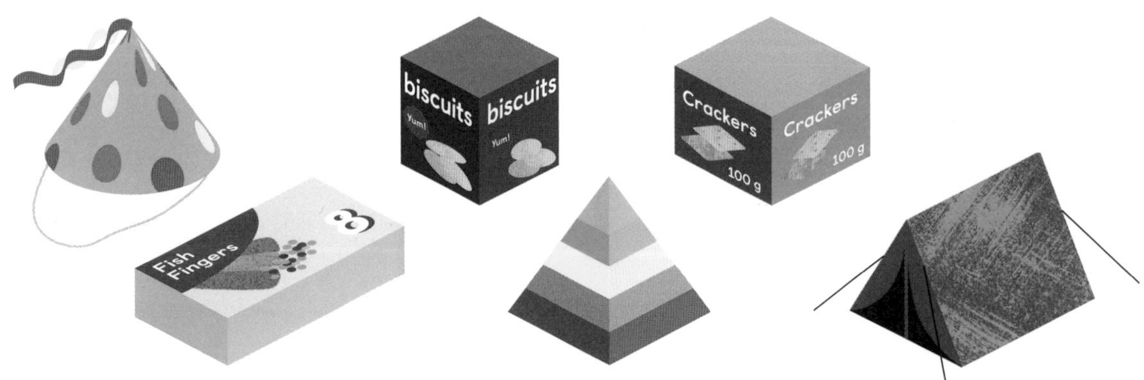

Example

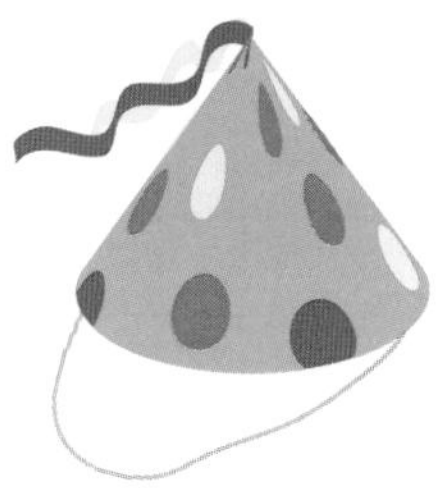

This hat is shaped like a **cone**.
A cone has a flat face and a curved surface.

We call a flat side a face. We call a curved side a surface.

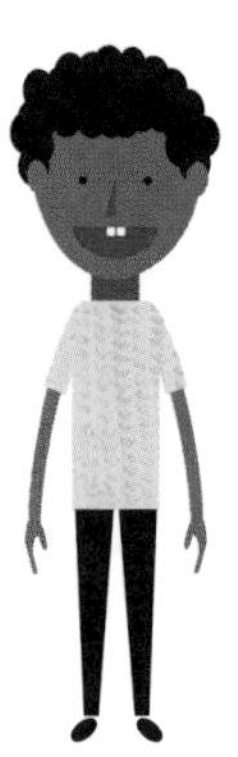

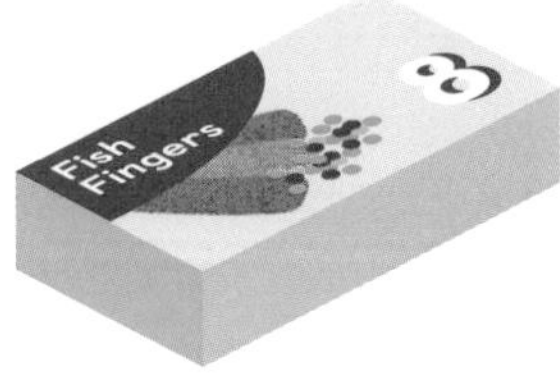

This box is shaped like a cuboid.
A cuboid has 6 faces.
The faces are rectangles.

This box is also a cuboid. The faces are squares and rectangles.

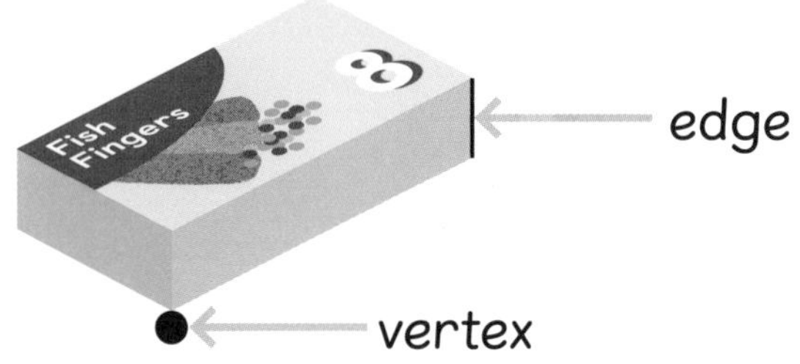

Count the number of edges and vertices on a cuboid.

It has 12 edges and 8 vertices.

A cube is a special cuboid.
It has 6 faces. All the faces are squares.
It has 12 edges and 8 vertices.

This is a pyramid. It has 5 faces.
1 face is a square and the other 4 faces are triangles.

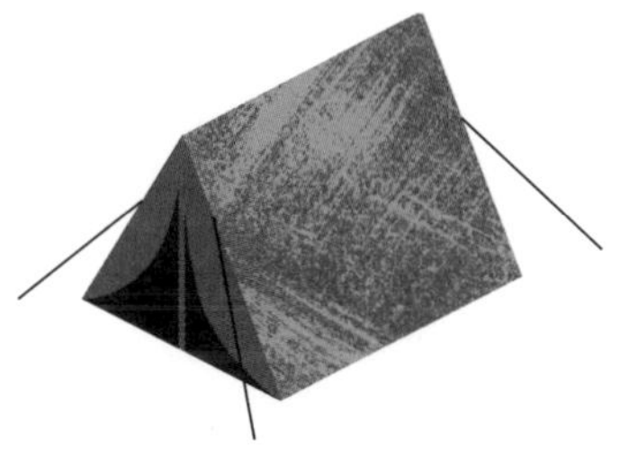

Can you describe the shape of this tent?
Look at the faces.
It is shaped like a prism.

A triangular **prism** has 9 edges and 6 vertices.

Practice

1 Match the objects with their shapes.

cuboid	•	•	
prism	•	•	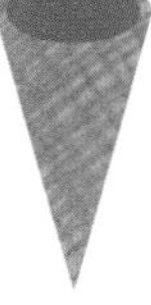
cube	•	•	
cylinder	•	•	
pyramid	•	•	
cone	•	•	

2 Describe each of the following shapes by completing the table.

Shape	Name	Number of faces	Number of vertices	Number of edges

3 What 3D shapes can you find in your home?
Record your findings in the table.

Item	Name	Number of faces	Number of vertices	Number of edges

Grouping 3D shapes

Lesson 14

Starter

How can we group these shapes?

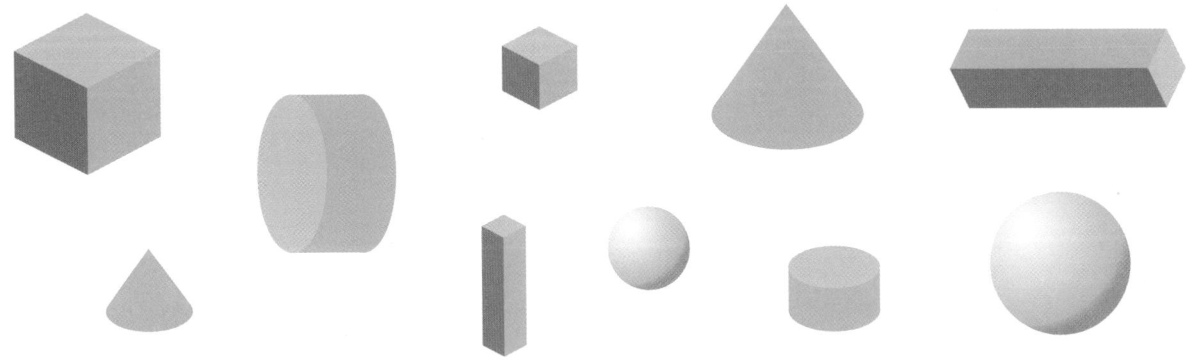

Example

We can group the shapes by the types of faces or surfaces they have.

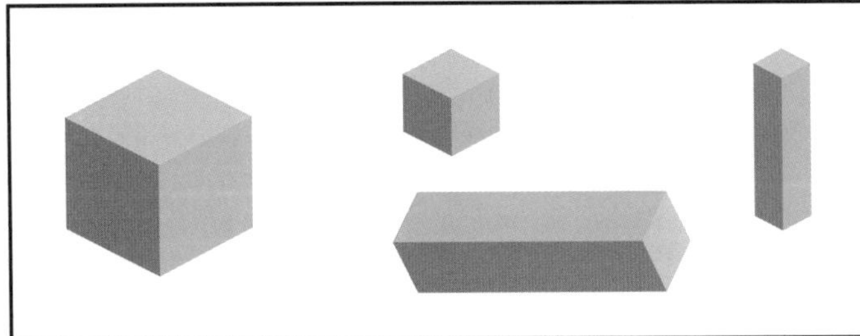

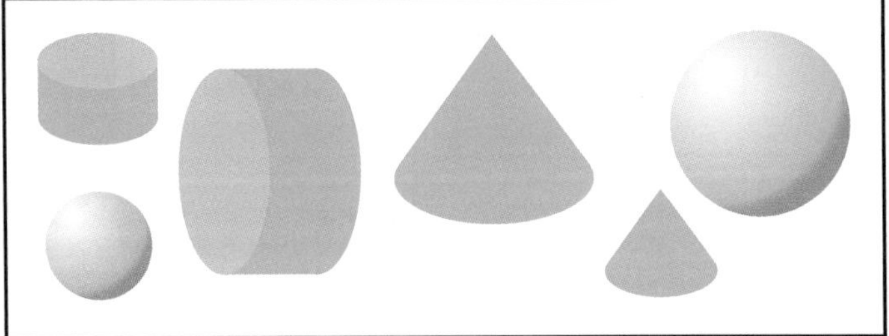

We can also group them by shape.

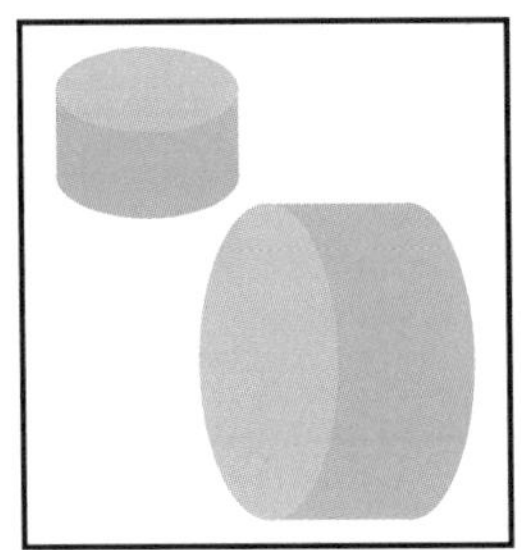

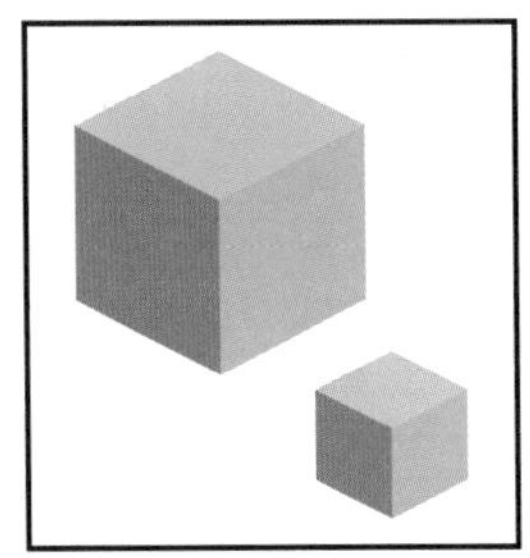

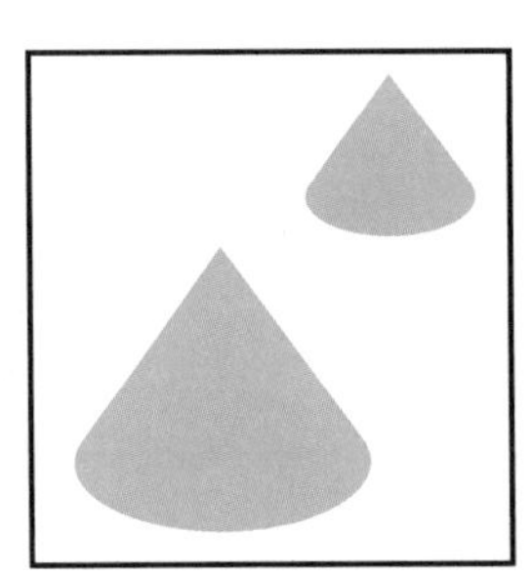

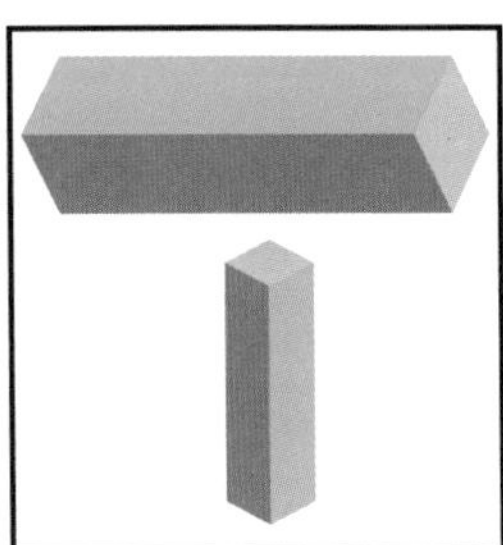

Practice

Match the objects with their shapes.

peanut butter

cuboid

prism

cube

cylinder

Forming 3D structures

Lesson 15

Starter

What structures can we make using these shapes?

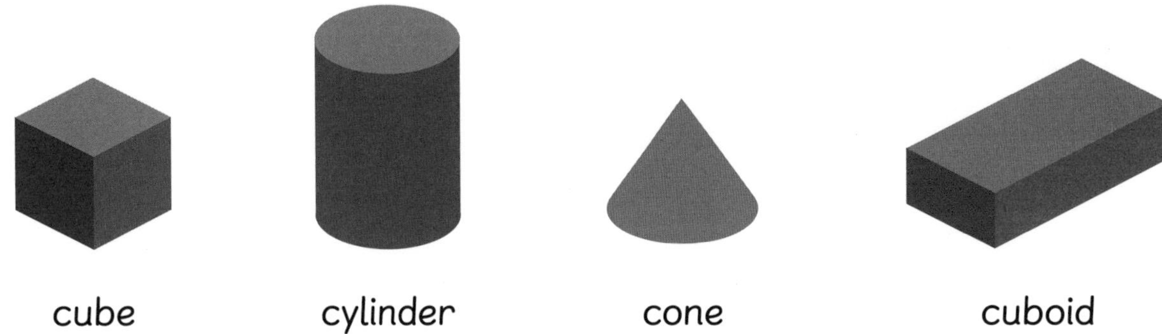

Example

I made this structure.

I made this structure.

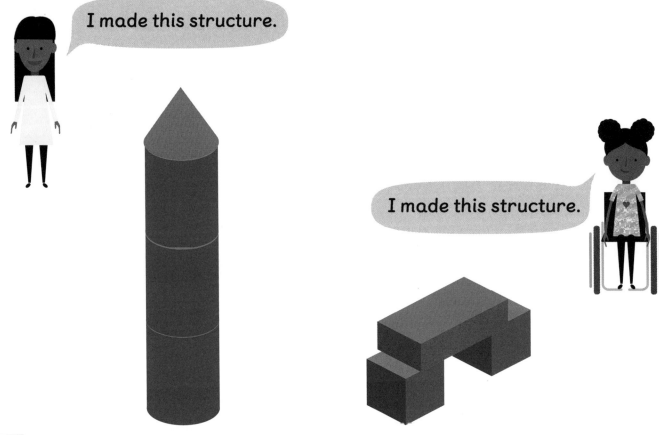

Practice

1. Look for 3D shapes in your home.
   What shapes did you find?

2. Make different structures from the shapes. Cover one of them with a cloth. Describe it to a member of your family. Can they make one exactly the same from your description without seeing it?

If you have a set of building blocks at home you can use those.

Matching 3D shapes to 2D nets

Lesson 16

Starter

Elliott unfolds a box to put into the recycling bin.
What shape will it make when it is flat?

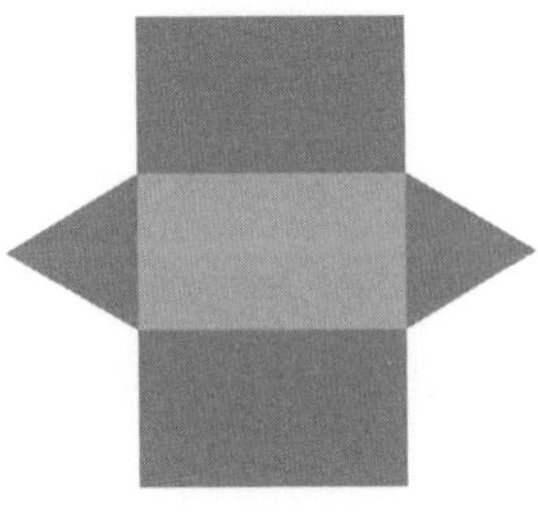

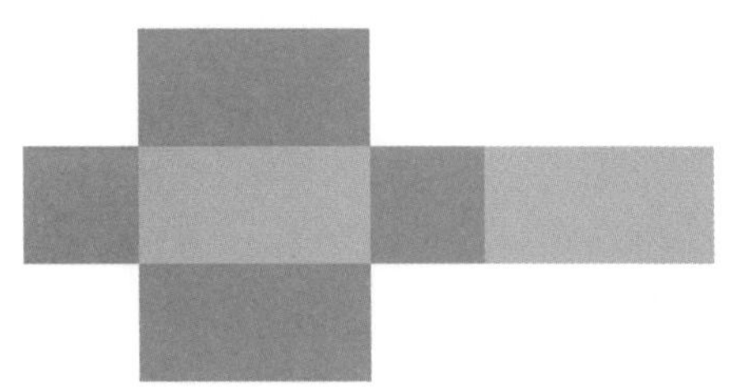

Example

 is a cuboid.

Elliott unfolds the cuboid.

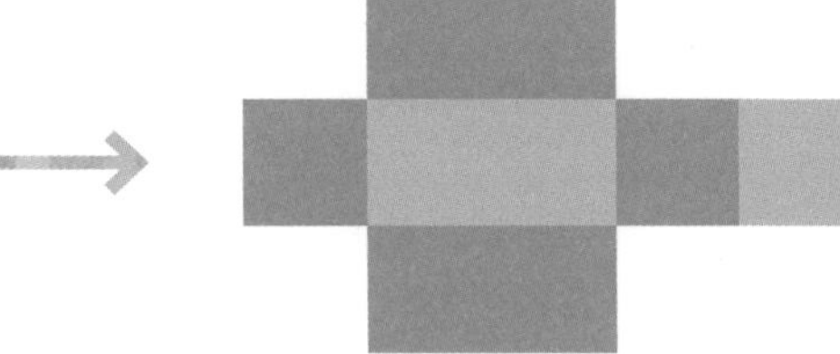

 is a cube.

Elliott unfolds the cube.

 is a prism.

Elliott unfolds the prism.

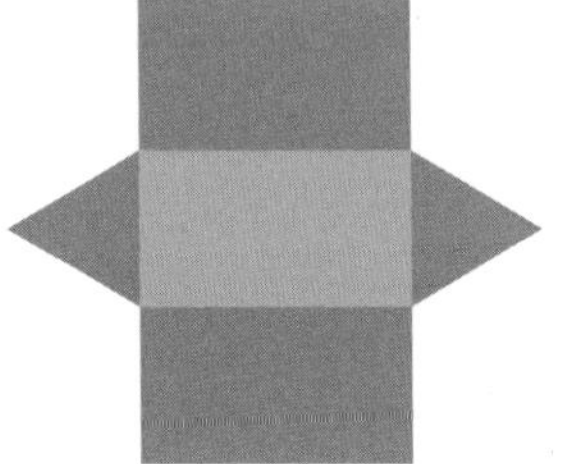

Practice

1. Match the nets to the 3D shapes.

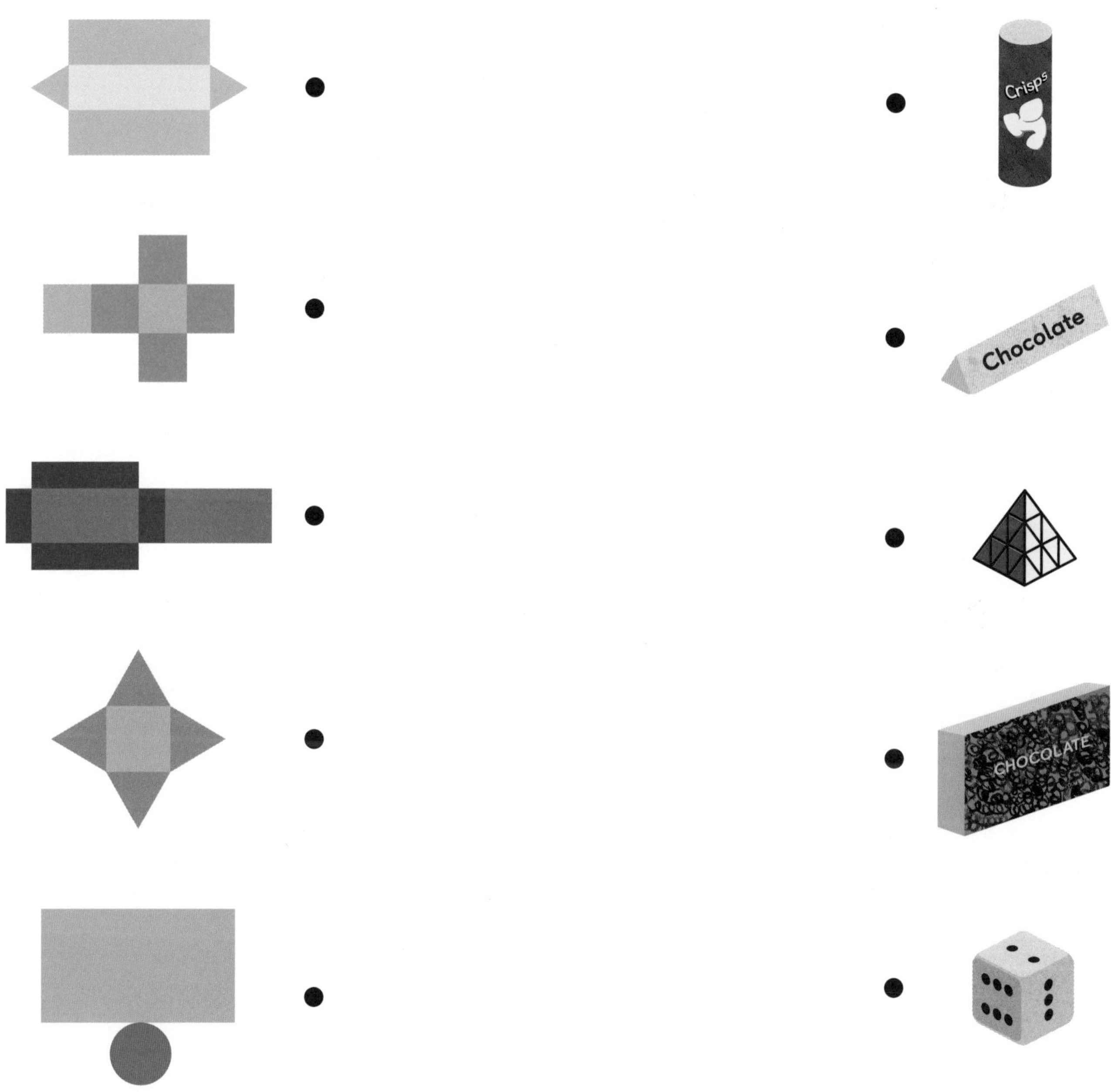

2. Find some boxes or cartons in your home and think about what their nets might look like.
Ask an adult to help you open up the boxes.

Making patterns (part 2)

Lesson 17

Starter

What shape is missing from this pattern?

Example

The repeating pattern is    .

          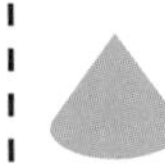  

I can see that the is missing.

Practice

1 Circle the next shape in these patterns.

(a)

 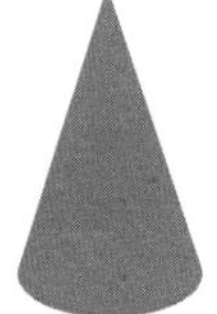     

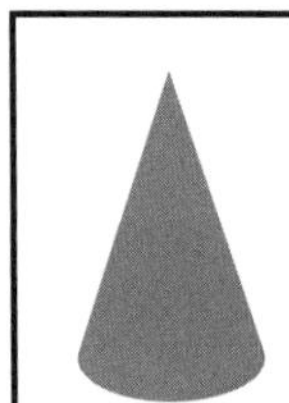

(b)

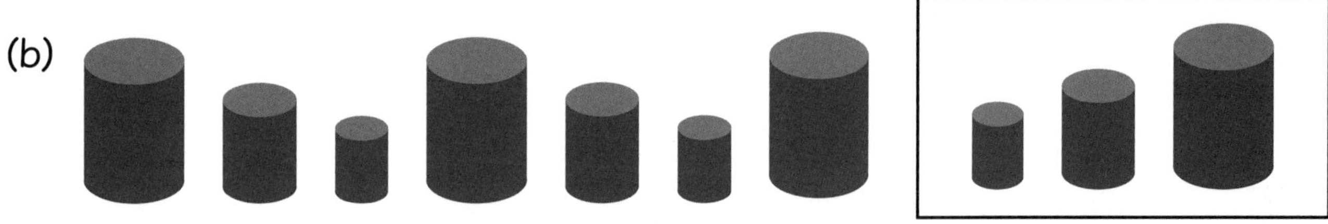

2 Circle the missing shape in these patterns.

(a)

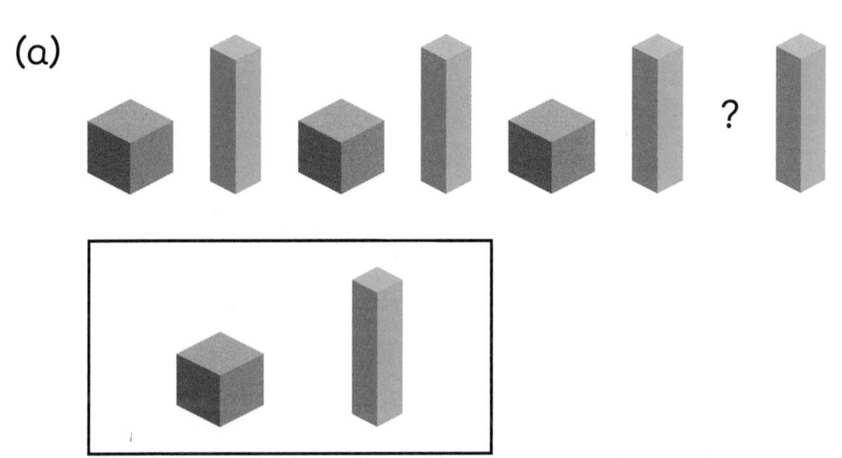

(b)

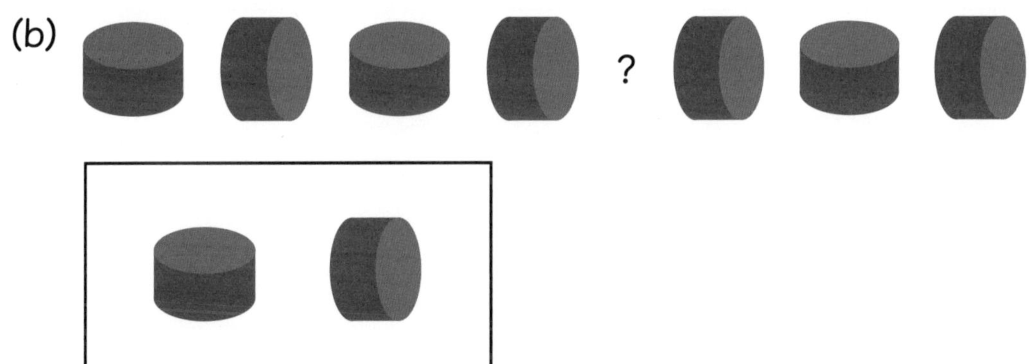

(c)

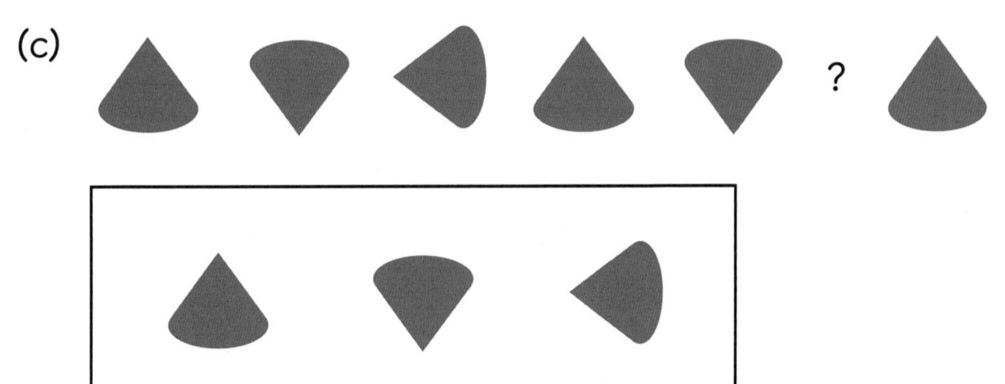

Review and challenge

1 Look at the shapes and complete the table.

Polygon	Name of polygon	Number of sides	Number of vertices
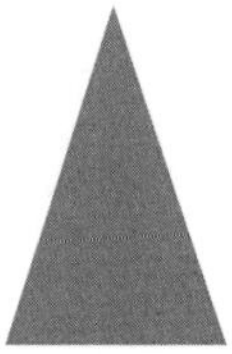			

2 Sort the shapes.

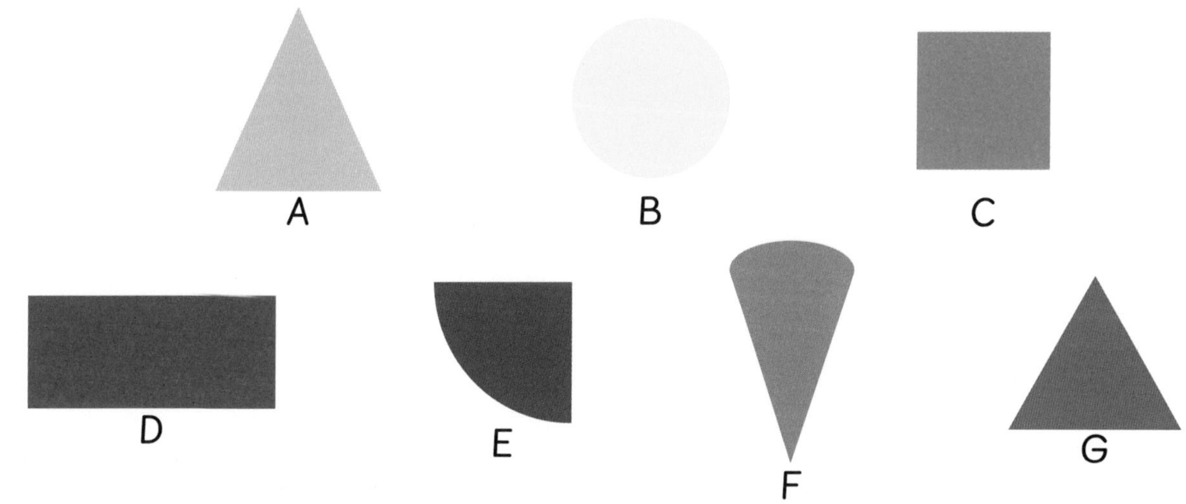

1 line of symmetry	More than 1 line of symmetry

3 Circle the figures that have a line of symmetry.

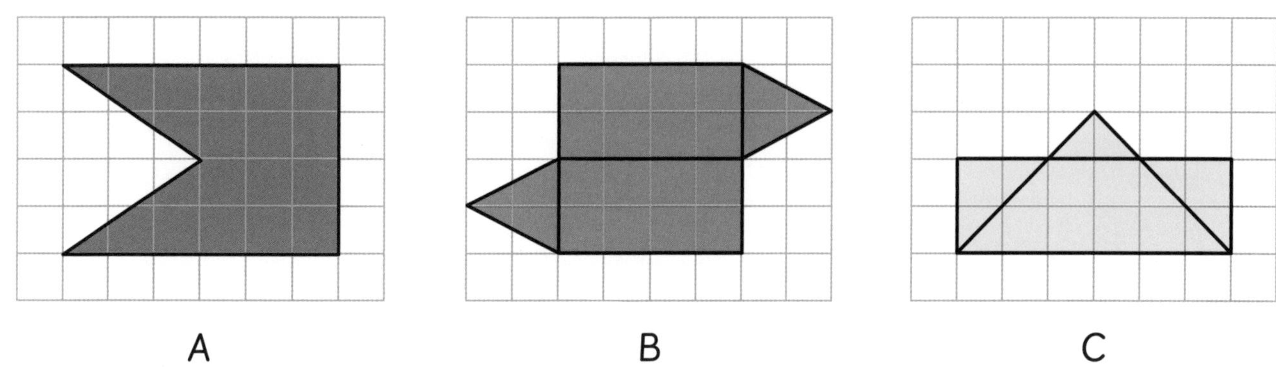

4 Copy these figures on the square grid paper below.

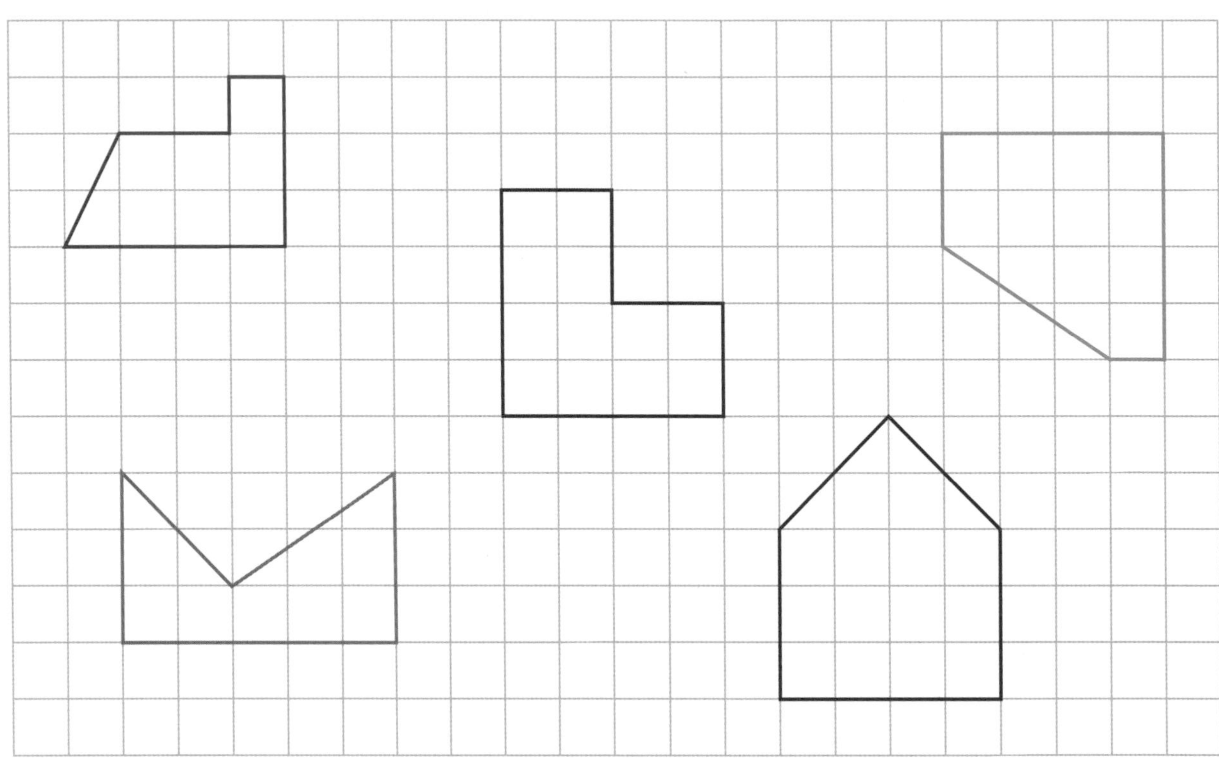

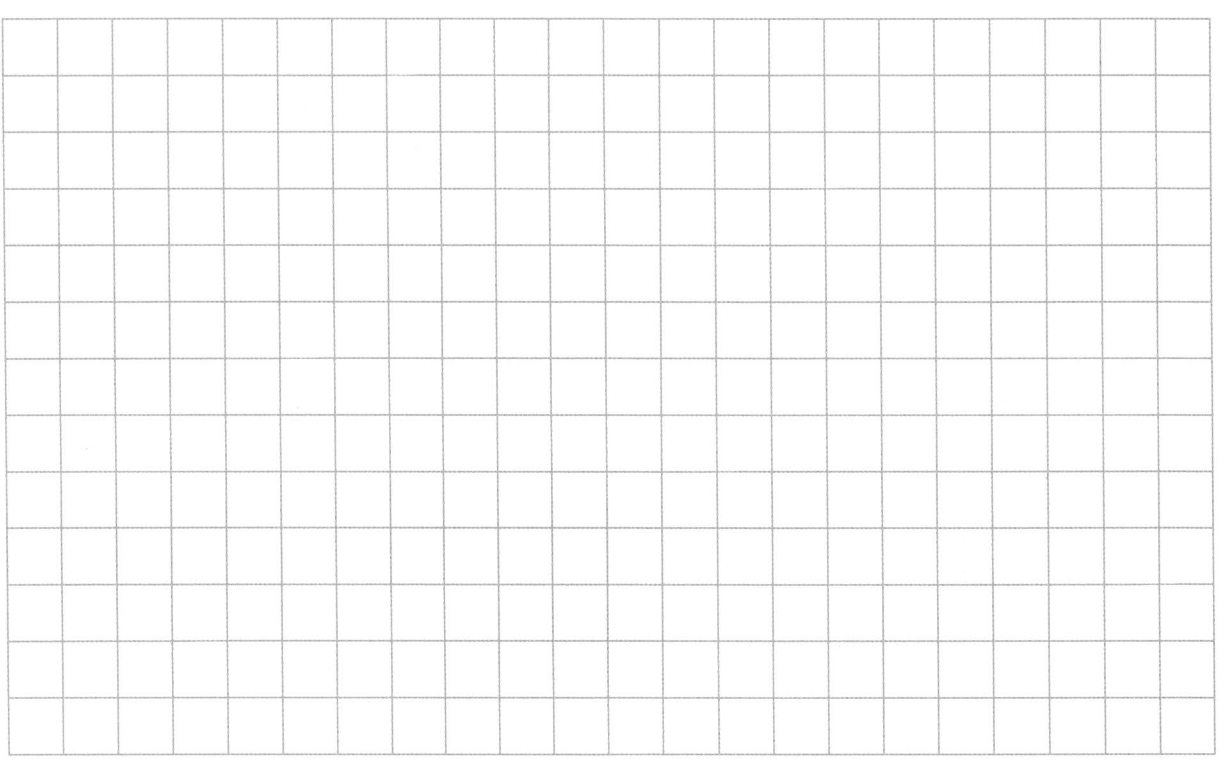

5 Circle the missing shape in these patterns.

(a) (b)

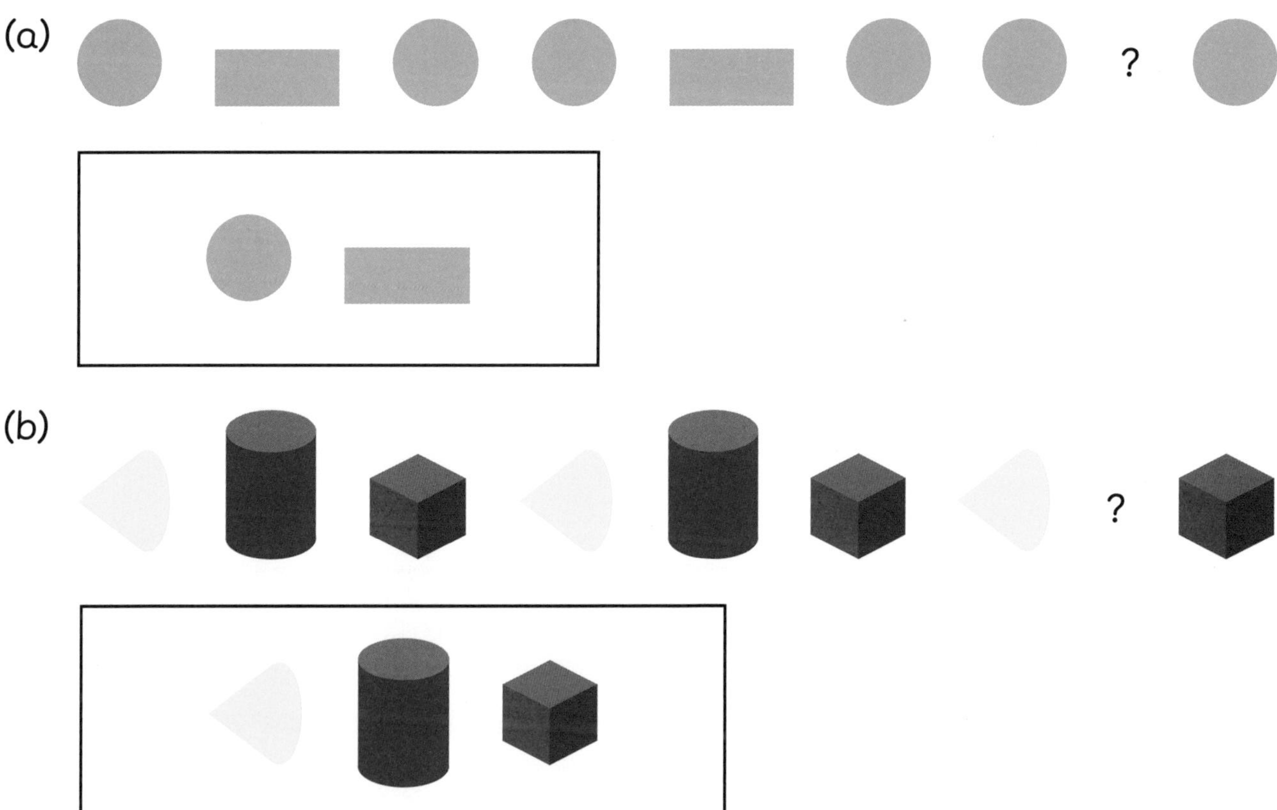

6 What is the 1st shape? Draw the shape in the space provided.

(a) (b)

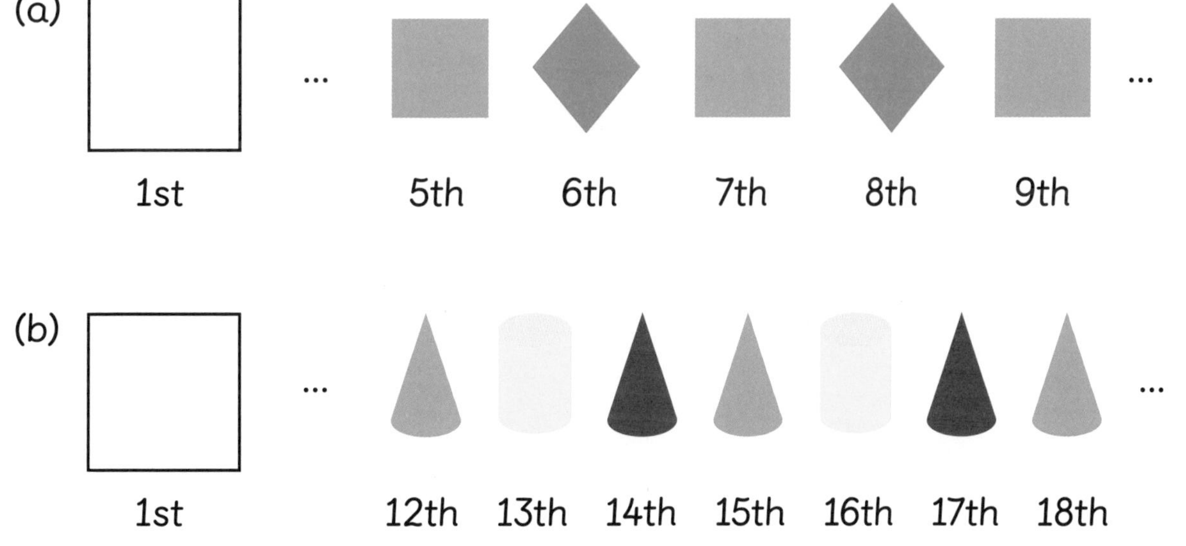

7 Circle the shape that does not belong in the group.

(a)

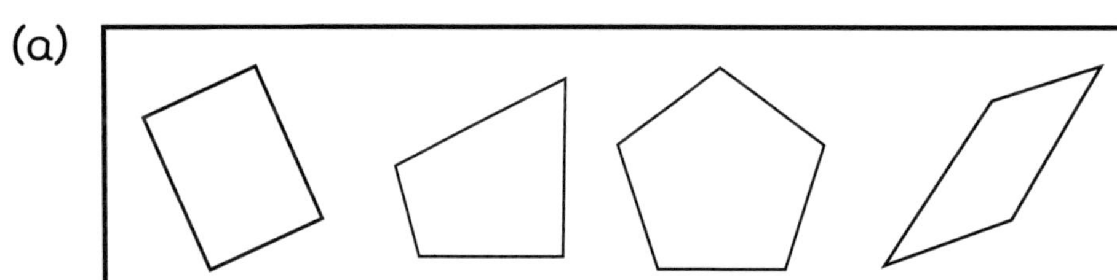

(b)

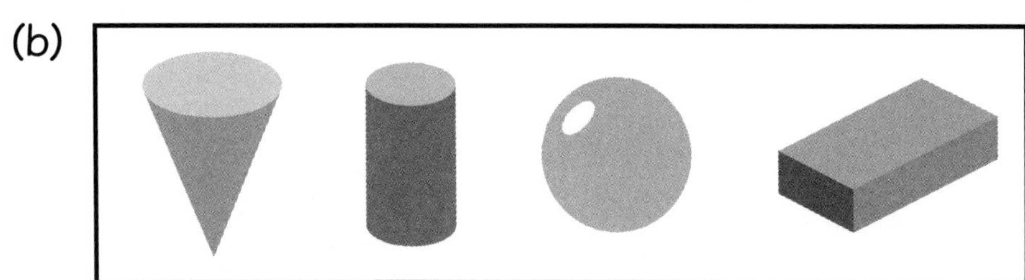

8 Name the 3D shapes made by folding these flat shapes.

(a)

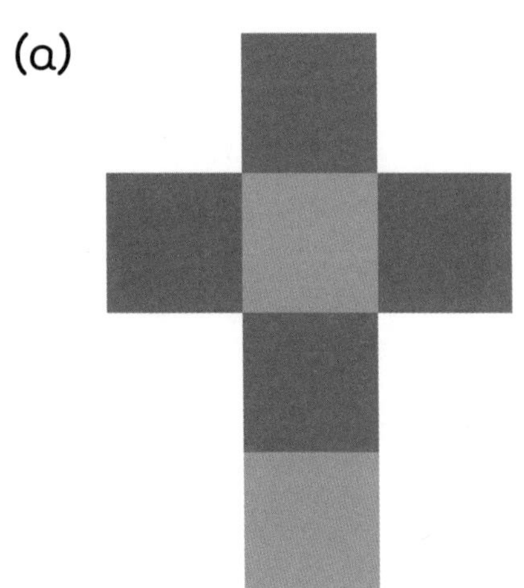

(b)

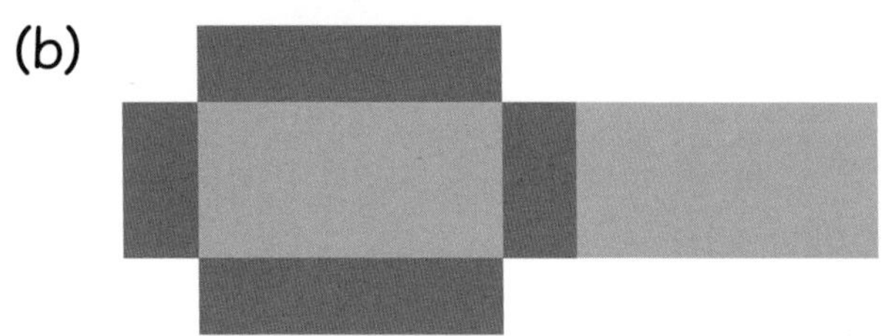

(c)

(d)

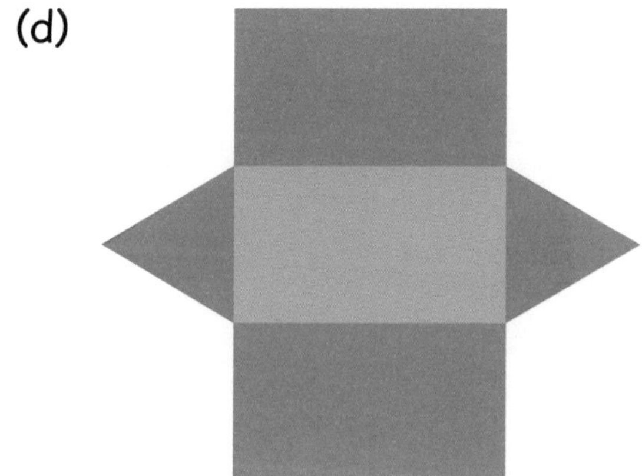

Answers

Page 5 **1 (a)** 4 sides **(b)** 4 sides **(c)** 3 sides **(d)** 3 sides

2 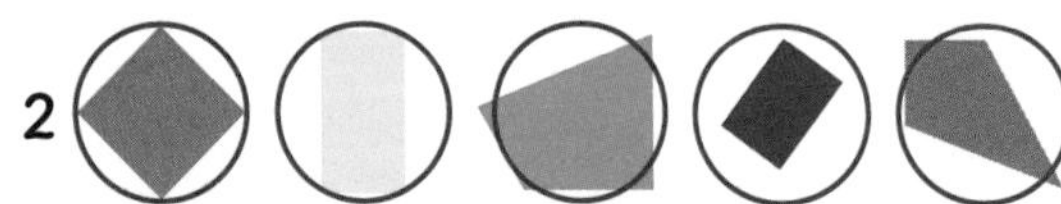

Page 7 **1** triangle 3, 3 **2** rectangle 4, 4 **3** heptagon 7, 7 **4** hexagon 6, 6 **5** pentagon 5, 5 **6** octagon 8, 8 **7** square 4, 4 **8** triangle 3, 3

Page 9 **1** tick **2** tick **3** tick **4** cross **5** cross **6** cross **7** tick **8** tick

Page 11 **1** Answers will vary. **2** Answers will vary.

3 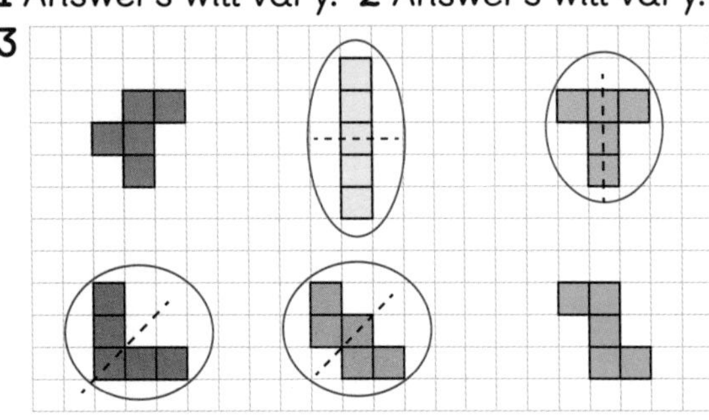

Page 13 **1** 3 vertices: C, E; 4 vertices: D, F, G, H; 5 vertices: A, B
2 no line of symmetry: D, E; one line of symmetry: A, B, C, F; more than one line of symmetry: G, H

Page 15 **1** Shapes correctly copied. **2** Answers will vary.

Page 17 **1** Answers will vary. **2 (a)** (b) (c)

Page 19 **1 (a)** (b) **2 (a)** (b)

3 Answers will vary.

Page 21 **1** 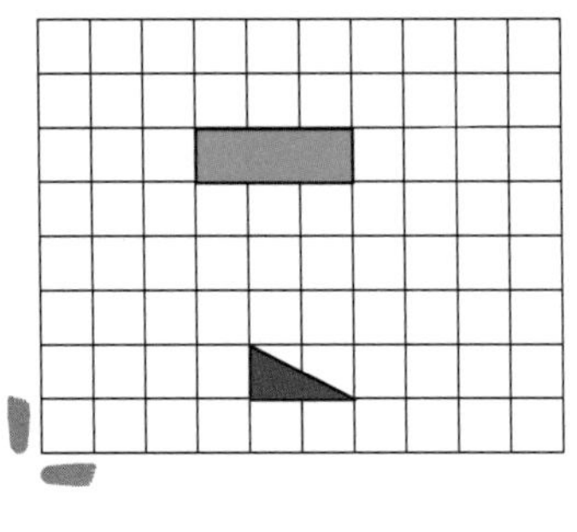 **2** 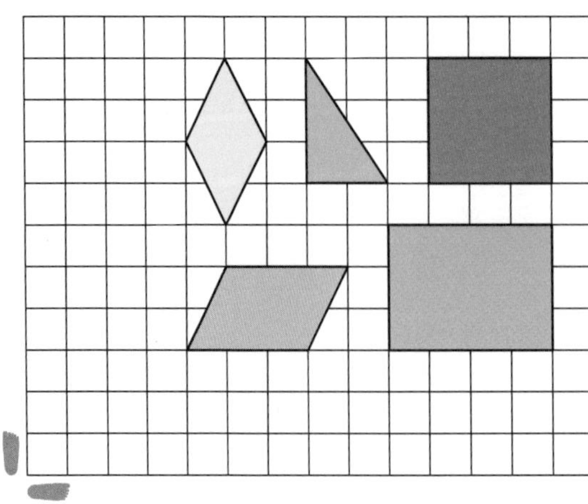

Page 23 1 (a) (b)

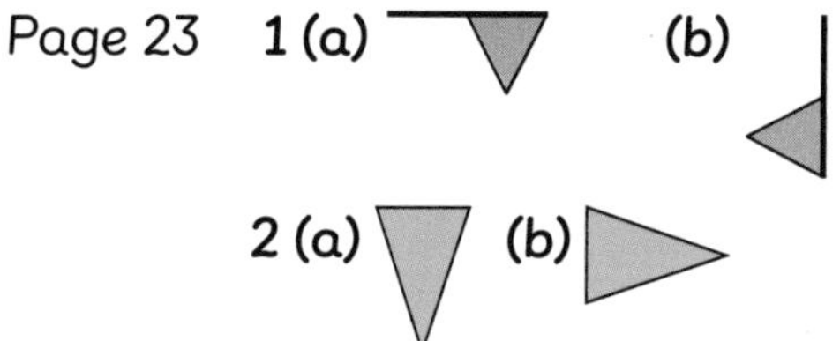

2 (a) (b)

Page 25 1 4 people can have a piece of cake.
2 The clock will show 12:15.
3 The pizza will serve 5 friends.

Page 27 1

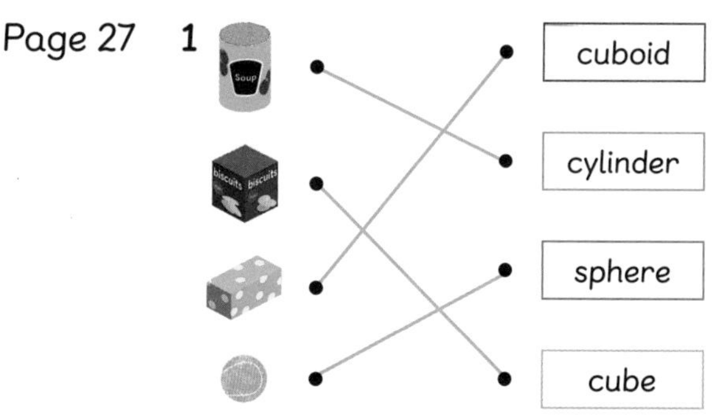

2 Answers will vary. 3 Answers will vary.

Page 30 1

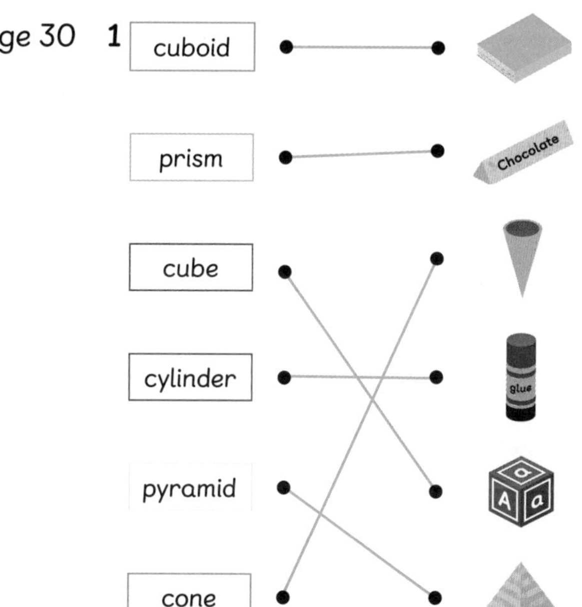

Page 31 2 pyramid, 5 faces, 5 vertices, 8 edges; cuboid, 6 faces, 8 vertices, 12 edges; cube, 6 faces, 8 vertices, 12 edges; triangular prism, 5 faces, 6 vertices, 9 edges 3 Answers will vary.

Page 33

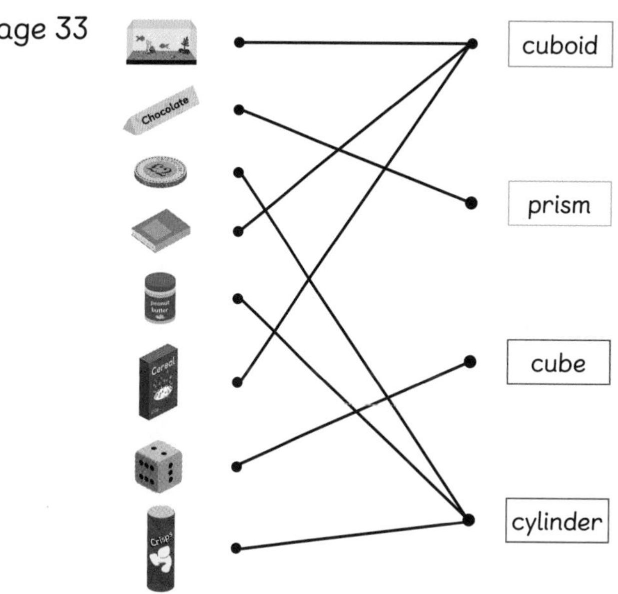

Page 35 1 Answers will vary. 2 Answers will vary.

Page 37 1

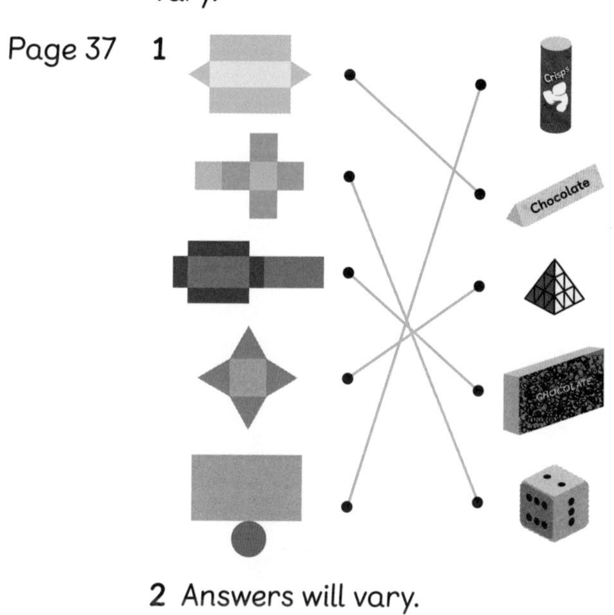

2 Answers will vary.

Page 38 1 (a)

Page 39 (b) medium cylinder

2 (a) (b) (c)

Page 40 1 square, 4 sides, 4 vertices; rectangle, 4 sides, 4 vertices; triangle, 3 sides, 3 vertices; triangle, 3 sides, 3 vertices.

Answers continued

Page 41 **2** 1 line of symmetry: A, E, F; more than one line: B, C, D, G

3 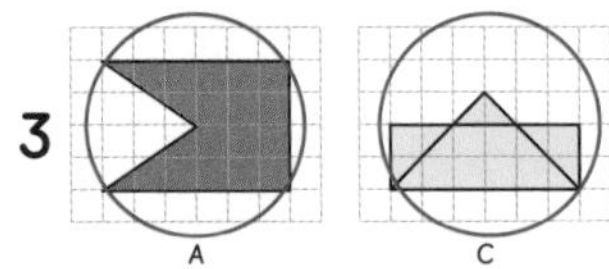

Page 42 **4** shapes correctly copied.

Page 43 **5 (a)** **(b)** **6 (a)** **(b)**

Page 44 **7 (a)** **(b)** **8 (a)** cube **(b)** cuboid

Page 45 **(c)** pyramid **(d)** triangular prism